DEMOCRACY AND LIBERTY

William Edward Hartpole Lecky

DEMOCRACY AND LIBERTY

by WILLIAM EDWARD HARTPOLE LECKY

Volume I.

LibertyClassics

INDIANAPOLIS

LibertyClassics is a publishing imprint of Liberty Fund, Inc., a foundation established to encourage study of the ideal of a society of free and responsible individuals.

The cuneiform inscription that serves as the design motif for our endpapers is the earliest known written appearance of the word "freedom" (ama-gi), or liberty. It is taken from a clay document written about 2300 B.C. in the Sumerian city-state of Lagash.

Photograph by Louis Mercier.

Democracy and Liberty was first published in March 1896 by Longmans, Green and Company in London. During that year it was printed three more times. This Liberty Classics edition of 1981 is based on the second edition of 1896.

Library of Congress Cataloging in Publication Data

Lecky, William Edward Hartpole, 1838–1903.
  Democracy and liberty.

  Originally published: London; New York: Longmans, Green, 1896
  Includes bibliographical references and index.
  1. Democracy. 2. Liberty. I. Title.
JC423.L4 1981 321.8 80-82371
ISBN 0-913966-80 (set) AACR2
ISBN 0-913966-82-7 (v. 1)
ISBN 0-913966-83-5 (v. 2)
ISBN 0-913966-81-9 (pbk. set)
ISBN 0-913966-84-3 (pbk.: v. 1)
ISBN 0-913966-85-1 (pbk.: v. 2)
10 9 8 7 6 5 4 3 2 1

CORRIGENDA
VOLUME I

Please note:

1

On line 22 of page 34, following the word "There" the reader must proceed to line 21 of page 36 and resume reading with the words "can be as little doubt . . ."

2

On lines 22-23 of page 43, the clause "Great Britain and that of her conquered adversary." is a repetition of part of the previous sentence.

CONTENTS OF THE FIRST VOLUME

CHAPTER 1

English Representative Government in the Eighteenth Century

CHAPTER 2

CHAPTER 3

CHAPTER 4
ARISTOCRACIES AND UPPER CHAMBERS

CHAPTER 5
NATIONALITIES

America a Test Case

The Italian Question

CHAPTER 6
DEMOCRACY AND RELIGIOUS LIBERTY

INTRODUCTION
by William Murchison

The veil of sentimentality long ago settled snugly over the 1890s, which have come to be regarded as dear, dead days of innocence, of straw boaters and bicycles built for two—a time so utterly unlike the depraved present as to horrify sensitive consciences.

Yet, to not a few of the sensitive consciences which inhabited them, the '90s were themselves an alarming decade. For a fact, industrial civilization seemed triumphant. Prosperity was widespread and the world in general at peace. But even in this blazing noonday, dark shadows seemed to be creeping 'round.

The underpinnings of 19th century civilization were, in the century's last decade, coming loose. Property was threatened. Crude, broadshouldered democracy was on the rise. The established leaders of affairs seemed about to be booted from the seats of power. What the 20th century would bring, should these trends come to fulfilment, was terrible to contemplate.

But what is a rigorous scholar to do, just because the world he esteems is beginning to crumble? Does he fastidiously avert his eyes? Or does he instead sound an alarm, to rally others around him and beat back the forces of turmoil? Eyeaversion was not for William Edward Hartpole Lecky, the Irish historian and political philosopher. He chose to write— and fight.

Lecky was born near Dublin on March 26, 1838. All his life he remained a staunch Irish patriot—though a conservative, not a radical, one. He was an ardent foe of Home Rule, as propounded by Parnell and Gladstone. He took degrees from Trinity College, Dublin, in 1859 and 1863. Despite early inclinations toward theology and politics, he found his niche in history, after the large success of his *History of Rationalism in Europe*, published in 1865. It was a book that exhibited most of Lecky's strengths and short-comings—powerful scholarship and a clean, clear literary style, marred by a tendency to go on at infinite length, scattering main points like diamonds in a field too heavily ploughed. The Victorians were undaunted, however, by large books, and Lecky's career prospered. His *History of European Morals, from Augustus to Charlemagne*, a sort of companion to the study of rationalism, likewise enjoyed success. But it was his 8-volume *History of England in the Eighteenth Century*, a work that took 19 years to research and write, that established Lecky's reputation. Each volume, as it appeared, won him new admirers. Lecky was not only lucid, but scrupulously objective throughout, even when treating of his beloved Ireland. Deeply interested in politics, he went to Parliament in 1895 as the Liberal Unionist member for Dublin University and sat until 1902. He became a privy councillor in 1897 and, in the year of his retirement from Parliament, received the Order of Merit. He died in London, October 22, 1903.

Lecky may have associated himself with the Liberal Party, but his political philosophy was tenaciously conservative. From his long study of the past, he had divined first principles. He saw how the affairs of men had been regulated before; he saw what had succeeded and what had failed. Change was not his enemy; he stood instead against change that went far beyond the simple righting of wrongs and redressing of grievances; wherein he was like his fellow Irishman, Burke, the

arch-foe of metaphysical tinkerings with deeply rooted institutions. Burke maintained that the success of an institution,
over years of growth and development, was tolerable proof of
its worthiness and utility. This, too, Lecky affirmed. Burke
asserted that some were fit to govern and others not. Likewise
Lecky. A century separated the two Irish philosophers but very
little else.

The revolution that Lecky saw raging around him was, as
revolutions go, a mild and peaceable affair; no lordly estates
plundered, no royal necks laid on the chopping block. Fit-
tingly enough, for the most literate age the world had yet seen,
the revolution was one more of words than of deeds. Such
deeds as were performed were normally of ink and paper.
They were laws, Acts of Parliament. For all that, the blaze they
kindled was brighter, both then and now, than incendiary
torches.

Democracy was the late Victorian age's great passion—a
concept not just to profess but to translate into reality. The
democracy professed was less radical than that of the French
revolutionaries who, in Burke's day, had cried, "Liberty,
Fraternity, Equality!"—and then had decapitated thousands
of their free and equal brethren. Democracy, to the Victorians,
meant something relatively high-minded—government by
the majority for the benefit of the majority. The principle was
amiable enough, certainly. It was in the practical application
that things began to go wrong, as Lecky and a few others easily
discerned. The implications of democracy for good government, for liberty—for precisely the values that democracy was
meant to assert—were deeply disturbing.

It was in 1896 that Lecky published his premonitions. *Democracy and Liberty* was issued by Longmans, Green, and Co.
in March and by October had run through four printings. The
reviews, while attentive and appreciative, were not uniformly
enthusiastic. Lecky's inveterate tendency to wander down
interesting bypaths, never mind how far removed from his
central theme, was frequently faulted.

In truth, *Democracy and Liberty* is about a great many things

besides democracy and liberty in purest form. To name only
a few of these things: the Irish land question, Indian suttee,
Mormonism and polygamy, England's Italian policy, gambling, drunkenness as a disease, divorce, and women's rights.
(The women's movement of the late 20th century would find
Lecky surprisingly sympathetic; he was a powerful advocate
of votes for women). *The Dictionary of National Biography* calls
Democracy and Liberty "a storehouse of admirable, if somewhat
disjointed, reflection." A. Lawrence Lowell, a future president
of Harvard University, writing in the *American Historical Review*, chided the author for supposedly blaming "all the ills
from which we suffer" on democracy alone. Still, like Sir
Henry Maine's *Popular Government* and Sir James Fitzjames
Stephen's *Liberty, Equality, Fraternity*,—learned, lucid protests
against the spirit of the new age—Lecky's two sturdy volumes
pointedly reminded Victorian England of the disaster it was
storing up for posterity.

The argument of the book is the incompatibility of two con-
cepts which, in the late 20th century, are regarded virtually as
twins—democracy and liberty. The one might seem, at first
glance, to reinforce and invigorate the other. But it was not
so, as Lecky proceeded to establish in detail.

Democracy demanded easy access to the ballot box, and
the Victorians had gone far toward complying. The electoral
reforms of 1867 had enfranchised the industrial workers,
those of 1884 the rural classes. Women would not gain the
ballot until after the First World War, but it could be said of
late Victorian Britain anyway that something like real democracy—the rule of The People—was being achieved. Whereas
in 1866 only 1.3 million Britons had been privileged to vote,
the right was shared by 5.7 million in 1886. The franchise had
in two decades more than quadrupled.

Theoretically, all this represented a great advance. But
Lecky was not so easy to convince. Like Burke, he never valued abstractions. That a thing worked, worked well, and gave
every evidence of continuing to do so, was more important
to him than speculative dreams. What had worked best for

Britain, so far as he was concerned, was the electoral system that prevailed from the Reform Bill of 1832 until the Reform Bill of 1867. In 1832, the middle class had been enfranchised. The change had, at the time, split the country asunder, but it had worked. This was because, in Lecky's view, it had admitted to power a class of men solid, trustworthy, educated, and hard-working. Their merits, not their abstract "rights," qualified them for the franchise. It was different with the millions granted the vote in 1867 and 1884. Sheer numbers was what mainly seemed to commend them as voters.

But what were mere numbers against intelligence, experience, and wisdom? "In every field of human enterprise," argued Lecky, "in all the competitions of life, by the inexorable law of Nature, superiority lies with the few, and not with the many, and success can only be attained by placing the guiding and controlling power mainly in their hands."[1]

In speaking of such matters, Lecky refused to mince words. "As far as the most ignorant class have opinions of their own, they will be of the vaguest and most childlike nature."[2] "One of the great divisions of politics in our day," he predicted, "is coming to be whether, at the last resort, the world should be governed by its ignorance or by its intelligence."[3] It is a measure of how much ideological water has flowed under the bridge since 1896, that a noted author, soon to become a member of Parliament, should write so frankly without giving public scandal. In the late 20th century, he would be picketed by college freshmen, pilloried by congressmen and TV talk show hosts, without anyone's stopping to inquire whether intelligence might, on the whole, be socially more useful than ignorance.

What Lecky feared was that his country's government would pass out of the hands of gentlemen and "into the hands

---

[1] W.E.H. Lecky, *Democracy and Liberty* (Indianapolis: Liberty Classics, 1980), Vol. 1, pp. 22–23.
[2] Lecky, Vol. I, pp. 19–20.
[3] Lecky, Vol. I, pp. 21–22.

of professional politicians"—like those to be found in the United States. (Lecky admired the American Constitution and the American Senate and compared Alexander Hamilton favorably to Burke; yet he winced to see democracy so far advanced in the Republic.) Already in Britain, since democracy had taken root, there was more bribe-taking, more apostasy, more flouting of principle.

Lecky was concerned, accordingly, that gentlemen should continue to govern. He was concerned especially for the future of the House of Lords, which fast was coming to be regarded as a feudal relic, occupying "a secondary position in the Constitution." "Man for man," he wrote, "it is quite possible that (the Lords) represents more ability and knowledge than the House of Commons, and its members are certainly able to discuss public affairs in a more single-minded and disinterested spirit."[4] The peers' "superiority of knowledge" was "very marked." They were more than ornamental; they contributed, along with the Throne, to the kingdom's "greatness and cohesion."

Do such notions sound snobbish and insufferable to 20th century ears? They sounded snobbish, in truth, to many a 19th century ear. Yet Lecky, a man of the middle class, was no snob. He reasoned that if liberty was to be maintained against the central state, someone other than the politicians, who were watering and nurturing the state, must do the job.

The state was in fact putting out roots in every direction, and not by happenstance either. A new kind of radicalism had arisen during the 1870s and 1880s. The older sort, the sort in which Englishmen like Lecky rejoiced, had asserted the rights of the individual against the state; the newer radicalism, whose voice was Joseph Chamberlain of Birmingham, insisted that to the contrary, individual freedom could only be guaranteed by the collective state. This was because individuals were being ground down by the weight of the capitalistic structure. Only the majesty of the state could rescue them.

---

[4] Lecky, Vol. I, p. 329.

Numerous rescue missions were launched in the 1870s and '80s. In 1871 and 1872, local government boards were created and given vast powers over public health and the poor—traditional concerns of the parish and squirearchy. By an act of 1888, justices of the peace, who were mostly squires bred in a tradition of public service, were denuded of their broad powers and replaced by 62 county councils. Education was made compulsory in 1876 and in 1891 was made free at the elementary level. The economist, Stanley Jeavons, in words that would have confounded Cobden and Bright, asserted that "the State is justified in passing any law, or even in doing any simple act, which in its ulterior consequences adds to the sum of human happiness"—with happiness, presumably, to be defined by the lawmakers themselves.

Even firmer in that conviction stood the Fabian Society, organized in 1884 by a coterie of middle-class intellectuals bent on converting the country, however slowly, to outright socialism. "The economic side of the democratic ideal," said one of the Fabians, Sidney Webb, "is in fact Socialism, itself."

Lecky, though the philosophical obverse of Webb, could not have agreed him with more. "No fact," he wrote, "is more incontestable and conspicuous than the love of democracy for authoritative regulation."[5] The increase of state power would mean "a multiplication of restrictions imposed upon the various forms of human action." It would mean more bureaucracy. It would mean something the 20th century can understand even better than these—constantly mounting taxes to finance the state. For Lecky, the tax question was "in the highest degree a question of liberty." The country was nearing a time when one class could impose the taxes and another class pay them. In that unhappy event, taxation would no longer serve the common good. It would be used "to break down the power, influence, and wealth of particular classes; to form a new social type; to obtain the means of class bribery."[6] Lecky, the historian, had shown that his eyes were as

---

[5] Lecky, Vol. I, p. 218.
[6] Lecky, Vol. I, pp. 219–220.

good for looking forward as for looking backward. For so it all came to pass in Britain, once the Labor Party finally acquired dominion.

The likelihood of actual socialist sway over his country, Lecky stoutly refused to admit. Socialism was an abstract, Teutonic program; the English were too sensible to have much truck with it, even if it was probable that Marxists might "in some degree and in more than one direction, modify the actions both of the State and of local bodies."[7]

It happened that the socialists came to power after all, but that they lacked the doctrinaire convictions necessary to build a thoroughly socialist nation. Though they increased taxes and nationalized key industries, they declined to drive the private sector entirely out of business. This was fortunate, for as Lecky had pointed out, "The desire of each man to improve his circumstances, to reap the full reward of superior talent, or energy, or thrift, is the very mainspring of the production of the world. Take these motives away; persuade men that by superior work they will obtain no superior reward; cut off all the hopes that stimulate, among ordinary men, ambition, enterprise, invention, and self-sacrifice, and the whole level of production will rapidly and inevitably sink."[8]

Lecky understood not just the practical arguments against socialism but likewise the theoretical ones. Capital was not robbery, as Marx alleged; nor was it the working man's enemy. Rather, it was "that portion of wealth which is diverted from wasteful and unprofitable expenditure to those productive forms which give him permanent employment."[9] Capital and labor were "indissolubly united in the creation of wealth," each one indispensable to the other.

All the eloquence and learning that Lecky mustered was shouted into the teeth of a gale. The England of his heart—

---

[7] Lecky, Vol. II, p. 340.
[8] Lecky, Vol. II, p. 310.
[9] Lecky, Vol. II, p. 276.

industrious, rational, above all free and unfettered—was passing away even as he wrote.

The 1890s, as one scholar has written, was "the decade of a thousand 'movements'." The people then living "were convinced that they were not only passing from one social system to another but from one morality to another, from one culture to another, and from one religion to a dozen or more!"[10] Liberty had been the supreme economic, political, and social value of the mid-Victorians. Nor had it been repudiated entirely by the late-Victorians. The term had simply come to mean something different than it meant in the '40s, '50s, and '60s, when the individual was viewed as a thing of wonder and might and endless possibility. In the '90s, liberty was more likely to be pursued through collective enterprises such as trade unions and local government councils, than through the removal of obstacles to personal achievement.

Lecky saw clearly the fallacy of the new "liberty," so defined. Far from ensuring a higher kind of freedom, collectivism—and the democracy that was its driving power—would enforce a lower kind of servitude. The democratic mass state would begin as man's servant and end as his master.

For decades after Lecky's death, such admonitions were muffled, if they were heard at all. The curtain had fallen on his values with a heavy thud but now and then a fold would be drawn back and a look stolen at the notions of the quaint past, when it still was possible to doubt that mere numbers was all that mattered.

Lecky, it can be more plainly seen now, was a man both behind and ahead of his times; which is often the case with those whose values are rooted in tradition and experience, not pinned precariously to the frenzies of the moment. He was a man eminently worth listening to in 1896. If anything, time has only deepened the value and pertinence of his conversation.

---

[10] Holbrook Jackson, *The Eighteen Nineties* (New York: Knopf, 1927), p. 31.

PREFACE

Many years ago, when I was deeply immersed in the History of England in the Eighteenth Century, I remember being struck by a saying of my old and illustrious friend, Mr. W. R. Greg, that he could not understand the state of mind of a man who, when so many questions of burning and absorbing interest were rising around him, could devote the best years of his life to the study of a vanished past. I do not think the course I was then taking is incapable of defence. The history of the past is not without its uses in elucidating the politics of the present; and in an age and country in which politicians and reformers are abundantly numerous, it is not undesirable that a few men should persistently remain outside the arena. But the study of a period of history as recent as that with which I was occupied certainly does not tend to diminish political interests, and a writer may be pardoned if he believes that it brings with it kinds of knowledge and methods of reasoning that may be of some use in the discussion of contemporary questions.

The present work deals with a large number of these questions, some of them lying in the very centre of party controversies. I had intended to introduce it with a few remarks on the advantage of such topics being occasionally discussed by writers who are wholly unconnected with practical politics, and who might therefore bring to them a more independent judgment and a more judicial temperament than could be easily found in active politicians. This preface I cannot now write. At a time when the greater portion of my book was already in the printers' hands an unexpected request, which I could not gratefully or graciously refuse, brought me into the circle of parliamentary life. But although my own position has been altered, I have not allowed this fact to alter the character of my book. While expressing strong opinions on many much-contested party questions, I have endeavoured to treat them with that perfect independence of judgment, without which a work of this kind can have no permanent value. Nor have I thought it necessary to cancel a passage in defence of university representation in general, and of the representation of Dublin University in particular, which was written when I had no idea that it could possibly be regarded as a defence of my own position.

One of the principal difficulties of a book dealing with the present aspects and tendencies of the political world in many different countries lies in the constant changes in the subjects that it treats. The task of the writer is often like that of a painter who is painting the ever-shifting scenery of the clouds. The great tendencies of the world alter slowly, but the balance of power in parliaments and constitutions is continually modified, and, under the incessant activity of modern legislation, large groups of subjects are constantly assuming new forms. I have endeavoured to follow these changes up to a very recent period; but in dealing with foreign countries this is sometimes a matter of no small difficulty, and I trust the reader will excuse me if I have not always altogether succeeded.

London:
February, 1896.

DEMOCRACY AND LIBERTY

CHAPTER 1

The most remarkable political characteristic of the latter part of the nineteenth century has unquestionably been the complete displacement of the centre of power in free governments, and the accompanying changes in the prevailing theories about the principles on which representative government should be based. It has extended over a great part of the civilised world, and, although it has had all the effects of a profound and far-reaching revolution, it has, in some of the most conspicuous instances, been effected without any act of violence or any change in the external framework of government. I have attempted in another work to describe at length the guiding principles on which the English parliamentary government of the eighteenth century was mainly based, and which found their best expression and defence in the writings of Burke. It was then almost universally held that the right of voting was not a natural right, but a right conferred by legislation on grounds of expediency, or, in other words, for the benefit of the State. As the House of Commons had been, since the Revolution of 1688, the most powerful element of the Constitution, nothing in the Constitution was deemed more important than the efficiency of the machine, and measures of parliamentary reform were considered good

1

or bad exactly in proportion as they conduced to this end.
The objects to be attained were very various, and they were
best attained by a great variety and diversity of representation. It was necessary to bring together a body of men of
sufficient intelligence and knowledge to exercise wisely their
great power in the State. It was necessary to represent, and
to represent in their due proportions, the various forms and
tendencies of political opinion existing in the nation. It was
necessary to represent with the same completeness and proportion the various and often conflicting class interests, so
that the wants of each class might be attended to and the
grievances of each class might be heard and redressed. It was
also in the highest degree necessary that the property of the
country should be specially and strongly represented. Parliament was essentially a machine for taxing, and it was therefore right that those who paid taxes should have a decisive
voice, and that those who chiefly paid should chiefly control.
The indissoluble connection between taxation and representation was the very mainspring of English conceptions of freedom. That no man should be taxed except by his own consent
was the principle which was at the root of the American Revolution. It was the chief source of all extensions of representative government, and it was also the true defence of the
property qualifications and voting privileges which concentrated the chief power in the hands of the classes who were
the largest taxpayers. No danger in representative government was deemed greater than that it should degenerate into
a system of veiled confiscation—one class voting the taxes
which another class was compelled to pay.

It was also a fundamental principle of the old system of representation that the chief political power should be with the
owners of land. The doctrine that the men to whom the land
belonged were the men who ought to govern it was held, not
only by a great body of English Tories, but also by Benjamin
Franklin and by a large section of the American colonists. It
was urged that the freeholders had a fixed, permanent, inalienable interest in the country, widely different from the

migratory and often transient interests of trade and commerce; that their fortunes were much more indissolubly blended with the fortunes of the State: that they represented in the highest degree that healthy continuity of habit and policy which is most essential to the well–being of nations. As Burke, however, observed, the introduction of the borough representation showed that the English Legislature was not intended to be solely a legislature of freeholders. The commercial and trading interests had also their place in it, and after the Revolution that place became exceedingly great. It was strengthened by the small and venal boroughs, which were largely in the hands of men who had acquired great fortunes in commerce or trade. The policy of the Revolution Government was, on the whole, more decidedly directed by commercial views than by any others, and it was undoubtedly the small boroughs which, during the first half of the eighteenth century, mainly kept the Hanoverian family on the throne.

Aristocratic influence in the Constitution was always very great, though it was never absolute. The House of Commons after the Revolution was a stronger body than the House of Lords. The most powerful ministers of the eighteenth century were commoners. Great popular movements in the country never failed to influence the Legislature, though they acted less promptly and less decisively than in later periods. On the other hand, a considerable proportion of the members of the House of Commons were returned by members of the House of Lords, and nearly every great family had at least one representative in the Commons. The aristocracy formed a connecting link between the smaller country gentry and the trading and industrial interests. Like the latter, but unlike the former, they were usually supporters of the system of government established by the Revolution, of the Whig interest, and of the Hanoverian dynasty. They possessed in many cases great fortunes in money; they had wider interests and more cosmopolitan tastes than the ordinary country gentlemen; and they shared with the commercial classes the ascendency in the boroughs. A few of them had risen from those classes, or were connected with them by marriage; while, on the other hand, they were the chief landowners, the natural leaders of the landowning classes.

It was contended that this system secured the harmony between the two branches of the Legislature, and that aristocratic ascendency brought with it many other advantages. The possession of land, more than any other form of property, is connected with the performance of public duties, and the great landowner was constantly exercising in his own district governing and administrative functions that were peculiarly fitted to give him the kind of knowledge and capacity that is most needed for a legislator. Men of this class may have many faults, but they are at least not likely in the management of public affairs to prove either reckless and irresponsible adventurers or dishonest trustees. To say this may not appear to be saying very much; but a country which has succeeded in having its public affairs habitually managed with integrity, and with a due sense of responsibility, will have escaped evils that have wrecked the prosperity of many nations. It was urged, above all, that the place which the aristocracy exercised in the Legislature had at least the advantage of reflecting the true facts and conditions of English life. In each county a great resident noble is commonly the most important man. He influences most largely the lives and happiness of the inhabitants, takes the leading part in local movements, exercises by general consent a kind of superintendence and precedence among his neighbours. It was therefore perfectly in accordance with the principles of representative government that his class should exercise a somewhat corresponding influence in the Legislature.

In order to attain these various ends the House of Commons was elected in a manner which showed the most complete absence of uniformity and symmetry. There were great differences both in the size of the constituencies and in the nature of the qualifications. In many places members were returned by a single man or by a small group of often venal freemen. In other constituencies there was a strong popular element, and in some places the scot-and-lot franchise approached nearly to universal suffrage. The difference of the political power vested in an individual voter in different parts of the country was enormously great, and even the House of Commons was only very partially a representative body. 'About one half of the House of Commons,' wrote Paley, 'obtain their seats in that Assembly by the election of the people; the other half, by purchase or by nomination of single proprietors of great estates.'[1]

The large share in the representative body which was granted to the two latter classes of members was defended by many arguments. It was said, with truth, that the small boroughs had introduced, and usually at an early age, into Parliament by far the greater number of the men of extraordinary ability who have adorned it, and also many useful and experienced men, not quite in the first rank, who from narrow circumstances, or from the turn of their own characters, or from some unpopular religious belief, or from the fact that they had spent much of their lives in obscure or remote fields of public duty, would never have been acceptable candidates in a popular constituency. To ministries they were of the utmost value. They gave a busy minister a secure and independent seat free from all local demands and complications, enabled him to devote his undivided energies to the administration of the country, and made it easy for him to bring into Parliament any colleague or valuable supporter who had failed at an election, and was perhaps under a cloud of transient unpopularity. In the eyes, too, of the best thinkers of the eighteenth century it was of the utmost importance that members of Parliament should not sink into simple delegates. On the broad lines and principles of their policy it was understood that they should reflect the sentiments of their constituents; but the whole system of parliamentary government, in the opinion of Burke and most other eighteenth–century statesmen, would degenerate

---

[1] *Moral Philosophy*, ii. 218.

if members were expected to abdicate their independent judgments, to submit to external dictation about the details of
measures, to accept the position of mere puppets pulled by
demagogues or associations outside the House. The presence
in Parliament of a large body of men who did not owe their
position to popular favour secured an independent element
in the House of Commons, and affected the tone of the whole
assembly. The borough system, also, concentrating power in
a few hands, greatly strengthened ministries. It gave them a
steady, calculable force, which in many circumstances, but especially in their foreign policy, was often of inestimable value.
Fluctuations of power were less frequent, less violent, less capricious than they afterwards became. Ministers could count
more confidently on persistent parliamentary support in lines
of policy of which the rewards were only to be looked for in a
distant future; amid the chequered fortunes and the ever-
changing aspects of a great struggle.

This system of representation was supported and consolidated by a tone of political feeling which has so completely
passed away that it is somewhat difficult to realise the power
which it once possessed—I mean that strong indisposition to
organic change, as distinguished from administrative reform,
which the best statesmen of all parties continually inculcated.
They were usually ready to meet practical evils as they arose,
but they continually deprecated any attempt to tamper with
the legislative machine itself, except under the most imperious
necessity. They believed that the system of the Constitution
had grown up insensibly in accordance with the wants of the
nation; that it was a highly complex and delicate machine,
fulfilling many different purposes and acting in many obscure
and far–reaching ways, and that a disposition to pull it to
pieces in the interests of some theory or speculation would
inevitably lead to the destruction of parliamentary government. A great part of its virtue lay in the traditionary reverence
that surrounded it, in the unwritten rules and restrictions that
regulated its action. There was no definite written constitution
that could be appealed to, but in no other form of government

did tacit understandings, traditional observances, illogical but serviceable compromises, bear so great a part.

It was claimed for this form of government that, with all its defects and anomalies, it had unquestionably worked well. I may again quote the words of Paley. 'Before we seek to obtain anything more,' he writes, 'consider duly what we already have. We have a House of Commons composed of 548 members, in which number are found the most considerable landholders and merchants of the Kingdom; the heads of the army, the navy, and the law; the occupiers of great offices in the State; together with many private individuals eminent by their knowledge, eloquence, and activity. If the Country be not safe in such hands, in whom may it confide its interests? If such a number of such men be liable to the influence of corrupt motives, what assembly of men will be secure from the same danger? Does any new scheme of representation promise to collect together more wisdom or to produce firmer integrity?'[2]

The English Constitution of the eighteenth century might also be tested in other ways. It is incontestable that under it England had enjoyed for a long space of time much prosperity, a far larger measure of steady freedom, and a far more equitable system of taxation than any of the great States of the Continent. Under this form of government she passed successfully through the dangerous internal crisis of a long–disputed succession; she encountered successfully foreign dangers of the first magnitude, from the time of Louis XIV. to the time of Napoleon; and although her history was by no means unchequered by faults and disasters, it was under this system of government that she built up her vast Indian Empire and largely extended and organised her colonial dominions.

The other great type of free government existing in the world was the American Republic, and it is curious to observe how closely the aims and standards of the men who framed the memorable Constitution of 1787 and 1788 corresponded

---

[2] *Moral Philosophy*, ii. 220 221.

with those of the English statesmen of the eighteenth century. It is true that the framework adopted was very different. In the true spirit of Burke, the American statesmen clearly saw how useless it would be to reproduce all English institutions in a country where they had no historical or traditional basis. The United States did not contain the materials for founding a constitutional monarchy or a powerful aristocracy, and a great part of the traditional habits and observances that restrained and regulated English parliamentary government could not possibly operate in a new country with the same force. It was necessary to adopt other means, but the ends that were aimed at were much the same. To divide and restrict power; to secure property; to check the appetite for organic change; to guard individual liberty against the tyranny of the multitude, as well as against the tyranny of an individual or a class; to infuse into American political life a spirit of continuity and of sober and moderate freedom, were the ends which the great American statesmen set before them, and which they in a large measure attained. They gave an elected president during his short period of office an amount of power which was, on the whole, not less than that of George III. They invested their Senate with powers considerably beyond those of the House of Lords. They restricted by a clearly defined and written Constitution the powers of the representative body, placing, among other things, the security of property, the sanctity of contract, and the chief forms of personal and religious liberty beyond the powers of a mere parliamentary majority to infringe. They established a Supreme Court with the right of interpreting authoritatively the Constitution and declaring Acts of Congress which exceeded their powers to be null and void; they checked, or endeavoured to check, the violent oscillations of popular suffrage by introducing largely into the Constitution the principle of double election; and they made such large majorities necessary for the enactment of any organic change that these changes became impossible, except where there was an overwhelming consensus of public opinion in their favour.

In dealing with the suffrage they acted in the same spirit. Chief Justice Story has treated this subject in a book which is, in my opinion, one of the most valuable ever written on the science of politics. He argues that 'the right of voting, like many other rights, is one which, whether it has a fixed foundation in natural law or not, has always been treated in the practice of nations as a strictly civil right, derived from and regulated by each society according to its own circumstances and interests.' On the ground of natural right it would be impossible to exclude females from voting, or to justify the arbitrary and varying enactments by which different countries have defined the age at which males attain their majorities. 'If any society is entrusted with authority to settle the matter of the age or sex of voters, according to its own views of its policy, or convenience, or justice, who shall say that it has not equal authority, for like reasons, to settle any other matters regarding the rights, qualifications, and duties of voters?' The truth is that 'there can be no certain rule' on these subjects 'for all ages and for all nations.' The right of suffrage will vary almost infinitely, according to the special circumstances and characteristics of a nation.[3]

The American Legislature acted on this principle. In the colonial period 'no uniform rules in regard to the right of suffrage existed. In some of the Colonies . . . freeholders alone were voters; in others, a very near approach was made to universal suffrage among the males of competent age; and in others, again, a middle principle was adopted, which made taxation and voting dependent upon each other, or annexed to it the qualification of holding some personal estate, or the privilege of being a freeman or the eldest son of a freeholder of the town or corporation.' When the Revolution separated the Colonies from the mother country the same diversity was suffered to continue. 'In some of the States the right of suffrage depends upon a certain length of residence and payment of taxes; in others, upon mere citizenship and residence;

---

[3] Story, *Commentaries on the Constitution of the United States*, ii. 55–58.

in others, upon the possession of a freehold or some estate of a particular value, or upon the payment of taxes, or performance of some public duty, such as service in the militia or on the highways. In no two of these State constitutions will it be found that the qualifications of the voters are settled upon the same uniform basis.' A proposal to establish a uniform system of voting on a common principle was brought before the Convention which framed the Constitution of 1787–88, but after full discussion it was resolved to leave the existing diversities untouched, and to confide to each State the power of regulating as it pleased the system of suffrage. All that the Convention established was, that the electors for the House of Representatives should, in each State, have the qualifications requisite for the electors of the most numerous branch of the State Legislature. As a matter of fact, for many years property qualifications were required in most States for electors, and a diversity in the system of election prevailed which was little, if at all, less than in England. In several of the State legislatures, though not in the Federal Legislature, a property qualification was required in representatives and in the Federal Legislature representatives, and direct taxes were apportioned by the same ratio.[4]

If we now pass from the two great English–speaking communities to France, we find ourselves in a different region of thought, over which Rousseau exercised the strongest influence. It is not necessary for me here to enter into a general examination of the political theories of Rousseau, or of the many inconsistencies they present. The part of his teaching which had most influence, and with which we are now specially concerned, is that relating to the suffrage. He held that absolute political equality was the essential condition of political freedom, and that no diversities of power, or representations of classes or interests should be suffered to exist in the Constitution. Every man should have a vote, and a vote of the same value; a representative should be nothing more than

[4] Story, ii. 59–66, 95, 96, 106.

a delegate under the absolute control of the constituency; and no law can have any binding force which has not been directly sanctioned by the whole community. His whole system rested on the idea of natural and inalienable rights.

These views did not at once pass into French legislation. The States-General which met in 1789 had been elected by orders, the nobles and the ecclesiastics voting separately and directly for their own representatives. For the third estate the system of double election was adopted, the electors being themselves elected by a very wide constituency, consisting of men of twenty-five who had a settled abode and who paid direct taxes. In the Constitution of 1791 the system of double election was maintained; the right of voting for the primary assemblies was restricted to 'active citizens' who, among other things, paid direct contributions to at least the value of three days' labour; while the men whom they elected, and who in their turn elected the representatives, were required to possess a considerable property qualification. It varied, according to the size of the constituencies and the nature of the property, from a revenue of the value of 500 days' to a revenue of the value of 100 days' labour. In 1792, however, the Legislative Assembly very nearly established manhood suffrage, though it was qualified by the system of double election. The connection of voting with property and taxation was abolished. All Frenchmen of twenty-one who had resided for a year in the department, and who were not in domestic service, might vote in the primary assemblies, and no other qualification was required, either for the elected electors or for the deputies, except that they should have attained the age of twenty-five. It was under this system that the Convention—the most bloody and tyrannical assembly of which history has any record—was elected. The Constitution of June 1793 completed the work of democratic equality. The Convention decreed that 'all Citizens have an equal right to concur in the enactment of the law and in the nominations of their delegates or agents'; that 'the Sovereign people is the universality of French citizens,' and that 'they should nominate directly their deputies.' Population was made the sole basis of national representation. All citizens of twenty-one years who had resided for six months in the electoral district were made voters, and every 40,000 voters were entitled to return one member. This Constitution itself was submitted to and ratified by direct universal suffrage.

The year when this Constitution was enacted was one of the most tragical in French history. It was the year when the ancient monarchy was overthrown; when the King and Queen were brought to the scaffold; when the flower of the French nation were mown down by the guillotine or scattered as ruined exiles over Europe; when the war with England began which raged, with one short intermission, for more than twenty years.

The Constitution of 1793 never came into force. It was adjourned till after the war, and long before the war had terminated France had passed into wholly different conditions. The downfall of the Jacobins in 1794 soon led to a restriction of the suffrage and a revival of the old system of double election, and in the strong reaction against the horrors of the Revolution France moved on by steady stages to the absolute despotism of Napoleon. The system of direct election of members of Parliament was not established in France till 1817, and universal suffrage, as it had been designated by the Convention in 1793, did not revive until 1848. But the theory that each change in the Constitution should be ratified by a direct popular vote showed more vitality, and successive Governments soon learned how easily a plebiscite vote could be secured and directed by a strong executive, and how useful it might become to screen or to justify usurpation. The Constitution of 1795, which founded the power of the Directors; the Constitution of 1799, which placed the executive power in the hands of three Consuls elected for ten years; the Constitution of 1802, which made Buonaparte Consul for life, and again remodelled the electoral system; the Empire, which was established in 1804, and the additional Act of the Constitution promulgated by Napoleon in 1815, were all submitted to a direct popular vote.[5]

A great displacement of political power was effected by the French Revolution of 1830 and by the English Reform Bill of 1832. Tocqueville, in a recently published book, has shown very clearly how the true significance of the French Revolution of 1830 was the complete ascendency of the middle, or, as the French say, bourgeois class. In that class all political powers, franchises, and prerogatives for the next eighteen years were concentrated; their good and evil qualities pervaded and governed the whole field of French politics; and, by a happy coincidence, the King in mind and character was in perfect harmony with the representatives of the people.[6] Constitutional government was carried out during these years faithfully, and in some respects even brilliantly, but it was tainted by much corruption, and it rested on an electorate of much less than a quarter of a million.

In England, a similar though not quite so decisive influence was established by the Reform Bill of 1832. Many causes contributed to this measure, but two predominated over all others, one of them being industrial and geographical, and the other political. The great manufacturing inventions of the eighteenth century had called into being vast masses of unrepresented opinion in the provincial towns, transferred the weight of population from the southern to the northern half of the island, and, partly by depleting old centres of power, and partly by creating new ones, added enormously to the inequalities and anomalies of English representation. On the other hand, the great wave of Toryism that overspread England after the French Revolution produced a greatly increased disinclination among the governing classes to all change, and especially to all measures of parliamentary re-

---

[5] See Jules Clère, *Hist. du Suffrage Universel*, 12–30, 33; Laferrière, *Constitutions de la France depuis 1789*.

[6] *Souvenirs de Tocqueville*, pp. 5–7.

form. The Royal prerogative of summoning new centres of
population to send members to Westminster had long since
become wholly obsolete. Pitt, with much prescience, had attempted in 1783 and 1785 to meet the growing inequalities of
representation and provide for a gradual diminution of the
nomination boroughs; but his scheme was defeated, and he
himself abandoned the policy of reform.

There can be little doubt that for many years after the horrors of the French Revolution the anti-reform party represented with perfect fidelity the true sentiments of the English
people, and no kind of blame should be attached to the ministers who resisted parliamentary reform during the continuance of the war. After that period, however, home politics
were for some years unskilfully conducted, and the reform
party grew steadily in strength. The reaction which the
French Reign of Terror had produced had spent its force. The
many forms of misery and discontent produced by the sudden fall of prices, by the enormous weight of the war taxation,
by the growth of the factory system, and by the vast and pain-
ful transformation of industry it involved, had all their influence on political opinion. Lord John Russell, dissociating
parliamentary reform from radical schemes of universal suffrage, electoral districts, and vote by ballot, repeatedly
brought forward the wise policy of disfranchising small boroughs which were found guilty of gross corruption, and
transferring their seats to the great unrepresented towns, beginning with Leeds, Birmingham, and Manchester. Such a
policy, if it had been adopted in time, and steadily pursued,
might have long averted a great and comprehensive change;
but it was obstinately resisted. Many mistakes, and perhaps
still more the establishment of peace, had dimmed the reputation which the Tory party had justly gained by their conduct of the war. On the other hand, the no less just discredit
which had fallen upon the Whig party on account of the profoundly unpatriotic conduct of a large section of its members
in the early years of the war had passed away. Most of its new
leaders were men who had no part in these errors, who were

untainted by French sympathies and revolutionary doctrines, who reflected the national feelings quite as truly as their opponents.

The triumph of Catholic Emancipation greatly accelerated the change. The Catholic question had been for many years that on which public opinion was mainly concentrated; and experience shows that the strength of public opinion which is needed to carry a great organic change in England can never be simultaneously evoked on two totally different questions. Some very acute judges, indeed, who cared nothing for Catholic Emancipation in itself, steadily resisted it because they saw that, once it was carried, the undivided enthusiasm of the country would flow into the channel of reform.[7]

After the settlement of the Catholic question the Whig party, having no longer the anti-Popery prejudice to contend with, acquired all the popularity its democratic tendencies would naturally give it, and obtained the undivided support of the Protestant Dissenters. A great Whig cause had triumphed, and it had triumphed by the Act of a Tory ministry. The struggle had demonstrated clearly the coercive power which might be exercised over Parliament by organised popular agitation. The Tory party was defeated, divided, discredited, and discouraged, and a new class of Irish reformers were introduced into Parliament. The cry for reform grew louder and louder, and the triumph of the cause in France greatly assisted it.

Under all these influences a movement of public opinion in favour of parliamentary reform was created which had probably never been equalled in England for its spontaneity and force. The country seemed for a time on the verge of revolution; but the measure was at last carried. To many contemporaries the destruction of the nomination boroughs and of the controlling power of the aristocracy over the House of

---

[7] Lord Russell used to relate that this was the reason which Lord Lonsdale in private always gave for his opposition to Catholic Emancipation. He said that he did not care about this measure, but he knew that, if it were carried, it would be impossible to resist the cry for reform.

Commons seemed destined to ruin the parliamentary system of England. But the men who chiefly presided over this great change were genuine patriots, profoundly imbued with the best political philosophy of the English school, and as far as possible from sympathy with the French apostles of liberty. It is curious to notice how deeply rooted the English sentiment of the necessity to well-ordered and enduring freedom of disparities of political power has been, even at the time when parliamentary government was in its infancy. No one expressed this feeling better than Shakespeare, in the noble words which he places in the mouth of Ulysses:

> Degree being vizarded,
> Th' unworthiest shows as fairly in the mask.
> The heavens themselves, the planets, and this centre,
> Observe degree, priority, and place.
> . . . .
> O ! when degree is shak'd,
> Which is the ladder in all high designs,
> The enterprise is sick. How could communities,
> Degrees in schools, and brotherhoods in cities,
> Peaceful commerce from dividable shores,
> The primogenitive and due of birth,
> Prerogative of age, crowns, sceptres, laurels,
> But by degree, stand in authentic place?
> Take but degree away, untune that string,
> And, hark, what discord follows! each thing meets
> In mere oppugnancy: the bounded waters
> Should lift their bosoms higher than the shores,
> And make a sop of all this solid globe:
> Strength should be lord of imbecility,
> And the rude son should strike his father dead:
> Force should be right; or rather, right and wrong
> (Between whose endless jar justice resides)
> Should lose their names, and so should justice too.
> Then everything includes itself in power,
> Power into will, will into appetite;
> And appetite, a universal wolf,
> So doubly seconded with will and power,

Must make perforce a universal prey,
And last eat up himself.[8]

Though the Reform Bill undoubtedly changed the centre of political power in England, it left the leading characteristics of the old system undestroyed. The constituencies were still very different in size and population. The suffrage in different parts of the kingdom was very variously arranged. All the old powers and influences were retained, though their proportionate weight was changed. The House of Lords still remained an important element in the Constitution. The landed interest was still powerful in the county constituencies. Property was specially and strongly represented, and the Reform Bill brought great masses of hitherto unrepresented property, as well as great centres of population, into the circle of the Constitution. The middle class, which now became the most powerful in the political system, was one which could be excellently trusted with a controlling power. Aristotle long since observed, that it is to this section of the community that the chief power in government may be most wisely and most profitably given. It is not the class most susceptible to new ideas or most prone to great enterprises, but it is distin-

---

[8] *Troilus and Cressida*, act i. scene 3. So Milton—
'If not equal all, yet free,
Equally free; for orders and degrees
Jar not with liberty, but well consist.'
Paradise Lost, Book V.1. 791.
Milton puts these lines in the mouth of Satan, but in his treatise on *Reformation in England* he expresses very similar sentiments in his own person. 'There is no civil government that hath been known—no, not the Spartan nor the Roman . . . more divinely and harmoniously tuned, more equally balanced as it were by the hand and scale of Justice, than is the Commonwealth of England, when, under a firm and untutored monarch, the noblest, worthiest, and most prudent men, with full approbation and suffrage of the people, have in their power the supreme and final determination of highest affairs' (Book II.). On the political opinions of English poets, see the interesting preface to Sir Henry Taylor's 'Critical Essays' (*Works*, v. xi–xix).

guished beyond all others for its political independence, its caution, its solid practical intelligence, its steady industry, its high moral average. It also, perhaps, feels more promptly and more acutely than any other class the effects of misgovernment, whether that misgovernment takes the form of reckless adventure and extravagant expenditure, or whether, in the not less dangerous form of revolutionary legislation, it disturbs settled industries, drives capital to other lands, and impairs the national credit, on which the whole commercial system must ultimately rest.

In England, however, this middle class, though it became after 1832 the most powerful, had not the same absolute empire as in France. The active administration of affairs was chiefly in the hands of the upper and most cultivated class. The chief controlling power lay with the great middle classes, and followed mainly the bent of their wishes and tendencies. At the same time, the suffrage was so arranged that it was, in some degree at least, within the reach of the skilled artisans—a great and intelligent class, who should have a distinct place and interest in every well-ordered government.

It does not appear to me that the world has ever seen a better Constitution than England enjoyed between the Reform Bill of 1832 and the Reform Bill of 1867. Very few parliamentary governments have included more talent, or represented more faithfully the various interests and opinions of a great nation, or maintained under many trying circumstances a higher level of political purity and patriotism. The constituencies at this time coincided very substantially with the area of public opinion. Every one who will look facts honestly in the face can convince himself that the public opinion of a nation is something quite different from the votes that can be extracted from all the individuals who compose it. There are multitudes in every nation who contribute nothing to its public opinion; who never give a serious thought to public affairs, who have no spontaneous wish to take any part in them; who, if they are induced to do so, will act under the complete direction of individuals or organisations of another class. The landlord, the clergyman or Dissenting minister or priest, the local agitator, or the public-house keeper, will direct their votes, and in a pure democracy the art of winning and accumulating these votes will become one of the chief parts of practical politics.

Different motives will be employed to attain it. Sometimes the voter will be directly bribed or directly intimidated. He will vote for money or for drink, or in order to win the favour or avert the displeasure of some one who is more powerful than himself. The tenant will think of his landlord, the debtor of his creditor, the shopkeeper of his customer. A poor, struggling man called on to vote upon a question about which he cares nothing, and knows nothing, is surely not to be greatly blamed if he is governed by such considerations. A still larger number of votes will be won by persistent appeals to class cupidities. The demagogue will try to persuade the voter that by following a certain line of policy every member of his class will obtain some advantage. He will encourage all his utopias. He will hold out hopes that by breaking contracts, or shifting taxation and the power of taxing, or enlarging the paternal functions of government, something of the property of one class may be transferred to another. He will also appeal persistently, and often successfully, to class jealousies and antipathies. All the divisions which naturally grow out of class lines and the relations between employer and employed will be studiously inflamed. Envy, covetousness, prejudice, will become great forces in political propagandism. Every real grievance will be aggravated. Every redressed grievance will be revived; every imaginary grievance will be encouraged. If the poorest, most numerous, and most ignorant class can be persuaded to hate the smaller class, and to vote solely for the purpose of injuring them, the party manager will have achieved his end. To set the many against the few becomes the chief object of the electioneering agent. As education advances newspapers arise which are intended solely for this purpose, and they are often almost the only reading of great numbers of voters.

As far as the most ignorant class have opinions of their own, they will be of the vaguest and most childlike nature. When personal ascendencies are broken down, party colours will often survive, and they form one of the few elements of real stability. A man will vote blue or vote yellow as his father did before him, without much considering what principles may be connected with these colours. A few strong biases of class or creed will often display a great vitality. Large numbers, also, will naturally vote on what is called 'the turn-about system.' These people, they will say, have had their turn; it is now the turn of the others. This ebb and flow, which is distinct from all vicissitudes of opinion, and entirely irrespective of the good or bad policy of the Government, has become of late years a conspicuous and important element in most constituencies, and contributes powerfully to the decision of elections. In times of distress the flux or reflux to the tide is greatly strengthened. A bad harvest, or some other disaster over which the Government can have no more influence than over the march of the planets, will produce a discontent that will often govern dubious votes, and may perhaps turn the scale in a nearly balanced election. In all general elections a large number of seats are lost and won by very small majorities, and influences such as I have described may decide the issue.

The men who vote through such motives are often most useful members of the community. They are sober, honest, industrious labourers; excellent fathers and husbands; capable of becoming, if need be, admirable soldiers. They are also often men who, within the narrow circle of their own ideas, surroundings, and immediate interests, exhibit no small shrewdness of judgment; but they are as ignorant as children of the great questions of foreign, or Indian, or Irish, or colonial policy, of the complicated and far-reaching consequences of the constitutional changes, or the great questions relating to commercial or financial policy, on which a general election frequently turns. If they are asked to vote on these issues, all that can be safely predicted is that their decision will not represent either settled conviction or real knowledge.

There is another and very different class, who are chiefly found in the towns. They are the kind of men who may be

seen loitering listlessly around the doors of every ginshop—
men who, through drunkenness, or idleness, or dishonesty,
have failed in the race of life; who either never possessed or
have wholly lost the taste for honest continuous work; who
hang loosely on the verge of the criminal classes, and from
whom the criminal classes are chiefly recruited. These men are
not real labourers, but their presence constitutes one of the
chief difficulties and dangers of all labour questions, and in
every period of revolution and anarchy they are galvanised
into a sudden activity. With a very low suffrage they become
an important element in many constituencies. Without knowledge and without character, their instinct will be to use the
power which is given them for predatory and anarchic purposes. To break up society, to obtain a new deal in the goods
of life, will naturally be their object.

Men of these two classes no doubt formed parts of the old
constituencies, but they formed so small a part that they did
not seriously derange the constitutional machine or influence
the methods of candidates. When they are very numerous
they will naturally alter the whole action of politicians, and
they may seriously impair the representative character of Parliament, by submerging or swamping the varieties of genuine
opinion by great uniform masses of ignorant and influenced
voters. That symptoms of this kind have appeared and increased in English politics since the Reform Bill of 1867 is, I
believe, the growing conviction of serious observers. The old
healthy forces of English life no doubt still act, and on great
occasions they will probably do so with irresistible power; but
in normal times they act more feebly and more uncertainly,
and are more liable to be overborne by capricious impulses
and unreasoning fluctuations. The evil of evils in our present
politics is that the constituencies can no longer be fully trusted,
and that their power is so nearly absolute that they have an
almost complete control over the well-being of the Empire.

One of the great divisions of politics in our day is coming to
be whether, at the last resort, the world should be governed
by its ignorance or by its intelligence. According to the one

party, the preponderating power should be with education and property. According to the other, the ultimate source of power, the supreme right of appeal and of control, belongs legitimately to the majority of the nation told by the head— or, in other words, to the poorest, the most ignorant, the most incapable, who are necessarily the most numerous.

It is a theory which assuredly reverses all the past experiences of mankind. In every field of human enterprise, in all the competitions of life, by the inexorable law of Nature, superiority lies with the few, and not with the many, and success can only be attained by placing the guiding and controlling power mainly in their hands. That the interests of all classes should be represented in the Legislature; that numbers as well as intelligence should have some voice in politics, is very true; but unless the government of mankind be essentially different from every other form of human enterprise, it must inevitably deteriorate if it is placed under the direct control of the most unintelligent classes. No one can doubt that England has of late years advanced with gigantic strides in this direction. Yet, surely nothing in ancient alchemy was more irrational than the notion that increased ignorance in the elective body will be converted into increased capacity for good government in the representative body; that the best way to improve the world and secure rational progress is to place government more and more under the control of the least enlightened classes. The day will come when it will appear one of the strangest facts in the history of human folly that such a theory was regarded as liberal and progressive. In the words of Sir Henry Maine, 'Let any competently instructed person turn over in his mind the great epochs of scientific invention and social change during the last two centuries, and consider what would have occurred if universal suffrage had been established at any one of them. Universal suffrage, which to-day excludes free trade from the United States, would certainly have prohibited the spinning-jenny and the power-loom. It would certainly have forbidden the threshing-machine. It would have prevented the adoption of the Gregorian Calendar; and it would have restored the Stuarts. It would have proscribed the Roman Catholics, with the mob which burned Lord Mansfield's house and library in 1780; and it would have proscribed the Dissenters, with the mob which burned Dr. Priestley's house and library in 1791."[9]

It is curious and melancholy to observe how Rousseau's doctrine of the omnipotence of numbers and the supreme virtue of political equality is displacing in England all the old maxims on which English liberty once rested. I have spoken of the great inequalities in the qualifications for the suffrage that existed in the United Kingdom. They secured a healthy diversity of character in the representatives, and they followed with rough but general fidelity the different degrees of political advancement. There was one suffrage for the towns, and another for the country—one suffrage for England, and another for Ireland. All these diversities have now been swept away. The case of Ireland is especially significant. Ireland was greatly over-represented in the Imperial Parliament, and by universal acknowledgment the Irish representatives formed the diseased spot in the parliamentary body, the disaffected and obstructive element most hostile to its healthy action. It was also absolutely certain that a lowering of the Irish suffrage would aggravate the evil, and introduce into Parliament a larger body of men who were completely alienated from the interests of the Empire, and utterly indifferent to the dignity of Parliament and the maintenance of the Constitution. No one who knew Ireland doubted that it would throw a still larger amount of power into the hands of a poor, ignorant, and disaffected peasantry, completely under the influence of priests and agitators; that it would weaken, and in many districts virtually disfranchise, loyalty, property, and intelligence; that it would deepen the division of classes; that it would enormously increase the difficulty of establishing any form of moderate and honest self-government. Nothing, indeed, is more certain than that the elements of good government must be sought for in Ire-

---

[9] Maine's *Popular Government*, pp. 35–36.

land in a higher electoral plane than in England. The men who introduced and carried the degradation of the Irish suffrage were perfectly aware of what they were doing. They acted with their eyes open; they justified themselves, in the true spirit of the Contrat Social, on the plea that they would not allow a political inequality to continue, and they probably believed that they were playing a good card in the party game.

A very similar illustration may be found in the language now commonly held in the Radical party about university representation. According to any sane theory of representative government, no form of representation can be more manifestly wise. I may here once more go to Ireland for an illustration. Nothing in the Irish representation is so manifestly wanting as a more adequate representation of loyalty and intelligence in three provinces. Loyal and well-educated men are to be found there in abundance; in nearly every form of industry, enterprise, and philanthropy, they take the foremost place; but they have no corresponding weight in the political representation, as they are usually swamped by an ignorant and influenced peasantry. Owing to the purely agricultural character of the greater part of Ireland, and the steady decadence of most of its county towns, the Irish boroughs are for the most part singularly small and insignificant. Among these boroughs a leading place must be assigned to the one university constituency. This great University has for many generations educated the flower of the intelligence of Ireland. It has sent into the Imperial Parliament a greater number of representatives of conspicuous ability than any other Irish constituency. It comprises more than 4,300 electors, and is, therefore, even in point of numbers, much more considerable than many Irish boroughs; and its voters consist of highly educated men, scattered over the whole surface of the country, taking a leading part in many professions and industries, and coming in close contact with an altogether unusual variety of interests, classes, and opinions. If the object of representation be to reflect faithfully in its variety and due proportion the opinions, the interests, and the intelligence of the community, what constituency could be more essentially and more usefully representative? Yet we are now told that, in computing the relative strength of parties in Ireland, the University representation must be subtracted, as 'it does not represent the nation.' This dignity, it appears, belongs more truly to the illiterates—more than one in five professedly unable even to read the names upon the ballot-papers[10]—who, in some remote western district, or in some decaying county town, are driven like sheep to the polling-booth by agitators or priests!

Surely it is impossible to exaggerate the fatuity of these attacks upon university representation; and the men who make them have rarely the excuse of honest ignorance. With many the true motive is simply a desire to extinguish constituencies which return members opposed to their politics, and at the same time, by depreciating the great centres of intelligence, to flatter the more ignorant voters. It is a truth which should never be forgotten, that in the field of politics the spirit of servility and sycophancy no longer shows itself in the adulation of kings and nobles. Faithful to its old instinct of grovelling at the feet of power, it now carries its homage to another shrine. The men who, in former ages, would have sought by Byzantine flattery to win power through the favour of an emperor or a prince, will now be found declaiming on platforms about the iniquity of privilege, extolling the matchless wisdom and nobility of the masses, systematically trying to excite their passions or their jealousies, and to win them by bribes and flatteries to their side. Many of those who are doing their best to reduce the influence of education and intelligence in English politics are highly cultivated men, who owe to university education all that they are, though they are now imitating—usually with awkward and overstrained effort—the rant of the vulgar demagogue. They have taken their line in public life, and some of them have attained their

---

[10] *Return showing the Number of Persons who voted as Illiterates at the General Election of* 1892 (Feb. 1893).

ends. I do not think that the respect of honest men will form any large part of their reward.

It is curious how often in modern England extreme enthusiasm for education is combined with an utter disregard for the opinions of the more educated classes. The movement against the influence of property is at least as strong as against the influence of education. One of the forms that it now chiefly takes is the outcry against plural voting. It is denounced as an abuse and an injustice that some great landlord who has property in several counties, or in several towns, should possess a vote for each constituency in which he possesses property. To me, at least, it appears that such an arrangement is most natural, expedient, and just. In each of these localities the voter has considerable material interests; in each of them he pays taxes; in each of them he discharges public duties; in each of them he probably exercises local influence as a landlord or an employer of labour. He takes part in each constituency in local charities, in local movements, in local business, and represents in each a clearly recognised, and often very considerable force. Can there be anything more reasonable than that he should have in each constituency a voice in the political representation? Can there be anything more irrational than to maintain that, in all these constituencies except one, he should be denied that minute fraction of political power which is accorded to the poorest day-labourer in his employment? Mill and some other advocates of universal suffrage have maintained that while every one should have a vote, plural voting should be largely extended, giving special privileges to special qualifications. It would be difficult to enact, and probably still more difficult to maintain, such privileges under a democratic ascendency; but plural voting connected with property is rooted by long-established custom in the habits of the country, and though its influence is not very great, it does something to make the Legislature a true picture and reflection of the forces in the country, and to qualify the despotism of simple numbers.

We may take another illustration of a different kind. Let the reader place himself in imagination at the Guildhall or at St. Paul's, and consider for a moment all that is included within a square mile taken from these centres. Probably no other spot on the globe comprises so many of the forms and elements of power. Think of all the wealth, all the varieties of knowledge, all the kinds of influence and activity that are concentrated in that narrow space. In the most distant quarters of the Empire men of enterprise and initiative turn to the city of London for assistance; each fluctuation of its prosperity is felt to the furthest confines of the civilised world. There is scarcely a Government that does not owe something to it, and its agencies radiate far beyond civilisation, among savage tribes and through unreclaimed deserts. It is the great heart of the Empire, beating in close, constant, active correspondence with all its parts. And yet, according to the democratic theory, a square mile of the City should have exactly the same weight in the political system as a square mile of Stepney or of Shadwell. Can any one suppose that a theory of representation so palpably and grotesquely at variance with the reality of things has any real prospect of enduring?

The complete submission of all taxation to the will of a mere numerical majority is an end which we have not yet fully attained, but towards which we are manifestly travelling. Every few years something is done in this direction, either by lowering the suffrage, or by abolishing ex-officio guardians of the poor, or by extinguishing plural voting, or by suppressing or weakening property qualifications. The inevitable result is to give one class the power of voting taxes which another class almost exclusively pay, and the chief taxpayers, being completely swamped, are for all practical purposes completely disfranchised. As I have already noticed, it would be difficult to conceive a more flagrant abandonment of that principle about the connection between taxation and voting which in former generations was looked on as the most fundamental principle of British freedom. It is curious to find men who are steadily labouring for this end declaiming on the iniquity of the aristocracy of the eighteenth century in attempting to tax America without her consent. Democracy pushed to its full consequences places the whole property of the country in the hands of the poorest classes, giving them unlimited power of helping themselves. At the same time, under its influence the effect of distant considerations on political action is steadily diminishing. Very naturally, every restraint of economy under such a system is weakened, and the sphere of Government activity and expense is rapidly increased. But evils much graver than mere extravagance and inequitable taxation are impending in a country which has no very extraordinary natural resources, and which owes its almost unique economical position mainly to its great accumulation of movable wealth, and to the national credit which secure wealth alone can give.

It is a saying of the great German historian, Sybel, that 'the realisation of universal suffrage in its consequences has always been the beginning of the end of all parliamentarism.' I believe that a large majority of the most serious and dispassionate observers of the political world are coming steadily to the same conclusion. Parliamentary government which is mainly directed by the educated and propertied classes is an essentially different thing from parliamentary government resting on a purely democratic basis. In all the instances in which this form of government has been conspicuously successful, the representative body was returned on a restricted suffrage. This is manifestly true of the British Parliaments of the past. The Italian Parliaments which displayed such eminent wisdom and forbearance after the war of 1859 and after the death of Cavour; the Austrian Parliaments which carried the singularly wise and moderate legislation that has transformed Austria from a reactionary despotism into one of the best-governed countries in Europe; the Belgian Parliaments which, in spite of furious religious animosities, established among a French-speaking population constitutional government which endured without organic change for sixty years, and which their more brilliant neighbours have wholly failed to rival; the Dutch Parliaments, which represent a country where self-government has long been as perfectly attained as in any portion of the globe—were all elected on a very high suffrage. All these nations have during the last years either entered upon the experiment of democracy or are now trembling on the verge. The result is already very apparent. In Italy, where the experiment has been longest tried, it has already led to a great and manifest deterioration in public life. In Belgium, its first effect was to break up the Parliament into groups, and to shatter the power of the Moderate Liberals.

In several countries pure democracy has been connected with extreme instability of government, with rapidly increasing taxation and debt, with broken credit, with perpetual military insurrections, with constantly recurring alternations of anarchy and despotism. In Mexico, it has been computed that in the thirty-two years between 1821 and 1853 no less than forty-eight different forms of government succeeded each other.[11] In Spain, democracy in its most exaggerated form has been repeatedly adopted. There was an extremely democratic constitution established in 1812, overthrown in 1814, re-established in 1820, again destroyed in 1823. After a long succession of insurrections and constitutional vicissitudes, which it is unnecessary to recount, universal suffrage was established by the Republican revolution of 1868. It prevailed, in spite of several revolutions of power, till 1877, and during this time the credit of the country was irretrievably ruined by the immense increase of the debt. In 1877 a high property electoral qualification was established. In 1887 it was somewhat modified. In 1890 universal suffrage, chiefly qualified by a two years' residence, was re-established.[12] In many cases where universal suffrage exists it has been rendered nugatory by the success with which the governing power has been able to manage and to drill it. There are said to have

---

[11] See Burke's *Life of Juarez*, p. 3.
[12] Dareste, *Constitutions Modernes*, i. 617, 619, 626.

been instances where a regiment of soldiers has been marched to the poll for the purpose of securing the majority for the Government candidate. The system has probably been least dangerous in countries like Germany and the United States, where the powers of the representative body are greatly limited, or in new and distant countries, inhabited by thinly scattered, prosperous, and self-reliant colonists, and where there are no old institutions to be destroyed. Yet, even in these cases the abuses and dangers that flow from it are very apparent.

France, which more than any other country claims the paternity of this form of government, deserves our special attention. In one important respect she seemed peculiarly fitted for it, for the great division of landed property secured a strong conservative basis, and erected the most formidable of all barriers against socialistic innovations. She was also, on account of her almost stationary population, much less exposed than other European nations to that pressure of population on means of subsistence which is one of the chief causes of political disturbances. At the Revolution of 1848 she passed at a single bound from an electorate of about 225,000[13] voters to universal manhood suffrage. For a few months the new electors turned with an overwhelming enthusiasm to Lamartine. At a time when France was peculiarly rich in great men he was pre-eminently the wonderful man of his age, possessing nearly all the qualities that are most fitted to dazzle great masses of men, though, unfortunately, not those which are most needed for the wise guidance of affairs. As a poet, he was by universal consent among the very greatest France had ever produced, and few men in all French literature have wielded the noble instrument of French prose with such consummate genius and skill. His 'History of the Girondins,' untrue, inaccurate, and misleading as it is, had, probably, a greater influence on immediate politics than any other historical work that has ever been written, and the passionate

---

[13] Clère, *Hist. du Suffrage Universel*, p. 59.

enthusiasm it aroused contributed very largely to the Revolution. He combined, too, as no one has done before or since, the most splendid literary gifts in poetry and prose with the power of enthralling assemblies by his spoken words, swaying and restraining the passions of vast multitudes of excited men. In a great crisis he proved brave, honest, humane, and well-meaning, and he could judge large social questions with wisdom and moderation; but he had neither the true strength nor practical talent that are needed in the government of men, and he was apt to be led astray by a childlike and unrestrained vanity.

His popularity was for a time so great that ten departments and more than two millions of voters simultaneously elected him to the National Assembly, without any solicitation on his part. But his star soon faded: socialistic attacks on property began to dominate at Paris, and under the terror of these attacks the great mass of voters began to turn towards a saviour of society. The election, by an enormous majority, of Louis Napoleon as President in December, 1848, clearly foreshadowed the future, and the extremely menacing character which the Paris elections assumed led to the law of 1850, which considerably restricted the suffrage. It made three years' residence in the constituency necessary for an elector, and it provided precise and stringent rules by which that resident must be ascertained. In spite of a furious opposition from the Radical party, this law was carried by 433 to 240, and it is said to have disfranchised more than three millions of voters, or about a third part of the electorate.[14]

Universal suffrage had lasted just two years; but in the conflict which ensued between the Legislative Assembly and the President, the latter clearly saw that it would be his best weapon. By a stroke of true political sagacity he sent down, in November 1851, a powerfully written presidential message, calling upon the Assembly to repeal the law of 1850, and to restore their franchise to the three million voters. The

---

[14] Clère, pp. 92–96.

Chamber received the message with some consternation, and after an agitated debate it resolved by a majority of seven to maintain the existing law. Less than a month later came the Coup d'État of December 2, when the chief statesmen and generals of France were arrested in their beds and carried in the dark winter morning to prison; when the Chamber was peremptorily dissolved; when its members, on their refusal to obey, were led between files of soldiers to the barracks, and thence conducted to prison; when all resistance was crushed by military force, martial law, and wholesale deportations. One of the first acts of Louis Napoleon was to announce in the proclamation that dissolved the Chamber that the electoral law of 1850 was annulled and universal suffrage re-established. Two days after the Coup d'État it was sanctioned by a plebiscite of the army, and within three weeks of the same event, when the greater part of France was still under severe martial law, the act of the President was ratified by universal suffrage. Nearly eight millions of electors are said to have voted for him.

From the Coup d'État of December 2 universal suffrage was duly installed in France. Another plebiscite, which took place in November 1852, made the Prince-President Emperor; while a fourth, only a few weeks before the outbreak of the disastrous war of 1870, once more sanctioned by overwhelming majorities the imperial rule. During the whole of this reign the Legislative Assemblies were elected by universal suffrage, yet during the greater part of it the government was an almost absolute despotism. Universal suffrage was drilled and disciplined into the most obedient of servants. Every official, from the highest to the lowest, was turned into an electioneering agent. The limits of constituencies were arbitrarily enlarged, modified, or contracted to secure the success of the Government candidate. All the powers of administration were systematically and openly employed in directing votes. Each constituency was taught that its prospect of obtaining roads, or bridges, or harbours, or other local advantages depended on its support of the Government, and that if the official candidate succeeded he would have the power of distributing among his supporters innumerable small Government places, privileges and honours. The powers of the Legislative Assembly were extremely limited. They came to little more than a right of sanctioning laws submitted to it by the Government, and voting taxes under great restrictions. Until 1860 its debates were not even fully reported, and for several years the Opposition consisted of five men.

In 1867 and 1868 the whole system was suddenly changed. The Emperor called one of the members of the old Opposition to power, and made a bold attempt, by large and liberal measures, to transform the character of the Empire. The right of interpellation was conceded to the Chamber. Liberty of the press, in almost the widest measure, and a large measure of liberty of meeting, were accorded, and the fierce political life which had been for some seventeen years suppressed burst out with a volcanic fury. Those who knew France in the last days of the Empire will, I think, agree with me that there has never been a more violent, a more dangerous, or more revolutionary press than then prevailed. The hope that active politicians would let bygones be bygones, and accept the compromise of a liberal empire, soon waned. Furious attacks on the main pillars of society attained an enormous popularity, and the very foundations of the Empire were persistently assailed. It was at this period that the works of M. Ténot on the Coup d'État exercised their great influence. The demonstrations at the tomb of Baudin, who had been shot on a barricade in December 1851, displayed the same spirit; and the defiant eloquence of Gambetta in defending those who were accused of riot in connection with these demonstrations first brought that tribune into public notice. The Emperor, not unnaturally, refused to abandon the whole system of official guidance at the election of the Chamber which met in 1869, and universal suffrage again returned a great majority in his favour. But the entire Parisian representation was won by the Opposition, and a great portion of it by its most violent and irreconcilable wing, while in the whole Chamber not much less than a third of the members and a great preponderance of the parliamentary talent were in opposition to the Government.

Most good observers felt that a state of things had been called into existence which could not possibly last. The Emperor, in opening the Chamber, while deploring the growth of subversive and anarchical passions, declared his determination to persevere in the path he had chosen, and, although he refused to abandon his action over the constituencies, and expressly reserved to himself the right of always appealing to his people independently of his ministers, he greatly enlarged the powers of the Assembly. In conjunction with himself it now obtained the right of initiating laws; it obtained the fullest powers of amending them, and the ministers became responsible to it. The Constitution was denounced by the Radical party as a worthless mockery, but it was sanctioned by the Plebiscite of 1870. There were about 7,350,000 votes in favour of the Government, and rather more than 1,500,000 votes against it.

There can be little doubt that the subversive passions that had been aroused and the grave internal dangers that had arisen bore a great part in impelling the Government into the disastrous Franco-German War. There is, therefore, wholly without that strong executive which is one of the most distinguishing characteristics of the great American republic.

Whatever else may be said of this Government, it has certainly not proved a brilliant one. Few French Governments have produced or attracted so little eminent talent, or have been, for the most part, carried on by men who, apart from their official positions, are so little known, have so little weight in their country, and have hitherto appealed so feebly to the imaginations of the world. As it seems to me, one of the characteristic features of our time is the absence of any political ideal capable of exciting strong enthusiasm. Political restlessness and political innovation are abundantly displayed, but there is nothing resembling the fervid devotion and the boundless hopes which the advent of democracy excited at the close of the eighteenth century. Democracy has completely triumphed in two forms—the American and the French—and we see it fully working before us. Men may like it or dislike it, but only rare and very peculiarly moulded minds can find in the Government of either republic a subject for real enthusiasm. The French Revolution, in its earlier days, excited such an enthusiasm nearly to the point of madness, and in 1830 and 1848 French politics exercised an almost irresistible attraction over surrounding countries. It has been one of the achievements of the present Republic to destroy this fanaticism. With our closer insight into American and French democracy, forms of government seem to have lost their magnetic power. The ideals and utopias that float before the popular imagination are of another kind. They point rather to great social and industrial changes, to redistributions of wealth, to a dissolution of the present fabric of society.

I do not know that this is altogether an evil. There is a constant tendency in the human mind to expect too much from Governments, and brilliancy in these spheres is often sought by violent constitutional innovations or military adventure. At the same time, when the Government of a country fails to excite enthusiasm, or even interest, there is apt to be some decline of patriotism, and there is much danger that the craving for excitement, which is so deeply implanted in human nature, and certainly abundantly present in French nature, may some day burst out in very dangerous forms. It has often been said that one of the causes of the popularity of military adventure in great despotisms is the absence of any interest in ordinary public life. In the light of the present condition of France, it is exceedingly curious to read the speeches of Lamartine, Crémieux, and the other men who played the chief part in the Revolution of 1848. The charge which they brought against the Government of Louis Philippe was much less that it was guilty of any positive fault, than that it failed to give France the brilliancy and the prominence in Europe which were her due. She appeared, they contended, like a dowdy,

ill-dressed figure in the concert of nations. Yet, who can doubt
that at that period the amount of brilliant talent in French
public life was incomparably greater than at present?

The characteristic function, however, of government is
business, and a Government that administers affairs with
steady wisdom, tolerance, and uprightness may well be pardoned if it does not appeal to the more poetic side of human
nature. I suspect, however, that most impartial judges will
greatly doubt whether modern French democracy fulfils these
requirements. One of the most conspicuous features has been
its extreme, its astonishing ministerial instability. Between
1870 and the closing days of 1893, when I write these lines,
France has had no less than thirty-two ministries. It may well
be doubted whether a form of government which leads to
such instability can be destined to endure, and whether it is
compatible with that continuity of policy which is one of the
most essential elements of national greatness. One of the
causes that make the power of Russia in the world so formidable is the steady persistence of its foreign policy. Designs
that may be traced to Peter the Great have been steadily pursued, and can be as little doubt that the same causes vastly
aggravated the calamity, for it was the fear of revolution that
prevented the Emperor from falling back on Paris after the
first defeat. When the news of Sedan arrived, and the people
of Paris learnt that the Emperor and his whole army were
prisoners in the hands of the Prussians, the Republic party
saw that their hour had arrived. Instead of rallying around
the Empress, they at once, on their own authority, destroyed
the Government which universal suffrage had so frequently
and so recently ratified, and drove the Regent into exile. Few
things in French history are more mournfully significant than
that the streets of Paris were illuminated the night after the
disaster of Sedan was known. In the eyes of the party which
now ruled, the triumph of the Republic more than compensated for the most terrible calamity that had ever befallen their
country. One of the principal streets in Paris still bears the
name of the Fourth of September, the day when this revolu-

tion was accomplished. It is, apparently, still regarded by some Frenchmen as a day of which they may be proud.

It deprived France of a settled Government at the moment when such a Government was most imperiously needed, and one of its most certain results was the useless prolongation of a hopeless war. There is little doubt that if the Empire had survived Sedan peace would have speedily been made, and, although Strasburg was irrevocably lost, Metz would have been saved; the war indemnity would have been far less; the vast expenditure of life and property and human suffering that marked the later months of the war would have been prevented, and France might have escaped the most hideous, shameful, and wicked of all insurrections—the Communist rising against a French Government under the eyes of a victorious invading army.

Happily, in this dark crisis of her fate France found a really great man, who in intellectual stature seemed to tower like a giant among his contemporaries; and it is a curiously significant fact that he was one of the few surviving statesmen who had been formed in the parliamentary conflicts under Louis Philippe, before the millennium of universal suffrage had dawned upon the land.

It is, perhaps, somewhat rash to discuss the Government which ensued, under which France still subsists. In the rapidly changing kaleidoscope of French politics it may soon take a new form, and something may easily occur which will give it a compexion somewhat different from my present judgment. Still, twenty-three years have elapsed since 1870 and the time at which I am writing, and this space is long enough to furnish us with some general conclusions. The French Republic is, not only in form, but in reality, a Government of universal suffrage, acting with very little control. Its democratic character is chiefly qualified by the position of the Senate, which has some special elements of strength, that will be considered in another chapter. The position of the President was for some time not very clearly determined. As interpreted by Thiers it carried with it great governing powers. Thiers was, indeed, essentially his own prime minister; he insisted upon the Chamber carrying out his policy; he corresponded directly with foreign ambassadors; he held the threads of foreign policy so exclusively in his own hands that the whole question of the evacuation of the territory was entirely managed by him, without reference to his ministers, and it is said that no documents relating to it were found in the Ministry of Foreign Affairs.[15] His ascendency, however, was mainly due to his great personality and reputation, and after his resignation, and especially after the constitutional laws of 1875, the French President assumed a position very little different from that of a constitutional monarch. Unlike the American President, unlike the French Emperor, the President does not owe his position to the direct and independent action of universal suffrage. He is elected by the Senate and Chamber of Deputies voting together. All his acts have to be countersigned by a minister. His ministers fall before a vote of the Assembly, and he cannot even dissolve the Chamber of Deputies without the assent of the Senate. The Government is, therefore, wholly without that strong executive which is one of the most distinguishing characteristics of the great American republic.

Whatever else may be said of this Government, it has certainly not proved a brilliant one. Few French governments have produced or attracted so little eminent talent, or have been, for the most part, carried on by men who, apart from their official positions, are so little known, have so little weight in their country, and have hitherto appealed so feebly to the imaginations of the world. As it seems to me, one of the characteristic features of our time is the absence of any political ideal capable of exciting strong enthusiasm. Political restlessness and political innovation are abundantly displayed, but there is nothing resembling the fervid devotion and the boundless hopes which the advent of democracy excited at

---

[15] Chaudordy, *La France en 1889*, p. 191.

the close of the eighteenth century. Democracy has completely triumphed in two forms—the American and the French—and we see it fully working before us. Men may like it or dislike it, but only rare and very peculiarly moulded minds can find in the Government of either republic a subject for real enthusiasm. The French Revolution, in its earlier days, excited such an enthusiasm nearly to the point of madness, and in 1830 and 1848 French politics exercised an almost irresistible attraction over surrounding countries. It has been one of the achievements of the present Republic to destroy this fanaticism. With our closer insight into American and French democracy, forms of government seem to have lost their magnetic power. The ideals and utopias that float before the popular imagination are of another kind. They point rather to great social and industrial changes, to redistributions of wealth, to a dissolution of the present fabric of society.

I do not know that this is altogether an evil. There is a constant tendency in the human mind to expect too much from Governments, and brilliancy in these spheres is often sought by violent constitutional innovations or military adventure. At the same time, when the Government of a country fails to excite enthusiasm, or even interest, there is apt to be some decline of patriotism, and there is much danger that the craving for excitement, which is so deeply implanted in human nature, and certainly abundantly present in French nature, may some day burst out in very dangerous forms. It has often been said that one of the causes of the popularity of military adventure in great despotisms is the absence of any interest in ordinary public life. In the light of the present condition of France, it is exceedingly curious to read the speeches of Lamartine, Crémieux, and the other men who played the chief part in the Revolution of 1848. The charge which they brought against the Government of Louis Philippe was much less that it was guilty of any positive fault, than that it failed to give France the brilliancy and the prominence in Europe which were her due. She appeared, they contended, like a dowdy, ill-dressed figure in the concert of nations. Yet, who can doubt that at that period the amount of brilliant talent in French public life was incomparably greater than at present?

The characteristic function, however, of government is business, and a Government that administers affairs with steady wisdom, tolerance, and uprightness may well be pardoned if it does not appeal to the more poetic side of human nature. I suspect, however, that most impartial judges will greatly doubt whether modern French democracy fulfills these requirements. One of its most conspicuous features has been its extreme, its astonishing ministerial instability. Between 1870 and the closing days of 1893, when I write these lines, France has had no less than thirty-two ministries. It may well be doubted whether a form of government which leads to such instability can be destined to endure, and whether it is compatible with that continuity of policy which is one of the most essential elements of national greatness. One of the causes that make the power of Russia in the world so formidable is the steady persistence of its foreign policy. Designs that may be traced to Peter the Great have been steadily pursued, and in the whole period from 1816 to 1895 only three ministers—Nesselrode, Gortschakoff, and Giers—have directed the foreign policy of the Empire. The great lines of French foreign policy were pursued with different degrees of energy and success, but with undeviating persistence, by Henry IV., by Richelieu and Mazarin, by Louis XIV., and by Cardinal Fleury. It is probable that in France, as in most democracies, the permanent service includes men greatly above the average which universal suffrage has brought to the front, and it is in this service that the old administrative traditions are preserved and the chief elements of good government are to be found. A good permanent service has often saved a country when its nominal rulers are utterly untrustworthy. But, excellent as the service has been, and, I believe, in many of its branches still is, in France, it is scarcely possible that it should not have been profoundly affected by constant fluctuations among its chiefs. Partly by a desire to weed out all officials who were not in accordance with the strictest Republican doctrine, and partly by the imperious desire felt by succeeding ministries to provide for their followers, a system of change has grown up in French official life much like that which has done so much to degrade American politics.[16] It is not, it is true, carried to the same extreme, but it has introduced much instability into spheres where steady continuity is of the highest importance.

It produces not only the evil of inexperience, but also the still greater evil of a lowered tone. No careful student of French politics can fail to have been struck with the many instances, since the establishment of the Republic, in which diplomatists and other officials have violated the cardinal article of professional honour by publishing to the world secrets they had learned in confidential Government posts. There can be no surer or more ominous sign of deterioration in official life; and it is not difficult to detect its causes. Much has been due to the frequency of revolutions, the functionaries of one dynasty regarding themselves as relieved from all obligation to secrecy when a new form of government was established. Much is also due to the character of the Republic. A prominent French politician who was for four years prefect of police published, almost immediately after he left office, two volumes of 'recollections,' full of anecdotes which would be considered in England scandalous violations of official con-

---

[16] Speaking of the Civil Service in France, M. Leroy-Beaulieu says: 'Plus la société approche du régime démocratique pur, plus cette instabilité s'accentue. . . . La France sur ce point se fait américaine. Pour ne citer qu'un petit fait qui est singulièrement significatif, en 1887 à l'enterrement d'un haut fonctionnaire du ministère des finances, l'un de ses collègues, bien connu d'ailleurs, prenait la parole en qualité de doyen, disait-il, des directeurs généraux du ministère. Ce doyen avait quarante-cinq ou quarante-six ans, si non moins. Que de révocations ou de mises prématurées à la retraite n'avait-il pas fallu pour amener ce décanat précoce!' (*L'Etat et ses Fonctions*, pp. 65–66.) See, too, Scherer, *La Démocratie et la France*, pp. 26–32.

fidence. The following significant lines are his own defence. 'After having found that all means were good for overthrowing the preceding *régimes*, the men who are now in power, in order to consolidate their own authority, claim to appropriate all the traditions of the monarchies they have destroyed. Under a monarchy, the functionary who returns to private life retains obligations of gratitude and fidelity towards the dynasty of which he was and will remain the subject. But in the system of our institutions, what permanent element is there in the name of which such obligations can be imposed on me? Do I owe anything to the existing Cabinet? Is it not composed of my adversaries? Does it not run counter to all the ideas that are dear to me? Does it not obstruct the path to the hopes of a better future? Does it not impose on my country a policy which I detest?'[17]

We may judge French democracy by other tests. Has it raised France to a higher plane of liberty than in the past? The latitude of speaking and writing and dramatic representation is, no doubt, extremely great, but few modern French Governments, in their religious policy and in their educational policy, have made more determined efforts to force upon great masses of the population a system of education they detested, or to deprive them of the religious consolation they most dearly prized. It is very doubtful whether the religious policy of Jules Ferry and the educational policy of Paul Bert were approved of by the majority of Frenchmen. They are, probably, among the many instances in which a resolute and well-organised minority have forced their policy on a majority who were for the most part languid, divided, or unorganised. If the opinions of women as well as of men be taken into account, as they surely should be in questions of religion and education, there can be little doubt that the Government policy was that of a not very considerable minority. The essential characteristic of true liberty is, that under its shelter many different types of life and character, and opinion and belief

---

[17] Andrieux, *Souvenirs d'un Préfet de Police*, ii. 53–54.

can develop unmolested and unobstructed. Can it be said that the French Republic represents this liberty in a higher degree than other Governments? It has been called a Government of the working-classes, but has it in this respect any extraordinary claim to our respect? On nearly all working-class questions, it will be found that France has been preceded on the path of progress by British legislation. At the present day, the hours of work of the French labourer are in general much longer than those of the Englishman; and I believe the English workmen, who have of late years so carefully examined continental legislations, have very generally concluded that they have nothing to envy in the industrial habits or legislation of the Republic.

Has it, at least, managed with peculiar wisdom the resources of France? The history of French finances in the nineteenth century is a very curious one, and a brief retrospect will not, I think, be irrelevant to my present purpose, for it throws much real and instructive light on the tendencies of democracies. We may start from the year 1814, when the great French war was concluded. There was then an extraordinary contrast between the financial condition of Great Britain and that of her conquered adversary. Great Britain and that of her conquered adversary. Great Britain seemed almost crushed by her enormous debt, while the debt of France was quite inconsiderable. Partly by unsparing levies on conquered nations, and partly by his own extremely skilful management of French resources, Napoleon had made his great wars almost self-supporting. Putting aside the debts of conquered or annexed countries, the whole debt of France created between 1800 and 1814 amounted only to an annual payment in interest of seven millions of francs, to a nominal capital of 140 millions, or less than six millions of pounds.[18]

The Hundred Days, the war indemnity exacted after Waterloo by the Allies for their expense in the war, the cost of the army of occupation, the large sums which were voted in

---

[18] Leroy-Beaulieu, *La Science des Finances* (ed. 1892), ii. 556.

compensation to the plundered 'émigrés,'[19] and the years of impaired and depreciated credit that followed the Restoration, added largely to the debt; but in the opinion of the best contemporary authority on French finance, the Government of the Restoration, in this branch of administration, was one of the most skilful, honourable, and economical France has ever known. The credit of the country was never so high as in 1830, and although the debt was increased, it was still very trifling in comparison with the resources of France. When Louis XVIII. came to the throne it involved an annual payment in interest of rather more than sixty-three millions of francs. In 1830 this payment had risen to 164½ millions. Rather more than four million pounds had thus been added to the annual debt-charge.[20]

The reign of Louis Philippe was conducted on much the same lines; and although the debt continued to grow, it grew at a far slower rate than the revenue of the country. In the eighteen years of his reign Louis Philippe added about twelve and a half millions of francs, or 500,000*l.*, to the annual debt-charge. When his Government fell, in 1848, the French debt was the second in Europe; but it was still only a fourth part of that of Great Britain, and if the French monarchy had been as stable as that of England, there can be little doubt that French credit would have attained the English level.[21]

Then came the democratic Republic of 1848. It lasted for three years, and in those three years France increased her debt more than in the twenty-five years between 1823 and 1848. In 1852, when the Empire began, the debt-charge was about 231 millions of francs. The French debt was now a little less than a third of that of England.[22]

During many years of the Second Empire the wealth of France increased perhaps more rapidly than in any other pe-

---

[19] Rather more than twenty-five millions of francs. Ibid. p. 495.
[20] Ibid. pp. 556–63.
[21] Leroy-Beaulieu, *La Science des Finances*, ii. 563-64.
[22] Ibid. p. 564.

riod of her history. Much of this prosperity was, no doubt, due to the astonishing impulse then given to all forms of production by Californian and Australian gold, but much also was due to the sagacious energy with which the Government assisted material development. The railway system, which had been very insufficiently developed under Louis Philippe, was now brought to great perfection. A policy of judicious free trade immensely stimulated industry, and nearly every kind of enterprise was assisted by the Government. Vast sums were expended, and usually with singular intelligence, on public works. The Constitution of 1852 reserved to the Emperor the right of authorising such works by simple decree, and also the right of transferring the credits voted for one department to another. But it was the policy of the Emperor through his whole reign to secure the popularity of his government by keeping the taxes low and unaltered, and meeting the growing expenditure by constant loans. Almost the whole cost of the Crimean War, the Italian War, and the Mexican expedition, and also an immense part of the habitual expenditure of the Government in times of peace, were raised in this way.The extravagance of this system was in part concealed by the complexity of French financial administration, under which several distinct budgets were usually put forward in a year, and also by the device of a very large floating debt. One of the most important steps taken under the Empire was the introduction of a new system of raising loans. Instead of appealing to a few great capitalists, the Emperor threw open the loans by direct subscription to the whole nation, dividing them in such small portions that nearly all classes could afford to subscribe. There is much difference of opinion about the economical advantages of this plan, but there can be no doubt of its extreme popularity. The small Government bonds were eagerly taken up, and loans became as popular as taxes were unpopular. There can also be no doubt that, by interesting an immense portion of the people in the security of the national debt, the new system greatly improved the national credit and strengthened the conservative element in France. It was computed that in 1830 there were at the utmost not more than 125,000 persons in France holding portions of the national debt. In 1869 the number had probably risen to between 700,000 and 800,000, and in 1881 it is believed to have been more than 4,000,000. Either in this way or as owners of land the great majority of the heads of families in France had a direct interest in the prosperity of the State.[23]

The system of government under the Second Empire, and especially in its first ten or twelve years, deserves more careful and impartial examination than it is likely to receive from the generation which witnessed the catastrophes of the Franco-German War. It was a government with no real constitutional freedom, no liberty of the press, no liberty of public meeting. It sheltered or produced great corruption, and repressed with arbitrary and tyrannical violence political opponents. It was detested by the educated classes, by the minority of the population who seriously cared for political freedom, and, in spite of the enormous sums that were expended in public works in Paris, it never succeeded in winning the affections of the Parisian workmen. On the other hand, the theory of paternal government exercised in a thoroughly democratic spirit had probably never before been carried out with equal energy and intelligence. The Emperor continually looked for his support to the great inarticulate masses of his people. To promote their immediate material well-being was the first object of his policy. No preceding Government had done so much to stimulate industry in all its forms, to develop latent resources, and to provide constant and remunerative employment. For many years he succeeded in an eminent degree,[24] and there is very little doubt that the last plebiscite which sanctioned his rule reflected the real feelings of the numerical majority of French-

[23] Leroy-Beaulieu, *La Science des Finances*, ii. 564-70.
[24] Full particulars about the industrial and financial history of the first ten years of the Empire will be found in a very able book, published in 1862, called *Ten Years of Imperialism in France*, by 'A Flâneur.' The writer had evidently access to the best sources of information.

men. If 100,000 more French soldiers had been present on the field of Wörth, and if the French commander had happened to be a man of genius, it is very possible that the Empire might have existed to the present day.

M. Leroy-Beaulieu calculates that in the beginning of 1870—the year of the war—the interest of the consolidated debt was about 129 millions of francs, or about 5,160,000 pounds sterling more than it had been in 1852, when the Emperor ascended the throne. The whole debt-charge was 360 millions of francs. It represented a nominal capital of rather less than twelve milliards of francs, or 480 millions of pounds; and there was in addition a floating debt, which at the beginning of 1870 had been recently reduced to somewhat less than thirty-two millions of pounds.[25]

But the Empire bequeathed to the Republic which followed it an appalling legacy. France was compelled to pay Germany an indemnity of 200 millions of pounds, and her own war expenses were only a very few millions below that sum. Nearly the whole of these colossal sums were raised by loans between 1870 and 1874, and added to the permanent capital of the debt.

The French debt had now greatly outstripped the English one. In the early years of the Republic, and especially during the ascendency of M.Thiers, French finances appear to have been managed with economy and skill. But in 1878 a new system of prodigality began which far exceeded that of the Second Empire, and which appears to have continued to the present time. A few plain figures will place the situation before the reader. The nominal value of the debt of France according to the Budget of 1892 was about thirty-two milliards of francs, or 1,280 millions of pounds. The annual debt-charge was about 1,000,250,000 francs, or fifty million pounds—about double the present interest of the debt of Great Britain; and in the twelve years of perfect peace from 1881 to 1892 France in-

[25] Leroy-Beaulieu, *La Science des Finances*, ii. 570; Chaudordy, *La France cn 1889*, pp. 52–53.

creased her debt by more than five milliards of francs, or 200 millions of pounds—a sum equal to the whole war indemnity which she had been obliged to pay to Germany after the war of 1870.[26] And this debt is irrespective of the large and rapidly growing debts of the communes and municipalities.

A great part of it was, no doubt, incurred for military purposes. The creation of a magnificent army; the fortification of a country which the loss of Strasburg and Metz had left very vulnerable, and the formation of a vast and costly navy, which was probably intended to intimidate Italy and overbalance the power of England in the Mediterranean, account for much. Much, too, was due to the great energy with which the French Republic has pushed on the work of national education; and the expense of this work was enormously increased by the anti-ecclesiastical spirit which insisted on building fresh schoolhouses where ecclesiastical schools were abundantly supplied, and which refused to make any use of the great voluntary institutions established by the Church. But, in addition to these things, there has been another great source of expense, on which the best French economists dilate with unfeigned alarm. It is the enormous and wasteful expenditure on public works which are, for the most part, unremunerative; which are intended, by giving employment, to conciliate the working-classes, and which are extended to every department, almost to every commune, as a reward for supporting the Government. Much of this kind was done—especially at Paris—under the Second Empire, but the system never acquired the enormous extension and extravagance that it has assumed under the Republic. The name of M. de Freycinet is specially attached to this great development of public works; but, as might be expected, it soon far outgrew the proportions which its author had originally assigned to it, though his first idea was to spend four milliards of francs, or 160 millions of pounds, on railways alone. Very naturally, such a system of artificial employment having been started, it was found im-

---

[26] Leroy-Beaulieu, *La Science des Finances*, ii. 578–81; see, too, Martin's *Statesman's Year-Book*, 1893 (France).

possible to abandon it. Very naturally, every locality desired its share of the beneficence of the Government. Countless millions were squandered, either in purely Government work or in tripling or quadrupling local subventions, or in rendering gratuitous public services which had once paid their expenses, or in multiplying inordinate Government posts. And the result was that, at a time when severe economy was imperiously required, the Republic added to its debt a sum which was little, if at all, less than the expense of the War of 1870.[27]

We can hardly have a more impressive illustration of the truth that universal suffrage wholly fails to represent the best qualities of a nation. No people in their private capacities are more distinguished than the French for their business talent, for their combination of intelligent industry with great parsimony, for the courage with which in times of difficulty they retrench their expenditure. Yet few Governments have been more lavishly and criminally extravagant than those which have emanated from universal suffrage in France.

The forms of corruption which are practised in a pure democracy are in general far more detrimental to the prosperity of nations than those which existed in other days. Sinecures, and corrupt pensions, and Court favours, and small jobs, and the purchase of seats of Parliament, may all be carried very far without seriously burdening the national revenues. A millionaire may squander with reckless profusion his shillings and his pence, but as long as the main lines of his expenditure are wisely ordered he will find no great difference at the end of the year. There are, it is true, occasional instances in which the extravagance of an individual or of a Court may have ruined a nation. The most amazing modern example has been that of Ismail Pasha, who, in the thirteen years between 1863 and 1876, raised the Egyptian debt from a little over three millions of pounds to eighty-nine millions, and who, mainly through his personal extravagance and reckless gambling,

---

[27] See on this subject, Scherer, La Démocratie et la France, pp. 29–33; Leroy-Beaulieu, L'Etat et ses Fonctions, pp. 137–74; Leroy-Beaulieu, La Science des Finances, ii. 277–78; Chaudordy, La France en 1889, pp. 54–62.

burdened a poor and struggling population of six million souls with an annual payment for interest of not less than seven millions of pounds.[28] Such prodigies of colossal selfishness, however, are, happily, rare; and if the world had not come to form a wholly false measure of the enormity of political crimes, both in rulers and subjects, they would lead to something very different from a simple deposition.

Corrupt Governments are not necessarily on the whole extravagant. The great corruption which undoubtedly prevailed in the French Government under Louis Philippe did not prevent that Government from managing French finances with an economy which, in the light of later experience, can only be regarded as admirable. The jobs and sinecures and pensions of the Irish Parliament in the eighteenth century were very notorious; yet Irish statesmen truly said that until the outbreak of the great French war Ireland was one of the least taxed nations, and its Government one of the cheapest Governments in Europe. These kinds of corruption do much to lower the character of Governments and to alienate from them the public spirit and enthusiasm that should support them; but except in very small and poor countries they seldom amount to a serious economical evil. Wars, overgrown armaments, policies that shake credit and plunder large classes, laws that hamper industry, the forms of corruption which bribe constituencies or classes by great public expenditure, by lavish, partial unjust, taxation—these are the things that really ruin the finances of a nation. To most of these evils unqualified democracies are especially liable.

Modern Radicalism is accustomed to dilate much upon the cost to a nation of endowing princes and supporting the pageantry of a Court. If there be a lesson which repeated and very recent experience clearly teaches, it is the utter insignificance of such expenditure, compared with the cost of any revolution which renders the supreme power in a State precarious, lowers the national credit, drives out of a country great masses of

[28] Milner's *Egypt*, p. 216.

capital, dislocates its industry and trade, or gives a false and extravagant ply to its financial policy. Brazil and Spain are poor countries, but the millions that have been lost to them by revolutions due to the selfish ambition of a few unprincipled adventurers would have gone far to pay for all the extravagances of all the Courts in Europe.

France can, no doubt, bear the burden of her enormous debt better than most countries. Her great natural advantages, her vast accumulated wealth, the admirable industrial qualities of her people, the wide distribution among them both of landed property and of portions of the national debt, and the fact that this debt is mainly held within the country, have all contributed to the high credit which she still enjoys. Great as is her present debt, it bears a much smaller proportion to her riches than the English debt did to the revenue of Great Britain at the Peace of 1815, than the debts of Italy and Russia still bear to their national resources. No one can doubt that, if a policy of strict economy and steady peace is pursued in France for the coming half-century, her finances will again become very sound. Some portions of her debt consist of terminable annuities. The good credit which is largely due to the wide diffusion of the debt among Frenchmen renders the policy of conversion at diminished interest possible; and in 1950 the railways of France will become national property. A country which was able in 1894 to convert without difficulty 280,-000,000l. of stock bearing 4½ per cent. interest into 3½-per-cent. stock is certainly in no desperate financial condition, and the cheapness and abundance of money, while it increases the temptation to borrow, diminishes the burden of debts.

But, in spite of all these things, no serious French economist can contemplate without alarm the gigantic strides with which both her debt and her taxation have of late years advanced. Such men well know that few national diseases are more insidious in their march, more difficult to arrest, more disastrous in their ultimate consequences. The immediate stimulus to employment given by a new loan masks its ultimate and permanent effects, and if the interest alone is paid out of taxation, the increase is at first scarcely perceptible. No one can suppose that France is destined for a long period to remain at peace, and there is very little prospect of serious retrenchment in her internal affairs. A policy which would involve greatly diminished expenditure in public works, and, at the same time, considerable increase of taxation, can never be popular with the great uninstructed masses, on whose votes all French Governments now depend. Few Governments would venture to propose it, and least of all feeble, transitory, and precarious Governments, like those which have existed in France since 1870. Such Governments necessarily take short views, and look eagerly for immediate support. All the lines of policy that are most fitted to appeal to the imagination and win the favour of an uninstructed democracy are lines of policy involving increased expenditure, and the whole tendency of European democracy is towards enlarging the functions and burdens of the State. When great sections of the people have come habitually to look to Government for support, it becomes impossible to withdraw, and exceedingly difficult to restrict, that support. Public works which are undertaken through political motives, and which private enterprise would refuse to touch, are scarcely ever remunerative. On the other hand, nothing can be more certain than that the evil of excessive taxation is not merely to be measured by the amount which is directly taken from the taxpayer; its indirect, remote consequences are much more serious than its direct ones. Industries which are too heavily weighted can no longer compete with those of countries where they are more lightly taxed. Industries and capital both emigrate to quarters where they are less burdened and more productive. The credit which a nation enjoys on the Stock Exchange is a deceptive test, for the finance of the market seldom looks beyond the prospect of a few years. A false security grows up, until the nation at last slowly finds that it has entered irretrievably on the path of decadence.

It is scarcely to be expected, under the conditions I have described, that the tone of public life should be very high. The disclosures that followed the Panama scandals, though the most startling, were by no means the only signs that have thrown ominous light on this subject. Scherer, in an admirable work, has described in detail the action of the present system on French political life. Nearly every deputy, he says, enters the Chamber encumbered with many promises to individuals; the main object of his policy is usually to secure his re-election after four years, and the methods by which this may be done are well known. There is the branch line of railroad which must be obtained for the district; there is the fountain that should be erected in the public place; there is, perhaps, even the restoration of the parish church to be effected. But it is not less important that all public offices which carry with them any local influence should be in the hands of his supporters. He therefore at once puts pressure on the Government, which usually purchases his support by giving him the patronage he desires. There is a constant shifting in the smaller local offices. Never, it is said, were there so many dismissals and changes in these offices as during the Republic; and they have been mainly due to the desire of the deputies to make room for their supporters or their children. The idea that a vote is a personal favour, establishing a claim to a personal reward, has rapidly spread. At the same time, any vote in favour of public works, and especially public works in his own constituency; any reorganisation that tends to increase the number of men in Government employment, increases the popularity of the deputy. The socialistic spirit takes different forms in different countries, and this is the form it seems specially adopting in France. The old idea, that the representative Chamber is pre-eminently a check upon extravagance, a jealous guardian of the public purse, seems to have almost vanished in democratic countries, and nowhere more completely than in France. In the words of Léon Say, a great proportion of the deputies are, beyond all things, 'agents for instigating to expense,' seeking to secure a livelihood out of the public taxes for the greatest possible number of their electors. The electoral committee, or, as we should say, the local caucus, governs the deputy, who, in his turn, under the system of small parliamentary groups and weak and perpetually fluctuating ministries exercises an exaggerated influence on the Administration.[29]

We may, in the last place, ask whether democracy has given France a nobler and more generous foreign policy. French writers have often claimed for their country that, more than any other, it has been governed by 'ideas;' that it has been the chief torchbearer of civilisation; that French public opinion is pre-eminently capable of rising above the limits of a narrow patriotism in order to support, popularise, and propagate movements of cosmopolitan liberalism. These cosmopolitan sympathies, it must be owned, sometimes fade into Utopia, and lead to a neglect of the duties of a rational patriotism; and not unfrequently they have either disguised, or served, or ended in, designs of very selfish military aggrandisement. Still, no impartial student will deny that France has for a long period represented in an eminent degree the progressive element in European civilisation; that her great influence has usually been thrown into the scale of freedom, enlightenment, and tolerance. Can this noble position be now claimed for her? Can it be denied that a policy of rancour and revenge has, in the later phases of her history, made her strangely false to the nobler instincts of her past? Let the reader follow, in the work of Sir Alfred Milner, the account of the way in which, through very unworthy motives, she has obstructed in Egypt all those reforms which were manifestly necessary to relieve the misery of the Egyptian fellah. Or, let him take a more conspicuous instance, and study that most hideous story of our century—the Russian persecution of the Jews—and then remember that it was on the morrow of this persecution that the French democracy threw itself, in a transport of boundless, unqualified enthusiasm, into the arms of Russia, and declared by all its organs that French and Russian policies were now identified in the world. Few sadder, yet few more significant spectacles have been witnessed in our time than this enthusiastic union, in 1893, of the chief democracy of

---

[29] Scherer, *La Démocratie et la France*, pp. 22–38.

Europe with its one great persecuting despotism. Could there be a more eloquent lesson on the tendencies of democracy than was furnished by the joyous and almost puerile delight with which France identified herself with the cause of reaction, and resigned to others her old supremacy in European liberalism? What a change since the days when George Sand heralded the triumph of democracy, in 1848, as introducing, by the initiative of France, a new era of progress and enlightenment among mankind; since Michelet described France as the armed sentinel of Europe, guarding its civilisation against the barbarians of the North; since Lamartine, in lines of exquisite beauty, proclaimed the cosmopolitan fraternity which was soon to make patriotism itself an obsolete sentiment, too narrow and too harsh for a regenerated humanity!

> Nations! Mot pompeux pour dire barbarie!
> L'amour s'arrête-t-il ou s'arrêtent vos pas?
> Déchirez ces drapeaux, une autre voix vous crie:
> L'égoïsme et la haine ont seuls une patrie,
> La Fraternité n'en a pas.

The conditions of American democracy are essentially different from those of democracy in France, and the effects of this great experiment in government must be profoundly interesting to every serious political inquirer. I have already referred briefly to its character. It would be impossible in a book like the present, it would be presumptuous on the part of a stranger, and after the great works which, in the present generation, have been written on the subject, to attempt to give a full account of the workings of American democracy, but a few salient facts may be gathered which will throw much light upon my present subject.

'La Marseillaise de la Paix.

One of the chief errors of English political writers of the last generation in dealing with this topic arose from their very superficial knowledge of American institutions, which led them to believe that the American Government was generically of the same kind as the Government of England, the chief difference being that a majority of the people could always carry out their will with more prompt, decisive, unrestrained efficiency. The English public have at last, it may be hoped, learned to perceive that this notion is radically false. In England, a simple majority of Parliament is capable, with the assent of the Crown, of carrying out any constitutional change, however revolutionary; and the House of Commons, in practice, has absorbed to itself all the main power in the Constitution. A chance majority, formed out of many different political fractions, acting through different motives, and with different objects, may change fundamentally the Constitution of the country. The Royal veto has become wholly obsolete. The Royal power under all normal circumstances is exercised at the dictation of a ministry which owes its being to the majority of the House of Commons, and if the Crown can occasionally exercise some idependent political influence, it can only be in rare and exceptional circumstances, or in indirect and subordinate ways. The House of Lords has, it is true, greater power, and can still, by a suspensive veto, delay great changes until they are directly sanctioned by the constituencies at an election. But after such sanction it is scarcely possible that such changes should be resisted, however narrow may be the majorities in their favour, however doubtful may be the motives by which these majorities were obtained.

In America the position of the House of Representatives is widely different from that of the House of Commons. It is a body in which the ministers do not sit, and which has no power of making or destroying a ministry. It is confronted by a Senate which does not rest on the democratic basis of mere numbers, but which can exercise a much more real restraining power than the House of Lords. It is confronted also by a President who is himself chosen ultimately by manhood suffrage, but in a different way from the House of Representatives, and who exercises an independent power vastly greater than a modern British sovereign. It is, above all, restricted by a written Constitution under the protection of a great, independent law court, which makes it impossible for it to violate contracts, or to infringe any fundamental liberty of the people, or to carry any constitutional change, except when there is the amplest evidence that it is the clear, settled wish of an overwhelming majority of the people. No amendment of the Federal Constitution can be even proposed except by the vote of two-thirds of both Houses of Congress, or of an application from the legislatures of two-thirds of the several States. No amendment of the Federal Constitution can become law unless it is ratified, in three-quarters of the States, by both Houses in the local legislatures, or by conventions specially summoned for that purpose. As a matter of fact, all amendments of the Federal Constitution have been ratified by the State legislatures; none of them have been submitted to conventions.

Changes in the constitutions of the different States may be effected in different ways, but never by a simple majority of a single legislature. In a few States, it is true, such a majority may propose such an amendment; but it always requires ratification, either by a popular vote, or by a subsequent legislature, or by both. In most States majorities of two-thirds or three-fifths are required for the simple proposal of a constitutional amendment, and in a large number of cases majorities of two-thirds, or three-quarters, or three-fifths, are required for the ratification. There is usually, however, a second method provided for revising or amending a State constitution, by means of a convention which is specially called for this purpose, and which proposes changes that must be subsequently ratified by a popular vote.[30]

The American Constitution, indeed, was framed by men who had for the most part the strongest sense of the dangers of democracy. The school of American thought which was rep-

---

[30] A detailed account of the methods of changing the State constitutions will be found in a Report on the Majorities required in Foreign Legislatures for changes in the constitution, presented to the House of Lords, April 1893.

resented in a great degree by Washington and John Adams,
and still more emphatically by Gouverneur Morris and Alexander Hamilton; which inspired the Federalist and was em-
bodied in the Federalist party, was utterly opposed to the
schools of Rousseau, of Paine, and even of Jefferson, and it has
largely guided American policy to the present hour. It did not
prevent America from becoming a democracy, but it framed a
form of government under which the power of the democracy
was broken and divided, restricted to a much smaller sphere,
and attended with far less disastrous results than in most European countries. Hamilton, who was probably the greatest
political thinker America has produced, was, in the essentials
of his political thought, quite as conservative as Burke, and he
never concealed his preference for monarchical institutions.
Democratic government, he believed, must end in despotism,
and be in the meantime destructive to public morality and to
the security of private property.[31]

To the eminent wisdom of the Constitution of 1787 much
of the success of American democracy is due; but much also
must be attributed to the singularly favourable circumstances
under which this great experiment has been tried. A people
sprung mainly from an excellent British stock, and inheriting
all the best habits and traditions of British constitutional government, found themselves in possession of a territory almost
boundless in its extent and its resources, and free from the
most serious dangers that menace European nations. The
habits of local government, the spirit of compromise and self-
reliance, the strong moral basis which Puritanism never fails
to establish, were all there, and during a great portion of
American history emigration was attended with so many
hardships that few men who did not possess more than average energy and resource sought the American shore. At the
same time a vast unpopulated, undeveloped country opened
limitless paths of adventure, ambition, and lucrative labour,
dispersed many peccant humours, attracted and employed

[31] Van Buren, *Political Parties in the United States*, pp. 80, 83.

much undisciplined and volcanic energy which, in other countries, would have passed into politics and bred grave troubles in the State. The immense preponderance of industrialism in American life is, indeed, one of its most characteristic features, and its influence on politics has been by no means wholly good. It has contributed, with other causes, to place political life on a lower plane, diverting from it the best energies of the country; but it has also furnished great safety-valves for discontented spirits and unregulated ambitions. The country was so situated that it was almost absolutely self-supporting, and had no foreign danger to fear. It might almost dispense with a foreign policy. It required no considerable army or war navy; and it has been able steadily to devote to the maintenance of an excellent system of national education the sums which, in less happily situated countries, are required for the purposes of self-defence. Although America has experienced many periods of acute commercial crisis and depression, the general level of her well-being has been unusually high. Property has been from the first very widely diffused. Her lower levels in their standard of comfort more nearly resemble the middle than the lowest class in European countries, and the great masses of unemployed pauperism in the large towns, which form one of the most serious political and social dangers of Europe, have been scarcely known in America until the present generation.

The chief steps by which the Government has moved in the direction of democracy may be briefly mentioned. Although the Constitution in most respects realised the anticipations of its founders, their attempt to place the President outside the play of party spirit, and to make him independent of democratic dictation, signally failed. The Constitution provided that each State was to choose a number of presidential electors equal to its representatives in Congress, and that these men should be entrusted with the task of electing the President. In accordance with its general policy on all matters of election, the Constitution left it to the different States to determine the manner of election and the qualifications of

these presidential electors; but it enacted that no member of
Congress and no holder of a Federal office should be eligible.
In this manner it was hoped that the President might be
elected by the independent votes of a small body of worthy
citizens who were not deeply plunged in party politics. But,
as the spirit of party intensified and the great party organisations attained their maturity, this system wholly failed.
Presidential electors are still elected, but they are elected under a distinct pledge that they will vote for a particular candidate. At first they were nearly everywhere chosen on party
grounds by the State legislatures. Soon this process appeared
insufficiently democratic, and they were chosen by direct
manhood suffrage, their sole duty being to nominate the candidate who had been selected by the party machine.

In the senatorial elections the principle of double election
has proved somewhat more enduring; but here, too, considerable transformations have taken place. The Senate, as is
well known, is composed of two senators from each State,
chosen for six years by the State legislatures, the largest and
the smallest States being in this respect on a par. For a long
time the mode of their election varied greatly. 'In some States
they were chosen *vivâ voce*; in others, by ballots; in some, by
a separate vote of each House; in others, by both Houses
meeting and voting as one body.'[32] By an Act of 1866 the
method of election has been made uniform, the senators
being nominated by a *vivâ voce* vote in each House; and if the
result is not attained in this manner, by a vote of the two
Houses sitting together. Very naturally and properly, these
are party elections; but of late years the senators appear to
have been rarely what they were intended to be—the independent choice of the State legislatures. 'The machines,' or,
in other words, the organisations representing the rival factions in each State, not only return absolutely the members
of the State legislature, but also designate the rival candidates
for the senatorships; and the members of the State legislature

---

[32] Ford's *American Citizen's Manual*, i. 13–14.

are returned under strict pledges to vote for these designated candidates. This servitude is not as absolute or universal as that under which the presidential elections are made, but it has gone very far to bring the election of senators under the direct control of those knots of wirepullers who rule all the fields of American politics, and direct and manage universal suffrage.[33] In the early stages of its history, when the States were very few, the Senate was a small body, deliberating in secret, and more like a Privy Council or a Cabinet than an Upper Chamber. After the first five years of its existence this system of secrecy was abandoned; with the multiplication of States the number of senators increased; and the Senate has now the chief characteristics of a legislative Chamber, though it possesses certain additional powers which are not possessed by the corresponding bodies in Europe.

The many restrictions on the suffrage by which the members of the House of Representatives were elected at the time of the Revolution have nearly all passed away, and America has all but reached the point of simple manhood suffrage. Maryland, in the first decade of the nineteenth century, led the way,[34] and the example was speedily followed. The management, restriction, and extension of the suffrage being left within the almost complete competence of the several States, form the chief field in which revolutionary change can be easily effected. The Federal Constitution only imposes two restrictions on the competency of the States to deal with this subject. The first is, that the electors for representatives in each State 'shall have the qualifications required for electors of the most numerous branch of the State Legislature.' The second, which was an amendment of the Constitution introduced after the Civil War, and carried at a time when the Southern States were still deprived of their normal political power, is that no one may be excluded from the suffrage 'on account of race, colour, or previous condition of servitude.'

---

[33] See Bryce's *American Commonwealth*, i. 131–32.
[34] Tocqueville, *Démocratie en Amérique*, i. 91.

The suffrage, it is true, is not absolutely universal. Besides the exclusion of women, children, criminals, insane persons, and unnaturalised immigrants, some easy qualifications of residence and registration are usually required; but property qualifications have almost wholly disappeared. The actual possession of property is no longer required for a voter in any American election, with the exception, it is said, of the municipal elections in a single district of Rhode Island.[35] A tax qualification existed in 1880 in six States, but it has since then been abolished in four of them.[36] Some States, however, still exclude from the right of voting those who are so illiterate that they are not able to read, and paupers who are actually supported by the State. With these slight and partial exceptions manhood suffrage generally prevails.

As far as I can judge, it seems to have been brought about by much the same means in America as in Europe. It has not been in general the result of any spontaneous demand, or of any real belief that it is likely to improve the Constitution; but it has sprung from a competition for power and popularity between rival factions. An extension of the franchise is, naturally, a popular cry, and each party leader is therefore ready to raise it, and anxious that his rival should not monopolise it. It is a policy, too which requires no constructive ability, and is so simple that it lies well within the competence of the vulgarest and most ignorant demagogue. A party out of office, and doubtful of its future prospects, naturally wishes to change the character of the electorate, and its leaders calculate that new voters will vote, at all events for the first time, for the party which gave them their vote. We are in England perfectly familiar with such modes of conducting public affairs, and it is probably no exaggeration to say that calculations of this kind have been the chief motives of all our recent

---

[35] Hart's *Practical Essays on American Government*, 1893, p. 28. There are still, however, some cases in which a property qualification is required from an office-holder.
[36] Ibid.

degradations of the suffrage. In one important respect the Federal system has tended to strengthen in America the democratic movement. Each State naturally wishes to have as much power as possible in the Confederation, and an amendment of the Constitution which was forced through during the temporary eclipse of the Southern States provides that while, as a general rule, representatives in Congress shall be apportioned among the several States according to their populations, the basis of representation in a State shall be reduced in proportion to the number of such citizens who are excluded from the suffrage, 'except for participation in rebellion and other crime.'

The system of popular election has extended through nearly all branches of American life. Perhaps its most mischievous application is to the judicial posts. The independence and dignity, it is true, of the Federal judges are protected by an article of the Constitution. They can only be appointed by the President with the consent of the Senate. They hold their office during good behaviour; and they possess salaries which, though small if compared with those of English judges, enable them to support their position. The Supreme Court is one of the most valuable portions of the American Constitution, and although even its decisions have not always escaped the suspicion of party motives, it is, on the whole, probably inferior in ability and character to no other judicial body on the globe. But in the States another system has spread which has both lowered and tainted the administration of justice. As recently as 1830 the judges in the different States owed their appointment to the governors, or to the State legislatures, or to a combination of the two. In 1878, in no less than twenty-four States they were elected by a popular vote.[37] When it is added that they only hold their office for a few years, that they are capable of re-election, and that their salaries are extremely small, it will not appear extraordinary

---

[37] Ford's *American Citizen's Manual*, i. 136.

that the judicial body in most of these States should be destitute of the moral dignity which attaches in England to all its branches. Deliberate personal corruption, which for generations has been unknown among English judges, has been in some cases proved, and in many cases suspected, in America, and the belief that in large classes of cases judges will act as mere partisans on the bench has extended much further. The prevalence of lynch law, which is so strangely discordant with the high civilisation of American life, is largely due to that distrust of justice in many States which is the direct, manifest, acknowledged consequence of the system of popular election.

No one, indeed, who knows the class of men who are wire-pullers in the different American factions will expect their nominees on the bench to be distinguished either for impartiality or integrity. One of the most extraordinary instances of organised crime in modern history is furnished by the Molly Maguires of Pennsylvania, an Irish conspiracy which, with short intervals, maintained a reign of terror between 1863 and 1875 in the anthracite coalfields of that State. The innumerable murders they committed with impunity, and the extraordinary skill and daring of the Irish detective who succeeded in penetrating into their councils and at last bringing them to justice, form a story of most dramatic interest; but one of the most curious facts connected with them is the political influence they appear to have obtained. They controlled township affairs in several districts; they applied to their own purposes large public funds; they had a great influence in the management of counties; they were courted by both political parties; and they only failed by a few hundred votes in placing one of their body on the judicial bench.[38] I can here hardly do better than quote the language of Mr. Bryce, who, writing with ample knowledge of the subject, is evidently desirous of minimising as much as possible the importance of the facts which he honestly but reluctantly relates.

[38] See that very curious book, Dewees's *The Molly Maguires* (Philadelphia, 1877), pp. 33, 92–93, 109, 221–29, 296.

'In a few States,' he writes, 'perhaps six or seven in all, suspicion has at one time or another, within the last twenty years, attached to one or more of the superior judges. Sometimes these suspicions may have been ill-founded. But though I know of only one case in which they have been substantiated, there can be little doubt that in several instances improprieties have been committed. The judge may not have taken a bribe, but he has perverted justice at the instance of some person or persons who either gave him a consideration or exercised an undue influence over him. . . . I have never heard of a State in which more than two or three judges were the object of distrust at the same time. In one State, viz. New York, in 1869–71 there were flagrant scandals, which led to the disappearance of three justices of the superior court who had unquestionably both sold and denied justice. The Tweed ring, when engaged in plundering the city treasury, found it convenient to have in the seat of justice accomplices who might check inquiry into their misdeeds. This the system of popular election for very short terms enabled them to do, and men were accordingly placed on the bench whom one might rather have expected to see in the dock—bar-room loafers, broken-down attorneys, needy adventurers—whose want of character made them absolutely dependent on these patrons. . . . They did not regard social censure, for they were already excluded from decent society; impeachment had no terrors for then, since the State legislatures, as well as the executive machinery of the city, was in the hands of their masters. . . . To what precise point of infamy they descended I cannot attempt, among so many discordant stories and rumours, to determine. It is, however, beyond a doubt that they made orders in defiance of the plainest rules of practice; issued in rum-shops injunctions which they had not even read over; appointed notorious vagabonds receivers of valuable property; turned over important cases to a friend of their own stamp, and gave whatever decision he suggested. . . . A system of client robbery sprang up, by which each judge enriched the knot of disreputable lawyers who surrounded him. He referred cases to them, granted them monstrous allowances in the name of costs, gave them receiverships with a large percentage, and so forth, they in turn either sharing the booty with him, or undertaking to do the same for him when he should have descended to the Bar and they have climbed to the Bench. Nor is there any doubt that criminals who had any claim on their party often managed to elude punishment. . . for governor, judge, attorney, officials, and police, were all of them party nominees. . . . In the instance which made much noise in Europe—that of the Erie Railroad suits—there was no need to give bribes. The gang of thieves who had gained control of the line and were 'watering' the stock were leagued with the gang of thieves who ruled the city and nominated the judges, and nobody doubts that the monstrous decisions in these suits were obtained by the influence of the Tammany leaders over their judicial minions'.[39]

Such is the state of things which flourished a few years ago in full exuberance in the capital of the great democracy of the West, and among a people who claim to be in the front rank of civilisation, and to have furnished the supreme pattern of the democracies of the future. Mr. Bryce does all that is in his power to soften the picture. He believes that the corrupt judges are only a small minority in a few States, and that there is no evidence that even the New York judges, in ordinary commercial cases, where no political interest came into play, and where the influence of particular persons was not exerted, decided unjustly or 'took direct money bribes from one of the parties.' He also takes a long historical flight over nearly three thousand years for the purpose of collecting parallel enormities. Hesiod complained of kings who received gifts to influence their decisions. Felix expected money for releasing St. Paul. Among the great despotisms of the East judicial corruption has always been common. In a single instance since the Revolution an English chancellor was found to have taken bribes; and in some of the more backward countries of Europe 'the judges, except, perhaps, those of the highest court, are not assumed by general opinion to be above suspicion.'

---

[39] Bryce's *American Commonwealth*, iii. 394–99.

Such arguments may be left to stand on their own merits. Of all the many functions which government is expected to discharge, the most important to the happiness of mankind is that of securing equal justice between man and man. No statesmen were more conscious of this truth than the great men who framed the Constitution of the United States; and, under the conditions of their time, they probably provided for it almost as perfectly as human prescience could have done. It would be a grave injustice to the American people to suppose that they were not in general a law-abiding people: they have more than once suppressed disorder in the States with an unflinching energy and a truly merciful promptness of severity which English Administrations might well imitate; and over a great part of the States honest justice is undoubtedly administered. But no one, I think, can follow American history without perceiving how frequently and seriously the democratic principle has undermined this first condition of true freedom and progress. As Mill justly says, the tyranny of the majority is not only shown in tyrannical laws. Sometimes it is shown in an assumed power to dispense with all laws which run counter to the popular opinion of the hour. Sometimes it appears in corrupt, tainted, partial administration of existing laws. Tyranny seldom assumes a more odious form than when judges, juries, and executives are alike the tools of a faction or a mob.

Closely connected with this great abuse has been the system of treating all the smaller posts and offices, both under the Federal and the State governments, as rewards for party services, and changing the occupants with each change of political power. This is the well-known 'spoils system,' and it has permeated and corrupted American public life to its very roots. It did not exist in the early days of the Republic. Washington, in the eight years of his presidency, only removed nine officials, and all for definite causes. John Adams made the same number of changes. Jefferson made thirty-nine; and the three Presidents who followed only removed sixteen in the space of twenty years. John Quincy Adams, the last of this line of Presidents, was in this respect scrupulously

just. 'As he was about the last President,' writes Mr. Goldwin
Smith, 'chosen for merit, not for availability, so he was about
the last whose only rule was not party, but the public service.
So strictly did he preserve the principle of permanency and
purity in the Civil Service, that he refused to dismiss from
office a Postmaster-General whom he knew to be intriguing
against him.'

The great evil which was impending was largely prepared
by an Act of 1820, which limited the term of office of a vast
number of subordinate officials to four years, and at the same
time made them removable at pleasure. The modern system
of making all posts under the Government, however unconnected with politics, rewards for party services was organised, in 1829, by Andrew Jackson. This President may be said
to have completed the work of making the American Republic
a pure democracy, which Jefferson had begun. His statue
stands in front of the White House at Washington as one of
the great men of America, and he assuredly deserves to be
remembered as the founder of the most stupendous system
of political corruption in modern history. It began on a comparatively small scale. About 500 postmasters were at once
removed to make room for partisans, and all the more active
partisans, including, it is said, fifty or sixty leading newspaper writers, received places, the propagation of Government
views through the press having now become, according to
Webster, 'the main administrative duty.' In a short time the
dismissals under this President numbered about 2,000.[40]

This was the beginning of a system which has spread like
a leprosy over all political life, and to which there is, I believe,
no adequate parallel in history. It is not easy to obtain exact
statistics about the extent to which it has been practised. A very
eminent American writer, who is distinguished not only for
his high character, but also for his scrupulous accuracy of statement and research, and who has himself taken a prominent

---

[40] Goldwin Smith, *The United States*, pp. 192–203; Ford's *American Citizen's Manual*, i. 138–40.

part in the work of Civil Service reform, mentions that a few years ago 'the army of Federal officials was roughly estimated at nearly 125,000, drawing annual salaries amounting to about eighty millions of dollars.' He notices that in the two years preceding 1887, out of 2,359 post-offices known as presidential, about 2,000 had been changed, and that out of 52,699 lower post-office clerks, about 40,000 had been changed. 100 out of 111 collectors of Customs, all the surveyors of Customs, all the surveyors-general, all the post-office inspectors-in-charge; 11 out of 13 superintendents of mints; 84 out of 85 collectors of internal revenue; 65 out of 70 district attorneys; 8 out of 11 inspectors of steam-vessels; 16 out of 18 pension agents; 190 out of 224 local land officers were changed in the space of two years, and under a President who had come to office as a supporter of Civil Service reform. These are but a few illustrations out of many of the manner in which, in the words of the writer I am citing, 'office is made the coin in which to pay political debts and gain the services of political *condottieri*,' and he estimates that this President had 'dismissed nearly 100,000 public servants for political ends.'[41]

Another very competent American author, who has written the best short account of American government with which I am acquainted, observes that 'in the Federal Administration alone there are nearly 90,000 office-holders who have no voice in the administration; but as chiefs of bureaux and clerks are necessary for the transaction of business, and as new territory is opened up, the number is constantly increasing.' These appointments are systematically filled up, not upon the ground of administrative capacity, but 'on the basis of nomination, influence, and official favour.' The practice of constant removals has, since Jackson's time, 'been followed by all parties in all elections, great and small, national and local.' A great part of this patronage is in the hands of senators and representatives, who claim as a right the power of advising the President

---

[41] See a remarkable essay on *Mr. Cleveland and Civil Service Reform*, by Henry C. Lea. Reprinted from the *Independent*, October 18, 1888.

in these appointments; who 'dictate appointments as if the
Federal patronage in their State or district was their private
property,' and who systematically use it to build up political
influence and reward political services.

And not only does this system turn into ardent politicians
countless officials whose duties should place them as far as
possible out of the domain of party politics; not only does it
furnish the staff of the great party organisations, and make
the desire of obtaining and retaining office the main motive in
all party conflicts—it also gives rise to the system of political
assessments, 'made on office-holders of all grades, by a perfectly irresponsible committee, to be expended in furthering
the objects of the party. . . . Although nominally such contributions to the campaign fund are made "voluntarily" by the
office-holders, yet their true nature is shown by many circumstances. Thus, in making its application, the committee fixes
the amount which each man is to pay. In 1882, 2 per cent. of
the amount which each man is to pay. In 1882, 2 per cent.
of the annual salary was required, and was levied on all, from
the chiefs of bureaux to the lowest labourer in the Govern-
Democrats. Moreover, in case the call was not responded to,
employés of the committee went among the departments and
made personal application to each delinquent. By experience
the clerk knows that he must pay or be discharged, a fact
which still more strongly brings out the "voluntary" nature
of the contribution. . . . The committee may expend the fund
thus collected as it sees fit, and need render an account of
such expenditure to no man. Truth compels us to say that it
forms a "corruption fund" for influencing elections; and the
manner of expending it is as vicious and debauching to the
public service as is the manner of collecting it. This matter
has also been made the subject of legislation, but without any
remedy being afforded.'[42]

---

[42] Ford's *American Citizen's Manual*, i. 130–41. Mr. Lea writes: 'It is in vain
that the Pendleton Act prohibits the levying of assessments on office-
holders, when circulars from democratic committees are as thick as
leaves in Vallombrosa, when the raffle for the Widow McGuiness's pig
proved so productive in the New York Custom House, when an office is

A third very competent American writer on the Constitution reminds us that, owing to the increased debt and taxation growing out of the Civil War, the number of office-holders in the United States quadrupled in the period from 1860 to 1870, and that these appointments are systematically made through mere party motives, and irrespective of the capacity of the claimant. 'This system,' he continues, 'not only fills the public offices of the United States with inefficient and corrupt officials in high station, and keeps out of political life the capable men who are disinclined to perform party work as a condition precedent to accession to office, but it also created the same system under those officials as to all their subordinates. . . . They were to a very large degree, and still are, regularly assessed to pay the political expenses of the campaign. Millions of dollars are thus raised from office-holders in the United States at every recurring Presidential election, or even local election. . . . Such assessments were paid because they knew that their official existence would be terminated in the event of a change of Administration, under the domination of an adverse party. . . . The evil of the abominable "spoils" system in the United States is not so much the incompetency of the officers—an American's adaptiveness enables him quickly to learn the routine duties of an office—nor in the waste of public money (because in a community so rich in productive power as that of the United States the amount which peculation can take from it is a burden easy to be borne)—but the main evil is that the spoils system demoralises both parties, and makes contests which should be for principle mainly for plunder.' Under its influence, this writer adds, the quadrennial presidential elections have become 'mere scrambles for office'. [43]

It will be observed that this system is very distinctly a product of democracy. It is called by its supporters the rotation of offices. It is defended on the ground that, by short tenures and constant removals, it opens the ranks of official life to the

---

ostentatiously opened in Washington, and every clerk is personally notified that it is ready to receive contributions' (*Mr. Cleveland and Civil Service Reform*, p. 4).

[43] Sterne's *United States Constitution and History*, pp. 227–31.

greatest possible number of the people; and although, in the words of Mr. Bryce, 'nobody supposes that merit has anything to do with promotion, or believes the pretext alleged for an appointment,'[44] its democratic character and its appeal to the self-interest of vast multitudes make it popular. It is also, as Mr. Bryce notices, a main element in that system of 'machine'-made politics which, in America, so successfully excludes the more respectable class from political life, and throws its whole management into the hands of the professional politicians. I can here only refer my readers to the instructive chapters in which Mr. Bryce has described the working of the 'machine.' He has shown how the extreme elaboration and multiplication of committees and organisations for the purpose of accumulating and directing votes, as well as the enormous number of local elections to office which are conducted on party lines, and which all add to or subtract from party strength, turn the politics of a State into a business so absorbing that no one can expect to have much influence in it unless he makes it a main business of his life. At the same time, the vast number of men who hold office, and the still larger number who are aspiring to office, furnish those organisations with innumerable agents, who work for them as men work for their livelihood, while the tribute levied upon officials supplies an ample fund for corruption. 'The great and growing volume of political work to be done in managing Primaries, conventions, and elections for the city, State and national Government . . . which the advance of democratic sentiment and the needs of party warfare evolved from 1820 down to about 1850, needed men who should give to it constant and undivided attention. These men the plan of rotation in office provided. Persons who had nothing to gain for themselves would soon have tired of the work. . . . Those, however, whose bread and butter depend on their party may be trusted to work for their party, to enlist recruits, look after the organisation, play electioneering tricks from which ordinary

---

[44] *American Commonwealth*, ii. 488.

party spirit might recoil. The class of professional politicians was, therefore, the first crop which the spoils system—the system of using public offices as private plunder—bore. . . . It is these spoilsmen who have depraved and distorted the mechanism of politics. It is they who pack the primaries and run the conventions, so as to destroy the freedom of popular choice; they who contrive and execute the election frauds which disgrace some States and cities, repeating and ballot-stuffing, obstruction of the polls, and fraudulent countings-in. . . . The Civil Service is not in America, and cannot under the system of rotation, become a career. Place-hunting is the career; and an office is not a public trust, but a means of requiting party services, and also, under the method of assessments previously described, a source whence party funds may be raised for election purposes'.[45] 'What characterises' American politicians, 'as compared with the corresponding class in Europe, is that their whole time is more frequently given to political work; that most of them draw an income from politics, and the rest hope to do so.[46]

One very natural result is, that while there is no country in the world in which great party contests are fought with more energy and tenacity than in America, there is no country in the world in which the motives that inspire them are more purely or more abjectly sordid. Great unselfish causes are, no doubt, advocated by groups of politicians in America, as elsewhere, but these lie usually within the limits of parties, and are not the true causes of party division. In other countries it is not so. Selfish and corrupt motives no doubt abound; but in the contest between Liberals and Conservatives, Unionists and Radicals, in England; in the great dynastic quarrels, or quarrels between monarchy and republicanism, between clericalism and anti-clericalism, between labour and capital, that divide parties on the Continent, there is always some real principle at issue, some powerful element of unselfish enthusiasm. In

---

[45] Bryce, ii. 485–89.
[46] Ibid. 399.

America this does not appear to be the case. This is partly, no doubt, due to the absence of great questions in a country which has few serious relations with other nations, which has almost wholly disconnected the interests of Churches and religion from national politics, and in which the Constitution opposes insuperable obstacles to organic change. But it is still more due to the enormous preponderance in politics of selfish interests, and of classes who are animated by such interests. I have quoted on this subject the emphatic language of Mr. Sterne. That of Mr. Bryce is very similar. 'Politics,' he says, 'has now become a gainful profession, like advocacy, stock-broking, the dry-goods trade, or the getting up of companies. People go into it to live by it, primarily for the sake of the salaries attached to the places they count on getting; secondarily, in view of the opportunities it affords of making incidental, and sometimes illegitimate, gains.' 'Republicans and Democrats have certain war-cries, organisations, interests enlisted in their support. But those interests are in the main the interests of getting or keeping the patronage of the Government. Tenets and policies, points of political doctrine and points of political practice, have all but vanished. They have not been thrown away, but have been stripped away by time and the progress of events fulfilling some policies, blotting out others. All has been lost except office or the hope of it.'[47]

There is scarcely any subject on which the best men in America are so fully agreed as upon the absolute necessity of putting an end to this spoils system, if American public life is ever to be purified from corruption. Unfortunately, this system appeals to so many interests and such strong passions, and has been so thoroughly incorporated in the normal working of both of the great parties, that the task of combating it is enormously difficult, and few active politicians have entered into it with real earnestness. There have been frequent efforts in this direction. There was an abortive attempt of Calhoun, in 1839, to prevent a large class of government officers from interfering in elections. There were Acts carried in

---

[47] Bryce, ii. 345, 392.

1853 and 1855 requiring examinations for some departments of the Civil Service at Washington, and another Act was carried in 1871: but they appear to have been little more than a dead-letter.[48] Though the subject was frequently before Congress, no really efficacious step was taken till the Act called the Pendleton Act, which was carried in 1883, and which applied to about 15,000 officials out of about 125,000. It introduced into some departments the system of competitive examinations, gave some real fixity of tenure, and attempted, though apparently with little or no success, to check the system of assessment for political purposes.

The system of competitive examinations has since then been in some degree extended. One of the latest writers on American politics says that about 43,800 servants of the Government, out of nearly 180,000 persons employed in all civil capacities by the United States, are now withdrawn from the spoils system, but he doubts much whether democratic opinion is, on the whole, in favour of an abandonment of the system of rotation and political appointment.[49] A considerable movement to abolish it has, however, been set on foot, and the reformers, who are known under the name of Mugwumps, are said to have acquired some real influence. In the opinion of Mr. Gilman, the independent element, which is 'opposed to any increase of the Civil Service of the State or the nation until a great reform has been accomplished, beyond dispute, in the distribution of the multitude of minor offices,' is, 'happily, coming to hold more and more the balance of power.' 'There is,' he adds, 'a powerful and growing tendency to take out of politics the public charities, the free schools, the public libraries, the public parks, and numerous other features of municipal administration.' To take an office 'out of politics,' Mr. Gilman very characteristically explains, means 'to take it out of corruption into honesty,' and to treat it 'as a public trust for the benefit of the whole people.'[50]

---

[48] Ford, i. 141–42; Bryce, ii. 490.
[49] Hart's *Essays on American Governments*, pp. 82, 83, 91–96.
[50] Gilman's *Socialism and the American Spirit* (1893), p. 178.

The growth of the number of minor officials, which is a natural consequence of the spoils system, and also of the prevailing tendency to extend the functions of government, is exciting serious alarm. A recent Civil Service Commission gives the number of 'employees' in the postal service of the United States, in 1891, as 112,800; the number of other 'employees' as 70,688. There has been, the commission says, 'a very startling growth in the number of Government employees, compared with the growth of population. . . . The growth of a service which can be used for political ends is a rapidly increasing menace to republican government.' Mr. Gilman quotes the statement of Mr. Curtis, that the first object of every reformer should be 'to restrict still further the executive power as exercised by party.' In America, that statesman says, 'the superstition of Divine right has passed from the king to the party,' and the belief that it can do no wrong 'has become the practical faith of great multitudes.' 'It makes the whole Civil Service a drilled and disciplined army, whose living depends upon carrying elections at any cost for the party which controls it.'[51]

On the whole, as far as a stranger can judge, there seem to be in this field real signs of improvement, although they may not be very considerable or decisive. It must be remembered that the period immediately following the War was one peculiarly fitted for the growth of corruption. The sudden and enormous increase of debt, the corresponding multiplication of officials, the paralysis of political life in a great part of the country, and the many elements of social, industrial, and political anarchy that still prevailed, all made the task of professional politicians easy and lucrative. One great improvement which has taken place, and which has spread very swiftly over the United States, has been an alteration in the ballot system. In my own opinion, the ballot, in any country where politics rest on a really sound and independent basis, is essentially an evil. Power in politics should never be dissociated

---

[51] Ibid, pp. 310–11.

from responsibility, and the object of the ballot is to make the elector absolutely irresponsible. It obscures the moral weight of an election, by making it impossible to estimate the real force of opinion, knowledge, and character that is thrown on either side. It saps the spirit of independence and upright- ness, and it gives great facilities for deception and fraud, for the play of mercenary, sordid, and malignant motives, and for the great political evil of sacerdotal influence. But the task of a statesman is, usually, to select the best alternative, and, where intimidation or corruption is very rife, the evils pro- duced by secret voting may be less serious than those which it prevents.

In America, the system of ballot secured no real secrecy, and seemed, and indeed probably was, specially intended to throw all electoral power into the hands of 'the machine.' The agents of each organisation were suffered to stand at the poll and furnish the elector with ballot-papers inscribed with the names of their party candidates, and watchful eyes followed him till he placed the paper in the ballot-box. He might, it is true, change the name on the paper, but in the immense ma- jority of cases the votes of the electors were dictated by and known to the party agent.[52] A powerful movement, however, grew up, chiefly in 1890 and 1891, for changing this system and introducing what is called the Australian ballot. Its prin- cipal feature is that the State has taken the manufacture and distribution of ballot-papers out of the hands of the different parties, and secures to the voter absolute secrecy and freedom from interference at the polling-booths. In five years the Aus- tralian ballot has been adopted in thirty-five States, and it appears to have done something to diminish the power of the caucus organisation and to check the various fraudulent prac- tices which had been common at elections.[53]

---

[52] See Bryce, ii. pp. 492–95. There were some varieties, however, in the system in the different States (Ford, *American Citizen's Manual*, i. 103–8).
[53] Gilman's *Socialism and the American Spirit*, pp. 169–70; *Political Science Quarterly* (New York), 1891, p. 386.

One great cause of the degradation of American politics has been the extreme facility with which votes have been given to ignorant immigrants, who had no experience in public life and no real interest in the well-being of the country. Most of the more intelligent American observers have agreed that the common schools, and the high level of knowledge and intelligence they secure, have been among the most important conditions of the healthy working of their institutions. For a long period the constituent bodies in America were certainly among the best educated in the world; but since the torrent of ignorant immigrants and negro voters has poured into them they can have no pretensions to this position.

In 1798, when revolutionary elements were very rife in Europe, and when their introduction into the United States excited serious alarm, a Naturalisation Act was carried increasing the necessary term of residence from five to fourteen years; but this Act was only in force for four years. The Know-nothing party, which played a considerable part in American politics in 1854 and the two following years, endeavoured to revive the policy of 1798. It grew up at the time when the evil effects of the great immigration that followed the Irish famine had become apparent, and it was assisted by a fierce anti-Popery fanaticism, which had been much strengthened by the hostility the Catholic clergy had begun to show to the common schools, and by the attempt of some of them to exclude Bible-reading from those schools. It was guilty of not a little lawless violence, and although it succeeded, in 1855, in carrying nine of the States elections, and in 1856 nominated presidential candidates, it soon perished, chiefly through its divisions on the slavery question, and through the transcendent importance that question was beginning to take in American politics. It is said that Washington, in some moment of great danger, gave the order, 'Put none but Americans on guard to-night,' and these words were taken by the Know-nothings as their watchword. Their fundamental object was the exclusion of foreigners and Catholics from all national, State, county, and municipal offices, and a change in the naturalisation laws providing that no immigrant should become a citizen till after a residence of twenty-one, or, at the very least, of fifteen years.[54]

Few persons would now defend the proposal to introduce a religious disqualification into the American Constitution; but if the Know-nothings had succeeded in lengthening the period of residence required for naturalisation, they might have given a different character to American political life and incalculably raised its moral tone. Their best defence is to be found in the enormous scandals in the government of New York that immediately followed their defeat. To one class especially, a change in the laws of naturalisation would have been a priceless blessing. It is difficult to say how different the Irish element in America might have been if the poor, ignorant, helpless, famine-stricken peasantry who poured by tens of thousands into New York had been encouraged to pass at once into honest industry, scattered on farms over the face of the country, and kept for fifteen or twenty years out of the corrupting influence of American politics. But the shrewd party managers soon perceived that these poor men were among the best counters in their game. The immediate prospect of much higher wages than they had been accustomed to kept an immense proportion of them in the great city where they landed. They had no one to guide them. They were hardly more fitted than children to make their way under new conditions in a strange land, and almost their only genuine political feeling was hatred of England. Like the Germans, they showed from the first a marked tendency to congregate in great towns. It was computed in 1890, that a third part of the Irish in America were still to be found in the ten largest towns; that, taking the population of those towns together, one out of every thirteen persons was Irish, and that in New York, out of a population of a little more than 1,200,000, 198,000 were

---

[54] Much information on the Know-nothing movement will be found in the second volume of Mr. Rhodes's *History of the United States from the Compromise of 1850*, and in an article by Mr. McMaster in *The Forum*, July 1894.

Irish.[55] Five years were required for naturalisation by the Federal law, but some State laws gave a vote after a shorter residence, and the Federal law was easily and constantly violated. Immense numbers, who were absolutely ignorant of all American public questions, and absolutely indifferent to public interests, were speedily drilled in the party organisation. They soon learned their lesson. They acquired a rare aptitude in running the machine, in turning the balance of doubtful elections, in voting together in disciplined masses, in using political power for private gain. There are few sadder histories than the influence of the Irish race on American politics, and the influence of American politics on the Irish race.

The enfranchisement of the negroes added a new and enormous mass of voters, who were utterly and childishly incompetent, and it applied mainly to that portion of the United States which had escaped the contamination of the immigrant vote. For some time after the war the influence of property and intelligence in the South was completely broken, and the negro vote was ostensibly supreme. The consequence was what might have been expected. A host of vagrant political adventurers from the North, known in America as carpet-baggers, poured into the Southern provinces, and, in conjunction with the refuse of the mean whites, they undertook the direction of the negro votes. Then followed, under the protection of the Northern bayonets, a grotesque parody of government, a hideous orgie of anarchy, violence, unrestrained corruption, undisguised, ostentatious, insulting robbery, such as the world had scarcely ever seen. The State debts were profusely piled up. Legislation was openly put up for sale. The 'Bosses' were in all their glory, and they were abundantly rewarded, while the crushed, ruined, plundered whites combined in secret societies for their defence, and retaliated on their oppressors by innumerable acts of savage vengeance.[56] At length the North-

[55] Hart's *Essays on American Government*, pp. 192, 204.
[56] See Bryce, ii. 520–21; Goldwin Smith, p. 300. M. Molinari, in his very interesting *Lettres sur les Etats-Unis et le Canada*, has collected a number

ern troops were withdrawn, and the whole scene changed. The carpet-baggers had had their day, and they returned laden with Southern booty to their own States. Partly by violence, partly by fraud, but largely also through the force of old habits of obedience and command, the planters in a short time regained their ascendency. Sometimes, it is said, they did not even count the negro votes. Generally they succeeded in dictating them, and by systematic manipulation or intimidation they restored the South to quiet and some degree of prosperity. A more curious picture of the effects of democratic equality among a population who were entirely unfitted for it had never been presented. The North, it is true, introduced all the apparatus of State education for the benefit of the negroes; but if there had ever been any desire for such things, it soon died away. Mr. Bryce, writing about twenty-three years after the termination of the Civil War, says: 'Roughly speaking, 75 per cent. of the adult coloured voters are unable to write, and most of the rest unaccustomed to read newspapers.'[57]

The system I have described has proved even more pernicious in municipal government than in State politics or in Federal politics. Innumerable elections of obscure men to obscure places very naturally failed to excite general interest, and they almost inevitably fell into the hands of a small ring of professional politicians. The corruption of New York, which has been the most notorious, is often attributed almost exclusively to the Irish vote; but as early as the first quarter of the nineteenth century, when Irish influence was quite imperceptible, the State and City of New York were in the hands of a clique called 'the Albany Regency,' which appears to have exhibited on a small scale most of the features of the later rings. 'A strong phalanx of officers, from the governor and the senators down to the justices of peace in the most remote

---

of facts illustrating the extraordinary reign of terror and plunder that existed in the South while the carpet-baggers were in power (see pp. 185–97, 270–72).
[57] Bryce, ii. 92–93.

part of the State,' we are told, governed New York for the sole
benefit of a small knot of corrupt politicians. 'The judiciaries'
were 'shambles for the bargain and sale of offices.' The justices of the peace were all the creatures of the party, and were
almost invariably corrupt.[58] Between 1842 and 1846, when the
great Irish immigration had not yet begun, an evil of another
kind was prevailing in New York. It was the custom to allow
the inmates of public almshouses to leave the institutions on
the days of election and cast their votes; and an American
writer assures us that at this time 'the almshouses formed an
important factor in the politics of the State of New York, for
the paupers were sent out to vote by the party in power, and
were threatened with a loss of support unless they voted as
directed; and the number was such as to turn the scale in the
districts in which they voted.'[59] It was abuses of this kind that
led to one of the greatest modern improvements in American
politics—the exclusion in several States of absolute paupers
from the franchise.

It is true, however, that the corruption never attained anything approaching the magnitude which it reached between
1863 and 1871, when all the powers of the State and town of
New York had passed into the hands of the Tammany Ring.
At this time four-ninths of the population were of foreign
birth. A vast proportion consisted of recent immigrants, and
the Irish Catholic vote seems to have 'gone solid' in favour of
the ring. The majority of the State legislature, the mayor, the
governor, several of the judges, almost all the municipal authorities who were empowered to order, appropriate, super-
vise and control expenditure, were its creatures, and I suppose
no other capital city in the civilised globe has ever, in time of
peace, witnessed such a system of wholesale, organised, continuous plunder. It was computed that 65 per cent. of the sums

---

[58] See an address of the well-known statesman, W. H. Seward, October
5, 1824: *Seward's Works* (New York, 1853), iii. 334–37. The first political
work of Mr. Seward was to resist the Albany Ring.
[59] Ford's *American Citizen's Manual*, i. 88–89.

that were ostensibly expended in public works represented fraudulent additions. Between 1860 and 1871 the debt of New York quintupled, and during the last two and a half years of the government of the ring it increased at the rate of more than five and a half millions of pounds a year.[60] A distinguished American writer, who is also a distinguished diplomatist and well acquainted with the conditions of European capitals, has drawn the following instructive parallel. 'The city of Berlin, in size and rapidity of growth, may be compared to New York. It contains twelve hundred thousand inhabitants, and its population has tripled within the last thirty years. . . . While Berlin has a municipal life at the same time dignified and economical, with streets well paved and clean, with a most costly system of drainage, with noble public buildings, with life, liberty, and the pursuit of happiness better guarded by far than in our own metropolis, the whole government is carried on by its citizens for but a trifle more than the interest of the public debt of the city of New York.'

'I wish,' says the same writer, 'to deliberately state a fact easy of verification—the fact that whereas, as a rule, in other civilised countries municipal Governments have been steadily improving until they have been made generally honest and serviceable, our own, as a rule, are the worst in the world, and they are steadily growing worse every day.'[61]

The case of New York was an extreme one, but was, indeed, very far from being unique. 'The government of the cities,' says Mr. Bryce, 'is the one conspicuous failure of the United States. . . . The faults of the State Governments are insignificant compared with the extravagance, corruption, and mismanagement which mark the administration of most of the

---

[60] See Mr. Goodnow's chapter on the Tweed Ring in New York City in Mr. Bryce's third volume. See especially pp. 179, 190, 195.
[61] *The Message of the Nineteenth Century to the Twentieth,* by Andrew Dickson White (Newhaven, 1883), pp. 14–15; see also an instructive article, by the same writer, on 'The Government of American Cities' (*The Forum,* December 1890).

great cities. For these evils are not confined to one or two cities. . . . There is not a city with a population of 200,000 where the poison-germs have not sprung into vigorous life, and in some of the smaller ones, down to 70,000, it needs no microscope to note the results of their growth. Even in cities of the third rank similar phenomena may occasionally be discerned; though there, as some one has said, the jet-black of New York or San Francisco dies away into a harmless grey.'[62] It should be added, that there is no country in the world in which this question is more important than in the United States, for there is no country in which town life during the present century has increased so enormously and so rapidly. The proportion of the population who live in towns of over 8,000 inhabitants is said to have risen in that period from 4 to more than 23 per cent.[63]

Mr. Bryce has enumerated from good American sources the chief forms which this municipal robbery assumes. There are sales of monopolies in the use of public thoroughfares; systematic jobbing of contracts; enormous abuses in patronage; enormous overcharges for necessary public works. Cities have been compelled to buy lands for parks and places because the owners wished to sell them; to grade, pave, and sewer streets without inhabitants in order to award corrupt contracts for the works; to purchase worthless properties at extravagant prices; to abolish one office and create another with the same duties, or to vary the functions of offices for the sole purpose of redistributing official emoluments; to make or keep the salary of an office unduly high in order that its tenant may pay largely to the party funds; to lengthen the term of office in order to secure the tenure of corrupt or incompetent men. When increasing taxation begins to arouse resistance, loans are launched under false pretences, and often with the assistance

---

[62] Bryce, ii. 281.
[63] See an essay on American cities in Hart's *Essays on American Government*, pp. 162–205; and an article by Mr. Springer, on 'City Growth and Party Politics,' *The Forum*, December 1890.

of falsified accounts. In all the chief towns municipal debts have risen to colossal dimensions and increased with portentous rapidity. 'Within the twenty years from 1860 to 1880,' says an American writer, 'the debts of the cities of the Union rose from about $100,000,000 to $682,000,000. From 1860 to 1875 the increase of debt in eleven cities was 270·9 per cent., increase of taxation 362·2 per cent.; whereas the increase in taxable valuation was but 156·9 per cent., and increase in population but 70 per cent.'[64] The New York Commissioners of 1876 probably understated the case when they declared that more than half of all the present city debts in the United States are the direct results of intentional and corrupt misrule.[65]

No candid man can wonder at it. It is the plain, inevitable consequence of the application of the methods of extreme democracy to municipal government. In America, as in England, municipal elections fail to attract the same interest and attention as great political ones, and when all the smaller offices are filled by popular election, and when those elections are continually recurring, it is impossible for busy men to master their details or form any judgment on the many obscure candidates who appear before them. Property qualifications are deemed too aristocratic for a democratic people. The good old clause, that might once have been found in many charters, providing that no one should vote upon any proposition to raise a tax or to appropriate its proceeds unless he was himself liable to be assessed for such tax, has disappeared. 'It is deemed undemocratic; practical men say there is no use in submitting it to a popular vote.'[66] The elections are by manhood suffrage. Only a small proportion of the electors have any appreciable interest in moderate taxation and economical administration, and a proportion of votes, which is usually quite sufficient to hold the balance of power, is in the hands of recent and most ignorant immigrants. Is it possible to conceive conditions more

---

[64] Sterne's *United States*, p. 267; see also Bryce, ii. 280.
[65] Bryce, ii. 278–87, 469–74, 521.
[66] Ibid, ii. 291.

fitted to subserve the purposes of cunning and dishonest men,
whose object is personal gain, whose method is the organisation of the vicious and ignorant elements of the community
into combinations that can turn elections, levy taxes, and appoint administrators?

The rings are so skilfully constructed that they can nearly
always exclude from office a citizen who is known to be hostile; though 'a good, easy man, who will not fight, and will
make a reputable figure-head, may be an excellent investment.'[67] Sometimes, no doubt, the bosses quarrel among
themselves, and the cause of honest government may gain
something by the dispute. But in general, as long as government is not absolutely intolerable, the more industrious and
respectable classes keep aloof from the nauseous atmosphere
of municipal politics, and decline the long, difficult, doubtful
task of entering into conflict with the dominant rings. 'The
affairs of the city,' says Mr. White, 'are virtually handed over
to a few men who make politics, so called, a business. The
very germ of the difficulty was touched once, in my presence,
by a leading man of business in our great metropolis, who
said: "We have thought this thing over, and we find that it
pays better to neglect our city affairs than to attend to them;
that we can make more money in the time required for the
full discharge of our political duties than the politicans can
steal from us on account of our not discharging them." '[68]

The evil has, however, undoubtedly, in many cases become
intolerable, and the carnival of plunder that culminated in
New York in 1871 gave a shock to public opinion and began a
series of amendments which appear to have produced some
real improvement. 'The problem,' says Mr. Sterne, 'is becoming a very serious one how, with the growth of a pauper
element, property rights in cities can be protected from confiscation at the hands of the non-producing classes. That the

[67] Bryce, ii. 469.
[68] White's *Message of the Nineteenth Century to the Twentieth*, pp. 15–16.

suffrage is a spear as well as a shield is a fact which many writers on suffrage leave out of sight; that it not only protects the holder of the vote from aggression, but also enables him to aggress upon the rights of others by means of the taxing power, is a fact to which more and more weight must be given as population increases and the suffrage is extended.'[69] Some good has been done by more severe laws against corruption at elections; though, in spite of these laws, the perjury and personation and wholesale corruption of a New York election appear far to exceed anything that can be found in the most corrupt capital in Europe.[70] A great reform, however, has been made by the extension of the term of office of the New York judges in the higher courts to fourteen years, and by a measure granting them independent salaries. The general impunity of the great organisers of corruption was broken in 1894, when one of the chief bosses in America, a man of vast wealth and enormous influence in American politics, was at last brought to justice and sentenced to six years' imprisonment.[71]

The most successful steps, however, taken in the direction of reform have been those limiting the power of corrupt bodies. One of the most valuable and most distinctive features of the American Constitution is the power of electing conventions independent of the State legislatures for the purpose of effecting amendments in the State constitutions. Being specially elected for a single definite purpose, and for a very short time, and having none of the patronage and administrative powers that are vested in the Legislature, these conventions, though the creatures of universal suffrage, have in a great degree escaped the influence of the machine, and represent the normal and genuine wishes of the community. They have

---

[69] Sterne, p. 271.
[70] See a striking account of the way in which New York elections are still conducted, by Mr. Goff, in the *North American Review*, 1894, pp. 203–10.
[71] A curious letter on the career of this personage, called 'The Downfall of a Political Boss in the United States,' will be found in *The Times*, March 2, 1894.

no power of enacting amendments, but they have the power
of proposing them and submitting them to a direct popular
vote. By these means a number of amendments have, during
the last few years, been introduced into the State constitutions. In New York, and in several other States, since 1874 the
State legislatures are only permitted to legislate for municipal
affairs by a general law, and are deprived of the much-abused
right of making special laws in favour of particular individuals
or corporations; but it is said that these restrictions are easily
and constantly evaded.[72] Restrictions have been imposed in
many States upon forms of corruption that had been widely
practised, in the guise of distributions of public funds in aid
of charities connected with religious establishments, and of
exemptions from taxation granted to charitable institutions.
In a few States some provision has been made to secure a representation of minorities,[73] and in many States limitations—
which, however, have been often successfully evaded—have
been imposed on the power of borrowing and the power of
taxing.[74] The theory of American statesmen seems to be, that
the persons elected on a democratic system are always likely
to prove dishonest, but that it is possible by constitutional
laws to restrict their dishonesty to safe limits. There has been
a strong tendency of late years to multiply and elaborate in
minute detail constitutional restrictions, and the policy has
also been widely adopted of making the sessions of State legislatures biennial instead of annual, in order to limit their
powers of mischief.

The following interesting passage from one of the chief living historians of America well represents the new spirit. 'It has

---

[72] Sterne, pp. 258–59.

[73] Ford, i. 113–15.

[74] See, on this subject, Bryce, ii. 293–94. One favourite form of restriction
has been that the debt of a country, city, borough, township, or school
district shall never exceed 7 per cent. of the assessed value of the taxable
property. In order to evade this the assessed value of property has almost
everywhere been largely increased.

become the fashion to set limits on the power of the governors, of the legislatures, of the courts; to command them to do this, to forbid them to do that, till a modern State constitution is more like a code of laws than an instrument of representative government. A distrust of the servants and representatives of the people is everywhere manifest. A long and bitter experience has convinced the people that legislators will roll up the State debt unless positively forbidden to go beyond a certain figure; that they will suffer railroads to parallel each other, corporations to consolidate, common carriers to discriminate, city councils to sell valuable franchises to street-car companies and telephone companies, unless the State constitution expressly declares that such things shall not be. So far has this system of prohibition been carried, that many legislatures are not allowed to enact any private or special legislation; are not allowed to relieve individuals or corporations from obligations to the State; are not allowed to pass a Bill in which any member is interested, or to loan the credit of the State, or to consider money Bills in the last hours of the session.'[75] In Washington, a still stronger measure has been adopted, and the whole municipal government is placed in the hands of a commission appointed directly by the Congress.

At the same time, another very different, and perhaps more efficacious, method has been adopted of checking municipal corruption, and Laveleye has justly regarded it as extremely significant of the future tendencies of democracy. There are two facts, as yet very imperfectly recognised in Europe, which American experience has amply established. The first is that, in the words of an American writer, 'there can be no question that one of the most prolific sources of official corruption and incompetence lies in the multiplication of elective offices.'[76] The second is, that this multiplication, instead of strengthening, materially diminishes popular control, for it confuses

---

[75] See an article, by Mr. McMaster, in *The Forum*, December 1893, p. 470.
[76] Ford, i. 129.

issues, divides and obscures responsibility, weakens the moral
effect of each election, bewilders the ordinary elector, who
knows little or nothing of the merits of the different candidates, and inevitably ends by throwing the chief power into
the hands of a small knot of wirepullers. The system has,
accordingly, grown up in America of investing the mayors of
the towns with an almost autocratic authority, and making
them responsible for the good government of the city. These
mayors are themselves elected by popular suffrage for periods
ranging from one to five years; they are liable to impeachment
if they abuse their functions; the State legislature retains the
right of giving or withholding supplies, and it can override,
though only by a two-thirds majority, the veto of the mayor.
But, in spite of these restrictions, the power vested in this
functionary, according to recent constitutional amendments,
is enormously great, far greater than in European cities. With
very slight restrictions, the mayor appoints and can remove
all the heads of all the city departments. He exercises a right
of veto and supervision over all their proceedings. He is responsible for the working of every part of municipal administration. He keeps the peace, calls out the Militia, enforces
the law, and, in a word, determines in all its main lines the
character of the city government. This system began in Brook-
lyn in 1882. It was extended, apparently with excellent results,
to New York in 1884; and the same highly concentrated responsibility is spreading rapidly through other States.[77] It is
curious to observe the strength which this tendency is assuming in a country which beyond all others was identified with
the opposite system; and it is regarded by some excellent political writers in America as the one real corrective of the vices
of democracy. In the words of one of the most recent of these
writers, 'the tendency is visibly strengthening in the United
States to concentrate administrative powers in the hands of
one man, and to hold him responsible for its wise and honest

---

[77] Bryce, ii. 264–65, 292, 304–5, iii. 196; Laveleye, *Le Gouvernement dans la
Démocratie,* i. 97–109.

use. Diffusion of responsibility through a crowd of legislators has proved to be a deceptive method of securing the public welfare.'[78]

It seems to me probable that this system will ultimately, and after many costly and disastrous experiments, spread widely wherever unqualified democracy prevails. In the election of a very conspicuous person, who is invested with very great prerogatives, public interest is fully aroused, and a wave of opinion arises which in some degree overflows the lines of strict caucus politics. The increasing power of organisations is a conspicuous fact in all countries that are gliding down the democratic slope. It is abundantly seen in England, where candidates for Parliament are now more and more exclusively nominated by party organisations; and in the United States the power of such bodies is far greater than in England. But while in obscure and comparatively insignificant appointments the managers of the machine can usually do much what they please, they are obliged in the more important elections to take average non-political opinion into account. The best candidates are not found to be men of great eminence or ability, for these always excite animosities and divisions; but it is equally important that they should not be men labouring under gross moral imputations. The system of double election also, though it has been greatly weakened, probably still exercises some influence in diminishing corruption. It is like the process of successive inoculations, by which physiologists are able to attenuate the virus of a disease. On the whole, corruption in the United States is certainly less prominent in the higher than in the lower spheres of government, though even in the former it appears to me to be far greater than in most European countries—certainly far greater than in Great Britain.

I can, however, hardly do better than give a summary of the conclusions of Mr. Bryce. They appear to me the more impressive because, in the somewhat curious chapter which

---

[78] Gilman, *Socialism and the American Spirit*, p. 82.

he has devoted to American corruption, it is his evident desire to minimise, as far as he honestly can, both its gravity and its significance. No President, he says, has ever been seriously charged with pecuniary corruption, and there is no known instance, since the presidency which immediately preceded the Civil War, of a Cabinet minister receiving a direct money bribe as the price of an executive act or an appointment; but several leading ministers of recent Administrations have been suspected of complicity in railroad jobs, and even in frauds upon the revenue. In the Legislature, both the senators and the members of the House of Representatives labour under 'abundant suspicions,' 'abundant accusations,' but few of these 'have been, or could have been, sifted to the bottom.' 'The opportunities for private gain are large, the chances of detection small.' All that can be safely said is, that personal dishonesty in the exercise of legislative powers, of a kind quite distinct from the political profligacy with which we are in our own country abundantly familiar, prevails largely and unquestionably in America. It is especially prominent in what we should call private Bills affecting the interests of railroads or of other wealthy corporations, and in Bills altering the tariff of imports, on which a vast range of manufacturing interests largely depend. 'The doors of Congress are besieged by a whole army of commercial and railroad men and their agents, to whom, since they have come to form a sort of profession, the name of Lobbyists is given. Many Congressmen are personally interested, and lobby for themselves among their colleagues from the vantage-ground of their official positions.'

The object of the lobbyist is to 'offer considerations for help in passing a Bill which is desired, or stopping a Bill which is feared.' There are several different methods. There is 'log-rolling,' when members interested in different private Bills come to an agreement that each will support the Bill of the others on condition of himself receiving the same assistance. There is the 'strike,' which means that 'a member brings in a Bill directed against some railroad or other great corporation merely in order to levy blackmail upon it. . . . An eminent

railroad president told me that for some years a certain senator regularly practised this trick.' 'It is universally admitted
that the Capitol and the hotels of Washington are a nest of
such intrigues and machinations while Congress is sitting.'
The principal method, however, of succeeding seems to be
simple bribery, though 'no one can tell how many of the members are tainted.' Sometimes the money does not go to the
member of Congress, but to the boss who controls him. Sometimes a Lobbyist receives money to bribe an honest member,
but, finding he is going to vote in the way desired, keeps it
in his own pocket. Often members are bribed to support a
railway by a transfer of portions of its stocks. Free passes were
so largely given with the same object to legislators that an Act
was passed in 1887 to forbid them. Mr. Bryce mentions a
governor who used to obtain loans of money from the railway
which traversed his territory under the promise that he would
use his constitutional powers in its favour; and members of
Congress were accustomed to buy, or try to buy, land belonging to a railway company at less than the market price,
in consideration of the services they could render to the line
in the House. It was clearly shown that, in one case within
the last twenty years, a large portion of a sum of $4,818,000,
which was expended by a single railway, was used for the
purpose 'of influencing legislation.' The letters of the director
who managed the case of this railway have been published,
and show that he found members of both Houses fully amenable to corruption. 'I think,' writes this gentleman in 1878,
'in all the world's history, never before was such a wild set of
demagogues honoured by the name of Congress.'

It is, of course, inevitable that only a small proportion of
transactions of this kind should be disclosed. These cases are
merely samples, probably representing many others. A great
additional amount of direct corruption is connected with the
enormous distribution of patronage in the hands of members
of Congress. There are about 120,000 Federal Civil Service
places, and an important part of each member's business is
to distribute such places among his constituents. It is easy to

imagine how such patronage would be administered by such men as have been described.

Mr. Bryce, however, is of opinion that there is much prevalent exaggeration about American corruption, and that Europeans are very unduly shocked by it. This is partly the fault of Americans, who have 'an airy way of talking about their own country,' and love 'broad effects.' It is partly, also, due to the malevolence of European travellers, 'who, generally belonging to the wealthier class, are generally reactionary in politics,' and therefore not favourable to democratic government. Englishmen, he thinks, are very unphilosophical. They have 'a useful knack of forgetting their own shortcomings when contemplating those of their neighbours.' 'Derelictions of duty which a man thinks trivial in the form with which custom has made him familiar in his own country, where, perhaps, they are matter for merriment, shock him when they appear in a different form in another country. They get mixed up in his mind with venality, and are cited to prove that the country is corrupt and its politicians profligate.' In the proceedings of Congress, Mr. Bryce says, 'it does not seem, from what one hears on the spot, that money is often given, or, I should rather say, it seems that the men to whom it is given are few in number. But considerations of some kind pretty often pass.' In other words, not actual money, but the value of money, and jobs by which money can be got, are usually employed.

Senators are often charged with 'buying themselves into the Senate,' but Mr. Bryce does not think that they often give direct bribes to the members of the State legislature to vote for them. They only make large contributions to the party election fund, out of which the election expenses of the majority are defrayed.[79] Bribery exists in Congress, but is confined to a few members, say 5 per cent. of the whole number.

---

[79] I may here quote the words of Mr. White, whose authority on such a question is at least equal to that of Mr. Bryce:—'I am not at all disposed to accept the prevalent cant about corruption; but suppose that any one

. . . The taking of other considerations than money, such as a share in a lucrative contract, or a railway pass, or a "good thing" to be secured for a friend, prevails among legislators to a somewhat larger extent. . . . One may roughly conjecture that from 15 to 20 per cent. of the members of Congress, or of an average State legislature, would allow themselves to be influenced by inducements of this kind. . . . Jobbery of various kinds, *i.e.* the misuse of a public position for the benefit of individuals, is pretty frequent. It is often disguised as a desire to render some service to the party; and the same excuse is sometimes found for a misappropriation of public money. Patronage is usually dispensed with a view of party considerations or to win personal support. But this remark is equally true of England and France, the chief difference being that, owing to the short terms and frequent removals, the quantity of patronage is relatively greater in the United States.'

On the whole, Mr. Bryce concludes, if 'we leave ideals out of sight, and try America by an actual standard, we shall find that while the legislative bodies fall below the level of purity maintained in England and Germany, probably also in France and Italy, her Federal and State Administration, in spite of the evils flowing from an uncertain tenure, is not, in point of integrity, at this moment sensibly inferior to the Administrations of European countries.'[80]

This judgment certainly does not err on the side of severity. If in England a great admirer of our parliamentary institutions, while boasting that no Prime Minister had been seriously charged with pecuniary corruption, and that no Cabinet Minister had been known for the last forty years to have taken

---

had told us in our college days, as we pondered the speeches of Webster, and Calhoun, and Clay, and Sumner, and Seward, and Everett, that great commonwealths would arise in which United States' senatorships would be virtually put up to the highest bidder term after term, until such a mode of securing a position in our highest council would be looked upon as natural and normal!' (*Message of the Nineteenth Century to the Twentieth*, p. 14).

[80] Bryce, ii. 509–25.

money as a bribe, was obliged to add that several Cabinet Ministers of both parties in the State were suspected of complicity in railroad jobs and frauds on the revenue; that the whole of that vast department of legislation which affects the interest of corporations and manufacturers was systematically managed, or at least influenced, by corruption; that about 5 per cent. of the members of both Houses of Parliament were accustomed to take direct money bribes; that one in every five or six members was pretty certainly open to corrupt jobs, while suspicion of dishonesty of some kind attached to a much larger number, we should scarcely, I think, consider our parliamentary government a success.

Many of the causes of the vices of American government are inherent in democracy, but there are two aggravating causes which I have not mentioned. The rule that the person elected to either House of Congress must be a resident in the State for which he sits abridges greatly the choice of able and efficient men, and much strengthens the power of the local machine; while the large salaries attached to the position of senator or representative make it—even apart from its many indirect advantages—an object of keen ambition to the professional politician. Members of each House have a salary of 1,000*l.* a year, besides some small allowance for travelling and other expenses. In 1873, the two Houses passed an Act increasing many official salaries and adding a third to their own salaries, and, by a curiously characteristic provision, the congressional salaries, and these alone, were made retroactive. The appropriation, however, by Congress of nearly 40,000*l.* to itself excited so much indignation that it was repealed in the next Congress.[81]

The members of the House of Representatives sit only for two years, which probably adds something to the desire for speedy gain. At the same time, it appears certain that the Federal Government is less deeply tainted with corruption than

---

[81] Bryce, i. 259–61.

a large proportion of the State legislatures, far less deeply than the Governments of nearly all the more important towns.

There is one thing which is worse than corruption. It is acquiescence in corruption. No feature of American life strikes a stranger so powerfully as the extraordinary indifference, partly cynicism and partly good nature, with which notorious frauds and notorious corruption in the sphere of politics are viewed by American public opinion. There is nothing, I think, altogether like this to be found in any other great country. It is something wholly different from the political torpor which is common in half-developed nations and corrupt despotisms, and it is curiously unlike the state of feeling which exists in the French Republic. Flagrant instances of corruption have been disclosed in France since 1870, but French public opinion never fails promptly to resent and to punish them. In America, notorious profligacy in public life and in the administration of public funds seems to excite little more than a disdainful smile. It is treated as very natural—as the normal result of the existing form of government.

I imagine that most persons who formed their opinions, as historians are apt to do, mainly by the examples of the past would judge very unfavourably the prospects of country where there was so much corruption and so much toleration of corruption in public life. The words of Jugurtha might well rise to their lips: 'Urbem venalem, et mature perituram si emptorem invenerit!' They would be inclined to conclude that, if the United States escaped great perils from without, this was mainly due to its extraordinarily advantageous position, and that internally it presented in a very marked degree the signs of moral dissolution which portend the decadence of nations. I believe, however, that the best judges, who are well acquainted with America, would concur in believing that such a judgment would be fallacious. America illustrates even more clearly than France the truth which I have already laid down, and which will again and again reappear in these volumes— that pure democracy is one of the least representative of governments. In hardly any other country does the best life and energy of the nation flow so habitually apart from politics. Hardly any other nation would be more grossly misjudged if it were mainly judged by its politicians and its political life.[82] It seems a strange paradox that a nation which stands in the very foremost rank in almost all the elements of a great industrial civilisation, which teems with energy, intelligence and resource, and which exhibits in many most important fields a level of moral excellence that very few European countries have attained, should permit itself to be governed, and represented among the nations, in the manner I have described. How strange it is, as an Italian statesman once said, that a century which has produced the telegraph and the telephone, and has shown in ten thousand forms such amazing powers of adaptation and invention, should have discovered no more successful methods of governing mankind! The fact, however, is as I have presented it, and there are few more curious inquiries than its causes.

The foregoing pages will, I think, have at least shown the chief sources from which the corruption has sprung. To quote

---

[82] The following remarks of Mr. Gilman appear to me well worthy of attention:—'Only one who has lived for some time in the United States, and has had considerable experience of the actual workings of American political institutions, will sufficiently realise the force of the curious contrast between "the people" and "the politicians." It is purely in imagination or theory that the politicians are faithful representatives of the people. The busy, "driving" American citizen is apt to feel that he has no time to watch the people who make a profession of running the political machine. His own private business, with which Government as a rule has little to do, tends to absorb his thoughts. He even prefers too often to be heavily taxed in direct consequence of political corruption, rather than to take the time from his private affairs which would be needed to overthrow the machine and keep it in permanent exile' (*The American Spirit of Socialism*, pp. 178–79). I may add the judgment of one of the most serious and impartial of American historians:—'It is certain that in no Teutonic nation of our day is the difference so marked between the public and private standards of morality as in the United States. The one is lower than it was in 1860; the other, inconsistent as it may seem, is higher' (Rhodes's *History of the United States from the Compromise of 1850*, iii. 113).

once more the words of Mr. Bryce: 'Every feature of the machine is the result of patent causes. The elective offices are so
numerous that ordinary citizens cannot watch them, and
cease to care who gets them; the conventions come so often
that busy men cannot serve in them; the minor offices are so
unattractive that able men do not stand for them. The primary
lists are so contrived that only a fraction of the party get on
them, and of this fraction many are too lazy, or too busy, or
too careless to attend. The mass of the voters are ignorant;
knowing nothing about the personal merits of the candidates,
they are ready to follow their leaders like sheep. Even the
better class, however they may grumble, are swayed by the
inveterate habit of party loyalty, and prefer a bad candidate
of their own party to a (probably no better) candidate of the
other party. It is less trouble to put up with impure officials,
costly city governments, a jobbing State legislature, an inferior sort of Congressman, than to sacrifice one's own business
in the effort to set things right. Thus the machine works on,
and grinds out places, power, and the opportunities of illicit
gain to those who manage it.'[83]

These things, however, would not be acquiesced in if it
were not that an admirable written Constitution, enforced by
a powerful and vigilant Supreme Court, had restricted to
small limits the possibilities of misgovernment. All the rights
that men value the most are placed beyond the reach of a
tyrannical majority. Congress is debarred by the Constitution
from making any law prohibiting the free exercise of religion,
or abridging the freedom of speech and of the press, or the
right of assembly, or the right of petition. No person can be
deprived of life, liberty, or property without due process of
law. All the main articles of what British statesmen would
regard as necessary liberties are guaranteed, and property is
so fenced round by constitutional provisions that confiscatory
legislation becomes almost impossible. No private property
can be taken for public use without just compensation, and

---

[83] Bryce, ii. 449.

the Federal Constitution contains an invaluable provision forbidding any State to pass any law impairing the obligation of contracts. The danger of partial or highly graduated taxation voted by the many and falling on the few has been, in a great measure, guarded against by the clauses in the Constitution providing that representatives and direct taxes shall be apportioned among the States according to their population; that no capitation or other direct tax shall be laid unless in proportion to the census, and that all duties, imposts, and excises shall be uniform through the United States. The judgment of the Supreme Court condemning the income-tax in 1894 brought into clear relief the full force and meaning of these provisions. Neither Congress nor the State legislatures can pass any Bill of attainder or any *ex post facto* law punishing acts which were not punishable when they were committed.

At the same time, the number and magnitude of the majorities that are required to effect any organic change in the Federal Constitution are so great that such changes become almost impossible. They have, in fact, never, since the earliest days of the Constitution, been effected on any important subject, except during the wholly abnormal period that immediately followed the Civil War, when the political independence of the Southern States was for a time destroyed. The concurrence of majorities in two-thirds, and afterwards in three-fourths, of the States which is required for such an organic change becomes more and more difficult to obtain as the States multiply, with increasing population. Other guarantees of good government—very notably, it is to be feared, the character of the Senate—have been enfeebled by time and corruption and the increasing power of the machine; but this one, at least, almost automatically strengthens.

In the State constitutions the same system of checks prevails. All men, in the language of several of the constitutions, have 'natural, essential, inalienable rights,' and among them that of 'enjoying and defending their lives and liberties, and acquiring, possessing and protecting property.' The Constitution of Alabama expresses admirably the best spirit of

American statesmanship when it states that 'the sole and only legitimate end of government is to protect the citizen in the enjoyment of life, liberty and property, and when the Government assumes other functions, it is unsurpation and oppression.' Politicians may job and cheat and maladminister, but they can only do so within narrow limits, and if the evils become too great, conventions are called, which impose restrictions on the State legislatures. These bodies are forbidden to borrow or to tax beyond certain limits, or to touch a long list of specified subjects, or to sit for more than once in two years or for more than a defined number of days.[84] If they contrive—as they undoubtedly do—to heap up a great deal of corrupt expenditure within these limits, the more respectable class consider that the country is very rich, and can afford it, and that it is better to allow this corruption to go on than to give up private business to prevent it. A curious kind of optimism also prevails largely in America. It is believed that, provided the most important things are secured, it is better to allow every one to vote and organise as he pleases; that there will ultimately be a survival of the fittest; that in course of time, and after prolonged and costly experiences, the turbid element of corruption will clarify, and its worst constituents sink like sediment to the bottom.

Another consideration, which has hardly, I think, been sufficiently recognised among the guiding influences of American politics, is the complete separation of Church and State. American writers, probably with good reason, consider this one of the great successes of their government. In spite of the Episcopal Church establishment that once existed in Virginia, and the intensely theocratic character which New England Governments for a long time presented, the idea of the connection of Church and State did not strike root in America, and public opinion, within as well as without the Churches, seems cordially to approve of the separation. But one con-

---

[84] See, *e.g.*, the long and curious list of the limitations imposed on the Pennsylvanian Legislature in Ford (i. 32–35).

sequence has been to diminish greatly the interest in national politics. Every one who knows England knows how large a proportion of the best men who are interested in politics are mainly interested in their ecclesiastical aspects, in questions directly or indirectly connected with Establishment or Disestablishment. All this class of questions is in America removed from the sphere of politics.

That public opinion can be powerfully aroused there in a worthy cause no one will question. Nowhere in the present century has it acquired a greater volume and momentum than in the War of Secession. The self-sacrifice, the unanimity, the tenacity of purpose, the indomitable courage displayed on each side by the vast citizen armies in that long and terrible struggle, form one of the most splendid pages in nineteenth-century history. I can well recollect how Laurence Oliphant, who had excellent means of judging both wars, was accustomed to say that no fighting in the Franco-German War was comparable to the tenacity with which in America every village, almost every house, was defended or assailed; and the appalling sacrifice of life during the struggle goes far to justify this judgment. Nor were the nobler qualities of the American people less clearly manifested by the sequel of the war. The manner in which those gigantic armies melted away into the civil population, casting aside, without apparent effort, all military tastes and habits, and throwing themselves into the vast fields of industry that were opened by the peace, forms one of the most striking spectacles in history; and the noble humanity shown to the vanquished enemy is a not less decisive proof of the high moral level of American opinion. It was especially admirable in the very trying moments that followed the assassination of Lincoln, and it forms a memorable contrast to the extreme vindictiveness displayed by their forefathers, in the days of the Revolution, towards their loyalist fellow-countrymen. America rose at this time to a new place and dignity in the concert of nations. Europe had long seen in her little more than an amorphous, ill-cemented industrial population. It now learned to recognise the true characteristics of a great nation. There was exaggeration, but there was also no little truth, in the words of Lowell:

> Earth's biggest country got her soul,
> And risen up Earth's greatest nation.

Jobbing and corruption and fraud flourished, indeed, abundantly during the war, but the lines of national greatness and genuine patriotism were far more conspicuous. In times of peace, no nation has ever been more distinguished than America for the generosity shown by her citizens in supporting public institutions and public causes.

Her treatment of her gigantic debt was also a great surprise to Europe. It was a common prediction among shrewd judges that the peace would speedily be followed by national bankruptcy, and that a democratic nation would never endure the burden of a national debt which was at that time by far the largest in the world. Hardly any one appears to have foreseen that this democracy would surpass all the monarchies in history in its unparalleled persevering and successful efforts to pay off its debt. It is true that its motives in doing so were far from being purely patriotic and disinterested. The payment of the debt was indissolubly connected with the adoption of a system of severe Protection. Manufacturers by such Protection made colossal fortunes. The working class in America seem to have very generally adopted the opinion that a protective system, by raising the price of the articles they make and excluding similar articles made in other countries, has an effect, in raising wages and increasing employment, which is very beneficial to their interests. Multitudes of Americans in the Northern States had purchased national bonds at a time when they were greatly depreciated, and they gained enormously by being paid off at par. At the time when the policy of paying off the debt was adopted, the section of the country where these bonds were exclusively held, where Protection was always most popular, and where manufactures chiefly existed, had acquired, through the war, a complete ascendency. These things do much to explain the course that was adopted, but it was a course which involved sacrifices that few nations could have endured, and it was carried out with an energy and perseverance that no nation could have surpassed.

The general legislation in America also ranks very high. Many of the worst abuses of British law either never existed there, or were redressed at a much earlier period than in England. Her penal code, her educational laws, her laws about the sale and transfer of landed property, were for a long period far better than those of Great Britain; and the fact that no religious disqualifications were recognised saved her from struggles that have largely occupied many generations of English reformers. I do not think that, in modern times, legislation has been better or the spirit of Reform more active in the republic than in the monarchy, but I believe the best observers on both sides of the Atlantic recognise the two systems as substantially on the same plane of excellence, though each country may learn many things from the other. The American type of legislator is eminently shrewd, business-like, and free from prejudice, and he is quite prepared to make good laws, as long as they do not affect injuriously his personal and party interests. Public opinion insists on this, and it makes, as we have seen, occasional spasmodic efforts to diminish the great corruption of American political life.

America, during the last three quarters of the nineteenth century, has changed greatly. It is very different from the country which Dickens and Mrs. Trollope described, and even the great work of Tocqueville occasionally wears an aspect of some unreality. The population of the United States has quadrupled since Tocqueville visited it, and it is not surprising that many conditions should have been changed and some predictions falsified. Tocqueville believed much more in the permanence of republican institutions in America than in the permanence of the Union. He predicted very confidently that the power of the Federal Government would steadily decline and the power of the separate States increase;

that any serious resistance of the States to the Federal Union must certainly succeed; that the Union would only endure as long as all the States continued to wish to form part of it.[85] The War of the Secession showed that he was mistaken, and it produced for some years a strong tendency in the direction of centralisation.

In many respects, however, he judged with singular accuracy both the dangers and the tendencies of American political life. He deplored the custom, which had already begun in his time, of making the judges elective. He predicted that the habit of treating representatives as mere delegates bound by imperative instructions would destroy the essence of representative government. He dwelt with much perspicuity on the dangers in a pure democracy of the multiplication of great towns; on the gradual displacement of power which would follow the rise of new territories eclipsing or superseding the old States; on the moral and political effects of slavery, and of the increase of the negro race; on the deep and menacing line of division which the combined influence of slavery and climate, and the resulting difference of character and habits were drawing between the Northern and the Southern States. He imagined, indeed, that slavery would make it the special interest of the latter to cling to the Union, as they had every reason to fear the consequences if they were left alone with their negroes; but he doubted whether this bond of interest would prove ultimately as strong as the antagonism of sentiment. The system of party in America he never seems to have clearly understood, and he altogether failed to foresee the enormous power and the corrupting influence of 'the Machine.'

The America he described was, in some respects, very unlike that of our own day. He speaks of a despotism of opinion which prevented all free expression of independent, eccentric,

---

[85] *Démocratie en Amérique*, ii. 351–55, 383–85. He suggests, however, in one place that a war, or a great internal crisis, might possibly arrest this tendency (p. 398).

or heretical ideas; of American dislike to general ideas and theoretical discoveries; of a jealousy of wealth which compelled rich men, like the Jews of the Middle Ages, to abstain from all the ostentation of luxury. These things are wholly changed. America is no longer a country without pauperism and without great wealth. It contains some of the largest fortunes in the world. American wealth is certainly by no means averse to ostentation, and is rather peculiarly apt to take forms that are dangerous and injurious to the community. We are accustomed to hear, in some quarters, the enormous landed properties possessed by a few English landlords described as a great evil; but as long as those who wish to buy land, or to take land on a long lease, have no difficulty in doing so, it is not easy to see what real interest is seriously injured. The power the great landlord possesses may, no doubt, be abused; but great abuse is neither easy nor common, while the benefits resulting to the nation from the existence of this class are very real and evident. But, of all forms that great wealth can take, I know of none that gives greater opportunities or temptations of abuse than that of the railway king, who controls for his own selfish purposes the chief lines of communication in the country. In no other country has this class of men been so prominent as in America, and in no other has their power been more hideously abused. Nowhere else have there been such scandalous examples of colossal, ostentatious fortunes built up by reckless gambling, by the acquisition of gigantic monopolies, by a deadly and unscrupulous competition bringing ruin into countless homes, by a systematic subordination of public to private interests, by enormous political and municipal corruption. If such men as Lincoln, and Emerson, and Lowell have, in our generation, represented with supreme perfection the distinctive beauty of the American type, such a career as that of Jay Gould has, in its own way, been not less truly characteristic.

Integrity in the management of great companies and corporations is certainly not, in these latter days, a characteristic of the Anglo-Saxon race on either side of the Atlantic, but I believe it is even less so in America than in England. The contrast between the management of railways in England and in the United States is extremely significant. America is now one of the richest countries in the world, and its people have certainly no superiors in business talent. Yet it has been stated on excellent authority that, in the fifteen years between 1875 and 1890, the aggregate foreclosure sales on the railways of the United States comprised 50,525 miles, with $2,865,000,000 of combined stocks and bonds, or an average of $191,000,000 per annum. In 1890, twenty-nine companies were subject to foreclosure sales.[86] A great railway authority, speaking in the beginning of 1894, said: 'There is no less than one-fourth of the American railways in extent of mileage and capital now under the control of the courts of law, and during the year 1893 alone seventy-four railway companies including a mileage of 30,000 miles and a capital of 360 millions sterling, passed into the hands of receivers.[87] Making the fullest allowance for trade depressions and vicissitudes, and for currency troubles, what an amount of gigantic and deliberate dishonesty, as well as unscrupulous gambling, does such a state of things represent! The system of monopolising articles of the first necessity, under the name of Trusts, in order to force up their price, which is one of the most mischievous forms that modern industry has assumed, has been especially American, and the origin of some of the greatest American fortunes.

These evils are certainly not unconnected with political conditions. In a country where there is no rank, and where political eminence gives little or no dignity, the thirst for wealth acquires a maddening power. Corrupt political organisations come in constant contact with great railway and industrial corporations, and each can do much to assist and to demoralise the other. Even independently of these mutual services,

---

[86] *North American Review*, 1891, p. 84; see, too, Professor Ely's *Socialism*, pp. 270–71.
[87] Speech of Sir Henry Tyler at a meeting of the Grand Trunk Railway Company, April 30, 1894, p. 4.

there is an analogy between the two things. To run a company is very like running the machine, and the low standard which public opinion admits in the one is, not unnaturally, extended to the other.

Slavery has passed away in America, and with it one great blot and danger has disappeared; but the negro race, with its doubtful future, remains. The character of the constituencies has been profoundly lowered by the negro voters, and the extraordinary prevalence and ferocity of lynch law seems to show that the old habits of violence which slavery did so much to foster are by no means extinct. A great improvement, however, has incontestably taken place in the character of American foreign policy since the close of the war. The many violent and unscrupulous acts that once marked that policy were nearly all distinctly traceable to the ascendency of Southern statesmen. Something was due to the character of the men, for the conditions of slave labour produce a type which is much more military and adventurous than pacific and industrial. But the main cause was the imperious necessity imposed on these States of acquiring new slave territories, in order to counteract the increasing preponderance which increasing population was giving to the Northern States, and thus secure their share of power in the Union. This was the origin of the annexation of Texas; of the conquest of New Mexico and California; of the filibustering expedition of General Lopez against Cuba in 1851; of the unscrupulous attempts to force a quarrel upon Spain in 1854, in order to find a pretext for seizing Cuba; of the shameless Ostend manifesto, in which American ministers declared their determination to acquire Cuba by force if they could not do so by purchase; of the countenance that was given to the filibustering expedition of William Walker to Nicaragua in 1857; of the renewed attempts to acquire Cuba in 1858 and 1859. Since the question of secession has been settled this spirit of aggression seems to have wholly passed out of American foreign policy. There have been occasions when American statesmen, in order to win the favour of some class of voters, have shown a disregard of the courtesies and decorum of international dealings which no European country would have displayed, but in the great lines of her foreign policy, America has of late years been in general eminently honourable and unaggressive. It is no small thing that this vast section of the human race, so rich in the promise of the future, has wholly escaped the militarism that is corroding the greatest Powers of Europe, and that its gigantic energies have been steadily directed in the paths of peace.

The feature of American civilisation which has most struck European observers has been its extremely one-sided character. It is a supremely great industrial civilisation, generating to the highest degree the qualities, capacities and inventions that are needed for industrial life, and bringing in its train widely diffused comfort, education and self-respect; but there are certain sides in which it still ranks much below the civilisations of Europe. Tocqueville and his generation were much struck with this. Tocqueville said that America had hitherto produced only a very small number of remarkable writers, that she had produced no great historians, and no poets, and that there were third-rate towns in Europe which published in a year more works of literature than all the twenty-four States of America.[88] Mill, writing in 1840, speaks of 'the marked absence in America of original efforts in literature, philosophy, and the fine arts;'[89] while Carlyle, a few years later, very roughly declared that America had still her battle to fight; that though the quantity of her cotton, dollars, industry and resources was almost unspeakable, she had as yet produced no great thought, or noble thing that one could worship or loyally admire; that her chief feat in history had been to beget, 'with a rapidity beyond recorded example, eighteen millions of the greatest bores ever seen in this world before.'[90]

---

[88] *Démocratie en Amérique*, ii. 233.
[89] *Dissertations*, ii. 42.
[90] *Latter-Day Pamphlets*: 'The Present Time.'

This last judgment is certainly more remarkable for its vigour than for its judicial impartiality. Since Carlyle wrote America has produced some admirable literature; it has produced several considerable historians, some graceful and justly popular poets, some excellent critics, novelists and moralists, and a vein of humour which is perhaps more distinctively American than any other element in its literature. It has, especially, produced some of the most beautiful literary lives in the whole history of letters—lives true, simple, laborious and affectionate, singularly free from the jealousies and extravagances that deface so many pages of literary biography, absolutely free from that taint of impurity which has passed so deeply into the contemporary literatures of Europe. But, when all this is said, we cannot but ask whether the America of the nineteenth century has produced much in the fields of thought, or literature, or art that is really great; anything comparable to what Germany or France has produced during the same period; anything comparable to what might have been expected from a rich, highly educated, and pacific nation, which now numbers more than sixty millions of souls, and is placed, in some respects, in more favourable circumstances than any other nation in the world. A curious passage in an essay on Channing which Renan wrote some forty years ago describes the impression which American civilisation at that time left on the mind of one of the most brilliant of Frenchmen. 'If it were necessary,' he says, 'that Italy with her past, or America with her future, should be blotted out of existence, which would leave the greater void in the heart of humanity? What has all America produced that can compare with a ray of that infinite glory that adorns an Italian town, even of the second or third order—Florence, Pisa, Sienna, Perugia? Before New York and Boston reach in the scale of human greatness a rank that is comparable to these towns, how many steps have they still to make!'[91]

---

[91] *Etudes d'Histoire Religieuse.*

There is, no doubt, exaggeration in such language; there are forms of very genuine human greatness that it fails to recognise. But it is impossible not to feel that, on the intellectual and æsthetic side, America has not yet fulfilled her part, and that an unduly large proportion of her greatest achievements belong to a time when she had not a tithe of her present population and wealth. Washington and Franklin and Hamilton, the Constitution of 1787, the Federalist and the Commentaries of Judge Story, have not been eclipsed.

Many causes have been assigned for this intellectual sterility, continuing long after America had taken her place among the great nations of the world. Tocqueville believed that there was no country with less intellectual independence and less real liberty of discussion than America, or in which the expression of unpopular opinion was more bitterly resented; and he said that there were no great American writers because 'literary genius cannot exist without liberty of thought, and there is no liberty of thought in America.'[92] Mill, expanding another passage from Tocqueville, described America as, 'intellectually speaking, a province of England—a province in which the great occupation of the inhabitants is making money, because for that they have peculiar facilities, and are, therefore, like the people of Manchester or Birmingham, for the most part contented to receive the higher branches of knowledge ready-made from the capital.[93] Maine attributed much to the long refusal of the Congress to grant an international copyright. The want of such copyright effectually crushed American authorship in the Home market by the competition of the unpaid and appropriated works of British au-

---

[92] *Démocratie en Amérique*, ii. 149, 152.
[93] *Dissertations*, ii. 43; compare Tocqueville, ii. 58. I do not think Mill's illustration a happy one. Most English books, no doubt, are published in London, but the intellectual life that produces them comes from all parts of the kingdom, and in a very large degree from the great provincial towns.

thors, and 'condemned the whole American community to a
literary servitude unparalleled in the history of thought.'[94]

In all this there is much truth; but it must, I think, be added
that modern democracy is not favourable to the higher forms
of intellectual life. Democracy levels down quite as much as
it levels up. The belief in the equality of man, the total absence
of the spirit of reverence, the apotheosis of the average judgment, the fever and the haste, the advertising and sensational
spirit which American life so abundantly generates, and which
the American press so vividly reflects, are all little favourable
to the production of great works of beauty or of thought, of
long meditation, of sober taste, of serious, uninterrupted
study. Such works have been produced in America, but in
small numbers and under adverse conditions. The habit, too,
which has so long existed in America, and which is rapidly
growing in England, of treating the private lives of eminent
men as if they were public property; of forcing their opinions
on all subjects into constant publicity by newspaper inter-
views; of multiplying demands upon their time for public
functions for which they have no special aptitude, adds greatly
to the evil. Among the advantages which England derives
from her aristocracy, not the least is the service it renders to
literature by providing a class of men who are admirably fitted
for presidential and other public functions, which in another
society would have been largely thrown on men of letters. No
one can fail to observe how large a proportion of the Americans
who have shown distinguished talent in literature and art have
sought in European life a more congenial atmosphere than
they could find at home.

In spite of all retarding influences, America will, no doubt,
one day occupy a far higher position than at present in the intellectual guidance of the world. It is probable that the concession of international copyright, placing American authors on
the same footing with foreign ones, will hasten that day, and

[94] Maine's *Popular Government*, p. 247.

there are clear signs that a school of very serious scholarship and very excellent writing is arising among them. Many of the peccant humours of the body politic will, no doubt, be ultimately dispersed. The crudest, most ignorant, most disorderly elements of European life have been poured into America as into a great alembic, and are being gradually transformed into a new type. The enormously corrupting influences which New York and some other immigration centres have exercised on American politics must diminish when they cease to be what Americans call 'pivot states,' holding the balance between rival parties, and when the centre of power moves onward towards the west. A people supremely endowed with energy and intelligence, and among whom moral and religious influences are very strong, can scarcely fail sooner or later to mould their destinies to high and honourable ends.

Optimism certainly reigns more widely in America than in Europe, and Americans are the best judges of their own institutions and future. Serious clouds seem to hang on their horizon. The decay, in some parts of America, of family life through the excessive facility of divorce; the alarming prevalence of financial dishonesty on a large scale; the strange and ominous increase of ordinary crime, which contrasts remarkably with its steady diminution in Great Britain[95] the profligacy that still reigns in political and municipal life, and the indifference with which that profligacy is contemplated, afford much ground for melancholy thought. It is contrary to all past experience that political corruption should be a mere excrescence in a nation, affecting either slightly or not at all the deeper springs of national morals. As the country fills up, as national expenses increase, as the problems of government become more difficult and delicate, the necessity of placing the Administration in all its branches in trustworthy and honest hands must be more felt, and the future of America seems

---

[95] See on this subject a remarkable article, by Mr. Lea, in *The Forum*, August 1894.

to me very largely to depend upon the success with which her reformers can attain this end. Something considerable, as we have seen, has been already done; yet some of the worst instances of corrupt rings have been posterior to the downfall of the Tammany rule at New York, which was supposed to mark the beginning of a new era. The evidence which was brought before the Senate of New York in 1894, disclosing the enormous and systematic corruption of the police force of that great city, is in itself sufficient to show how little this hope has been fulfilled.[96]

The policy of Protection in America, which has been carried to such a high point since the war, is no new thing. It existed, though with some fluctuations, through a great part of earlier American history;[97] the high duties imposed during the war were amply justified by the necessity of obtaining money for its support, and their continuance for some years after the peace was probably justified by the transcendent importance of reducing rapidly an unparalleled debt. With the ideas that are now floating through the world, nothing could be more dangerous than for a pure democracy, in times of difficulty or poverty, to find itself burdened with an enormous debt taxation for the fulfilment of ancient contracts. The statesmen who followed the war have at least secured America from this danger. But the immense increase of Protection, which began with the Woollen Act of 1867 and the Copper Act of 1869, and which culminated in the McKinley tariff, was largely due to other motives. If the best American authorities may be trusted, it includes as much purely class legislation, intended to support class interests and carried by corrupt means, as can be found in the most effete monarchy of Europe.

The wonderful surplus which for many years existed in consequence of the high protective duties astonished Europe, but not more so than the manner in which it was expended. I

---

[96] Many particulars about this will be found in *The Forum*, August 1894.
[97] On the early history of American Protection, see Taussig's *Tariff History of the United States* (New York, 1888).

suppose there is no page in the financial history of the world more extraordinary than the history of the American pension list. At the close of the war pensions were, very properly, given to soldiers who were disabled in the course of it, and to wives of soldiers who had been married during the war, and who were left widows. It was naturally supposed that in America, as elsewhere, the war pensions would diminish as time rolled on and as the actors in the struggle passed away. For some years there seemed every prospect that this would have been the case; and there can be no doubt that it would have been so if the Protectionist interest had not found it necessary to maintain and expend an enormous surplus. The result of that necessity is, that in a long period of unbroken peace a war pension list has been created in the United States which far exceeds in magnitude any other that is known in history. Fifty-seven years after the war of 1812 pensions were voted to its surviving soldiers and to their widows; thirty-nine years after the Mexican War a similar measure was taken in favour of the survivors of that war. The list was made to include men who had been disabled long after the war, and by causes totally unconnected with it, and widows who had not been married, who in many cases had not been born when the last shot was fired. Personation, and other frauds almost grotesque in their cynicism and enormity, became notoriously common, and were practised with the most absolute impunity. Multitudes of young women formed real or pretended connections with old men for the purpose of qualifying for a pension. It appears from official documents that, in 1892, there were on the pension list 165 persons pensioned as survivors of the war in 1812, and there were no less than 6,657 women who were pensioned as widows of the soldiers in that war. The pension list trebled between 1880 and 1884. In 1893, it was stated that half a million of dollars a day were distributed on account of a war which had terminated nearly thirty years before. In 1893 there were 960,000 names on the pension list, and 165 millions of dollars, or thirty-three million pounds, was appropriated by Congress to the pension service.

It is not surprising that such an administration of public money should have produced a great financial revulsion, and that the period of enormous surpluses should have been followed by a period of almost equally enormous deficits. No other country, indeed, could have borne such an expenditure, and certainly public opinion in no other country would have tolerated it.[98]

It would be perhaps a paradox to say that the government of a country which is so great, so prosperous, and so pacific as the United States has not been a success; but, on the whole, American democracy appears to me to carry with it at least as much of warning as of encouragement, especially when we remember the singularly favourable circumstances under which the experiment has been tried, and the impossibility of reproducing those conditions at home. There is one point, however, on which all the best observers in America, whether they admire or dislike democracy, seem agreed. It is, that it is absolutely essential to its safe working that there should be a written constitution, securing property and contract, placing serious obstacles in the way of organic changes, restricting the power of majorities, and preventing outbursts of mere temporary discontent and mere casual coalitions from overthrowing the main pillars of the State. In America, such safeguards are largely and skilfully provided, and to this fact America mainly owes her stability. Unfortunately, in England the men who are doing most to plunge the country into democracy are also the bitter enemies of all these safeguards, by which alone a democratic government can be permanently maintained.

---

[98] A great deal of information about the American pensions will be found in *The Forum*, May and June, 1893, and in the *North American Review*, April and May, 1893; see, too, the *Times*, January 29, 1894. It appears, however, that in the year ending June 30, 1894, the expenditure on the pension list had sunk to 27,960,892*l*. (*Times*, October 30, 1894).

CHAPTER 2

The power given in England to a simple majority of a single Parliament to change, with the assent of the Crown, any portion of the Constitution is not a common thing among free nations. Italy and Hungary, it is true, appear in this respect to stand on the same basis as England. In Spain there is a written Constitution that makes no special mention of provision for its own reform, and it is a disputed question whether the text of the Constitution can be modified by a simple legislative measure of an ordinary Cortes, or must be submitted to a Constituent Cortes specially summoned for this purpose. But in most constitutions there is a distinct line drawn between organic constitutional changes and ordinary legislation, and careful provisions establish the manner in which alone the former can be carried into effect. In a large number of constitutions, of which those of the Austrian Empire, Belgium, and Bavaria may be cited as examples, two-thirds majorities are required for constitutional changes. In several constitutions it is necessary that such changes should be sanctioned by two successive Parliaments. In the Netherlands they may be demanded by a simple majority in one Parliament, but must be sanctioned, after a dissolution, by two-thirds majorities in its successor. In the German Empire

there is a provision that fourteen hostile votes in the Federal
Council constitute on these subjects an absolute veto. In
France, constitutional changes, after being voted by majorities in each of the two Houses, must be approved by a majority in a National Assembly consisting of the two Houses
sitting and voting together. In Switzerland they may be proposed by either Legislative Chamber, or by 50,000 vote-pos-
sessing citizens, but they cannot become law until they have
been sanctioned by a direct popular vote taken in the form of
a Referendum.[1]

Probably none of these provisions are as really efficacious
as those which are contained in the Constitutions of the
United States. None of them exist in the British Constitution,
or in the constitutions of the great colonial democracies that
are growing up under the English sceptre. One remarkable
attempt to introduce the American principle into an English
colony was, indeed, made by the great Australian statesman,
Wentworth, who, in 1853, introduced into his scheme for the
Constitution of New South Wales a clause providing that
alterations in the Constitution could only be carried by two-
thirds majorities. Unfortunately, this clause ultimately mis-
carried in England, and in this, as in the other Colonies, the
power of an upper Chamber and the small measure of restraint involved in connection with the mother country alone
restrict the power of unbridled democracy.[2]

Nothing, indeed, is more remarkable in our constitutional
history than the small stress which has been placed in England
upon mere legislative machinery, upon Constitutional laws
definitely tracing the respective limits and powers of different
institutions. The system of checks and counterchecks which
it has been the object of written constitutions to maintain has
been roughly maintained in England by the great diversities
that long existed in the constituencies; by the powerful orga-

---

[1] Report on the Majorities required in Foreign Legislatures for Constitutional Changes, presented to the House of Lords, April 1893.

[2] Rusden's *History of Australia*, iii. 71-137.

nisation of many distinct, and sometimes conflicting interests; by the great influence and essentially representative character of the House of Lords. It has been supported by a network of usages, traditions, compromises, and understandings which have no real or sufficient basis in the letter of the law, but which have long been universally accepted. Many of the most important working elements in the Constitution—the nature of the Cabinet, the functions of the Prime Minister, the dignity and the attitude of the Speaker, the initiative of the Government in matters of finance, the extent to which the House of Lords may use its veto—rest essentially on the foundation of custom. It is absolutely indispensable to the working of the whole machine that it should be in the hands of honest and trustworthy men, of men determined to subordinate on great occasions their personal and party interests to the interests of the State; imbued with a genuine spirit of compromise, and cordially in harmony with the general spirit of the Constitution. As long as such a spirit prevails in Parliament and governs the constituencies, so long the British Constitution will prove a success. If this spirit is no longer found among rulers and Parliaments and constituencies, there is no constitution which may be more easily dislocated, and which provides less means of checking excesses of bad government.

'Upon the power,' wrote Adam Smith, 'which the leading men, the natural aristocracy of every country, have of preserving or defending their respective importance depends the stability and duration of every system of free government.'[3] This truth has been always strongly felt in England, and it has sometimes been pushed to very extreme consequences. Thus, in the debates upon the abolition of the Corn Laws, some of the most considerable defenders of these laws refused to argue the question on merely economical grounds. They maintained that the preponderance of the landed interest was a political end of the first magnitude. They argued that it secured for the nation a governing class whose interests were

---

[3] *Wealth of Nations*, Book iv. ch. 7.

indissolubly connected with the permanent prosperity of England; whose class standard of honour placed them above all suspicion of personal corruption, and who, by living among their people and conducting the local government of their counties, had acquired in a high measure the kinds of knowledge and of capacity that are most needed in political life. Long after the sceptre of power had passed from the landed gentry to the middle classes, the old belief, or prejudice, or superstition that the administration of government ought to be chiefly entrusted to gentlemen, prevailed, and, in spite of all democratic agitations, it is certainly very far from extinct.

As I have already intimated, this belief, like many others which are now often very disdainfully treated, is by no means incapable of defence. The position of a public man is essentially that of a trustee, and interests of the most enormous importance depend largely on his character. To place the direction of affairs in the hands of honest, trustworthy, and competent men, though it is not the sole, is certainly the most important end of politics, and an immense proportion of the calamities that politicians have brought upon the world are due to the management of great political interests having passed into the hands of mere scheming adventurers. Honesty and dishonesty belong to all ranks and to all grades of fortune, but in dealing with masses of men we must judge by averages and probabilities, and chiefly by the strength of temptation and the pressure of interest. 'How easy it is,' as Becky Sharp said, 'to be virtuous on 5,000*l.* a year!' The fact that a trustee who is entrusted with vast money interests is himself not a needy, struggling, embarrassed man, but the possessor of a competent fortune, is generally recognised as furnishing some guarantee, though, unfortunately, by no means a sufficient one, that he will not dishonestly abuse his trust. And the strength of this presumption is greatly increased if the character of his fortune is not fugitive and movable, but permanent and stationary, and if he holds a desirable social position which depends mainly upon opinion, and would be inevitably destroyed by an act of private dishonesty.

This is the mode of reasoning on which men invariably act in the transactions of private life, and it is equally applicable to politics. The code of honour which the conventionalities of society attach to the idea of a gentleman is, indeed, a somewhat capricious thing, and certainly not co-extensive with the moral law. It may be, and often is, compatible with acts that are, in truth, profoundly base and immoral. Without forfeiting this position in the eyes of the world, men have plunged their country, through motives of mere personal ambition, into the horrors of war; have sought for honours, or power, or party triumphs, by shameful acts of political apostasy and shameful incitements to class warfare; have purchased majorities by allying themselves with dishonest men pursuing dishonest ends; have framed constitutions to enable their allies to carry those ends into effect. Men of old families and ample means may be found among the active agents or the servile tools in some of the worst political transactions of our time. All this is profoundly true; and it is also true that when any one class, be it high or low, obtains an uncontrolled, or even a greatly preponderating, power, its policy will exhibit a class bias. At the same time, it is no less true that on special subjects, and within a restricted sphere, the code of honour of a gentleman is the most powerful of all restraining influences, more powerful even than religion with ordinary men. Wherever it pervades the public service men will soon learn to recognise that public servants cannot be bribed or corrupted; that in dealing with public money they will not be guilty of malversation; that their word may be trusted, that they are not likely to act by tortuous or intriguing methods. The credit of England in the world depends largely upon this conviction, and that credit has been no small element of her prosperity. Imputations against men in high office, which in many countries are constantly made, easily believed, and sometimes proved, are in England at once felt to be incredible. One thing, at least, is very apparent to all serious observers—if the government of England passes altogether out of the hands of the kind of men who have hitherto directed it, it will speedily fall into the hands of professional politicians. What the character and tendencies of such politicians are likely to be, the example of the United States abundantly shows, and it shows also how different must be the constitution under which alone they can be safely restrained.

I do not think there is any single fact which is more evident to impartial observers than the declining efficiency and the lowered character of parliamentary government. The evil is certainly not restricted to England. All over Europe, and, it may be added, in a great measure in the United States, complaints of the same kind may be heard. A growing distrust and contempt for representative bodies has been one of the most characteristic features of the closing years of the nineteenth century. In some countries, as we have already seen, the parliamentary system means constantly shifting government, ruined finances, frequent military revolts, the systematic management of constituencies. In most countries it has proved singularly sterile in high talent. It seems to have fallen more and more under the control of men of an inferior stamp: of skilful talkers and intriguers; or sectional interests or small groups; and its hold upon the affection and respect of nations has visibly diminished. Laveleye has truly noted the sigh of relief that is felt in many lands when a Parliament is prorogued, and the growing feeling that America has acted wisely in restricting many of her State legislatures to biennial sessions. He observes, with some cynicism, that Italy has one special advantage in her capital—the Roman malaria effectually abridges the sessions of her Parliament.

This great decline in the weight of representative bodies, which has made 'parliamentarism' almost a byword in many nations, has advanced contemporaneously with the growth of democracy. In a large degree, at least, it may be clearly traced to the general establishment of universal suffrage as the basis of representation. It is being generally discovered that the system which places the supreme power in the hands of mere majorities, consisting necessarily of the poorest and most ignorant, whatever else it may do, does not produce Parliaments of surpassing excellence. One thing, however, must be observed. Ignorance in the elective body does not naturally produce ignorance in the representative body. It is much more likely to produce dishonesty. Intriguers and demagogues, playing successfully on the passions and the credulity of the ignorant and of the poor, form one of the great characteristic evils and dangers of our time.

In England, no one can be insensible to the change in the tone of the House of Commons within the memory of living men. The old understandings and traditions, on which its deliberations have been for many generations successfully conducted, have largely disappeared, and new and stringent regulations have been found necessary. Scenes of coarse and brutal insult, of deliberate obstruction, of unrestrained violence, culminating on one occasion in actual blows, have been displayed within its walls to which there have been few parallels in other legislatures. Perhaps the nearest are to be found in the American Congress in the years of fiercely excited passions that preceded the Civil War. It is true that these scenes may be chiefly traced to one party, which made it its avowed object to degrade, dislocate, and paralyse the parliamentary machine till their objects were attained; but the contagion of their example and the connivance, through party motives, of other members have been very evident.

On the other hand, the power of arbitrarily closing debates, which has been placed in the hands of majorities, has been grossly abused. It has been made use of not merely to abridge, but to prevent, discussion on matters of momentous importance. Many clauses of a Home Rule Bill which went to the very root of the British Constitution; which, in the opinion of the great majority of competent British statesmen, would have proved the inevitable prelude to the dismemberment and downfall of the Empire; which was supported by a party depending on the votes of men who were ostentatiously indifferent to the well-being of the Empire, and was strenuously opposed by a great majority of the representatives of England, and by a considerable majority of the representatives of Great

Britain, were forced through the House of Commons by the application of the Closure, and without any possibility of the smallest discussion. Nothing but the veto of the House of Lords prevented a measure of the first importance, carried by such means and by a bare majority, from becoming law.

And while this change has been passing over the spirit of the House of Commons, its powers and its pretensions are constantly extending. The enormous extension of the practice of questioning ministers has immensely increased the intervention of the House in the most delicate functions of the Executive. It insists on measures and negotiations, in every stage of their inception, being brought before it, and resolutions emanating from independent sections have more than once exercised a most prejudicial influence, if not on foreign affairs, at least on the government of India. At the same time, the claim is more and more loudly put forward that it should be treated as if it were the sole power in the State. The veto of the sovereign has long since fallen into abeyance. Her constitutional right of dissolving Parliament if she believes that a minister or a majority do not truly represent the feelings of the nation, and are acting contrary to its interests, might sometimes be of the utmost value, but it is never likely to be put in force. Her slight power, in the rare cases of nearly balanced claims, of selecting the minister to whom she will entrust the government, and the slight influence she still retains over the disposition of patronage, are regarded with extreme jealousy; while every interference of the House of Lords with the proposed legislation of the Commons has been, during a considerable part of the last few years, made the signal of insolent abuse. It would be difficult to conceive a greater absurdity than a second Chamber which has no power of rejecting, altering, or revising; and this is practically the position to which a large number of members of the House of Commons, and of their supporters outside the House, would reduce the House of Lords.

We can hardly have a more grotesque exhibition of this spirit than was displayed during the discussion of the Parish Council Bill in 1894. The Bill came for the first time before Parliament. It was one on which the House of Lords, consisting of the great proprietors of the soil, could speak with pre-eminent knowledge and authority, while a vast proportion of the majority in the House of Commons had not the remotest connection with land, and were notoriously acting under mere motives of party interest. The Bill of the Commons, in its principle and main outlines, was accepted by the Lords, and they went no further than to alter it in a few of its details. But because they exercised in this manner their clearest and most indisputable constitutional right, on a subject with which they were peculiarly competent to deal, they were denounced as if they had committed an outrage on the nation. The last ministerial speech with which Mr. Gladstone closed his long political career[4] was an abortive attempt to kindle a popular agitation against them on that ground.

The enormous and portentous development of parliamentary speaking, which has so greatly impeded public business, is due to many causes. In the first place, the House of Commons of 670 members is far too large for the purposes for which it is intended. It is larger than any other legislative body in the world, and the nineteenth century has added greatly both to its numbers and its speakers. At the beginning of the century it received an important addition in the Irish members who were brought in by the Union. The abolition of the small boroughs and the increasing power of the constituencies over their members greatly increased the average attendance, by making the members much more directly dependent upon their electors. The Reform Bills of 1867 and 1885 gave an opportunity for some reduction. But, as is usually the case, the interests of party and popularity prevailed, and the number of members was not diminished, but even slightly increased. The scenes of violence, anarchy, and deliberate obstruction that have been so frequent during late years have done much to destroy that respect for the House,

---

[4] March 1, 1894.

that timidity in appearing before a fastidious audience, which once weighed heavily on nearly all new members, and imposed a useful restraint on idle speaking. At the same time, the development of the provincial papers has made it an easy and desirable thing for each member to be reported at full in his own constituency as a prominent speaker; and the vast increase of stump oratory by members of Parliament in every town and almost every village has given nearly all members a fatal facility. Something, also, has been due to the fact that the House of Commons was led or profoundly influenced during many years by a very great orator, who possessed every form of eloquence except conciseness, and who could rarely answer a question without making a speech.

This diffuseness and incontinence of speech has not been the characteristic of the deliberative assemblies that have left the greatest mark on the history of the world. Jefferson observes in his 'Memoirs,' 'I served with Washington in the Legislature of Virginia, before the Revolution, and during it, with Dr. Franklin, in Congress. I never heard either of them speak ten minutes at a time, nor to any but the main point which was to decide the question.'[5] In our own House of Commons, old members still remember the terse, direct character of the speeches of Russell, Palmerston, and Disraeli, and many men who have exercised great weight and influence in English politics have been singularly deficient in the power of speech. The names of Lord Althorp, Sir Charles Wood, and the Duke of Wellington in the past generation, and of W. H. Smith in our own, will at once occur to the reader. The dreary torrent of idle, diffusive, insincere talk that now drags its slow lengths through so many months at Westminster certainly does not contribute to raise the character of the House of Commons. It is a significant sign that parliamentary reporting has of late years greatly declined, and that newspapers which would once have competed for the fullest reports of parliamentary speeches now content themselves

---

[5] *Life of Jefferson*, i. 179.

with abridgments, or summaries, or even with sketches of the speakers.

On the whole, however, it may be questioned whether, in the existing state of the British Constitution, this diffuseness is an evil. There is some weight in the contention of Bagehot, that one great advantage of government by debate is, that much talking prevents much action, and if it does little to enlighten the subject, it at least greatly checks the progress of hasty and revolutionary legislation. There are worse things than a wasted session, and, in times when the old restraints and balances of the Constitution have almost perished, the restraint of locquacity is not to be despised.

It makes the House of Commons, however, a perfectly inefficient instrument for some of the purposes it is expected to fulfil. There are large questions, such as the reform and codification of great branches of the law, which bristle with points of difficulty and difference, but which at the same time do not fall within the lines of party or affect the balance of power. To carry highly complex measures of this kind through a body like the present House of Commons is utterly impossible, and these much-needed reforms are never likely to be accomplished till the Constitution is so far changed as to give much larger powers to Committees.

The independence of Parliament has at the same time almost gone. Since the country has committed itself to democracy the caucus system—which is but another name for the American machine, and which, like the American machine, is mainly managed by a small number of active politicians—has grown with portentous rapidity. It nominates the candidates for elections. It dictates their policy in all its details. It applies a constant pressure by instructions, remonstrances, and deputations at every stage of their task. It reduces the ordinary member of Parliament to the position of a mere delegate, or puppet, though at the same time it tends, like many other democratic institutions, to aggrandise enormously the power of any single individual who is sufficiently powerful and conspicuous to enlist the favour of the nation and dominate and direct the caucus machinery. What is called 'the one-man power' is a very natural product of democracy. Mr. Bright once said that the greatest danger of our present system of government is surprise—the power which a bold and brilliant leader possesses of committing his party by his own will to a new policy which had never been maturely considered or accepted. It is notorious that the most momentous new departure made by the Liberal party in our day—the adoption of the policy of Home Rule—was due to a single man, who acted without consultation with his colleagues.

At the same time, a great change has taken place in the relations of Government to the House of Commons. In order to guard against the dangers to be feared from an unrestrained House, opposite methods have been employed in the United States and in England. In the former, the ministers form no part of the representative Chamber, and the vote of that Chamber is incompetent to overthrow them. In England, on the other hand, the Ministry is the creature of the House of Commons; but the organised force of a united Cabinet is the most powerful restraint upon its proceedings. Most of the old power of the sovereign, as it has been truly said, has now passed to the Cabinet, and a solid body of the leaders of the majority, whose guidance is indispensable to the ascendency of their party, is able to exercise a strong controlling influence on all parliamentary proceedings. But the situation is much modified when Parliaments break up into small groups. All over the world this has been one of the most marked and significant tendencies of democratic Parliaments, and it will probably eventually lead to a profound change in the system of parliamentary government. In France, in Germany, and in Italy, as well as in many minor States, this disintegration may be shown to its full extent; in Great Britain it has made considerable progress. Not many years ago Belgium was said to be the only European country where the Legislature was still divided into only two distinct parties.[6] One of the first results

---

[6] Laveleye, *Le Gouvernement dans la Démocratie*, ii. 101.

of her lowered suffrage has been the introduction into her Parliament of a new and powerful Socialist group.

The results of this disintegration are very manifest. Government in its relation to the House of Commons loses its old commanding and controlling authority. The Cabinet had already lost much of its initiating power by the growth of the caucus system, which dictates the policy of the party. In a Parliament divided into several groups its strength is still further diminished. A coalition may at any time overthrow it. It depends upon the concurrence of many distinct groups, governed by different motives, aiming at different objects, representing different shades of political feeling. It is obliged to conciliate by separate bribes these different sections, or to discover some cry that may rally them, some active and aggressive policy that may secure their support, and to which they will subordinate their special objects.

This evil is greatly accentuated by the modern discovery that the disintegration of parties is exceedingly conducive to the triumph of minor sectional objects. A group of men representing opinions and aiming at objects which are only those of a small minority of the nation, may obtain a decisive influence if it keeps apart from the great party organisations, subordinates all other considerations to its own objects, and at times when parties are evenly balanced, and when a few votes can save or destroy a Government, makes the attainment of those objects the price of its adhesion. Where there are only two strongly organised parties these minor questions fall into their natural place; but in a Parliament broken into many fractions, each fraction can exercise a power utterly disproportionate to its numbers and to its real hold upon the country. The action of the independent Irish Home Rule party in the parliamentary system has been the most remarkable instance of this truth, and other groups are evidently constituting themselves in the same way, and are likely to pursue their objects by the same parliamentary methods.

The consequences of all this are very far-reaching. If my forecast is not erroneous, it must end in the destruction of that ascendency of the House of Commons which was built up in the days of middle-class supremacy and of strong party organisation. It produces also a weakness and an instability in the executive power which is often very injurious to the interests of the nation. On the whole, however, this weakness seems likely to be greater under Liberal than under Conservative Governments, as the Conservative party is far more homogeneous than its rival. The great revolt of the nation against Radical policy in 1895 has created one of the most powerful ministries of the century, resting upon an enormous and substantially homogeneous majority in both Houses. But, with the fluctuations to which parliamentary government is now so liable, no one can suppose that such a majority can be permanent. All the signs of the times point to the probability in England, as elsewhere, of many ministries resting on precarious majorities formed out of independent or heterogeneous groups. There are few conditions less favourable to the healthy working of parliamentary institutions, or in which the danger of an uncontrolled House of Commons is more evident.

One consequence of this disintegration of Parliament is a greatly increased probability that policies which the nation does not really wish for may be carried into effect. The process which the Americans call 'log-rolling' becomes very easy. One minority will agree to support the objects of another minority on condition of receiving in return a similar assistance, and a number of small minorities aiming at different objects, no one of which is really desired by the majority of the nation, may attain their several ends by forming themselves into a political syndicate and mutually co-operating. The kind of politics which was notoriously adopted on the question of Home Rule illustrates both the nature and the danger of this system. The Home Rule Bill had been decisively condemned by the constituencies, and the Government which proposed it saw clearly that on that issue alone it was not likely to obtain a favourable verdict. It was argued, however, that if a Home Rule Government could win the support of the electors who desired local option, and the disestablishment of the Welsh and Scotch Churches, and the abolition of the hereditary element in the House of Lords, and legislation shortening the hours of labour, and other measures of a democratic character, these different parties would constitute a majority that would enable the ministers to carry Home Rule in spite of the wishes of the nation.

Probably still more dangerous is the necessity, which the existing state of parliamentary representation establishes, of seeking for a popular cry, which generally means some organic and destructive change in the Constitution. An appetite for organic change is one of the worst diseases that can affect a nation. All real progress, all sound national development, must grow out of a stable, persistent national character, deeply influenced by custom and precedent and old traditional reverence, habitually aiming at the removal of practical evils and the attainment of practical advantages, rather than speculative change. Institutions, like trees, can never attain their maturity or produce their proper fruits if their roots are perpetually tampered with. In no single point is the American Constitution more incontestably superior to our own than in the provisions by which it has so effectually barred the path of organic change that the appetite for such change has almost passed away. No one who observes English politics with care can fail to see how frequently, when a statesman is out of office and his party divided, his first step is to mark out some ancient institution for attack in order to rally his followers. Personal vanity here concurs powerfully with party interests, for men who are utterly destitute of real constructive ability are capable of attacking an existing institution; and there is no other form of politics in which a noisy reputation can be so easily acquired. Instead of wisely using the machinery of government for the benefit of the whole nation, English politicians have of late years been perpetually tampering with it, and a spirit of feverish unrest has passed into English politics which, if it is not checked, bodes ill for the permanence of parliamentary government.

Both parties have in this respect much to answer for. A weak Conservative Government is often tempted to outbid its rival and win the support of some discontented fragment of the Opposition; and there is no Radicalism so dangerous as this, for it finds no external body to restrain it, and the Opposition is bound by its position to aggravate it. Few pages in our modern political history are more discreditable than the story of the 'Conservative' Reform Bill of 1867. A weak Liberal Government, on the other hand, depends for its support on the concurrence of many semi-detached groups, among which extreme politicians often exercise a disproportionate power. The Home Rule schism, by depriving the party of the greater part of its restraining and moderating element, has much increased the danger.

There are few things, also, more disheartening in English politics than what may be called the unintelligent conservatism of English Radicalism. It moves persistently in a few old, well-worn grooves. The withdrawal of the control of affairs from the hands of the minority who, in the competitions of life, have risen to a higher plane of fortune and instruction; the continual degradation of the suffrage to lower and lower strata of intelligence; attacks upon institution after institution; a systematic hostility to the owners of landed property, and a disposition to grant much the same representative institutions to all portions of the Empire, quite irrespectively of their circumstances and characters, are the directions in which the ordinary Radical naturally moves. In hardly any quarter do we find less constructive ability, less power of arriving even at a perception of the new evils that have arisen or of the new remedies that are required. To destroy some institution, or to injure some class, is very commonly his first and last idea in constitutional policy.

Another tendency which is very manifestly strengthening in English politics is that of attempting to win votes by class bribery. With very large democratic constituencies, in which a great proportion of the voters are quite indifferent to the main questions of party politics, some form of corruption is certain to arise. The kinds of bribery, it is true, which prevailed in England under an unreformed Parliament have either disappeared or greatly diminished. The number of the electors, the secrecy of the vote, and the stringency of recent legislation against corruption, have had in this respect a salutary effect. The gigantic corruption which exists in America under the name of the 'spoils system' has not taken root in England, though some recent attempts to tamper, in the interests of party, with the old method of appointing magistrates in the counties, and some claims that have been put forward by members of parliament to dictate the patronage in their constituencies, show that there are politicians who would gladly introduce this poison-germ into English life. Happily, however, the system of competitive examination places most branches of the Civil Service out of the reach of politicians. But a form of bribery which is far cheaper to the candidate, yet far more costly to the nation, than that to which our grandfathers were accustomed, has rapidly grown. As Sir Henry Maine has truly said, the bribery which is most to be feared in a democracy is that of 'legislating away the property of one class and transferring it to another.'[7] Partial, inequitable taxation, introduced for the purpose of obtaining votes, is an evil which in democratic societies is but too likely to increase.

It has been rendered easier by the great fiscal revolution which took place in England after the abolition of the Corn Laws. A number of widely diffused indirect taxes, which were paid in the form of enhanced prices, were abolished; taxation has been more concentrated, and it has become very easy to vary both its amount and its incidence. It is remarkable that, at a time when this process was rapidly advancing, a note of warning and of protest was sounded by one of the wisest leaders of the Liberals. Sir C. Lewis, in the memorable Budget speech which he made as Chancellor of the Exchequer in 1857, quoted the following striking passage from Arthur Young: 'The mere circumstance of taxes being very numerous in order

---

[7] *Popular Government*, p. 106.

to raise a given sum is a considerable step towards equality in the burden falling on the people. If I were to define a good system of taxation, it should be that of bearing lightly on an infinite number of points, heavily on none. In other words, that simplicity in taxation is the greatest additional weight that can be given to taxes, and ought in every country to be most sedulously avoided.' 'That opinion,' said Sir Cornewall Lewis, 'though contrary to much that we hear at the present day, seems to me to be full of wisdom, and to be a most useful practical guide in the arrangement of a system of taxation.'[8]

These remarks of Sir Cornewall Lewis were much censured at the time; but I believe that many of our best contemporary thinkers will agree with me that they contain much truth, and that the concentration of taxation into a very few forms has been carried in England to an exaggerated extent. In times when prosperity is rapidly advancing and when taxation is easily borne the evil may be little felt; but in times of receding prosperity it is of no small advantage that the burden of taxation should be diffused in many forms and over a wide area. As it is much easier in times of adversity to raise than to impose a duty, it is often wiser in times of prosperity to lower than to abolish it. Low duties on articles of general consumption, showing themselves in a slightly enhanced price, pass almost unnoticed, and usually cause far less friction and discomfort than direct taxes. They are very equitable, for they are strictly proportioned to consumption or enjoyment; and this system of taxation makes it easy for the taxpayer, according to his improving or declining means, to vary his taxation by varying his consumption, while it secures that some portion of the national burden shall be diffused over a wide area. An excel-

---

[8] Northcote's *Twenty Years of Financial Policy*, pp. 309–10. There is a remarkable speech of Thiers in favour of a great variety of moderate taxes, delivered January 19, 1831. He contended that this is the only system of really equitable taxation that has been yet devised, as those who escaped one tax fall under another, and taxation adjusts itself almost insensibly to expenditure.

lent writer on this subject has truly said: 'If only our fiscal burdens are equitably apportioned, and so contrived as neither to fetter industry nor to repress enterprise, that mode of levying them must be the best which is the least unpleasant and the least felt;' and the same writer gives good ground for believing that there is much exaggeration, and even positive error, in the popular notion that the cost of collecting indirect taxes is greater than that of collecting direct ones.[9] Two other considerations must also be remembered. One is, that the remission of a direct tax is usually felt to its full extent by the whole body of taxpayers affected, while a wholly disproportionate amount of the benefit arising from the remission of a duty is in most cases intercepted by middlemen. The other is, that the remission of a direct tax is usually an unmixed benefit, while the remission of an indirect tax, by stimulating competition, often produces acute suffering to particular classes. Thus, to give a single example, the kelp manufacture, on which the poorest inhabitants of the most barren coast-lands in Scotland and Ireland are largely supported, was for many years wholly dependent for its existence on a tax which was imposed on Spanish barilla.

I do not intend by these remarks to dispute the immense advantages which England has derived from her Free-trade legislation. This legislation has vastly stimulated both production and consumption; it has lightened many burdens; and in many cases the Treasury has derived a far greater revenue from a low duty than it had ever received from a high one. But the political evil of narrowing the basis of taxation is a real one, and, even in its purely economical aspects, the reaction against the abuses of the old fiscal system seems to have been carried too far. It is not probable that a single loaf of bread was made the cheaper by the abolition, in 1869, of the shilling registration duty on corn, though that small duty at the time it was repealed by Mr. Lowe brought more than

[9] Greg's *Political Problems*, p. 304.

900,000*l.* into the national exchequer, and would, probably, at the present day have brought in double that sum. Not one Londoner in a hundred even knew of the existence of the small duty on coal which was abolished in the present generation. It had existed in one form or another for more than six hundred years, and was almost the oldest of our taxes. It furnished an income of more than 500,000*l.* a year, raised without complaint, for the purpose of effecting metropolitan improvements; and there is no reason to believe that any human being, except a few rich coalowners and middlemen, derived any benefit from its abolition.[10]

We have a striking instance—though it was not of a democratic character—of the manner in which changes in taxation may be made use of for electioneering purposes in the conduct of Mr. Gladstone in making the abolition of the income-tax his election-cry at the general election of 1874. The circumstances of this election may be briefly told. Mr. Gladstone was not obliged to go to the country. In spite of his defeat on the Irish University question in the preceding year, he had still a considerable and unbroken majority, though several defeats at bye-elections showed clearly that his power was declining, and especially that the upper and middle classes, who were the payers of income-tax, were profoundly shaken in their allegiance to him. The income-tax-payers, it is true, were not even then an absolute majority of the electors, but they formed a much larger proportion than after the Reform Bill of 1885. They included the great majority of the voters who could influence other voters; and they were a body so large and so powerful that there was no reasonable doubt that a general movement among them would decide the fate of the election. The fortune of the ministry was tolerably certain to turn upon the question whether the defection in this notoriously wavering class could be arrested.

---

[10] The facts relating to these coal dues will be found in a report issued by the Coal, Corn, and Finance Committee of the Corporation of London, on *The Results in the way of Fluctuations and Alterations of the Price of Coal in London since the Abolition of the Coal Dues.*

It was under these circumstances that Mr. Gladstone, much to the surprise of the country, suddenly dissolved Parliament; and he issued a programme to his electors which, if the report of those who are likely to be best informed is not wholly erroneous, was as much a surprise to most of his colleagues as to the public. The times were very prosperous, and a great surplus was gathering in the Exchequer. Mr. Gladstone, throwing all other political questions into the background, resolved to utilise this surplus for election purposes, and to stake his chances at the election upon large direct offers of financial relief made to the electors, but especially to that class of the electors who were known to be wavering in their allegiance. One portion of his election address consisted of a general and undefined promise to reduce duties and assist rates; but the part which at once and especially riveted the attention of the country by its conspicuous novelty and boldness was a definite pledge that if he won the election he would abolish the income-tax. This promise at once became the leading feature of the election. It was urged from a hundred Liberal platforms and in a hundred Liberal newspapers as the great reason why the income-tax-payers should support the ministry. Every elector of this class, as he went to the poll, was clearly informed that he had a direct personal money interest in the triumph of the Government.

It is true that the promise of Mr. Gladstone was qualified by the following vague passage in his election address: 'I have said nothing to preclude the government from asking Parliament to consider, in conjunction with these great remissions, what moderate assistance could be had from judicious adjustments of existing taxes.' It is true also, that in a later speech, being pressed with the impossibility of repealing the income-tax without imposing other taxation, he admitted that, in consideration of the repeal of the income-tax and the reduction of rates, 'property ought in some shape and to some considerable and equitable extent to make some fair contribution towards the public burdens.' But the nature and magnitude of this contribution, the form it was to take, and the area over which it was to be distributed, were never revealed up to the day of the election. Everything relating to it was left perfectly vague and shadowy. One point only was brought before the electors in clear, vivid, unmistakable relief. It was, that if Mr. Gladstone won the day the income-tax would cease. Such a promise, unaccompanied by any distinct statement of equivalent burdens to be imposed, could only have operated as a direct bribe addressed to that great section of the electorate whose growing alienation from the Government was the chief cause of the dissolution. No politician, I believe, seriously doubted that when Mr. Gladstone placed the abolition of the income-tax in the forefront of the battle, his object was to win the income-tax-payers to his side.

Some strictures that I ventured to make on this transaction in the former book elicited from Mr. Gladstone two articles of indignant defence.[11] No one who judged solely from those skilful and plausible pages would imagine that any question of winning votes, or arresting a political defection, or gaining a party triumph, could have entered even distantly into his calculations. He was merely, he said, 'consulting' the nation 'upon the exercise of its chief and primary right of giving or withholding taxes;' upon 'a great subject of financial readjustment.' 'The rights of the people,' as he truly said, 'in respect to taxation are older, higher, clearer than in respect to any other subject of government.' He at the same time asserted that his censor 'ought to have known, and to have stated, that with the proposal to repeal the income-tax came a proposal to reconstruct and enlarge the death duties. Direct taxation of a kind most vexatious to trade and industry was to be removed—direct taxation, the least of all unfavourable to trade and industry, . . . was to be imposed.'

The assertion so confidently made in this passage was simply untrue, and is a curious instance of the lapse of memory into which, by too hasty writing, its author has sometimes been betrayed. No proposal of this kind was made. Mr. Glad-

---

[11] *Nineteenth Century*, June and August 1887. A brief article of my own will be found in the July number.

stone was obliged in his second article to confess that on this
point his memory had betrayed him, and that his critic was
right; but he at once changed his ground, and argued that it
would have been exceedingly prejudicial to the public service
if he had disclosed at the election the 'readjustment' of taxation which he had contemplated, as such a disclosure would
have enabled the tax-payer to evade the coming burden. 'The
disclosure of the particulars of the plan would have been both
wholly novel and in the highest degree mischievous to the
public interest.' It is, surely, sufficiently obvious to reply that
this fact is a very conclusive argument against the propriety
of throwing such a matter into an election programme. 'The
ancient right' of the people to be consulted on adjustments
of taxation can hardly be very valuable when the condition of
the consultation is that the nature of the adjustment should
be concealed. Stated fully to the electors, Mr. Gladstone's
proposal would, according to his own showing, have defeated itself. Stated as it was stated, it amounted to little more
than a naked promise, that if a certain class of voters would
maintain the Government in power, they should be freed
from a burdensome tax.

But Mr. Gladstone takes a much higher ground than that
of mere apology, and assures us that his real motive in this
transaction was 'the fulfilment of a solemn duty.' He considered the income-tax unjust, unequal, and demoralising;
twenty-one years before he had formed part of a ministry
which promised to abolish it. This pledge, after a long slum-
ber, revived in its full vitality at the eve of the election, and
he offered the electors 'the payment of a debt of honour.'

I have little doubt that Mr. Gladstone succeeded in persuading himself that this mode of reasoning was legitimate,
but the answer to it is very simple. It was perfectly open to
him to have introduced into Parliament a Budget abolishing
the income-tax and carrying out, after full exposition and discussion, such other financial arrangements as he deemed desirable. Had he pursued this usual and regular course, no
shadow of blame or discredit could have been attached to

him, and he would, very probably, have rendered a real service to the country. But it was a wholly different thing to throw a half-disclosed and fragmentary Budget before the constituencies at a general election, making the simple abolition of a specific tax the main ground for asking the votes of those who paid it. A Minister who, seeing the popularity of his Government visibly declining, determined to dissolve Parliament before introducing his Budget, and to make his election-cry a promise to abolish the chief direct tax paid by a great wavering body of electors, may have been actuated by no other object than 'the fulfilment of a solemn duty.' But in ordinary men such conduct would imply other motives; and such men undoubtedly co-operated with Mr. Gladstone in the struggle, and such men will, for their own purposes, follow his example. In my opinion, few worse examples could have been given, and the constituencies in defeating Mr. Gladstone at this election rendered no small service to political morality.

Another argument of a curiously ingenious and characteristic nature must be noticed. I had said that the meaning of Mr. Gladstone's address was, that if he won the day the income-tax would cease. The statement is literally and incontestably true; but Mr. Gladstone very dexterously met it by declaring that it is an entire misrepresentation and an evidence of extreme ignorance to describe the election as if it was fought on the issue of the income-tax. It was not a question of one party supporting and the other opposing the abolition. 'This supposed historical fact is a pure historical fiction.' Both parties promised the abolition, and both parties, therefore, stood on the same footing.

A few words of explanation will, I think, place this matter in its true light. When Mr. Gladstone issued his election address, Mr. Disraeli was evidently taken by surprise. He was much alarmed lest this novel and unprecedented course might produce a great wave of popularity, and sweep the main body of income-tax-payers into his rival's net. He, accordingly, promptly replied that he also was in favour of the abolition of the income-tax, and had always been opposed to it. This implied promise was thought by many good judges at the time to have been an exceedingly improper one; and I am in no way bound to defend it, though it is but justice to add that Mr. Disraeli stated that he was only in favour of the abolition in case the surplus was sufficiently large to make it possible without the imposition of fresh taxation.[12] But surely it is mere sophistry to argue that the conduct of Mr. Disraeli affects the character of Mr. Gladstone's original address. Is it not perfectly notorious that the popularity which Mr. Gladstone's promise was expected to produce in this great wavering portion of the constituencies was the element of success on which his followers most confidently relied? Did they not, after Mr. Disraeli's reply, still urge (and with much reason) the special claim which Mr. Gladstone had established on the voters by forcing the question into the van, and also that he was much more competent than his rival to carry the proposal into effect? Is the fact that Mr. Gladstone's example was so speedily followed a proof that it was not pernicious, and was not likely to be contagious?

A much more serious argument is, that among the questions that have at different times been brought, with general consent, before the constituencies there have been many, such as the abolition of the corn laws, or local taxation, or economical reform, in which a private pecuniary interest, as well as a public interest, must have been presented to the elector. The statement is perfectly true, and I have no wish to dispute or evade its force. Public and private interest are, undoubtedly, often so blended in politics that it is not possible wholly to disentangle them. The difference between an election which is mainly governed by low motives of private interest, and an election which is mainly governed by high motives of public spirit, is very great, but it is essentially a difference of proportion and degree. All that can be said is, that it will depend largely on a minister to determine at an election which of these classes of motives preponderate. Each dubious case must be judged by the common sense of the community on its own merits, and in the light of its own special circumstances. In former days, private interest was chiefly brought to bear upon elections by the process of corruption applied to individual voters. In modern days, bribery has changed its character, and is much more likely to be applied to classes than to individuals. Manipulations of taxation, and other legislative offers dexterously adapted to catch in critical times the votes of particular sections of the electorate, are the evils which are chiefly to be feared, and, of this kind of evil, the course adopted by Mr. Gladstone in 1874 still appears to me to have been a conspicuous example.

Many other illustrations might be given. No one who has carefully followed Irish politics during the period of the Land League agitation can doubt that appeals to the cupidity of electors formed the mainspring of the whole machine. Other motives and elements, no doubt, entered largely into the calculations of the leaders; and with them a desire to drive the landlord from his property was not in itself an end, but rather a means of obtaining political ascendency and separation from England. But it is notorious that the effectual inducement they held out to the great body of the farming class to support them was the persuasion that it was possible by the use of political means to break contracts, lower rents, and confiscate property. Nor can it be denied that the legislation of the Imperial Parliament has gone a long way to justify their prevision.

I do not include in this charge the Land Act of 1870, which appears to me to have been, in its main lines, though not in all its parts, a wise and comprehensive effort to deal with one of the most difficult and complicated questions that have appeared in English politics. The elements of the problem were very numerous. There was the imperfect sympathy between the land-owning and land-cultivating classes, arising originally from historical causes, from differences of religion, politics, and, in some degree, of race, and in modern times strengthened by the Famine and the Encumbered Estates Act, which created a multitude of new landlords, largely drawn from the trading classes, who had no knowledge of the traditions and customs of the estates they acquired, and who often purchased with borrowed money and as a commercial investment. Improvements, too, in Ireland were for the most part made by the tenant, and not by the landlord; and although the rents were in general proportionately lower than in England, although on most old estates a long tenure at low rents amply compensated the tenant for his outlay, there were, undoubtedly, cases where the advent of a new proprietor, or a sudden rise in rents or depreciation in values, led to a virtual confiscation of tenants' improvements. Leases had been for some years diminishing, and tenancies at will became general. The custom of tenant-right was general in Ulster and occasional in other provinces, though it subsisted without the smallest sanction or protection of the law. Usage unsanctioned by law played a large part in Irish agrarian life; and there was a bad custom of allowing rents to be paid, in many parts of the country, with extreme irregularity, according to the good or bad seasons, and leaving the arrears of many years outstanding, not claimed, and not wiped away. It must be added, that the small number of manufactures had thrown the population, to an unhealthy extent, for subsistence on the soil; that political agitation had already done much to inflame class animosities and accentuate class divisions, and that there were grave faults on both sides. Wretched farming; thriftless, extravagant, unbusinesslike habits in all classes; a great want of enterprise and steady industry; much neglect of duty, and occasional, though not, I think, frequent, acts of oppression and extortion, all contributed to complicate the task of the legislator.

In my own opinion, it should have been his object to secure to the tenants compensation for all future improvements; to bring back by special inducements a land system resting on definite written contracts; to give legal character to tenant-right when it was generally acknowledged; and to assist by

Government measures in the formation of a peasant proprietary, or, what was politically scarcely less valuable, of a class of tenants holding land for ever at a low fixed rent.

The question of tenants' improvements especially was of vital importance, and it is one of the most real of Irish grievances that Parliament, in spite of the clearest warnings, so long neglected to attend to it.

Some years before the Famine Sharman Crawford had devoted himself with much zeal to the subject, and had repeatedly brought into the House of Commons a Bill which would have effectually met it. He proposed that when a tenant made improvements which were of a nature to produce an increased rent, and which had not been included in the terms of his existing lease, these improvements should be duly valued; that the tenant, at the expiry of his term, should have the right to claim either immediate money compensation from the landlord or a prolongation of his tenancy; and that, in fixing the new rent, the value of unremunerated improvements should be taken into account, so that the tenant might be repaid for them in the course of the succeeding tenancy.[13]

The Devon Commissioners, who sat under a commission ordered at the end of 1843, collected a great deal of valuable information on the subject, and treated it in an eminently judicial spirit. They acknowledged that 'there had not been brought many cases to show that it had been the practice of land-proprietors to take advantage of improving tenants who had invested money without a lease or other security.' They acknowledged also, that 'it had not been shown that tenants possessing long and beneficial leases of the lands had in general brought them to a high state of improvement;' that, in fact, there was evidence 'that lands let upon very long terms, and at very low rents, were in a worse condition, and their occupiers even more embarrassed, than others.' On the other hand, they urged that cases of the confiscation of tenants' im-

---

[13] See the *Digest of the Evidence of the Devon Commission*, pt. i. 164–66.

provements had occurred; that a tenant at will or a tenant with
a very short lease was always liable to them; that 'a single instance occurring in a large district would naturally paralyse
exertion to an incalculable extent;' that the possibility and extreme facility of such confiscation in the existing state of the
law was a gross injustice to the tenant, discouraged in the most
powerful manner a kind of investment which was naturally
very profitable both to the tenant class and to agriculture in
general, and directly or indirectly contributed largely to most
of the social evils of Ireland. They recommended, as of the
highest importance to Ireland, a law giving tenants in the future compensation for permanent and productive improvements, and framed upon the following principles. Agreements
between landlord and tenant relative to such improvements
were to be duly registered, and, in cases where it was found
impossible to arrive at such agreement, a tenant was to serve
a notice on the landlord of his intention to make suitable improvements. Mutually chosen arbitrators were to report upon
them, and the assistant barrister, after such report, and after
examination, was to certify the maximum cost, not exceeding
three years' rent. If the tenant was ejected, or if his rent was
raised within thirty years, the landlord was to pay such a sum,
not exceeding the maximum fixed, as the work shall be then
valued at. The improvements were to be completed within a
limited time, and the landlord was to have the option of making them himself, charging 5 per cent. on the outlay.[14]

A Government measure based on this report was introduced by Lord Stanley, in a speech of great power, in 1845,
and by Lord Lincoln in 1846. In the first case it was abandoned
in the face of very determined opposition. In the second, it
fell through on account of the overthrow of the Government
of Sir Robert Peel, which had introduced it. Several attempts
in the same direction were made in the following years, the
most remarkable being the Bill of Mr. Napier, the Irish

---

[14] *Digest of the Evidence of the Devon Commission*, pt. ii. 1124–1125.

Democracy and Liberty

Attorney-General of Lord Derby's Government, in 1852, which had a retrospective character applying to all past improvements. None of these measures, however, ultimately succeeded, and the advice of the Devon Commission was neglected.

Besides the question of improvements, it was clearly recognised that something must be done to prevent the too frequent evictions, or threatened evictions, and the Land Act of 1860 did something in this direction. This Act, which was passed by a Liberal Government, affirmed in the clearest terms that the relations of landlord and tenant in Ireland rested solely 'on the express or implied contract of the parties, and not upon tenure or service;' but it at the same time provided that the landlord could bring no ejectment for non-payment of rent till a year's rent under the contract of tenancy was in arrear; and that, even after the ejectment had taken place, and the landlord was in possession of the farm, the tenant might apply to the court for his reinstatement if, within six months after his ejection, he paid his rent and costs. A clause which appears to have been imitated from the French Civil Code[15] uthorised the tenant to remove 'all personal chattels, engines, machinery, and buildings accessorial thereto affixed to the freehold by the tenant at his own expense,' provided this could be done without injuring the freehold as it existed when he first received it; and another clause established the right of the tenant to cut turf, in the absence of any express agreement to the contrary, on any unreclaimed turf bog on his tenancy. It may be added, that Acts of the old Irish Parliament had long since given the leaseholder a right of property in the trees he had planted, provided they were duly registered.

The very comprehensive and elaborate Act of 1870 went much further, and it was inspired by an evident desire to do justice to all parties; though, in the vast range of its provisions, there were some which have proved prolific in dangerous con-

---

[15] See Richey on *The Irish Land Laws*, pp. 50–51.

sequences not, I believe, clearly foreseen by its authors. One valuable portion of the Act followed and extended the policy, which had been adopted in the Church Act, of endeavouring to create a peasant proprietary. It authorised advances not exceeding two-thirds of the purchase money, and repayable by an annuity of 5 per cent. in thirty-five years, to any tenant who desired to purchase his holding. Another portion recognised, in the largest and fullest terms, the right of the tenant to compensation for his improvements, which are defined as works adding to the letting value of the holding, and suitable to it, and also to his crops and his unexhausted manure. This right was not destroyed by an ejection for non-payment of rent. It was not confined to improvements made subsequent to the Act. With certain clearly defined exceptions, it applied to all improvements made by the tenant or his predecessors in title. In the case of permanent buildings and reclamation of waste land there was no limit of time. In the case of other improvements there was a limit of twenty years. It was enacted that improvements, except in certain specified instances, should be deemed to have been made by the tenant or his predecessors, unless the contrary had been proved, thus reversing the old legal presumption that whatever is added to the soil belongs to the landlord. Durable and written contracts and tenant-right were encouraged by clauses limiting the improvements for which a landlord was liable whenever he granted a long lease, and permitting a departing tenant to dispose of the interests of his improvements to an incoming tenant on terms that were approved of by the court.

The Ulster tenant-right—or, in other words, the right of a tenant to sell his interest in his farm—received the force of law, and it was extended to all parts of Ireland. In Ulster the existing tenants had purchased their tenant-right, and they only obtained legal security for what was already theirs by usage. In the other parts of Ireland a saleable property which they had not bought was conferred upon them. One consequence of this was, that the boon was a much greater one to the first generation of tenants, who received it as a gift, than it was likely to be to their successors, who would in due course purchase their tenant-right. Another consequence, which was probably not foreseen, was that the tenants borrowed largely on their new security; and it was from this time that the 'gombeen man,' or local usurer, obtained his great prominence in Irish life. A provision, to which, I believe, there was then no parallel in the legislation of the world, provided that a tenant who had accepted a tenancy from year to year could not be removed, except at a ruinous cost, at the date at which his tenancy was terminable. Except in case of non-payment of rent, bankruptcy, or violation of specified conditions of tenancy, the landlord had no power of resuming possession of his land without paying the tenant a fine for 'disturbance,' which might, in some cases, amount to seven years' rent. It will be observed that this 'disturbance' was not an illegal act. It was simply the enforcement by the landlord of a plain and incontestable right secured to him by the contract under which he freely parted from his land. As Judge Longfield has observed, it was possible for a landlord under this law to put a tenant in possession as tenant from year to year, to leave him in the enjoyment of it for five years, and then to be obliged to pay him seven years' rent as a fine for removing him from it.[16] This compensation was quite distinct from that given for improvements in the shape of permanent buildings or reclamation of the soil. A landlord might, however, free himself from this claim by giving a long lease.

The statesman who introduced the Act very clearly stated that it was not intended to give the tenant at will a proprietary right in his holding, but the provisions relating to disturbance plainly and unquestionably had this effect. Some faint and distant analogy may be discovered between this legislation and the English tenure of copyhold, which grew out of tenancies at will that had existed undisturbed in the same families for many generations, and which the law at last rec-

---

[16] *Systems of Land Tenure* (Cobden Club), p. 78.

ognised as a permanent tenure, to be enjoyed by the tenants and their heirs, subject to the conditions prescribed by immemorial custom in the manor. The Irish law, however, applied to the newest as well as to the oldest tenancies. It was defended, partly on the ground that usage in most parts of Ireland made a yearly tenant secure that he would continue undisturbed in his tenancy as long as he paid his rent; partly as a measure intended to discourage the great political evil of unnecessary evictions; partly on the ground that it was likely to be beneficial to both landlord and tenant, by giving the tenant strong additional reasons for punctually observing the conditions of his tenancy. It was said that it merely gave the tenant of a bad landlord the security which the tenant of a good landlord already enjoyed, and that, in the case of small farmers, an increased stability of tenure would be not only a great political advantage, but also a great incentive to better agriculture. Even eviction for non-payment of rent might be deemed a 'disturbance' establishing a claim for compensation if, in the opinion of the Land Court, the rent was an exorbitant one, or if the arrears that were demanded had not wholly accrued within the previous three years. The right of compensation for disturbance applied to all tenancies from year to year, or held on leases for less than thirty-one years created after the Act had passed, and also to all tenancies from year to year existing when the Act was passed which were under the value of 100*l.* a year.

The Legislature considered, with some reason, that the smaller tenants were too poor to make their own bargains. Agreements between landlord and tenant, under which the latter gave up their rights to certain privileges granted by the Act, were in a large number of cases made null and void. These clauses prohibiting grown-up men from making their own bargains have been the fruitful parents of much later legislation. The principle passed into England in the Ground Game Act of 1880, which made it impossible for an English tenant to divest himself by agreement with the landlord of the right of killing hares and rabbits; and a tendency to introduce the same principle of compulsion into the largest possible number of contracts relating to land and trade seems fast becoming a distinctive feature of advanced English Liberalism.

The Irish Land Act of 1870, in its consequences, was certainly one of the most important measures of the present century. It appears to me to have been introduced with much integrity of motive, and in many of its parts it proved very beneficial. The recognition of a tenant's right to the improvements he had made; the recognition of the Ulster tenant-right; the encouragement given to the substitution of written leases and contracts for the system of tenants at will; the measures taken to create a peasant proprietary, were all marked with much wisdom. Capricious notices to quit, or notices to quit given for the mere purpose of accelerating the payment of rent, were discouraged by the imposition of a stamp duty, and there was a useful provision granting loans of public money for the reclamation of waste land. I cannot, however, reconcile with the rights of property the retrospective clause making a landlord liable for improvements made by tenants at a time when no such liability was recognised by law, and with a clear knowledge of that fact; and the clause giving a yearly tenant compensation for simple disturbance if he was removed at the end of the year seems to me essentially dishonest, and the germ of much evil that followed. It was not altogether a new importation into Irish politics. In 1866, Sir Colman O'Loughlin brought in a Bill for discouraging annual letting and precarious tenancies, and one of its clauses gave compensation to a yearly tenant if he was ejected for any other cause than nonpayment of rent. This Bill was thrown out by a large majority.[17]

It is probable that the Act of 1870 would have been more successful if it had been less ambitious, and had aimed at a smaller number of objects. The difficulty, however, of the task was extremely great, and much allowance must be made for the statesmen who framed it. The two features of the old Irish

[17] See Sir William Gregory's *Autobiography*, p. 243.

land system which made the position of the Irish tenant most precarious were the general absence of leases, and the custom of the tenant, not the landlord, making most improvements. Neither of these points was, in most cases, a matter of much dispute between landlord and tenant. Those who are best acquainted with the conditions of Irish land before the recent legislation will I believe, agree with me that the majority of smaller tenants preferred a yearly tenancy, which was rarely changed, to a definite lease, which usually involved stricter covenants, and was likely when it expired to be followed by a revaluation and rise of rents; and that they preferred making their improvements in their own economical, and generally slovenly, way, rather than have them made in the English fashion by the landlord, who compensates himself by adding a percentage to the rent. If the rent is sufficiently low, and the tenure sufficiently long to compensate the tenant for his outlay, there is nothing in this system that is unjust; nor is it unjust that, after the tenant has been so compensated, the land should be rented according to its improved value. But it is easy to understand how this custom strengthened that notion of the joint ownership of the soil which had such a deep root among Irish ideas. In many of the poorest parts of Ireland the cabin built by the peasant, the clearing of stones, and the erecting of fences, constituted much the greater part of the value of the farm. These little farms of barren land were, indeed, essentially unsupporting. They furnished the small tenant with shelter and with potatoes for his subsistence. His rent, which was usually not more than about 4*l*. a year, and very irregularly paid, was earned sometimes by fishing, more frequently as a migratory labourer, and often by harvest-work in England or Scotland.

In the fertile districts the conditions were different and very various. Probably the greater number of the original improvements had been made under the old system of very long leases at very low rents. In many cases the erection of certain buildings was expressly stipulated in the lease, and was one of the elements in regulating the price. A great part of the cost of drainage which has been made under Government loans has been paid by the landlords, and in very many cases they have contributed a proportion to the cost of buildings; but, as a general rule, the improvements were made by the tenant, under the belief that he would enjoy his tenancy for a sufficient time and at a sufficiently low rent to compensate him for them. The immense deterioration of Irish land through bad and wasteful farming forms, however, a considerable offset against these improvements.

That rents in Ireland before 1870 were not in general extortionate, and were, indeed, much below the competition value, is abundantly proved.[18] It is proved by the fact that wherever tenant right was permitted this right of occupation sold for a large sum; by the fact that wherever subletting was permitted the tenant almost invariably let the whole, or portions of his tenancy, at much higher rents than he paid. It is proved by the evidence of men of the greatest authority on Irish land, such as Judge Longfield and Master Fitzgibbon, and by the direct testimony of the Bessborough Commission in 1881, which, after a long and careful investigation, arrived at the conclusion that in Ireland it was 'unusual to exact what in England would have been considered as a full and fair commercial rent.'[19] It

---

[18] Comparisons between Irish and British rents are apt to be very fallacious, on account of the different systems of farming and payment for improvements. The following passage, however, from a pamphlet by one of the greatest modern authorities on statistics, may be given : 'Before the period of distress,' writes Sir Edwin Chadwick in 1886, 'the rents in Ireland appeared to average 15s. an acre for tillage land (it is now declared to be on an average under 10s.); in England, 23s. an acre. In Scotland, on inferior tillage lands to those of England, the rents were 40s. and more' (Chadwick's *Alternative Remedies for Ireland*, p. 19). On the comparison between Irish and foreign rents I may cite M. Molinari one of the most competent judges on the Continent. His conclusion is: 'Le taux général des rentes est modéré; autant que j'ai pu en juger, il est á qualité égale de terrain, de moitié plus bas que celui des terres des Flandres' (*L'Irlande, le Canada, Jersey* (1881), p. 138).

[19] See *Report of the Inquiry into the Working of the Landlord and Tenant Act, 1870*, p. 3; Judge Longfield's essay, in the Cobden Club volume, on 'Systems of Land Tenure;' Fitzgibbon's *Ireland in 1868*, pp. 268–70. Judge

is proved by comparison with English and with foreign rents, and by the slow increase of Irish rents, as compared both with the prices of the chief articles of agricultural produce and with the increase of rents in other parts of the kingdom. Arthur Young, in his day, considered the rents paid in Ireland to the owner of land unduly, and often absurdly, low; and in bringing in the Land Bill of 1870, Mr. Gladstone stated that, in the ninety years that had elapsed since Arthur Young wrote, the rents of Ireland had just doubled, and, if Ulster were excluded, had much less than doubled, while in ninety-eight years the rental of England had trebled, and in ninety-nine years the rental of Scotland had sextupled.[20] If we take a shorter period, and a period of great prosperity, we shall come to much the same conclusion. Mr. Caird, who is one of the best modern authorities on agriculture, computed that in the seven years before 1869 'the land rental of England has risen 7 per cent., that of Scotland 8 per cent., while that of Ireland appears in the same time to have advanced, from its lowest point, not more than 5½ per cent.'[21] Taking Ireland, indeed, as a whole, it is probably the portion of the United Kingdom in which the benefit of the great rise in the price of agricultural produce in the third quarter of the nineteenth century has fallen most largely to the labourers and tenants, and in the smallest degree to the landlords.[22]

But although it is not true that Irish rents were in general unduly high, it is true that the position of the great body of

---

Longfield was for many years judge of the Landed Estates Court, and probably the first authority on land in Ireland. The authority of Master Fitzgibbon is scarcely less, for as Master of Chancery he had for many years no less than 452 estates, with more than 18,000 tenants and a rental of more than 330,000*l*., under his jurisdiction.

[20] See Mr. Gladstone's published speech on introducing the Land Bill of 1870, pp. 26–27.

[21] *The Irish Land Question*, by James Caird (1869), p. 15.

[22] Sir R. Giffen speaks of 'the stationariness of rents in Ireland for a long period, notwithstanding the great rise in the prices of the cattle and dairy products which Ireland produces;' and he adds: 'The farmer and the labourer together have, in fact, had all the benefit of the rise in agricultural prices' (*Progress of the Working Classes in the last Half-century*).

the Irish tenants was utterly precarious; that in three provinces of Ireland many causes had conspired to break down the good feeling between landlord and tenant which was essential to a sound agrarian state; and that cases of gross oppression and extortion, though they were a small minority, did exist, and were not infrequent. Subletting, it is true, had much diminished, and with it the chief cause of extravagant rents. No fact is more clearly stamped upon every page of Irish agrarian history than that men of the farmer class have always been far harsher masters than men of the gentleman class; and in these latter days there have been instances of tenants holding at very moderate rents under the landlord, and actually having their rents reduced by the Land Court, at the very time when they were themselves extorting for portions of the same land extreme rack rents from their labourers. To no spot of the globe, indeed, is the parable of the servant who, having been forgiven his debt by his own master, exacted the last penny from his fellow-servant, more applicable than to Ireland.

But among rents paid to the actual owner of the soil two classes were often extortionate. There were small properties in the hands of men of narrow means, either of the trading or farming classes, and there were tracts—often extensive tracts—which had been bought by speculators under the In-cumbered Estates Act, usually with borrowed money. There were cases in which the purchasers at once sought, by extensive clearances and greatly raised rents, to recoup themselves for their outlay. In the sale of these estates the tenants had usually been unprotected by lease. The law under which the estates had been sold recognised in them no right in their improvements, and rents were sometimes raised, in estates which had derived most of their value from recent tenants' improvements, in a manner that was positively fraudulent. The purchaser thought only of his legal rights. He knew nothing and he cared nothing about the history of his property.[23]

---

[23] See some good remarks on this subject by Sir W. Gregory, *Autobiography*, pp. 157–59.

Sometimes, too, on older estates, particular farms might be found rented at a strangely higher rate than those around them. The explanation is, usually, that these rents had formerly been paid to a middleman, and had not been revised when the middleman was removed.

The Act of 1870 had many merits, but it admitted, as I believe, a dangerous and dishonest principle. The Act of 1881 appears to me one of the most unquestionable, and indeed extreme, violations of the rights of property in the whole history of English legislation. In order to realise its character it is only necessary to remember that before the legislation of Mr. Gladstone the ownership of land in Ireland was, like that in France and in America, as absolute and undisputed as the ownership of a house, or a horse, or a yacht. The Incumbered Estates Act, and all the proceedings connected with it, brought this fact into the clearest relief. It had been the policy of the Whig Government, supported in its day by the loud applause of the Liberal party, to place landed property in Ireland on the strictest commercial basis. The measure was carried in 1849, at a time when Ireland was reduced to the lowest depths of misery by the great Famine, and when the newly imposed poor law in many cases equalled, in some cases even exceeded, the whole valuation income of an estate, and it was pressed on by the Liberal party with extreme harshness, to the ruin of countless landlords and creditors.

By this Act, at a time when Irish land had sunk to a mere fraction of its normal value, the first incumbrancer of an estate, or any other creditor who believed that the estate would fetch a price large enough to meet the payment of his own demand, might force the estate by a summary proceeding, and before a newly constituted court, into the market, utterly regardless of the interests of the other creditors and of the owner. Every creditor except the petitioner who was forcing the sale was at liberty to bid; and even the petitioner, by leave of the court (which was easily procured), might become the purchaser of the depreciated property. 'By this new process,' writes a very competent lawyer, 'estates were sold to the amount of many millions, during the years 1849, 1850, 1851, and 1852, for less

than half their value, and less than half the prices which the
same estates would bring had the sale been deferred till the
end of 1863. Some of the most ancient and respected families
in the country, whose estates were not incumbered to much
more than half their value, were sold out and beggared; thousands of creditors whose demands would have been paid if
the sales had not been accelerated were not reached, and lost
the money which they had lent upon what was ample security
at the time it was lent, and would again have become sufficient security had the property not been ruined by the poor
law and sold in that ruined condition, in a glutted market,
under an enactment devised for the professed purpose of
improving the condition of Ireland. The law's delay, which in
ordinary circumstances is a grievance and a vexation, would
have had a salutary and a just effect in those calamitous times.
There was no justice in exonerating the early incumbrancers
from all participation in the effects of the visitation which had
come upon the country, and every feeling of humanity and
every principle of equity demanded temporary indulgence
from them. There was cruel injustice in turning a destructive
visitation of Providence into an advantage to them which they
could not have had if the law had been left as it stood when
they made their contracts and took their securities, and as it
still stands in England.'[24]

This measure, however, was at that time put forward by
the Whig party as the supreme remedy for the ills of Ireland.
It was pushed on against all remonstrances, and with many
insults to the broken and impoverished landlords, who were
now fast sinking into the shades of night. Political economy,
it was said, was vindicated, and with a chorus of self-con-
gratulation the Whig leaders proclaimed that Irish property
was at last placed on its true basis, that all feudal superstitions
had been effectually exorcised, and that a new and energetic
class of landlords would replace the old thriftless, apathetic
landlords of the past. During the last twenty-five years the

---

[24] Fitzgibbon's *Ireland in 1868*, p. 208.

main object of the leaders of the Liberal party has been to
undo the work of 1849.

Let us now look at the Incumbered Estates Act from another
side. The purchaser purchased from the Government, and at
the invitation of the Government, the complete and absolute
ownership of the estate, subject only to the existing contracts
under which it had been hired out to the tenants. He bought
every acre of the land, every stone of the buildings. If there
were improvements on the land, these improvements were
specifically mentioned in the printed advertisements that
were issued by the Land Court, and they were sold to the
purchaser by a judge who was appointed by the Government,
and under the direct sanction of the Imperial Parliament. If
the property was let on very easy terms; if the leases were
soon to expire; if there was a possibility of making a considerable rise of rents, these facts were constantly put forward
by the court as inducements to the purchaser, and they entered largely into the price which he gave. He was guaranteed
the complete and absolute possession of the land and buildings on the termination of the tenancies in the schedule, the
full legal right of determining the existing yearly tenancies.
One of the special advantages attributed to the Act was, that
it was perfectly clear; that the title which it conferred was
absolutely indisputable. It was a parliamentary title, and
highest known to English law; a security of the same kind
and of the same force as that by which the fundholder or
other Government creditor is guaranteed the interest of his
loan. Between 1849 and 1870 more than fifty-two millions of
pounds had been invested on this security in the purchase of
Irish land. About an eighth part of the soil of Ireland is said
to be held under this parliamentary title.

Let us now pass for a moment to the position of the existing
landlords as it is established by the legislation of Mr. Gladstone. In the first place, the improvements which had been
purchased under the Incumbered Estates Act have, by a naked act of confiscation, and without the smallest compensation, been taken from the purchaser, and are now the property

of the tenant. A great part of what the State had sold to him, and what the State had guaranteed to him, is no longer his; and it has ceased to be his, not by an act of honest purchase, but by an act of simple power. In the next place, his clear and indisputable right to resume possession of his land when the tenancies upon it had expired has been taken from him. The tenant who was in possession when the Land Act was passed has acquired fixity of tenure. Subject to the periodical revision of rents by the Land Court, and the fulfilment of certain easy statutory conditions, he cannot be removed unless the landlord should purchase from him, by permission of the Land Court, and on conditions which the court prescribes, that right of resuming possession of his land which before the new Act was indisputably his own. The landlord has ceased to be the owner. He has become merely a rent-charger. Again and again in the debates of 1870, when the question of fixity of tenure was raised, the leaders of the Liberal party acknowledged the very obvious truth that such a provision simply amounted to the transfer of the ownership of the soil from the landlord to the tenant, and that such a transfer could only be honestly effected by paying for it in money. 'By such a provision,' said Mr. Gladstone, 'the landlord will become a pensioner and rent-charger upon what is now his own estate. The Legislature has, no doubt, the perfect right to reduce him to that condition, giving him proper compensation for any loss he may sustain in money.' 'Inasmuch as perpetuity of tenure on the part of the occupier is virtually expropriation of the landlord, and as a mere readjustment of rent according to the price of produce can by no means dispose of all contingencies the future may produce in his favour, compensation would have to be paid to the landlord for the rights of which he would be deprived.'[25] I shall not go into argument on that subject,' said Sir Roundell Palmer when speaking of this proposal, 'because that point was exhausted by the Head of the

---

[25] *Speech of Mr. Gladstone in Proposing the Irish Bill*, February 15, 1870 (Murray).

Government when he spoke of fixity of tenure, which, in plain English, means taking away the property of one man and giving it to another. My right honourable friend said that, according to the principles of justice, if we transferred property in that way we must pay for it. No doubt we may take a man's property, but in that case we must compensate him for it.'[26]

These principles appear to me perfectly true, and indeed self-evident; but they did not prevent the legislators of 1881 conferring fixity of tenure on the present tenant without granting compensation to the landlord, and from that time the first principle of much reasoning in Parliament about Irish land has been that it is a dual ownership; that the landlord is nothing more than a partner, or, as it is now the fashion to say, 'a sleeping partner,' in a joint possession, whose interests in every question of dispute should be systematically subordinated to those of the other partner. And this phraseology represents with much truth the position which the holders of land under parliamentary or other title in Ireland now hold.

In the last place, the Legislature has deprived the landlord of the plainest and most inseparable rights of ownership— the power of making contracts, offering his farms at the market price; selecting his tenants; prescribing the period and the terms for which he will let his land. A court is established with an absolute power of deciding the amount of rent which the tenant is to pay, and the landlord has no option of refusing, or seeking another tenant. It is often argued that the reduction enforced by the Land Courts is, on an average, somewhat less than that which has taken place in England, and that the Irish landlord has, in consequence, no reason to complain. There is, however, a great difference between a country which is mainly pasture and a country which is in a large degree wheat-growing; between a country where farms are constantly thrown into the hands of the landlord, as no tenant will take them, and a country where the average price

---

[26] *Hansard*, cxix. 1666.

of tenant-right is more than ten years' purchase of the existing rental. There is also a clear difference between a reduction imposed by an act of mere power, and a reduction which is the result of the free bargaining of two contracting parties.

It might have been supposed that a legislature, in conferring this tremendous power upon a new court, would take great care at least to minimise its injustice by strictly defining the principles on which it was to act, and insisting that the reasons for its decisions should be clearly and fully given. Mr. Gladstone, however, with great skill, succeeded in persuading Parliament to abstain from giving any definition or any approximation to a definition of a fair rent, leaving this matter completely, or almost completely, to the arbitrary and unregulated action of the court. The single exception was a provision that no rent must be allowed for improvements made either by the tenant or by his predecessor in title. The one real test of the value of a thing is what men are prepared to give for it, and this market test was absolutely excluded from the valuation. Another possible test was the long continuance of the existing rent. The Bessborough Commission, which laid the foundation of the Act of 1881, proposed 'that a rent which was paid at any time within the last twenty years, and which continued for not less than ten years to be regularly paid,' should be always assumed to be a fair rent, unless the conditions had altered to the detriment of the tenant. Another proposal was, that rents should be deemed fair, and should be exempted from the jurisdiction of the court, if they had not been raised during the preceding twenty years. In spite of the great and almost unparalleled increase of prosperity in Ireland during that period, it appears that this proposal would be applied to no less than 4,700,000 acres of Irish soil.[27]

Both of these proposals, however, were rejected. Many rents were reduced which had been paid without a murmur for thirty or forty years, and in spite of clear evidence that the

---

[27] See the speech of the Right Hon. E. Gibson on the second reading, April 5, 1881.

chief articles of Irish agricultural produce had during that period largely risen, and that the opening of new markets and the improvement of communications had materially added to the value of the farms.[28] Many rents were reduced although it was shown that, within the last few years, the right of occupying the farms at these rents had been purchased by the tenant at a large sum under the Act of 1870.[29] The decisions were virtually and mainly in the hands of the subcommissioners, who were to a large extent young barristers and county attorneys; many of them with scarcely any previous knowledge of land, or of the conditions of agriculture in the province in which they were adjudicating. They were sent to their task—or, as one of the ablest of them expressed himself, 'let loose upon property'—without any instructions;[30] and they usually gave their decisions without assigning any reasons. It was clearly understood that their business was to reduce, and not to regulate, rents. Their popularity or unpopularity depended on the amount of their reductions, and they knew that the wildest expectations were excited. One of the great perplexities of the lawyers who practised before them arose from the extreme difficulty of discovering the principle or reasoning on which they acted. One fact, however, which was clearly shown was, that the artificial depreciation of land arising from agrarian agitation and outrage entered largely into their estimate.[31] It would be impossible to conceive a greater encouragement to such agitation; while the landlords were fined by the Government because the Government had failed to discharge adequately its elementary duty of suppressing anarchy and securing property. A hasty visit to the farms was made, and rents were settled according to their present condition. In this way, in a country

---

[28] See on this subject the striking evidence in the *Third Report of the Committee of the House of Lords on the Land Act*, 1883, p. 18; see, too, p. 101.

[29] Ibid. pp. 17, 43.

[30] Ibid. pp. 104, 132.

[31] Ibid. p. 86.

where farming was already deplorably backward, slovenly and wasteful farming received a special encouragement in the form of the greatest reduction of rents.

It is not surprising that such decisions carried with them little moral weight. When complaints were made, the ministers dilated on the indecency of questioning 'judicial decisions;' as if such arbitrary proceedings as I have described bore any real resemblance to the judgments of a law court, where a judge is guided at every step by the clearly defined provisions of the law, and where his task is simply to decide or explain its relations to the facts that are before him. It may be observed, too, that while competition for rents was extinguished by the law, and rentals greatly reduced, the competition for tenant-right was practically unrestrained, and the price of tenant-right rapidly rose.[32] There could be no better proof that the reductions did not represent the real market depreciation of value, but were in a large degree simply the transfer of property from one class to another.

I have no wish to put forward any extreme or exaggerated view of the sanctity of landed property. In my own opinion, the Legislature has a perfect right, if the public welfare requires it, to take possession of all such property, and to sell or hire it on such terms as it pleases, on the single condition of giving full compensation to the owners. The recommendation of Mill, that Irish landlords should be altogether expropriated, receiving full compensation, seems to me very doubtful in point of policy, but in no degree objectionable in point of principle. Mill will certainly not be suspected of any undue leaning towards landowners, but his doctrine differs little, if at all, from that which I am maintaining. 'The claim of the landowners,' he writes, 'is altogether subordinate to the general policy of the State. The principle of property gives them no right to

---

[32] For full statistics on this subject, see the *Statements of the Irish Landowners' Convention*, addressed to H.M.'s Ministers, February 3, 1888, p. 23, and the reply to the *Report of the Land Acts Committee of 1894*, pp. 102–13.

the land, but only a right to compensation for whatever portion of their interest in the land it may be the policy of the State to deprive them of. To that their claim is indefeasible. It is due to landowners, and to owners of any property whatever, recognised as such by the State, that they should not be dispossessed of it without receiving its full pecuniary value, or an annual income equal to what they derived from it. . . . When the property is of a kind to which peculiar affections attach themselves, the compensation ought to exceed a bare pecuniary equivalent. . . . The Legislature, which, if it pleased, might convert the whole body of landlords into fundowners or pensioners, might, *à fortiori*, commute the average receipts of Irish landowners into a fixed rent-charge, and raise the tenants into proprietors, supposing always (without which these acts would be nothing better than robbery) that the full market value of the land was tendered to the landlords in case they preferred that to accepting the conditions proposed.'[33]

I should myself state the claims of the landlord in somewhat different terms. As much land in these islands is held in trust, it seems to me that the Government, if it deprives the landlord, for purposes of public policy, of the whole or a portion of his property, is bound in equity to compensate him by such a sum as would produce, if invested in a trust fund, an income equal to that of which he was deprived.

The course which was pursued by the British Legislature towards Irish land was different, and if the terms 'honesty' and 'dishonesty' apply to the acts of Parliaments or Governments as truly as to individuals, it was distinctly and grossly dishonest. Under the Constitution of the United States, the greater part of this legislation, being a direct violation of contract, would have been beyond the competence of Congress. Nor is there, I believe, anything in the legislation of the great European countries that is parallel to it. It has been described by one of the best continental writers upon government as an attack on the principle of property more radical than any

---

[33] *Political Economy*, Book ii. chap. ii. § 6.

measure of the French Revolution, or even of the Reign of Terror.[34] It is, indeed, much less like ordinary legislation than like extraordinary legislation of the nature of Acts of attainder or confiscation. There is, it is true, one material difference. Acts of attainder are usually passed for the purpose of confiscating the property of men who have been guilty of treason or rebellion. As the Parnell Commission abundantly showed, the true crime of the Irish landlords was their loyalty. It was for the avowed purpose of ruining and driving from the country 'the English garrison' that the Fenian party organised the agrarian agitation that led to the legislation of 1881.

The Bill was defended by some very serious statesmen on the ground of necessity. A gigantic agrarian conspiracy, including the bulk of the Irish peasantry, the great transfer of political power that had taken place in Ireland under English legislation, and an acute and protracted agricultural crisis, produced by bad seasons and wretched prices, had, they said, brought Ireland into a state in which some such measure was inevitable. It must be added that its character and effects were much misunderstood. It was believed that the free sale clause, which enabled a tenant who was in difficulties to sell his tenant-right to a solvent farmer, and, after paying all debts, to emigrate or set up business with a substantial capital, would operate to the great advantage of all parties. It would, it was thought, give the broken tenant a new start, secure the rent of the landlord, put an end to all necessity for evictions, and at the same time attract farmers of energy and industry; and it was not foreseen how completely it could be paralysed by violence and intimidation.

---

[34] Les lois agraires que M. Gladstone a fait voter pour l'Irlande et que l'on trouve déjà insuffisantes portent au principe de la propriété et du libre contrat une atteinte plus radicale que ne l'ont fait la révolution française et même la Terreur. . . . A moins de confiscation on ne peut guère aller plus loin' (Laveleye, *Le Gouvernement et la Démocratie*, i. 31–32). M. Léon Say cites recent Irish agrarian legislation as the most striking modern instance of State Socialism (*Socialisme d'Etat*, p. 7). See, too, the remarks of M. Stockquart, *Revue de Droit International*, xxvii. 145.

It is also tolerably certain that a considerable number, at least, of the most important ministers never anticipated that the provisions for settling rents by the authority of the court would be applied to the bulk of Irish tenancies, or made use of to create a new level of rental. It would, they believed, simply reduce to the general average those exceptional and extortionate rents which, in every county, undoubtedly existed. If it had not been for the assurances to this effect given by the ministers, it is very improbable that the Bill would have passed. 'My view,' said Mr. Bright, 'is, that in reality the rents in Ireland will for the most part, in nine cases out of ten, be fixed very much as they are now.'[35] 'The Government,' said the Attorney-General for Ireland, 'did not admit that there would be any loss to the landlord except the loss of a power which he ought not to exercise.'[36] 'I deny,' said the English Chancellor, 'that it [the Bill] will, in any degree whatever, diminish the rights of the landlord, or the value of the interest he possesses.'[37] 'I think,' said Mr. Forster, 'the final result of the measure within a few years will be, that the landowners of Ireland, small and large, will be better off than they are at this moment.'[38] It was believed that rents would be often raised as well as often lowered, that the tenants who were moderately rented would, in consequence, abstain from going into the court, and that the Act would in practice apply only to a small number of over-rented tenancies. Lord Carlingford, who spoke with especial authority on all Irish questions, and who took the chief part in carrying the measure through the House of Lords, was very explicit. 'My lords,' he said, 'I maintain that the provisions of this Bill will cause the landlords no money loss whatever. I believe that it will inflict upon them no loss of income, except in those cases in which a certain number of landlords may have imposed upon their tenants

---

[35] *Hansard*, cclxi. 103.
[36] Ibid. cclxi. 1379.
[37] Ibid. cclxiv. 532.
[38] Ibid. cclxiii. 1685.

excessive and inequitable rents, which they are probably vainly trying to recover.'[39]

I am far from presuming to fathom the true meaning or design of the statesman who is chiefly responsible for this legislation. In introducing the Bill of 1870, with its dangerous principle of compensation for disturbance, Mr. Gladstone had specially and repeatedly maintained that he was conferring a benefit upon the owners as well as the occupiers of the soil. He deplored the fact that the selling value of Irish land was much lower than that of British land, and predicted that the effects of his legislation would make it 'not merely worth twenty or twenty-five years' purchase, but would raise it altogether, or very nearly, to the value of English or Scotch land.'[40] In 1881 he used similar language. When introducing a measure establishing fixity of tenure he was confronted with his own very plain words in 1870, which I have already quoted, about the confiscatory character of such a measure; but it was not difficult for so supreme a master of the art of evasion to extricate himself from his difficulty. He skilfully met the demands for compensation for property and legal rights that were clearly taken away by alleging that he was not injuring, but, on the contrary, benefiting the landowner. In many cases, he said, the probable effect of the Bill would be to raise rents; and although he would not say 'whether the action of the court in fixing a judicial rent may not, on the whole, lower the rents rather than raise them in the first operation,' he was convinced that the increased value of land derived from the greater solidity of the social state which he was bringing about would speedily 'repay the landlord for any incidental mischief of the Act twofold or threefold.'[41] As was his usual custom on such occasions, he pitched his tone very high, and appealed

---

[39] Ibid. cclxiv. 252.

[40] *Hansard*, cc. 1263.

[41] Ibid. cclxiii. 1696–1697. See on this subject an excellent pamphlet, called *The Working of the Land Law*, February 1882, published by the Irish Land Committee.

in noble language to the loftiest motives. 'Justice, sir, is to be our guide; and as it has been said that love is stronger than death, even so justice is stronger than popular excitement, stronger than the passions of the moment, stronger even than the grudges, the resentments, and the sad traditions of the past. Walking in that light, we cannot err. Guided by that light—the Divine Light—we are safe.'

Probably no one who was present when, with uplifted eyes, and saintly aspect, and exquisitely modulated intonation, the great speaker poured out these sonorous sentences, predicted that in a few short years he would identify himself with the men whom he had truly described as preaching 'the doctrine of public plunder;' demoralising a people by 'teaching them to make the property of their neighbour the objects of their covetous desire;' attempting to substitute 'an anarchical oppression' for the authority of law; making rapine their first object; seeking 'to march through rapine to the dismemberment of the Empire;' destroying the peace of life; aiming at 'the servitude of good men, the impunity and supremacy of bad men.' Few persons could have imagined that this virtuous statesman would soon be endeavouring to place the government of Ireland in the hands of those who were guilty of such things; that he would be employing all the resources of his matchless dialectic to attenuate their misdeeds; that he would denounce as coercion measures for the enforcement of the criminal law against the most merciless of oppressions, which were largely copied from his own legislation; that he would spend the evening of his long and brilliant public life in inflaming class animosities and reviving the almost extinct embers of provincial jealousies. It is perhaps somewhat less surprising that the Irish landlords continued to be attacked just as if the Acts of 1870 and 1881 had never been carried, and as if capricious evictions and rack-rents had not been rendered impossible.

The Act was, indeed, as far as possible from appeasing Ireland. Probably the worst period of the land agitation followed its enactment, and hopes of plunder were excited to the utmost, while falling prices and ever-deepening agricultural distress vastly aggravated the crisis. The stability which was supposed to have been given by the Act of 1881 had been represented as one of its great merits; but every year the cry for revising it acquired fresh force, and after the utter political demoralisation that followed the apostasy of 1886, when the main section of the Liberal party purchased the votes by adopting the policy of the National League, this cry became probably irresistible. Some of those who had consented to the Act of 1881 now looked with consternation at their work. 'I would rather have cut off my hand,' said Lord Selborne, 'than been a party to the measure of 1881, giving the House the reasons and assurances which I then gave, if I had known that within five years after its passing it would have been thrown over by its authors, and that the course they had now taken would have been entered on.'[42]

The Land Act of 1887, however, which reopened the settlement, was carried by a Unionist Government, and it again lowered rents which only four or five years before had been judicially fixed. It was said that the State, having undertaken to regulate rents, could not remain passive when prices had so greatly fallen, and that the political condition of the country imperatively demanded its intervention. It is true that, under the Act of 1881, the State, while reducing the rents of the Irish landlords, had guaranteed those reduced rents for fifteen years.[43] It was a distinct, formal promise, resting on the national faith and on the authority of the Imperial Parliament. The promise was broken, but it was asked whether this was in truth a very different thing from what had already been done in 1881, when parliamentary and hereditary titles had been torn into shreds. The existing leaseholders were at the same time brought, for the first time, within the provisions of the clause for reducing rents. Mr. Gladstone had refused

---

[42] *Hansard*, cccxix. 18.
[43] 'An alteration of judicial rent shall not take place at less intervals than fifteen years' (Sect. viii.)

to do this in 1881; but it was said that it was intolerable that the flower of the Irish tenantry should alone be excluded from benefits which all other tenants so abundantly enjoyed, and that there was little chance of conciliating the Irish farmers if their leading and most intelligent members were left embittered by an exceptional disability.

The force of this argument is incontestable, but the gravity of the step that was taken is not less so. One great object, as we have seen, of the Act of 1870 had been to induce landlords to grant leases by giving them an assurance that they would in this way place themselves beyond the many entanglements and penal clauses of the new legislation. No one could pretend either that the Irish leaseholders were a helpless class, incapable of making their own bargains, or that their position rested on any other foundation than a distinct written contract. They were the most substantial and intelligent farmers of Ireland. The lease which regulated their tenancies was a fully recognised legal document, bearing the Government stamp, carrying with it all the authority and protection that English law could give. Its first clause was, usually, that at the expiry of the assigned term the tenant should hand back the land to its owner. This provision had been already torn to pieces by the Act of 1881, which provided that in cases of all leases of less than sixty years the tenant, at the expiry of the lease, if resident on his farm, need not hand it back according to his contract, but should remain a 'present tenant,' with all the rights of permanent occupancy attaching to that position.[44] The next clause stipulated in very explicit terms the rent in consideration of which the landlord had, in the exercise of his full legal rights, hired out his farm. This also was broken, and the leaseholder had now the right of bringing

---

[44] There was an exception in case of *bonâ-fide* reversionary leases made before the law had passed; *e.g.*, if the landlord had already granted to C. D. the lease of a farm on the expiry of the lease of A. B., in whose hands it now was, this arrangement was suffered to stand. See Kisbey *On the Land Act of 1881*, pp. 64–65.

his landlord into a court where, as the result of proceedings which always brought with them heavy legal costs to the landlord, the rent was authoritatively and judicially reduced.

It will be observed that the State did not in this matter annul or dissolve a legal contract, leaving the two parties free to make fresh arrangements. It left one party wholly bound by the terms of the contract; it contented itself with releasing the other; and, it need scarcely be added, it did this without granting the smallest compensation to the defrauded partner. There were other provisions, into which I need not enter, diminishing the few remaining powers of the landlord of recovering rent, and somewhat improving the position of the ordinary tenant. The Act was described by a leading Unionist statesman as 'the most generous boon' ever conferred by the Imperial Parliament on the Irish tenant. This 'generosity' which impels legislators, without the smallest sacrifice to themselves, to seek to conciliate one class by handing over to them the property of another is likely to be a growing virtue in English politics.

We can hardly, indeed, have a better example of the manner in which a subversive principle, once admitted into politics, will grow and strengthen till it acquires an irresistible power. When the principle of compensation for disturbance was introduced into the measure of 1870, it was carefully explained that this was not intended to invalidate in any degree the indisputable title of the landlord to the sole ownership of his property; that it was intended to be strictly limited in its application; that it was essentially a measure for the maintenance of public order; that its only object was to make a few bad landlords do what all good landlords were already doing; that it was certain to be as beneficial to the landlord as to the tenant class. Probably, few persons cearly foresaw that it was the first step of a vast transfer of property, and that in a few years it would become customary for ministers of the Crown to base all their legislation on the doctrine that Irish land was not an undivided ownership, but a simple partnership.

As might be expected, the Irish landlords claimed compensation for property that was manifestly confiscated, for vested and reversionary interests and clearly recognised legal rights which, for reasons of public policy, had been taken away. In an eminently moderate and closely reasoned statement they showed how invariably and rigorously the Imperial Parliament, following the general custom of civilised communities, had itself recognised this right, and imposed the obligation of compensation on all public bodies, companies, and individuals to whom it had granted a compulsory power of acquiring or interfering with property or vested interests. They suggested especially two forms of compensation. One of them was the reduction of the tithe rent-charge which was paid to the Government by the landlord. They strengthened their case by reminding the ministers that before 1872 the tithe rent-charge could be revised every seven years, according to the price of corn, which was then much higher than at the time they wrote; that before 1838 the tithe was paid by the occupier, and not by the owner, and that the duty of paying it, or, as it was then said, collecting it, was transferred in that year to the landlord, on the understanding that he could recoup himself in the rent. This rent was now arbitrarily reduced, and the landlord had lost all power over it.

The other suggestion was, that Government might lend money at low interest to pay off the heavy charges which rested on Irish land, and which had been incurred on the faith of legal rights that were now destroyed. Great sums had been already advanced in Ireland for public purposes on such terms, and it was noticed that this policy had very recently been adopted in Russia to relieve the embarrassments of the Russian landlords. As the normal rate of interest on charges on Irish property was little, if at all, below 5 per cent., and as, with Imperial credit, State loans might be granted at an annuity not exceeding 3½ per cent., repaying capital and interest in about sixty-five and a half years, this measure would have very materially lightened the burden, and probably saved many landlords and many creditors from ruin.[45]

---

[45] Statement submitted on the part of the Irish Landowners' Convention to Her Majesty's ministers, February 3, 1888.

Such proposals, however, never had the least chance of being accepted. It was certain that the Liberal party, which now depended on the National League, would be steadily opposed to them, and it was quite powerful enough to prevent them. There was, indeed, a melancholy unreality about all such discussions. The two parties moved on different planes. Arguments of justice, precedents, clear statements by Liberal leaders, were put forward by the representatives of the Irish landlords, but every politician knew in his heart that the real question was one of votes and power, and political power had passed away from the Irish landlords.

It is not necessary to follow this story any further, and to describe the almost annual attempts that have been made to grant, through political pressure, to the occupying class in Ireland a larger share of the property of the nominal owners. It cannot be denied that this legislation has redressed some hard cases and benefited a large number of tenants; and as few men look beyond immediate consequences, or rightly estimate those which are indirect and remote, this fact is accepted by many as its justification. For my own part, I believe that it will one day be found that the evils resulting from this policy have greatly outweighed its benefits, and that they will fall far more heavily on another class than on the small class which was directly injured. In a poor country, where increased capital, improved credit, and secure industry are the greatest needs, it has shaken to the very basis the idea of the sanctity and obligation of contract; made it almost impossible to borrow any considerable sum on Irish land; effectually stopped the influx of English gold; paralysed or prevented nearly all industrial undertakings, stretching into a distant future. It has reacted powerfully upon trade, and thus contributed to impoverish the Irish towns, while it has withdrawn the whole rental of Ireland from the improvement of the soil, as the landlord can have no further inducement or obligation to spend money on his estate. In combination also with the Home Rule movement it has driven much capital out of the land. Probably only a small portion of the money which is now received for the sale of land under the Government Acts is invested in Ireland. Prudent men have learned the wisdom of placing their savings, and at least a portion of their realised property, outside a country where the dominant political influences are on the side of dishonesty; where the repudiation of debts and the intimidation of creditors have become leading features of popular politics; where the protection of property and the administration of justice may one day fall into the hands of the authors of the 'No Rent Manifesto' and of the Plan of Campaign.

Under such conditions, the difficulty of establishing any system of safe and honest self-government has been immensely aggravated. Ireland must indeed be greatly changed if the withdrawal from her country districts of the presence and influence of her most educated class proves a real benefit; if local institutions are more wisely and honestly administered by passing from the hands of country gentlemen into the hands of the professional politician; if the labourer and smaller tenant find it to their advantage to be more directly under the power of farmers, gombeen men, and local attorneys. Fair rents and free sale, as has been often observed, are mutually destructive, and after a few sales the burden of interest paid to the moneylender will be far heavier than the rent which was taken from the landlord; while the conflict between the farmer and the labourer is likely to reproduce in an aggravated form the conflict between the landlord and the farmer.

Three things, indeed, may be confidently asserted about Irish rents. The first is, that it has never been the custom of the great body of Irish landlords to exact the full competitive rents from their tenants, although a considerable minority have done so. The second is, that it has been the invariable practice of Irish tenants, in selling to one another their tenant-right and in subletting plots of ground to their labourers, to demand the full competitive price. The third is, that in order to make the system of what is practically rack-rent general, no better way could be devised than the recent land legislation. If you give the tenant fixity of tenure at a judicially fixed rent

which is considerably below the market price, and at the same
time give him a practically unlimited power of selling his tenancy with no restriction of price, the result must be two rents—
one paid to the landlord, the other paid to the money-lender
in the shape of interest on the money borrowed to purchase
the tenant-right. And these two combined will represent the
extreme value of the land.

The moral effects on the Irish people of the land legislation
and of the agitation that produced it have been still more pernicious. If we ask what are the chief services that a Government can render to national morals, we shall probably obtain
different answers. Some men will place the greatest stress on
the establishment by the State of the religion which they believe to be true; on the infusion into national education of a
large measure of religious teaching; on laws restraining private
vices or controlling trades, institutions, or amusements that
may produce them. On all these points there may be much
controversy about the true province of the State, and there is
probably much exaggeration about the good that it can do. To
me, at least, the first and greatest service a Government can
render to morals seems to be the maintenance of a social organisation in which the path of duty and the path of interest
as much as possible coincide; in which honesty, industry,
providence, and public spirit naturally reap their rewards, and
the opposite vices their punishment. No worse lesson can be
taught a nation than that violence, intimidation, conspiracy,
and systematic refusal to pay debts are the natural means of
rising to political power and obtaining legislative concessions.
No worse habit can be implanted in a nation than that of looking for prosperity to politics rather than to industry, and forming contracts and incurring debts with the belief that a turn of
the political wheel may make it possible to cancel them.

It is, indeed, a curious and melancholy study to trace the
effects of recent legislation on different classes in Ireland. The
landlords who have suffered least have probably been those
who simplified their properties by the wholesale evictions,
the harsh clearances, that too often followed the Famine. Next

in the scale came those who exacted extreme rack-rents from their tenants. Those rents had been received for many years, and though they were ultimately more reduced than rents which had always been low, they still, in innumerable cases, remained somewhat higher than the others. The large class who regarded land simply as a source of revenue, and, without doing anything harsh, or extortionate, or unjust, took no part or interest in its management, have suffered very moderately. It is the improving landlord, who took a real interest in his estate, who sank large sums in draining and other purposes of improvement, who exercised a constant and beneficent influence over his tenants, who has suffered most by the legislation that reduced him to a mere powerless rent-charger, and in most cases rendered the sums he had expended an absolute loss. As I have already noticed, the careless and slovenly farmer had his rent more reduced than the farmer who, by good cultivation, had maintained his farm at its full value. An Arrears Act was carried conferring great benefits on the farmer who had allowed his rent to fall many years into arrear, but doing nothing for the farmer who, by steady, conscientious industry, had in bad times honestly paid his way. Even the land purchase Acts, though they are by far the most valuable parts of recent Irish land legislation, had a similar tendency. As the tenant is no longer asked to advance any portion of the purchase money, no premium is given to industry and thrift; the value of the purchased land has been artificially depreciated by agitation and attacks upon property; and as the landlord whose income has already been twice reduced by a land court knows that in most cases, in addition to heavy legal expenses, a sale will reduce each remaining 100*l.* a year to 60*l.* or 70*l.*, he is, not unnaturally, unwilling to sell when his tenants are honest and solvent, though he may be ready to do so on easy terms when they are dishonest, troublesome, and unpunctual.

To crown the edifice, a measure was introduced by the Government, in 1894, for the purpose of reinstating, at the cost of 250,000*l.* of public money drawn from the funds of the Irish

Church, those tenants who, in spite of judicial reductions and all the delays and indulgences of the law, had been either unable or unwilling to pay their rents, and had been in consequence evicted. By this measure it was proposed to invest three men nominated by the Government, and uncontrolled by any right of appeal, with an arbitrary and almost absolute power of reinstating any Irish tenant, or the representative of any Irish tenant, who had been evicted for any cause since 1879. The only restriction was that the consent of the present tenant must be obtained; but in a great part of Ireland he could not withhold it without imminent danger to his life. The tenant might have been evicted for dishonesty, for violence, for criminal conspiracy, for hopeless and long-continued bankruptcy. He might be living in America. The owner of the soil might have delayed the eviction for years after the law had empowered him to carry it out, and he might have at last taken the land into his own possession, and have been, during many years, farming it himself. He had no right of refusing his consent, and his only alternative was to take back the former tenant, or to sell to him the farm at whatever price a revolutionary and despotic tribunal might determine.

The explanation of the measure was very plain. It was specially intended for the benefit of the 'Plan-of-campaign' tenants, who had placed money which was actually in their possession, and which was due to their landlords for benefits already received, in the hands of 'trustees,' for the express purpose of defrauding their creditors. This 'Plan of Campaign' had been authoritatively pronounced by the highest law court in Ireland to be 'clearly and absolutely illegal.' It had been condemned by the head of the Catholic Church as distinctly immoral. It had been avowedly 'a political engine,' devised by political conspirators for the purpose of defeating the Government, proving that the Land League was stronger than the law, and persuading the peasantry that its directors were the real rulers of Ireland. The instigators of this conspiracy were now in Parliament. The Government depended for their majority upon their votes, and their terms were that the Plan-of-campaign conspiracy should be triumphantly vindicated. The proposed measure was not a mere measure of amnesty closing an old controversy, granting indulgence to poor men who had been duped by men far more dishonest than themselves. It was a measure of triumph, giving special and exceptional favour to defaulting tenants. No solvent tenant could become the owner of his farm without the consent of his landlord. This privilege was reserved for the evicted tenant.

In the light of this clause and of the persistence with which it was maintained, no reasonable man could doubt the character, the origin, and the motive of the measure. The Government bought the Irish vote by a Bill to carry out their design, and it resolved to devote a large amount of public money to the purpose. It is true that this scandalous instance of political profligacy was defeated by the House of Lords, and that in the Land Bill of the succeeding year the compulsory clause was dropped; but the fact that a British minister could be found to introduce, and a party majority to vote it, is not likely to be forgotten in Ireland. Never, indeed, did a minister of the Crown propose a measure more distinctly calculated to encourage dishonesty, and to persuade a deluded people that a sufficient amount of voting power was all that was needed to make it successful. It has been truly said, that the worst feature of the old penal code against Irish Catholics was that some of its provisions placed law in direct opposition to religion and to morals, and thus tended powerfully to demoralise as well as to impoverish. A system of government has, in our day, grown up in Ireland not less really and scarcely less widely demoralising. Those who have examined its effects will only wonder that so much honesty and virtue have survived it.

It has been well said by Senior, that 'the most revolting, and perhaps the most mischievous, form of robbery is that in which the Government itself becomes an accomplice; when the property of whole classes of individuals is swept away by legislative enactments, and men owe their ruin to that very institution which was created to ensure their safety.'[46] Probably the most serious aspect, however, of this Irish legislation is to be found in the precedents it created. I have not concealed the difficulties under which it grew up, and which explain and palliate the conduct of the legislators, and if a comparison were made between the losses English landlords have undergone through economical causes, and the losses of Irish landlords under the action of the law, it is very doubtful whether the position of the former would appear the more desirable. But, when all this is said, it is impossible reasonably to deny that this legislation involves as distinct instances of national faith violated, of property guaranteed by law taken without compensation, as can be found in the proceedings of any of those defaulting governments of South America on which English public opinion has so often and so largely expended its indignation. If Parliament passed a law repudiating its railway guarantees, or the whole or part of the interest of the National Debt, or limiting by an act of power the profits of tradesmen, or compelling a London lodging-house keeper to give fixity of tenure at a reduced rent to a London workman, or placing the debentures and preference shares of a railway on the same basis as the ordinary shares, or obliging a railway company to expend the whole or nearly the whole of its profits in cheapening fares, instead of increasing dividends, it would not be invading the rights of property more clearly.

It is idle to suppose that such a precedent can be confined to Ireland, or Irish land, or Irish landlords. With a suffrage that gives the predominant power to the very ignorant and the very poor; in an age when every kind of predatory theory relating to property is in the air, and when the province of State interference is continually extending, and under a Constitution which gives no special protection to contracts, such a precedent is certain to grow. A departure from sound principle in legislation is nearly always advocated, in the first

---

[46] *Journals, &c., relating to Ireland*, i. 2.

instance, on the ground that it is entirely exceptional, strictly limited in its application, certain to do no practical harm, and intended to secure some practical benefit. Once admitted, it soon becomes a starting-point or logical premise, and is pushed into new fields and to new consequences.

There are very few forms of confiscation which an ingenious man may not justify by the Irish precedent. Irish landlordism is far from being an exceptional thing, and oppressive rents and harsh evictions will be found in greater abundance in the poorer quarters of London, Paris, or New York, than in Mayo and Connemara. The well-known American writer, Mr. George, compares Irish landlords to useless, ravenous, destructive beasts, but he acknowledges, a few pages later, that they are in no degree harder than any similar class; that they are less grasping towards their tenants than the farmers who rent of them are towards the labourers to whom they sublet; that it is pure 'humbug' to pretend that 'Irish landlordism is something different from American landlordism;' and that the position of an American tenant is, in fact, not better, but worse, than that of an Irish one. 'In the United States the landlord has, in all its fulness, the unrestricted power of doing as he pleases with his own. Rackrenting is with us the common, almost the exclusive, form of renting. There is no long process to be gone through to secure an eviction, no serving notice upon the relieving officer of the district. The tenant whom the landlord wants to get rid of can be expelled with the minimum of cost and expense.' Mr. George quotes with approval the statement of an American judge that there are few months in which at least 100 warrants of ejection are not issued against poor tenants in the more squalid quarters of New York.[47]

In countless instances, indeed, the rents of poor men's houses, the value of poor men's investments, and the burdensomeness of poor men's contracts, are affected by circumstances which they could neither foresee nor control. How

[47] George's *Social Problems*, chap. xi.

often does some great quarter of houses for the poor grow up in the neighbourhood of a flourishing industry, but a change of fashion, a new invention, a migration of population or capital, destroys the industry: work ebbs away, prices and wages change, contracts which were once easy and natural become overwhelmingly oppressive, and with diminishing or disappearing profits, the interest of money borrowed to carry on the business ruins the worker. Ought the State under such circumstances to constitute itself a kind of Providence, to break contracts and regulate anew the conditions of industry? And if it begins to do this, without giving compensation for rights that it takes away, and under mere political pressure, at what point is it likely to stop?

Reflections of this kind must have occurred to every thinking man who observes the course of modern politics, and the alacrity and complaisance with which schemes of the most wholesale plunder are in many quarters received. One favourite form has consisted of attacks on the private ownership of land, and the popularity attained by the writings of Mr. George, who preaches on this subject the most extreme doctrine, is a striking sign of the times. Nothing, indeed, in history or in economics is more plain than that the strong stimulus of an exclusive personal interest can alone attract to land the labour and the capital that make it fully productive, and that the productiveness of the soil is one of the first conditions of the wellbeing of the whole community. The transition from the common ownership of land which existed when mankind were thinly scattered nomads and hunters, to a divided land cultivated and fertilised by individual industry, was one of the first and most valuable steps in the progress of civilisation. Nothing also in morals is more plain than that to abolish without compensation that private ownership which has existed unquestioned for countless generations, and on the faith of which tens of thousands of men in all ages and lands, and with the sanction and under the guarantee of the laws of all nations, have invested the fruits of their industry and their thrift, would be an act of simple, gross, naked, gigantic robbery. Were it not so, indeed, the words 'honesty' and 'dishonesty' would have no real meaning. Yet such a proposal has been warmly welcomed, such a measure has been eagerly advocated, by many who would be very indignant if they were described as the accomplices of thieves, and who would probably be perfectly incapable in their private capacities of an act of dishonesty. If, on the other hand, the State simply purchased honestly the land of the country, and placed itself in the position of the landlord, it is easy to show that the whole transaction could only end in a ruinous loss. The position of the occupying tenant would be unchanged, except that he would pay his rent, not to a private individual, but to the representative of the State. The purchase money could only be raised by a colossal loan, which would have to be paid for in the shape of interest. The returns from land are so small that, far from furnishing a surplus for the relief of taxation, they would, in most cases, be insufficient to pay the simple interest of this loan, even if it could be raised on ordinary terms. But every competent judge must know the utter impossibility of raising such a loan at the ordinary price, and without producing a financial convulsion probably more tremendous than any that the world has seen.[48]

Another doctrine which, in different forms, has spread widely through public opinion is that of Mill about 'the unearned increment.' Starting from the belief that the value of land has a natural tendency to increase through the progress of society, and without any exertion or sacrifice on the part of the owner, Mill proposed that this 'unearned increment' should be steadily intercepted and appropriated by the State in the form of taxation. It was true, Mill acknowledged, that men had long bought land, which brings a smaller return than almost any other form of investment, through a belief that

---

[48] Mr. Fawcett has dealt fully with this aspect of the question in an admirable pamphlet called *State Socialism and the Nationalisation of Land* (1883).

their income would gradually increase, and with an implied assurance that they would only be taxed in proportion to other incomes. Mill, however, very honestly met this objection by maintaining that the confiscation of the increment should only take place from the present time and with due notice, and that the landlord should have the alternative of receiving from the State the present market value, which includes the present value of all future expectations.

In the long period of agricultural depression through which England and most other countries have passed the doctrine of 'an unearned increment' wears an aspect of irony. For many years the market value of agricultural land, instead of rising, has been steadily falling, and history clearly shows that the same phenomenon has taken place in many long periods and in many great countries. If the State takes from the owner by exceptional taxation the normal rise in the value of his land, it may very reasonably be expected by exceptional legislation to compensate him for its fall.

No statement can be more palpably untrue than that 'unearned increment' is a thing in any degree peculiar to land. The growth of population and the development of civilisation exercise exactly the same influence on the shares of a railway or a dockyard; on the wages of the labourer; on the fees of the professional man; on the masterpieces of art; on the value of innumerable articles of commerce. In countless cases property is increased, or industry and ability reap larger rewards in consequence of changes which do not lie within themselves, and to which they have contributed nothing, but which are wholly due to extraneous and surrounding circumstances. Ask any rich man which of his investments, without any sacrifice or exertion on his part, have doubled or trebled in value, and you will find that in the great majority of cases they have no connection with land. What reason is there, therefore, for selecting for exceptional and penal taxation the single form of property which usually produces the least return, and which is associated to the greatest degree with the discharge of duties that are eminently useful to the State? And this proposal is made in a country where so large an amount of money has been sunk in land by many generations of proprietors that the actual rent would represent, in very many instances, nothing more than the lowest interest on the outlay; in a country where the value of personal property enormously exceeds that of land, and has been, during the last century and a half, advancing with a vastly greater rapidity. According to Sir Robert Giffen, land in England constituted in 1690 about 60 per cent. of the national wealth, and in 1800 about 40 per cent. In the United Kingdom it constituted, in 1812, 44 per cent.; in 1865, 30 per cent.; in 1875, 24 per cent.; in 1884, only 17 per cent.[49]

The true explanation of such proposals is political. It is to be found in that almost rabid hatred of the landed interest, growing out of political antagonism, which has characterised large bodies of English Radicals, and which, in a time when the deep agricultural depression forms probably our most serious national evil and danger, makes the increased taxation of land one of the most popular of Radical cries.

One argument, upon which much stress has been put, but which has now, in a great degree, lost its force, is that the land of the country is the source of the food on which its people depend, and that special legislation ought therefore to prevent it from being in the uncontrolled power of the few. As I have already said, I believe that, if any clear case of public welfare can be established, the Government has the right to take complete or partial possession of the land, on condition of compensating the owners. If England were surrounded by a brass wall, and if its people depended for their subsistence on the crops raised within that wall, severe restrictions should undoubtedly be placed on the use of great portions of the soil for parks or sporting purposes. But the situation is much modified when the main supply of food for the people is not derived from English soil, but comes from the United States, from the Colonies, from India, and from Russia, and when this supply pours in with such abundance and at such prices

---

[49] Giffen's *Growth of Capital*, pp. 111–12.

that the best English land is almost crushed by the competition, while the inferior lands have become, as food-producing land, almost useless.

The unreality, however, of the speculation that would separate landed property by a sharp generic distinction as an object of spoliation from all other property speedily became apparent. The same class of reasoners soon found that similar or analogous arguments may be applied to other branches of property, and to defence of other forms of dishonesty. It is a significant fact that while Mr. George in his first book only proposed to rob the landowner, in his second book he proposed equally to rob the fundowner, being now convinced that the institution of public debts and private property in land rested on the same basis. In nearly all the Socialist programmes that are now issued on the Continent the 'nationalisation of land' is included, but it is always coupled with proposals for the nationalisation of all capital and means of production, and for the repudiation of national debts.

Jefferson had already anticipated these writers in their advocacy of the repudiation of national debts; and it must be acknowledged that the arguments for this course are quite as plausible as those in favour of land spoliation. It is said that one generation cannot bind another and impose on it the interest of its debts. We are reminded that these debts were incurred at a time when the masses, who now consider themselves, by a kind of right divine, the rulers of the State, were almost wholly unrepresented, and for objects of which they altogether disapprove. Demagogues are not wanting to persuade them that the war of the American Revolution and the war of the French Revolution, which are responsible for the greater part of the debt, were mere crimes of the aristocracy, and crimes directed against the people. Are the people, it is asked, for ever to bear the burden of debts so incurred, and incurred, too, when the national credit was so low that not more than 70*l.* or 60*l.* was paid to the Exchequer for bonds which now bear the value of 100*l.*?

As democracy advances, the precedents of spoliation pass into legislation, doctrines of this kind are likely to find an increasing number of adherents. This prospect renders peculiarly alarming the enormous increase of national debt that has taken place in Europe during the last few decades. It justifies the wisdom of the policy of America in paying off, even by very drastic measures, the bulk of its debt, and also the great and praiseworthy efforts that have been made by British Governments in the same direction.

Mining royalties stand on the same footing as private property in land. They are a kind of property which has been for generations bought, sold, mortgaged, and bequeathed with the full sanction of the law, and they have been estimated in the British Isles at the enormous sum of eight millions a year. There is a party, though happily not a large one, who openly advocate their simple confiscation. Thus the Glasgow Trade Council passed a resolution, 'That this Council instructs the secretary to state to the (Mining Royalties) Commission that it is in favour of mining royalties becoming national property without compensation being given.' Similar views are frequently expressed in Socialist literature, and they were put forward by some witnesses before the Labour Commission, the most conspicuous upholder of this shameless dishonesty being a Radical member of Parliament.[50]

Another kind of property which has been the subject of much more or less ingenious sophistry is literary property. The right of an author to the profits of the book he has written rests on the highest and simplest title by which property can be held—that of creation. The author made it. His title to what he has himself created, like that of the labour to what he himself earned, is certainly more direct, if it is not of a higher kind, than that of any species of property which is simply hereditary. But the peculiarity of literary property is, that while it may be of great value to its author, and of great utility

---

[50] Spyers, *The Labour Question*, pp. 128–30.

to mankind, it may be stolen with peculiar facility, and in a different way from most other kinds of property. Like a bank-note, its value is destroyed if every one is allowed to reproduce it, and hence laws of copyright have been found necessary to protect it. Among all the forms of property, few are so imperfectly protected as this; but there are some who would abolish it altogether, refusing all legal protection to literary property. One of their arguments is, that an author merely gives a form to ideas and knowledge which are floating in the intellectual atmosphere around him, and which are the common property of all men, and has, therefore, no exclusive right to what he has written. If this be true—and it is far from being absolutely so—the simple answer is, that it is to the form alone, which is his own work, that he claims an exclusive right. A sculptor's right of property in his statue is not destroyed by the fact that the clay and the marble existed before he touched them with his chisel. An author claims no monopoly in his ideas; but the form in which he moulds them is so essentially the main element in the question, that the distinction is for all practical purposes trivial. There is no idea in Gray's Elegy which has not passed through thousands of minds. Gray alone gave them the form which is immortal.

It is said that an author is a 'monopolist' because he claims an exclusive right of selling his book, and that his claim is therefore opposed to the doctrine of free trade. But this is a pure confusion of thought. In the sense of political economy, a man is a monopolist who prevents others from pursuing a form of industry which they might have pursued independently of him, and had he not existed. He is not a monopolist if he only prevents them from appropriating what he alone has made, and what would not have existed without him. An author is a monopolist in no other sense than a proprietor or labourer who claims the exclusive possession of his own earnings or his own inheritance. If I write the history of a particular period, I claim no legal right of debarring others from writing about the same period, or using the materials that I have used. I claim only an exclusive right in that specific work which I have myself made. A fisherman would be rightly called a monopolist if he excluded all others from fishing in the sea. He is not rightly called a monopolist if he only claims an exclusive right to dispose of the fish which he has himself caught in the sea, which is open to all.[51]

But the author, it is said, is under a special obligation to the State because his property is protected by a special law. The answer is, that the very object for which all governments are primarily created, and for which all taxes are paid, is the protection of life and property. A government in protecting property is simply discharging its most elementary duty. Different kinds of property may be invaded, and must therefore be protected in different ways; and, as a matter of fact, the protection of literature costs the State much less in labour, in money, and in popularity than the protection of pheasants.

Others again contend for what they call the nationalisation of the means of communication, or, in other words, the appropriation of the railways and all other public conveyances by the State. If by this term is meant that the Government should either construct, or purchase at a fair price, the railways within its dominion, there is no objection of principle to be raised. The system of State railways exists in many countries. In judging whether it is for the advantage of the nation as a whole, we have to consider a large number of conflicting and closely balanced advantages and disadvantages, and the preponderance in each country must be decided according to its own special economical circumstances. It is also univer-

---

[51] Locke's remarks about landed property appear to me very eminently applicable to copyright. 'Whatsoever a man removes out of the state that Nature hath provided and left it in, he hath mixed his labour with, and joined to it something that is his own, and thereby makes it his property. It being by him removed from the common state Nature hath placed it in, it hath by this labour something annexed to it that excludes the common right of other men. For, this labour being the unquestionable property of the labourer, no man but he can have a right to what that is once joined to, at least where there is enough and as good left in common for others' (Locke *On Civil Government*, c.v.).

sally admitted that the State, having given great privileges and powers to a railway company, is perfectly justified in imposing upon it many restrictions. But when it is claimed that the State may, without purchase, or at a rate of compensation below its real value, take possession of a railway, depriving of their property the shareholders at whose risk and cost it was made, it can only be answered that such a claim is simple and naked robbery. And the same thing may be confidently asserted of many other ambitious schemes for 'nationalising' all great industrial undertakings and absorbing all capital into the State. If the element of just purchase enters into these transactions, they would only result in a great financial catastrophe. If purchase or compensation be refused, the catastrophe would not be averted, but the process would be one gigantic robbery.

Such schemes for turning the State into the universal landlord, the universal manufacturer, the universal shopkeeper, reorganising from its foundations the whole industrial system of the world, excluding from it all competition and all the play of individual emulation and ambition, can never, I believe, be even approximately realised; but no one who watches the growth of Socialist opinion in nearly all countries can doubt that many steps will be taken in this direction in a not remote future.

The question in what degree and in what manner the demands that are rising may be wisely met is of the utmost importance. The subject is one which I propose to discuss at some length in later chapters. Two things may here be said. One is, that in an overcrowded country like England, whose prosperity rests much less on great natural resources than on the continuance of a precarious and highly artificial commercial and manufacturing supremacy, any revolution that may lead to a migration of capital or the destruction of credit is more than commonly dangerous. The other is, that this class of questions is eminently one in which consequences that are obscure, intricate, indirect, and remote are often, in the long run, more important than those which are obvious and immediate.

Is the parliamentary system in the democratic form which it has of late years assumed well fitted for wisely dealing with these difficult and dangerous questions? Let any one observe how steadily and rapidly the stable forces, which in old days shaped and guided the course of English politics, are losing their influence. Let him watch closely a great popular election, and observe how largely the chance of a candidate depends upon his skill in appealing to the direct and immediate interests, or supposed interests, of large sections of the electorate; in making use of claptrap and popular cries; in inflaming class animosities and antipathies, and pledging himself so far as to conciliate many distinct groups of faddists. Let him then observe how Parliament itself is breaking into small groups; how the permanent forces of intelligence and property, which once enabled governments to pursue their paths independently of fluctuating or transient gusts of ignorant opinion, are weakened; how large a part of legislation, especially in the closing period of a Parliament, is manifestly intended for mere electioneering purposes; how very few public men look much beyond the interests of their party and the chances of an election. He must be a sanguine man who can look across such a scene with much confidence to the future.

He will not, if he is a wise man, be reassured by the prevailing habit, so natural in democracies, of canonising, and almost idolising, mere majorities, even when they are mainly composed of the most ignorant men, voting under all the misleading influences of side-issues and violent class or party passions. 'The voice of the people,' as expressed at the polls, is to many politicians the sum of all wisdom, the supreme test of truth or falsehood. It is even more than this: it is invested with something very like the spiritual efficacy which theologians have ascribed to baptism. It is supposed to wash away all sin. However unscrupulous, however dishonest, may be the acts of a party or of a statesman, they are considered to be justified beyond reproach if they have been condoned or sanctioned at a general election. It has sometimes happened that a politician has been found guilty of a grave personal offence by an intelligent and impartial jury, after a minute investigation of evidence, conducted with the assistance of highly trained advocates, and under the direction of an experienced judge. He afterwards finds a constituency which will send him to Parliament, and the newspapers of his party declare that his character is now clear. He has been absolved by 'the great voice of the people.' Truly indeed did Carlyle say that the superstitions to be feared in the present day are much less religious than political; and of all the forms of idolatry I know none more irrational and ignoble than this blind worship of mere numbers.

It has led many politicians to subordinate all notions of right and wrong to the wishes or interests of majorities, and to act on the maxim that the end justifies the means quite as audaciously as the most extreme Jesuit casuists. This new Jesuitism has, indeed, much real affinity with the old one. The root idea of the old Jesuitism was a strongly realised conviction that the Catholic Church is so emphatically the inspired teacher of mankind, and the representative of the Deity upon earth, that no act can be immoral which is performed in its service and is conducive to its interests. The root idea of the new Jesuitism is the belief that the moral law has no deeper foundation and no higher sanction than utility, and that the greatest happiness of the greatest number is its supreme test and ideal. From this it is easily inferred that minorities have no rights as against majorities. In both cases, too, the love of power plays a great part. The old Jesuit found in his doctrine a strong lever for governing the Church and influencing the world. The new Jesuit finds his doctrine peculiarly useful in a society in which all political power is obtained by winning the votes of a majority. Many good Catholics will maintain that the old Jesuit misread the teaching of the Church, and some of them believe that religion has had no worse enemy than a society which has associated the most sacred Name given among men with falsehood, imposture, unscrupulous tyranny, and intrigue. Many good utilitarians will say that the new Jesuit has calculated falsely the balance of utilities, and that no course of policy which shakes the security of property or contract, and the rights of minorities, can be, in its far-off results, for the benefit of the majority. But in each case the inference of the Jesuit is plausible and natural, and it is an inference that is certain to be drawn.

Some of my readers will probably consider it fanciful to attribute to theories of moral philosophy any influence over political conduct. In England, speculative opinion has not usually much weight in practical politics, and English politicians are very apt to treat it with complete disdain. Yet no one who has any real knowledge of history can seriously doubt the influence over human affairs which has been exercised by the speculations of Locke, of Rousseau, of Montesquieu, of Adam Smith, or of Bentham. The force and the intensity which the doctrine of nationalities has of late years assumed throughout Europe is not unconnected with the new importance which speculative writers have given to race affinities and characteristics, and something of the current Radical notions about land is certainly due to our increased knowledge of the wide diffusion, in the early stages of society, of joint or communal ownership of the soil.

So, too, I believe the views of many politicians have been not a little coloured by the doctrines of moral philosophy, which have of late years been widely popular, which reduce our conceptions of right and wrong, of justice or injustice, to mere general utility, or a calculation of interests. Philosophy has its fanatics as well as religion, and to this conception of ethics may be largely traced the utter unscrupulousness in dealing with the rights of minorities which is sometimes found among men who are certainly not mere unprincipled self-seekers. In every conflict of interests between the few who own a thing, or have produced it, or paid for it, or run the risks attending it, and the many who wish to enjoy it, this bias may be discerned. In the eyes of many politicians, all differences between the landlord and his tenants, between the author and his readers, between railway-shareholders and the travelling public, between the producer and the con-

Democracy and Liberty

sumers, are simply regarded as conflicts between the few and the many, and the rights of the few cease to have any binding force if their destruction is likely to confer an immediate benefit on the many.

Herbert Spencer has said, with profound truth and wisdom, that 'the end which the statesman should keep in view as higher than all other ends is the formation of character.' It is on this side that democratic politics seem to me peculiarly weak. Let us once more look at the representative body. Even taking the lowest test, can it be confidently said that its moral level is what it was? Too much stress may perhaps be laid on the many grave private scandals that have taken place among its members within the last twenty or thirty years. It is impossible, however, not to be struck by the number of cases in which members of that House have during this space of time been found guilty of acts of financial dishonesty that brought them within the scope of the criminal law, or of other forms of immorality sufficiently grave to come before the law courts. The House of Commons consists of 670 members. About the year 1892 the committee of a great London club containing nearly twice as many members had their attention called to the fact that, by a curious omission in their rules, no provision had been made for the expulsion of any member who, without breaking the precise rules of the club, had been guilty of any of those gross scandals which make men unfit for the society of gentlemen. The omission had been unnoticed because, although the club had existed since 1824, no such case had arisen among its members. It would be unreasonable to expect from a body elected under such stormy and contentious conditions as the House of Commons a standard as high as that in the Athenæum Club, but surely the contrast is too great and too marked to be lightly dismissed. And if we extend our survey beyond England, and count up the instances of gross profligacy or dishonesty which have been detected, often in very high places, in the Parliaments of the Continent, of the United States, and of the Colonies, in the present generation, the evidence will accumulate, showing how little democratic election secures a high standard of integrity and morality.

The House of Commons, however, as I have before said, is essentially a body of trustees, and it is by their performance of their public duty that its members must be chiefly judged. Is it too much to say that, in the opinion of the great body of educated men, there has been in this respect a marked decline? I am anxious on this subject to avoid all exaggeration. It is not yet true of England, as it is of America, that the best men in intellect and character avoid public life, though there are ominous signs that this may before long be the case. Parliament still contains a large body of such men, and there have been several conspicuous modern instances showing how much the weight of character still tells in public life. Probably a large proportion of my readers will be of opinion that the year 1886 witnessed the worst act of modern English politics; but it at least brought with it the consoling spectacle of a large body of public men, several of them of the highest political eminence, deliberately and without any possible selfish motive breaking old ties and sacrificing political ambition rather than take part in a disgraceful scene. But, on the whole, can any one doubt that apostasies have been more shameless, class bribes more habitual, and the tone of the House of Commons less high, than in the last generation; that principles are more lightly held and direct party interests more habitually followed; that measures of great and far-reaching importance are more recklessly launched for mere electioneering purposes; that men to whom, in private conversation, not one educated man out of a hundred would ascribe any real sincerity or weight of conviction are playing a more leading part in English public life? I have elsewhere dwelt on the profound and indelible impression made in the last century by the coalition between Fox and North. These two able, honourable, and in most respects patriotic, politicians, had been fiercely divided on the question of the American War, and Fox had used the strongest language against his opponent, denouncing him as the enemy of British freedom, and describing him as worthy of death upon the scaffold. The American War ceased; the controversies it produced were closed, and then Fox made an alliance with North for the purpose of keeping out of office a statesman whom they disliked and distrusted. Nothing in the English parliamentary history of the eighteenth century more profoundly shocked the public mind and conscience than this transaction, and Fox, at least, never recovered the discredit which the coalition left upon his character. Yet, after all, both of these statesmen were men undoubtedly devoted to the interests of the great empire they ruled, and after the termination of the American War there was no capital subject of present difference between them.

Compare this transaction with the alliance which gave the Liberal leaders eighty-five Home Rule votes in 1886, and placed them in a close bond of union with the very men whom they had so lately denounced and imprisoned for treason to the Empire, and for most deliberately inciting to dishonesty and crime. Those who will judge public men by their acts, and not by their professions, can have little difficulty in pointing the moral.

Few persons will question that this transaction would have been impossible in the Parliaments before the Reform Bill of 1867. In the days of middle-class ascendency every politician found it necessary to place himself in general harmony with average educated opinion. A very slight shifting of that opinion, especially in the smaller boroughs, could be decisive. There was always an ultimate court of appeal, which could be relied on to judge promptly, with shrewdness and patriotism, and some real knowledge of the facts of the case. Mere rhetoric and claptrap; brilliant talent, unallied with judgment; coalitions to carry some measure which the country condemned by uniting it with a number of bribes offered to many different classes; policies in which great national interests were sacrificed to personal ambition or to party tricks; the dexterity which multiplies, evades, or confuses issues, had seldom even a temporary success. The judgment of average educated men on the whole prevailed; and although that judgment may not be very quick or far-seeing, or open to new ideas, it rarely failed to arrive at a just estimate of a practical issue.

But the changes that introduced into the constituencies a much larger proportion of ignorance, indifference, or credulity soon altered the conditions of politics. The element of uncertainty was greatly increased. Politicians learned to think less of convincing the reason of the country than of combining heterogeneous and independent groups, or touching some strong chord of widespread class interest or prejudice. The sense of shame to a remarkable degree diminished. It would once have been intolerable to an English public man to believe that, in spite of all differences of opinion, he was not followed through life and to the grave by the respect of the great body of his educated fellow countrymen. This sentiment has greatly faded. Men have now become very indifferent to what they would nickname the opinion of the classes or the clubs, provided they can succeed, by the methods I have described, in winning a majority and obtaining power and office. The party game is played more keenly and more recklessly, and traditional feelings as well as traditional customs have greatly lost their force.

This tendency is increased by the extreme rush and hurry of modern life, which naturally produces some levity of character. A constant succession of new impressions and ideas takes away from societies, as from individuals, the power of feeling anything deeply and persistently. Disgrace never seems indelible when it is so soon forgotten, and the strong, steady currents of national sentiment and tendency, on which the greatness of empires depends, become impossible. Continuity of policy is more difficult, and, with a jaded political palate, the appetite for experiment and sensation becomes more powerful.

In the whole field of politics, personal and class interests seem to have grown stronger; and the latter are often not even those of a very large class. The objects of an ordinary trade strike have begun to blend powerfully with national politics. In the dockyard towns, it has long been said that questions of wages, salaries, or employment dominate over all others. There have been instances in which the political votes of the police force, of the Post-office officials, of the Civil Service clerks, have been avowedly marshalled for the purpose of obtaining particular class advantages.[52] In county councils and other small elective bodies, it is probable that these motives will, in England as in America, be easily and efficaciously employed. When the votes of a body of men in a nearly balanced contest may be purchased with public money, or at least lost if public money is withheld, a higher standard of public virtue than is now general is required to resist a mode of bribery which is at once cheap, easy, and not illegal. A powerful trade union may capture a small elected body, and a weak government resting on a fluctuating and a disintegrated majority is strongly tempted to conciliate every detached group of voters.

The reader must judge for himself whether this picture is untrue or overcharged; if he believes it to be true, he will hardly question its gravity. The evil I have described is much aggravated by the very inadequate sense of the criminality of political misdeeds that prevails widely in contemporary thought. In the case of those acts of open violence and treason which are commonly described as political crimes, this may be largely traced to the time when power was in the hands of a very few, when religious liberty, and personal liberty, and liberty of expression were all unknown, and when much of the highest and purest heroism was displayed in resisting intolerable oppression. Much of the poetic glamour which was thrown over the revolutionists of those days still remains, though in nearly all countries the circumstances have wholly changed. Under the popular governments of modern times revolution is nearly always a crime, and usually a crime of the first magnitude. No one, as I have elsewhere said, 'Who has any adequate sense of the enormous mass of suffering which the

---

[52] A remarkable paper, giving instances in which this kind of pressure has been employed, will be found in the *Times*, October 15, 1892.

authors of a rebellion let loose upon their country will speak lightly of this crime, or of the importance of penalties that may deter others from following in their steps. . . . In the great lottery of civil war the prizes are enormous; and when such prizes may be obtained by a course of action which is profoundly injurious to the State, the deterrent influence of severe penalties is especially necessary. In the immense majority of cases, the broad distinction which it is now the fashion to draw between political and other crimes is both pernicious and untrue. There is no sphere in which the worst passions of human nature may operate more easily and more dangerously than in the sphere of politics. There is no criminal of a deeper dye than the adventurer who is gambling for power with the lives of men. There are no crimes which produce vaster or more enduring suffering than those which sap the great pillars of order in the State, and destroy the respect for life, for property, and for law on which all true progress depends.'

Let any one examine the chief revolutionary movements of our time, and he may soon convince himself that by far the greater number of them have been led by some ambitious soldier, or politician, or pretender, simply actuated by a desire for wealth and power, by a wish to defeat and overthrow a competitor, by overweening vanity, or by a mere love of excitement, adventure, and notoriety. A man who through such motives makes a revolution which destroys a multitude of lives, ruins the credit and commerce of a nation, scatters far and wide the seeds of anarchy, disaster and long-continued depression, and perhaps begins the decadence of his nation, surely deserves a prompt and ignominious death as much as the man who, under the influence of want, or passion, or drink, has committed an ordinary murder. A public opinion is very morbid which looks on these things as venial. It is the custom in England to assert that such crimes as the murders in the Phœnix Park, or the massacre or attempted massacre by an Anarchist's bomb of a number of innocent persons in some place of public amusement, are not 'political.' It does not appear to me reasonable to deny this character to acts which were inspired by no motive of private gain or malice, and were directly and exclusively intended to produce political ends. But the fact that they were political does not attenuate their atrocity, nor ought it to mitigate the punishment of the criminal.

In home affairs, while the widest toleration should be accorded to all honest diversities of opinion and policy, there are courses of conduct which involve the deepest turpitude, and which, at the same time, bring with them no legal penalties, and can only be restrained and punished by opinion. If a man, for the mere purpose of winning votes, seeks to plunge his country into an unrighteous or unnecessary war, or to prolong a war which might be terminated with honour; to set class against class and deepen the lines of division and animosity; to place the power of government in the hands of dishonest or disloyal men, and assist them in carrying out their designs; if for the sake of an office, or a pension, or a peerage, he supports a policy which he knows to be unrighteous or unwise, he is certainly committing a moral offence of the deepest dye. Judgments which relate to motives are, no doubt, always uncertain, and ample allowance should be made for the eccentricities of honest opinion. A course which seems to most men very iniquitous may appear to some men positively good, or the lesser of two evils, or the necessary fulfilment of an old engagement, or an inevitable result of preceding policy. Yet still public opinion can, with a rough but substantial justice, estimate the characters and the motives of public men, and it is a very evil sign when it looks without serious reprobation on those whom it believes to be acting without convictions; to be playing with great national interests for party or personal ends, as if they were cards in a game or horses in a race.

This consideration is quite compatible with the fact that men acting in parties are frequently obliged, on public grounds, to subordinate their own judgment on minor questions to that of their party. They are often confronted with the question whether supporting a bad measure is not a less evil than displacing a good government or breaking up or enfeebling a useful organisation, and they are often obliged to vote for or against one measure with a view to carrying or defeating a totally different one. They must look to the whole results of their conduct, ulterior as well as proximate. In France, a large number of the best men of our century have successively supported more than one dynasty and republic, and they were not wrong in doing so. Though they preferred one or other form of government, they considered that the evils of instability and revolution were so great that it was the part of a patriotic man to strengthen the existing form, if it was only a tolerable one, and endeavour to graft upon it the best characteristics of the other forms.

In party parliamentary government, questions of ethics of a much more perplexing character continually arise. Some men differ from the dominant tendencies of their party, but not so strongly or universally as to induce them to break formally the ties of long-standing engagements; or they remain in it because they believe that it would be a great public calamity if it were deprived of its moderating element, and thrown altogether into the hands of extreme men. Usually, while the extremes of rival parties differ widely, there is a frontier line where the two parties almost blend. Sometimes, as in the latter days of Lord Palmerston's life, the lines of party have been so faintly drawn that a rising politician might very reasonably consider it a matter of great indifference to which party he attached himself. At other times parties are deeply sundered by questions vitally affecting the wellbeing of the nation. In practical politics there must always be much compromise and mutual concession; and, as Hallam long since said, the centrifugal and the centripetal forces, which correspond roughly to the rival party tendencies, are both needed to preserve the due balance of affairs. There are great evils, as well as great advantages, attending the party system, and there are periods when these evils seem brought into a more than common prominence.

All this, however, is clearly distinct from the conduct of a politician who, in matters of grave national concern, regulates his actions with an exclusive view to his own interests. In English opinion, very glaring instances of political profligacy are distinguished broadly from acts of private and personal dishonesty, such as malversation in the administration of public funds. But the distinction is, in truth, an unreal one, and it is not likely to last. A man who remains in a party which he would otherwise have abandoned, or votes for some important measure which he would have otherwise opposed, because he has been bought by the offer of a peerage or a place, would probably be incapable of swindling and cheating at cards, but his conduct is not really less dishonourable. The false trustee to the public will easily, under sufficient temptation, turn into the fraudulent bankrupt, and a public opinion which is lax and indulgent in dealing with one form of dishonesty will soon learn to look with toleration on the other. The same type of character which produces the unscrupulous professional politician produces also the too familiar fraudulent director. We need not look beyond the Atlantic for examples.

There is hardly any field, indeed, in which moral notions are more confused and inconsistent than in politics. Let any one, for example, read the report of the judgment of the Parnell Commission, and the sworn testimony on which it was based, and let him then remember that the men who were distinctly proved to have organised, encouraged, stimulated, and profited by all the violence, fraud, intimidation, and crime that is there recorded received the support of the great body of the Catholic priests in Ireland, and of the great body of Nonconformist ministers in England. There were, it is true, noble exceptions. The names that had most weight in the Nonconformity of our time—the names of Spurgeon, and Fraser, and Allon, and Dale—stand in this respect beyond reproach. But the majority of the English and Welsh Nonconformists took a different course, and their ministers have in the present generation been ardent politicians, prominent on the platform, and not unfrequently introducing their politics into the pulpit. They were, apparently, entirely unmoved by the judicial inquiry which proved beyond all possibility of doubt the complicity of the men they supported with crime. The boycotting, the Plan of Campaign, the incendiary speeches, the open advocacy of public plunder, the connection with American dynamiters, the concealed accounts, the many instances of hideous cruelty and oppression of the weak that were distinctly traceable to the Irish Land League, all left these religious teachers completely undisturbed. These things were regarded as merely 'political.' At last, however, it was shown that the prime mover of the Irish agitation had been guilty of adultery. It was a very ordinary case, without much special aggravation, and such as might be found in almost every newspaper. Then, for the first time, the Nonconformist conscience was aroused. It was intolerable that a truly religious party should be in alliance with a politician guilty of such an act; and the explosion of moral indignation, which began in the Nonconformist ranks, soon shook the land, and detached by successive impacts the Prime Minister, the Irish bishops, and most of the Irish members from their old connection. Can those who witnessed this grotesque exhibition wonder at the charge of Pharisaism and hypocrisy which foreign observers so abundantly bring against English public opinion? Can they be surprised that 'the Nonconformist conscience' is rapidly becoming a byword in England, much like the 'moral sentiments' of Joseph Surface?

My readers will not, I hope, so far misunderstand these remarks as to attribute to me any indifference to the private morals of public men. The example of men who hold a high and responsible position before the world exercises a more than common influence, and it is therefore specially desirable that they should be men of untarnished honour and blameless lives. There have been instances of men of very lax domestic morals who have been excellent politicians, and of men of exemplary private characters who have in Parliament been unprincipled and corrupt; but still private virtue is at least some guarantee for the right performance of public duty; while a man who has lost his position in the world through a great moral scandal would be almost more than human if he did not subordinate all political convictions and public interests to regaining it. But, after all, it is not the private vices of public men that are most dangerous to the community. It may be a curious question of casuistry whether it is a more immoral thing to commit adultery, or to incite to intimidation which leads to crime and outrage, persisting in it 'with knowledge of its effect.'[53] There can, at least, be no doubt which of these two acts is more injurious to the State.

The maintenance of a high standard of right and wrong in the field of politics is certainly one of the first of national interests, and it becomes increasingly difficult with the democratic tendency to throw public affairs more and more into the hands of professional politicians. To other classes the House of Commons has lost much of its old attraction. The extraordinary prolongation of its sessions; the growth of mere obstruction in its debates; the increased prominence of parliamentary manœuvre, requiring a more incessant attendance; the vast amount of stump oratory, and other wearisome work, which is now expected both from a candidate and a member, are making public life far more burdensome than in the past, and are gradually alienating from it men who have no strong personal object to gain. The influences that have begun to dominate at elections neither attract nor favour the best men. Such men will not readily consent to be mere delegates or puppets of a caucus, and they are not likely to be skilful in conciliating by vague promises groups of impracticable theorists, and in employing the language of class bribery.

The withdrawal of nearly all forms of local government from magistrates and from nominated bodies, and the great multiplicity of elected and democratic bodies, tend in the same direction. In the cases—happily, in the present century, very rare in England—in which public funds were corruptly administered for the benefit of the few, the introduction of the elective system on a broad basis may be a valuable corrective,

---

[53] *Special Commission Report*, pp. 88, 92.

though no one would maintain that local administration is, on the whole, purer in America than it has long been in England. It is contended, however, with justice, in favour of the elective system that it forms one of the best schools or training-grounds for the politician; that it gives an intelligent interest in public affairs to multitudes who had long been very indifferent to them; that it furnishes a security that the wants of all classes should be brought to light, and at least discussed; and that it infuses a new strength and energy into local administration.

All this is, I believe, very true, and very important. At the same time there are manifest and serious drawbacks. One of them is increased expense, which nearly always follows when a nominated or magisterial body is replaced by a democratic elected one; another is a great multiplication of antagonisms and dissensions. In many quiet country parishes, where Churchmen and Dissenters, Liberals and Conservatives, long lived in almost perfect amity, social fissures are now deepening, and constantly recurring elections are keeping up a permanent fever of contention. The elections for the school board, for the county council, for the parish council, the parliamentary elections, which now imply constant party meetings extending through the greater part of the session, are ranging the different parties more and more in hostile committees and opposing platforms, and whatever good may result is certainly produced by a great deal of ill-feeling and discomfort. Nothing, too, as we have already seen, is more clearly established by American experience than that very frequent contested elections tend to lower the moral tone of politics, and to throw them more and more into the hands of the professional politician.

It would, I believe, be a mistake to suppose that under the new conditions wealth will disappear, or even exercise a greatly diminished power in politics, but the rich men who will chiefly enter Parliament are not the kind who are most desirable. Three classes appear to have an increasing prominence. There are those who, having amassed large fortunes in trade, commerce, or manufacture, desire above all things social position, and are prepared to sacrifice large sums to attain it. The social precedence which a seat in Parliament affords, and the possibilities of rank which are open to every rich man who steadily supports his party, become their guiding motives, and very often shape the whole course of their political calculations. There are also prosperous lawyers who enter Parliament for professional objects, knowing that it is the path which leads directly to the chief honours in their profession; and there is the large class of business men connected with public companies, who find a political position useful to their financial enterprises. The increasing number of directors in Parliament, and the desire of companies to have members of Parliament for their directors, are significant signs, not, I think, of good omen for the purity of politics. As State functions multiply, including many things that were once left to private commercial enterprise, the position of member of Parliament is likely to have an increasing value in the fields of patronage, industry, and finance. Men of these different classes are often among the most dangerous of demagogues. Private aims predominate with them over public ones. If they can attain them, they care little for a large expenditure or sacrifice of money, and their special interests are usually only very slightly identified with the permanent interests of the country.

Two or three measures which are much advocated would confirm the power of the professional politician. I have already spoken of the abolition of university representation. It is not a measure which would have very extensive consequences, but it would at least expel from Parliament a small class of members who represent in an eminent degree intelligence and knowledge diffused throughout the country; who, from the manner of their election, are almost certain to be men of political purity and independent character, and who, for that very reason, are especially obnoxious to the more unscrupulous type of demagogue. Their expulsion would be a considerable party advantage to one faction in the State, and it is therefore likely to be steadily pursued.

A more considerable measure would be that of throwing the whole or a large part of the expenses of elections on the rates. There is much to be said in its defence. It is not a natural thing that men should be expected to pay largely for discharging what should be a public duty, for rendering what should be a public service. Payment from the rates would render it much easier for men of moderate fortunes to enter the House, and it would very possibly diminish the appetite for place, or for the less legitimate forms of gain, which are often sought merely for the purpose of recovering an expenditure already made. Men who have paid much for a position easily persuade themselves that it is legitimate to make profit out of it, and to regard their expenditure as an investment. But, unless payment from public sources were restricted to candidates who obtained a considerable amount of support at the poll, it would multiply useless and mischievous contests, and, like the payment of members, which would probably follow it, besides adding largely to the cost of government, it would greatly smooth the path of the professional agitator or wirepuller.

The reader will, I hope, understand that in the foregoing remarks I am describing tendencies which appear to me to be in operation and not fully accomplished facts. It would take a long time, and many disastrous revolutions, to break down the firm texture of English political life. The old feelings of traditional reverence; the long-established organisations of property and class and corporate existence; the shrewdness and sobriety of judgment, and, above all, the sound moral feeling which a long and noble history has implanted in all classes of the British people, have not disappeared, though power is passing mainly into the hands of the most uninstructed, and therefore least intelligent, classes, and though low motives are in consequence acquiring a greater prominence in English politics. Still, there have been encouraging signs that a politician who is ready to sacrifice his character in order to win power or popularity may make the sacrifice without obtaining the reward. Manufactured and organised agitations; ingenious combinations of heterogeneous elements; skilful attempts to win votes by distributing class bribes or inflaming class or national animosities, have not always proved successful. The deliberate judgment of the constituencies on a great question which strongly arouses national feeling will, I believe, seldom be wrong, though there is an increased danger that they may be for a time misled, and that such influences as I have described may obtain a temporary ascendency in the House of Commons.

The high standard, both of professional honour and of competence, that has long prevailed in our permanent services is certainly unimpaired, and, in days when parliamentary government is in its decadence, the importance to national well-being of a good permanent service can hardly be overrated. Parliament itself, though it shows many evil signs, has escaped some which may be detected in other legislatures. It would be difficult to exaggerate the value of the standing order which provides that the House of Commons shall make no money grant except at the initiative of the responsible Ministers of the Crown. Probably no other provision has done so much to check extravagance and to place a bound to that bribery by legislation which is one of the distinctive dangers of democracy; and the absence of such a rule has been justly described as one of the great sources of the corruption and extravagance of French finance. The Committee system also, which seems likely to become in England, as it has already become in America, the most important thing in parliamentary government, is still essentially sound. The House of Commons as a whole is becoming so unfit for the transaction of the details of business that it will probably more and more delegate its functions to Committees; and these Committees submit great questions to a thorough examination, bring together the most competent practical judges and the best available information, weaken the force of party, and infuse into legislation something, at least, of a judicial spirit.

I have already alluded to the great political value of the competitive system of examination as applied to the public services. It has undoubtedly many and grievous drawbacks, and few good judges will deny that examinations have been overdone in England, and that in these examinations mere book knowledge has been too prominent. Sometimes, indeed, there has been an almost grotesque dissimilarity between the character of the examination and the career to which it leads; as, for example, when questions about Spenser's 'Faerie Queene,' or about English parliamentary history, or about classical literature, are said to have turned the scale for or against a candidate who is examined for the army. Many of the qualities that are most useful in the administration of affairs and the management of men can be neither given nor tested by examination. Tact, knowledge of men, sound judgment, promptitude and resolution in times of danger, and that charm of manner which adds so much, especially in Eastern nations, to the success of administrations, lie wholly beyond the range of the examination hall. There are positions in life in which the wild, idle, high-spirited boy, whose natural bent is all to sport and to adventure, but who is utterly without the turn of mind or character that triumphs in examinations, is more likely to succeed than the plodding, industrious boy who will win the prize. The competitive system is in theory a very democratical one, but, like many democratic measures, it does not altogether fulfil its promise. It is a system which gives a wholly disproportionate share of the world's goods to a small minority who are endowed with a particular kind of capacity. It is a system also in which money plays a great part, for it has become all but impossible for boys to succeed in the most keenly contested examinations unless they have had the advantage of special and expensive teaching. It is curious to observe how often, under the old aristocratic system of patronage, a poor man gained a place on the ladder of promotion which he could not have reached under the present system. An officer who, like so many of his profession, found himself towards the close of a useful and honourable life with only a very humble competence, could, under the old system, always obtain for his son a commission without purchase in the army. His son must now enter by an examination, and he will hardly succeed unless the father is able to give him the advantage of an experienced crammer.

In India the competitive system may prove a serious danger. In that country the nimbleness of mind and tongue which succeeds in examinations is, to a degree quite unknown in Europe, separated from martial courage, and from the strength of nerve and character that wins the respect of great masses, and marks out the rulers of men. In the opinion of the best judges, a system which would bring to the forefront the weak, effeminate Bengalese, to the detriment of the old governing races of India and of the strong, warlike populations of the North, would be the sure precursor of a catastrophe.

But, with all its drawbacks, the competitive system has been, I think, in England a great blessing, and the disadvantages that attend it have been mitigated by more intelligent kinds of examination and by a judicious mixture of patronage and competition, which gives some power of selection to men in responsible positions. The competitive system realises, on the whole, more perfectly than any other that has been yet devised the ideal of the Revolution: '*La carrière ouverte aux talents.*' If patronage were always exercised with perfect wisdom and public spirit, it would, no doubt, bring forward better men, but there is no real reason to believe that the class who, in Great Britain, are produced by the competitive system are, on the whole, at all inferior to their predecessors. At the same time, its value in keeping the public services pure from corruption can hardly be overstated. It is the one real protection against the complete dominance of the 'spoils system,' and it is a protection which is likely to last. In a democratic age it is very difficult to correct democratic evils except by democratic remedies. It would be impossible to measure the corruption which would ensue if all the powers of patronage and nomination that were once in the hands of governments and aristocracies were placed in the hands of popular bodies, to be scrambled for by professional politicians or used as bribes by contending factions.

It is a truth which is not sufficiently recognised, that the general character of a nation cannot always be fairly judged by the character of its public men or of its political actions. In a really sound representative system this remark would not apply. One of the truest tests of a good constitution is, that it brings into habitual political action the best characteristics of the nation. But in the extremes both of despotism and of democracy political action is often a strangely deceptive guide to national character. Governments sometimes pursue a constantly aggressive, military, and violent policy, simply because power is in the hands of a small class, and because the bulk of the nation are so mild, peaceful, and loyal that they can be easily led. In democracies, as America has abundantly shown, politics may be an equally faithless mirror of the best side of the national character. The politics of a nation and the character of its public men may deteriorate, not because the aggregate intelligence or virtue of the nation has diminished, but simply because the governing power has descended to classes who are less intelligent, less scrupulous, or more easily deceived.

If it be true—as there seems great reason to believe—that parliamentary government in England has entered on its period of decadence, it becomes a question of the highest importance to ascertain whether this implies a general decadence in the national character. I do not myself believe it. It appears to me hardly possible to compare the present generation of Englishmen with the generation of our grandfathers and great-grandfathers without believing that, on the whole, English character has improved. The statistics of crime are, no doubt, in this respect an imperfect test, for the criminal class always forms only a small section of the community, and an increase or diminution of actual criminal offences often depends upon circumstances that are only very slightly connected with the average morals of the community. As far, however, as this test goes, it is eminently satisfactory, for there can be no doubt that most forms of grave crime, in proportion to population, have, in the present generation, greatly diminished. Nor is this surprising, for no feature of our century is more remarkable than the skill with which, by reformatories and industrial and other schools, by factory laws, by the diminution of insanitary dwellings, and by the better regulation of the drink traffic, modern philanthropy has succeeded in restricting or purifying the chief sources of national crime. As a single illustration of the change that has taken place, I may mention that in 1834 it was officially stated in Parliament that not less than one-fifth of the army stationed in England had, in the two preceding years, passed through the common goals.[54] The great diminution of ordinary crime in England is especially remarkable, because both in France and in the United States there has been, in the present generation, a great and deplorable increase.

Not less conspicuous is the improvement that has taken place in the decorum, civilisation, and humanity of the bulk of the poor; in the character of their tastes and pleasures; in their enlarged circle of interests; in the spirit of providence which, under the influence of savings banks and kindred institutions, has arisen among them. The skilled artisans in our great towns, within the memory of living men, have become, not only the most energetic, but also one of the most intelligent and orderly elements, in English life. No one who has come into close contact with their political organisations, or trade unions, or mechanics' institutes, or free libraries, or who has watched the working-class audience of some great scientific lecturer, will deem this an exaggeration. The spirit of humanity has immensely increased, both in the form that shrinks from the infliction of suffering and in the form that seeks out suffering in order to alleviate it. Churches and creeds will come and go; but the best index of the moral level of a community is to be found in the amount of unselfish action that is generated within it. I do not believe that there has ever been a period in England, or in any other country, when more time, thought, money, and labour were bestowed

---

[54] *Hansard*, xxv. 281.

on the alleviation of suffering, or in which a larger number of men and women of all classes threw themselves more earnestly and more habitually into unselfish causes. Both within and without the Church the passion for social reform and philanthropic action has, to a large extent, displaced theological enthusiasm; but, at the same time, the increased activity of the Established Church is very apparent, the standard of duty among its clergy is appreciably raised, and its patronage is administered in a far better and purer spirit than in the past.

All this is, no doubt, compatible with the growth of some special forms of vice. It may perhaps be compatible with a decline of those stronger and more robust qualities that chiefly lead to political greatness. Whether in this last field there has been any decadence in England is a question on which it is difficult to pronounce. The last occasion in which England was engaged in a life-and-death struggle against overwhelming odds was in the Indian Mutiny; and, in that now distant crisis, it must be owned that there was no failing in the stronger, fiercer, and more tenacious qualities that have made England what she is. Amid all the much obtruded sentimentalisms of our time there are indications that the fibre of the race is still unimpaired. The old love of manly sports was never more abundantly displayed; in the great fields of adventure and discovery, in the forms of commercial and industrial enterprise that most tax the energies and resources of men, modern Englishmen bear their full part, and no other people are doing so much to explore, subdue, and civilise far-distant and savage lands.

Have their governing qualities declined? Have the Englishmen of our day learnt to prefer words to things and plausibilities to facts, and men who are cunning in the arts of parliamentary fence and political manœuvre to men of wise judgment and solid character? Carlyle believed that they had, and there have been symptoms in these later days that support his opinion. I believe, however, that they will nearly all be found in close connection with the influence of a demo-

cratic Parliament. When Englishmen escape from its interference and its contagion, their old high governing qualities
seldom fail to shine. No piece of more skilful, successful, and
beneficent administration has been accomplished in our day,
under circumstances of great difficulty, than the English
administration of Egypt, and no achievement of secular government since the Roman Empire can compare in its magnitude and splendour with the British Empire in India. The men
who built up that gigantic empire, who have maintained for
so many generations and over so vast an area peace and prosperity and order, who have put a stop to so many savage wars
and eradicated so many cruel customs, are the statesmen of
whom England should be most proud. There is no sign that
they have lost their cunning; and if such men and such modes
of government could have been employed nearer home,
many old injustices and discontents would have long since
passed away.

He would be a sanguine man who ventured to predict with
confidence the long duration of this supreme monument of
the genius and the character of our race; but most good judges
will agree that the great danger that menaces it is to be found
neither at Calcutta nor at St. Petersburg, but at Westminster.
It is to be found in combinations of fanaticism with intrigue
that are peculiarly dangerous in a country ruled by feeble
governments, and disintegrated parliaments, and ignorant
constituencies; it is to be found in the introduction into India
of modes and maxims of government borrowed from modern
European democracies, and utterly unsuited to an Oriental
people; it is to be found in acts of injustice perpetrated by
Parliament in obedience to party motives and to the pressure
of local interests. Two shameful instances of this kind are very
recent. The Commission sent out to India to inquire into the
opium traffic in 1893 was wholly due to the action in the
House of Commons of a little knot of fanatics and agitators
in England, unprompted by any voice in India, and carried
contrary to the whole force of experienced Indian opinion.
Yet it was at first determined that a great part of its cost should

be thrown on the Indian taxpayer. Still graver in its probable effects was the policy which forbade India, in a time of deep financial distress, to raise a revenue by import duties on English cotton, in accordance with the almost unanimous desire of her administrators and her educated public opinion. No one ever doubted that, if India possessed representative institutions, or if the opinions of English administrators in India or of Indian administrators at home had been taken, such duties would have been imposed. But votes might have been lost, an agitation might have been raised in England, and both parties feared to run the risk.

Fortunately, in these two cases the false steps that had been taken did not prove irrevocable. The Minister for India (Sir Henry Fowler), to his infinite credit, had the courage to insist at all hazards upon revising them, and he found sufficient patriotism in the Opposition to enable him to secure the support of a large majority in the House of Commons. Seldom indeed in recent years has the chord of genuine public spirit in that House been so powerfully and so successfully struck. But the original faults were very grave, and they illustrate the dangers to which democratic parliamentary government with a weak executive exposes the great interests of the Empire.

The blame must be divided between both parties. In both parties the minister representing India has, I believe, usually done his best, short of resigning his office; but when a small group of voters may turn the balance, the great interests of India are but too likely to be sacrificed to the party game. It is often said that England holds India by the sword; but this, though largely, is not wholly true. If the belief of the great masses of the Indian people in the essential integrity and beneficence of English rule is ever shaken, one of the chief pillars of our power will have been destroyed.

Our Indian experience, however, at least shows that the governing qualities of the race remain; and the same truth is taught by the admirable corporate government which has grown up in our great towns. It is very doubtful whether the spirit of municipal and local patriotism was more strongly developed either in ancient Greece, or, during the Middle Ages, in the great towns of Italy and Flanders or along the Baltic, than it now is in Birmingham, or Liverpool, or Manchester. The self-governing qualities that are displayed in these great centres, the munificence and patriotism with which their public institutions are supported, the strong stream of distinctive political tendency that emanates from them, are among the most remarkable and most consolatory facts of English life. In France, the ascendency of Paris has almost atrophied political life in the provincial towns, and the capital has again and again shown itself sufficiently powerful to reverse the decision of the country. In America, the corruption of municipal government in nearly all the more important cities is the worst side of the national life. England has hitherto escaped both of these evils, and the political weight of the chief provincial towns is unquestionable. The Manchester school of the last generation, and the Birmingham school of the present generation, have been among the most powerful influences in modern politics.

The growth of an independent provincial spirit has been much accelerated by the telegraph. The political influence of this great invention, though various and chequered, has been scarcely less powerful than that of the railway. It has brought the distant dependencies of the Empire into far closer connection with the mother country; but it is very doubtful whether the power it has given to the home ministers of continually meddling with the details of their administration is a good thing, and there have been times of disagreement when a rapid communication between foreign countries might have led rather to war than to peace. Government by telegraph is a very dangerous thing; and it has been often said that if an Atlantic telegraph had connected England with the United States in the first excitement of the 'Trent' affair, enabling the two nations, when their blood was still hot, to exchange their impressions, a war could scarcely have been averted. The telegraph, on the other hand, has greatly strengthened the Central Government in repressing insurrections, protecting property, and punishing crime. It has at least modified the Irish difficulty, by bringing Dublin within a few minutes' communication of London. It has had enormous economical consequences, equalising prices, stimulating speculation, destroying in a great measure the advantage of priority of time which the inhabitants of great centres naturally had in many competitions.

The effect, however, on which I would now specially dwell is its great power in decentralising politics. The provincial press, no doubt, owes much to the repeal of the stamp duty and the paper duty; but the immense development and importance it has assumed within the lifetime of men who are still of middle age are mainly due to the existence of telegraphic communication. All kinds of foreign and domestic news, and even full reports of debates in Parliament that are of any local interest, are printed in an Irish, or Scotch, or Liverpool paper as early as in London. The local newspaper is thus able, in its own district, to anticipate the news of the London papers, and in consequence, over large areas of the country where the metropolitan press once exercised an enormous influence, a London newspaper is now seldom seen. With its increased importance and circulation, the provincial press can command far more talent than in the past, and it has become one of the most important agencies, both in indicating and in forming national opinion.

I do not know that it was ever clearly foreseen that while railways were doing so much to centralise, the telegraph would do so much to decentralise, multiplying in England powerful and independent centres of political thought and education, building up a provincial press which often fully rivals in ability that of the metropolis, while, within its own spheres of influence, it exercises a far greater ascendency. This has been one of the great political facts of our time, and, on the whole, it seems to me to have been a beneficial one. Representative institutions will probably perish by ceasing to be representative, genuine opinion being overlaid and crushed by great multitudes of ignorant voters of one class. In our day, the press is becoming far more than the House of Commons the representative of the real public opinion of the nation.

Its growth is but one of the many signs of the intense and many-sided intellectual and moral energy that pervades the country. There are fields, indeed, both of thought and action, in which the greatest men of our generation are dwarfed by their predecessors; but if we measure our age by the aggregate of its vitality, by the broad sweep of its energies and achievements, the England of our century can hardly fail to rank very high. In art, in science, in literature, in the enlargement of the bounds of knowledge, in the popularisation of acquired knowledge, in inventions and discoveries, and in most of the forms of enterprise and philanthropy, it has assuredly done much. It has produced in Darwin a man who has effected a greater revolution in the opinions of mankind than anyone, at least since Newton, and whose name is likely to live with honour as long as the human race moves upon the planet; while in Gordon it has produced a type of simple, self-sacrificing, religious heroism which is in its own kind as perfect as anything, even in the legends of chivalry. A country which has produced such men and such works does not seem to be in a condition of general decadence, though its Constitution is plainly worn out, though the balance of power within it has been destroyed, and though diseases of a serious character are fast growing in its political life. The future only can tell whether the energy of the English people can be sufficiently roused to check these evils, and to do so before they have led to some great catastrophe.

CHAPTER 3

I do not think that any one who seriously considers the force and universality of the movement of our generation in the direction of democracy can doubt that this conception of government will necessarily, at least for a considerable time, dominate in all civilised countries, and the real question for politicians is the form it is likely to take, and the means by which its characteristic evils can be best mitigated. As we have, I think, abundantly seen, a tendency to democracy does not mean a tendency to parliamentary government, or even a tendency towards greater liberty. On the contrary, strong arguments may be adduced, both from history and from the nature of things, to show that democracy may often prove the direct opposite of liberty. In ancient Rome the old aristocratic republic was gradually transformed into a democracy, and it then passed speedily into an imperial despotism. In France a corresponding change has more than once taken place. A despotism resting on a plebiscite is quite as natural a form of democracy as a republic, and some of the strongest democratic tendencies are distinctly adverse to liberty. Equality is the idol of democracy, but, with the infinitely various capacities and energies of men, this can only be attained by a constant, systematic, stringent repression of their natural development.

Whenever natural forces have unrestricted play, inequality is certain to ensue. Democracy destroys the balance of opinions, interests, and classes, on which constitutional liberty mainly depends, and its constant tendency is to impair the efficiency and authority of parliaments, which have hitherto proved the chief organs of political liberty. In the Middle Ages, the two most democratic institutions were the Church and the guild. They first taught the essential spiritual equality of mankind, and placed men taken from the servile class on a pedestal before which kings and nobles were compelled to bow; but it also formed the most tremendous instrument of spiritual tyranny the world has ever seen. The second organised industry on a self-governing and representative basis, but at the same time restricted and regulated it in all its details with the most stringent despotism.

In our own day, no fact is more incontestable and conspicuous than the love of democracy for authoritative regulation. The two things that men in middle age have seen most discredited among their contemporaries are probably free contract and free trade. The great majority of the democracies of the world are now frankly protectionist, and even in free-trade countries the multiplication of laws regulating, restricting, and interfering with industry in all its departments is one of the most marked characteristics of our time. Nor are these regulations solely due to sanitary or humanitarian motives. Among large classes of those who advocate them another motive is very perceptible. A school has arisen among popular working-class leaders which no longer desires that superior skill, or industry, or providence should reap extraordinary rewards. Their ideal is to restrict by the strongest trade-union regulations the amount of work and the amount of the produce of work, to introduce the principle of legal compulsion into every branch of industry, to give the trade union an absolute coercive power over its members, to attain a high average, but to permit no superiorities. The industrial organisation to which they aspire approaches far more nearly to that of the Middle Ages or of the Tudors than to the ideal of

Jefferson and Cobden. I do not here argue whether this tend-ency is good or bad. No one at least can suppose that it is in the direction of freedom. It may be permitted to doubt whether liberty in other forms is likely to be very secure if power is mainly placed in the hands of men who, in their own sphere, value it so little.

The expansion of the authority and the multiplication of the functions of the State in other fields, and especially in the field of social regulation, is an equally apparent accompaniment of modern democracy. This increase of State power means a mul-tiplication of restrictions imposed upon the various forms of human action. It means an increase of bureaucracy, or, in other words, of the number and power of State officials. It means also a constant increase of taxation, which is in reality a con-stant restriction of liberty. One of the first forms of liberty is the right of every man to dispose of his own property and earn-ings, and every tax is a portion of this money taken from him by the force and authority of the law. Many of these taxes are, no doubt, for purposes in which he has the higest interest. They give him the necessary security of life, property, and in-dustry, and they add in countless ways to his enjoyment. But if taxes are multiplied for carrying out a crowd of objects in which he has no interest, and with many of which he has no sympathy, his liberty is proportionately restricted. His money is more and more taken from him by force for purposes of which he does not approve. The question of taxation is in the highest degree a question of liberty, and taxation under a de-mocracy is likely to take forms that are peculiarly hostile to liberty. I have already pointed out how the old fundamental principle of English freedom, that no one should be taxed ex-cept by his consent, is being gradually discarded; and how we are steadily advancing to a state in which one class will impose the taxes, while another class will be mainly compelled to pay them. It is obvious that taxation is more and more employed for objects that are not common interests of the whole com-munity, and that there is a growing tendency to look upon it as a possible means of confiscation; to make use of it to break down the power, influence, and wealth of particular classes; to form a new social type; to obtain the means of class bribery.

There are other ways in which democracy does not harmonise well with liberty. To place the chief power in the most ignorant classes is to place it in the hands of those who naturally care least for political liberty, and who are most likely to follow with an absolute devotion some strong leader. The sentiment of nationality penetrates very deeply into all classes; but in all countries and ages it is the upper and middle classes who have chiefly valued constitutional liberty, and those classes it is the work of democracy to dethrone. At the same time democracy does much to weaken among these also the love of liberty. The instability and insecurity of democratic politics; the spectacle of dishonest and predatory adventurers climbing by popular suffrage into positions of great power in the State; the alarm which attacks on property seldom fail to produce among those who have something to lose, may easily scare to the side of despotism large classes who, under other circumstances, would have been steady supporters of liberty. A despotism which secures order, property, and industry, which leaves the liberty of religion and of private life unimpaired, and which enables quiet and industrious men to pass through life untroubled and unmolested, will always appear to many very preferable to a democratic republic which is constantly menacing, disturbing, or plundering them. It would be a great mistake to suppose that the French despotic Empire after 1852 rested on bayonets alone. It rested partly on the genuine consent of those large agricultural classes who cared greatly for material prosperity and very little for constitutional liberty, and partly on the panic produced among the middle classes by the socialist preaching of 1848.

The dangers to be apprehended from democracy are enormously increased when the transformation is effected by sudden bounds. Governments or societies may be fundamentally changed, without producing any great convulsion or catastrophe, if the continuity of habit is preserved, if the changes are made by slow, gradual, and almost imperceptible steps. As I have already said, it is one of the evils of our present party system that it greatly accelerates this progress. Very few constitutional changes are the results of a genuine, spontaneous, unforced development. They are mainly, or at least largely, due to rival leaders bidding against each other for popularity; to agitators seeking for party purposes to raise a cry; to defeated statesmen trying, when they are condemned by existing constituencies, to regain power by creating new ones. The true origin of some of the most far-reaching changes of our day is, probably, simply a desire so to shuffle cards or combine votes as to win an election. With a powerful Upper Chamber and a strong organisation of property in the electorate, the conservative influences are sufficient to prevent a too rapid change. But when these checks are weakened and destroyed, and when there are no constitutional provisions to take their place, the influences working in the direction of change acquire an enormously augmented force, the dangers of the process are incalculably increased, and the new wine is very likely to burst the old bottles.

It is impossible to foretell with confident accuracy in what form societies will organise their governments if, under the pressure of democracy, our present system of parliamentary government breaks down. A study of the methods which many different countries have adopted, and especially of the manner in which America has dealt with the dangers of democracy, furnishes us with perhaps the best light we can obtain. But, within the framework of the British Constitution, a few remedies or mitigations of existing evils have been suggested, which may be easily, or at least without any insuperable difficulty, introduced.

The first and most obvious is a change in the Irish representation. The presence in the House of Commons of a body of men who are entirely detached from the general interests of the Empire, and prepared to subordinate all Imperial concerns to their own special policy, must always bring with it some danger; and there could hardly be a greater folly than to allow such an element to possess an abnormal and wholly excessive share in the representation. Few more foolish or wicked acts have been done in modern times than the lowering of the suffrage in Ireland, by which this great evil and danger was deliberately raised to its present magnitude, while not a single step was taken, either by curtailing representation, or redistributing seats, or securing a representation of minorities, to mitigate the evil. Such a policy, indeed, would seem simple madness if party interest did not furnish an explanation. It is acknowledged that the Irish representation, if measured by the test of numbers alone, is about twenty-three seats in excess of its proper number. If the far more rational test of numbers and taxation combined be taken, the excess is still greater. It is an excess, too, which is mainly in one portion of Ireland, and in one class—the most ignorant, the most disloyal, the most amenable to sinister influence. The steady action of this party has been to disintegrate and degrade parliamentary government, to support every measure in the direction of anarchy or plunder. Yet it is well known that for some years the Government of England depended for its existence, not only on the Irish vote, but on the illegitimate strength of that vote. If we look through the more revolutionary and dangerous measures of the last few years, we shall find that very few have been carried through all their stages by an English majority and not many by a British majority, while some of the worst measures could never have been carried by the votes of the whole kingdom if the Irish representatives had not been disproportionately large. And the men who have kept a Government in power, and largely influenced its policy, have been men who are avowedly and ostentatiously indifferent to the welfare of the Empire, men whose votes on questions vitally affecting British or Imperial interests are notoriously governed by considerations in which these interests have no part. It is owing to the excessive number of such men in Parliament that a system of taxation has been carried through the House of Commons which may break up the social organisation on which a great part of the wellbeing of England has depended for nearly a thousand years. No one supposes that the Irish surplus which turned the balance felt the smallest interest in the result.

It would be difficult to conceive a situation either more dangerous, or more absurd, or more humiliating than this. According to all rational conceptions of constitutional government, it should be the object of the legislator to strengthen the influence of intelligence, loyalty, and property in the representation, and in every change to improve, or not to injure, the character of Parliament. If, however, such ideas are discarded as obsolete and behind the age, if the new worship of mere numbers prevails, to the utter disregard of all the real interests of the State, the present representation of Ireland is still completely indefensible. The argument from the 100 votes stipulated by the Union treaty has been torn to pieces by the legislation of the last few years. A party which has abolished the Established Church of Ireland, which the Irish Parliament made 'an essential and fundamental part of the Union,' and which threatens to abolish the Established Church of Scotland, which was guaranteed with equal solemnity at both the Scotch and the Irish Unions, cannot avail itself of such an argument. And the absurdity becomes still more manifest when it is remembered that the great industrial counties in Ireland, which represent its most progressive and loyal portions, are not over-represented, but under-represented, and that, as the result of the present system, in three provinces property, loyalty, and intelligence are practically disfranchised.

There can be little doubt that a reduction, and at the same time a rearrangement, of the Irish representation would greatly improve the constitution of parties, and it would certainly be a great blessing to Ireland. Should this reduction be effected, it is to be hoped that the seats taken from Ireland may not be added to Great Britain, and that statesmen will avail themselves of the opportunity to effect some slight diminution of the numbers of the House.

Nearly all the methods by which it has been attempted to secure in Parliament a representation of the various classes and interests of the community seem passing away under the influence of democracy. Unequal constituencies, restrictions of the suffrage, property qualifications, special representations of property, are all denounced as opposed to the spirit of the age. Direct class representation also, which has borne a large part in the history of representative government, has been steadily declining, though it has in our own day some able defenders,[1] and though it is, I think, by no means impossible that in some future stage of the world's history it may be largely revived. The apportionment of political power between distinctly separated classes has, indeed, been one of the oldest and most fruitful ideas in political philosophy. It existed in Athens even before the days of Solon, and Solon, in his revision of the Athenian Constitution, divided the citizens into four classes, according to the amount of their property, subjecting each class to a special proportion of taxation, and giving each class special and peculiar privileges in the State.[2] In the Roman republic the citizens were divided into six different classes, according to the amount of their property, the lowest class comprising the poorest citizens; and each class was subdivided into a number of 'centuries,' proportioned to what was considered their importance in the

---

[1] See, *e.g.*, the remarkable book of M. Adolphe Prins, *L'Organisation de la Liberté* (Brussels, 1895). M. Prins observes: 'Il est incontestable que le suffrage universel sans cadres, sans organisation, sans groupement, est un système factice; il ne donne que l'ombre de la vie politique. Il n'atteint pas le seul but vraiment politique que l'on doive avoir en vue, et qui est non de faire voter tout le monde, mais d'arriver à représenter le mieux les intérêts du plus grand nombre. . . . On peut avoir le droit de vote sans être représenté. C'est le fait de toutes les minorités électorales sous le régime de la majorité numérique. . . . Le suffrage universel moderne c'est surtout le suffrage des passions, des courants irréfléchis, des partis extrêmes. Il ne laisse aucune place aux idées modérées et il écrase les partis modérés. La victoire est aux exaltés. La représentation des intérêts, qui contient les passions par les idées, qui modère l'ardeur des partis par l'action des facteurs sociaux, donne à la société plus d'équilibre' (pp. 186, 187, 201).

[2] See Grote's *History*, iii. 118–21.

State, and each century had a single vote in enacting laws and electing magistrates. Cicero claims for this system that it gave some voice to every class, but a greatly preponderating voice to those who had most interest in the wellbeing of the State.[3] A similar idea inspired the special representation of the three estates of Lords, Clergy, and Commons, which grew up in the Middle Ages, and which played a great part in the early constitutional history of England, France, and Spain. The four orders of Nobles, Clergy, Burgesses, and Peasants were separately represented in Sweden up to 1866, and the same system still survives in the Constitution of Finland. In the Prussian Constitution of 1850 an attempt is made to maintain a balance of classes by dividing the electors 'of the first degree' into three different classes, according to the direct taxes they pay, and giving each class a separate and equal power of election. In the still more recent Constitution of Austria the electors are divided into four great classes—the large territorial proprietors, the towns, the chambers of commerce, and the rural communes—and each category returns its own members to the Chamber of the Deputies. But it is evident that the present stream of political tendency is not flowing in this direction, and it is remarkable that the legislators who framed the Constitution for the German Empire did not follow the example of Prussia, but based the representative chamber on direct universal suffrage. It is now chiefly in the upper chambers that class representation may be found.

The question, however, of proportionate representation, or the representation of minorities, stands on a different basis from the representation of classes. It can hardly be contended that the substitution of a representation of the whole nation for a representation of a mere majority is contrary to demo-

---

[3] 'Ita nec prohibebatur quisquam jure suffragii, et is valebat in suffragio plurimum, cujus plurimum intererat esse in optimo statu civitatum' (Cicero, *de Republica*, ii. 22). This Constitution is attributed to Servius Tullius, but probably acquired its most characteristic features much later. It was for some time greatly abused by the first class, who possessed the majority of centuries, and voted first.

226 *Democracy and Liberty*

cratic principles. It is manifest that, under the existing system, multitudes of electors are in effect permanently disfranchised and unrepresented because they are in a permanent minority in the constituencies in which they live. The majority possess not merely a preponderance, but a monopoly; and in a constituency where three-fifths vote one way and two-fifths the other, the whole representation is in the hands of the former. Where constituencies are very unequal in their magnitude it is quite possible that a majority of the representatives may be returned by a minority of the electors, as the minority in a large constituency will often outnumber the majority in a small one. With equalised constituencies and widely extended suffrage another, but not less serious, evil will prevail. A single class—the most numerous, but also the most ignorant—will generally exceed all others, and other classes in large numbers of constituencies will be wholly unrepresented. In such a state of things, the importance of providing some representation for minorities is extremely great, and it continually happens that the proportion of parties in the representation differs very widely from the proportion in the electorate. When two-thirds of a constituency vote for one party, and one-third for the other, it is obviously just that the majority should have two-thirds, and the minority one-third, of the representation.

The importance of this question has been widely felt during the last few years in many countries, especially since the powerful chapter in which Mill discussed it. 'In a really equal democracy,' he wrote, 'every or any section would be represented, not disproportionately, but proportionately. A majority of the electors would always have a majority of the representatives, but a minority of the electors would have a minority of the representatives. Man for man, they would be as fully represented as the majority. Unless they are, there is not equal government, but government of inequality and privilege, . . . contrary to the principles of democracy which professes equality as its very root and foundation.'[4]

---

[4] Mill *On Representative Government*, p. 133.

There are several methods by which this representation of minorities may be obtained with more or less perfection. The most perfect is that which was first proposed by Mr. Hare in 1859. It has undergone several slight modifications, at the hands either of Mr. Hare or of his disciples; but it will here be sufficient to state its principle in the simplest form. The legislator must first ascertain the number of voters who are entitled to return a member; which is done by the easy process of dividing the number of voters in the kingdom, or in one portion of the kingdom, by the number of seats. Every candidate who can gain this number of votes is to be elected, whether these votes come from his own or from other constituencies. It is proposed that each elector should have one vote, but should vote on a paper on which the candidate he prefers stands first, while the names of other candidates follow in the order of preference. If, when the paper is drawn, the candidate at the head of the list has already obtained the requisite number of votes, the vote is to pass to the first of the succeeding candidates who is still deficient. No candidate is to be credited with a greater number of votes than is required for his election, and his superfluous votes are in this manner to be transferred to other candidates to make up their quota. And this transfer is to be made quite irrespectively of the locality for which they stand.

It cannot, I think, be said that there is anything very mysterious or perplexing in this proceeding, though it would probably be some little time before the electors became accustomed to it, and though it would impose some difficulties of detail and some rather complicated calculations upon the officials who worked it. An element of chance would always remain, as the direction of the votes would partly depend upon the order in which the papers were drawn; and it would probably be found impossible to adapt the system to bye-elections, which might continue as at present. If all the seats were not filled by candidates who had obtained the requisite number of votes, those who approximated most nearly to the number might be chosen to fill the vacancies. The plan is not put forward as absolutely perfect, but it is contended for it that it would give at every general election a far more accurate representation of the wishes of the electorate than our present system; that it would utilise a great number of votes which are now lost or wasted; that it would rekindle political life among large classes who are at present in a hopeless minority in their constituencies; that it would diminish the oscillations of politics, by preventing the wholly disproportionate change of power that so often follows a slight shifting in the electorate; and that it would greatly improve the intellectual level of the House of Commons, by making it the interest of party managers to select candidates of acknowledged eminence, and by giving such candidates far greater chances of success. It has been said that it would destroy local representation; but it is answered that a strong local candidate would usually have most chance of obtaining the required number of votes, and that it would be mainly the voters who are in a minority in their constituency, and are now virtually disfranchised, who would transfer their votes. On the great majority of papers a local candidate would almost certainly head the list. It is urged that the system realises more perfectly than any other the democratic principle of absolute equality, while it at the same time secures the representation of all considerable minorities. Under no other system would the representative chamber reflect so truly, in their due numerical proportion, the various classes, interests, and opinions of the nation.

There have been, as I have said, several slight modifications of this system—usually, I think, not improvements. M. de Girardin has urged that all local constituencies should be abolished, and that the whole country should be treated as one great constituency. Another proposal is, that each candidate should have a right to have the votes for him that are in excess of those required for his election transferred to some other candidate whom he had previously named. I do not think that, if Mr. Hare's system were adopted, there would be any great difficulty in working it, and it would probably materially improve the Constitution; but it is very doubtful whether, in a democratic age, public opinion would ever demand with sufficient persistence a representation of minorities, or whether the British nation could ever be induced to adopt a system which departs so widely from its traditional forms and habits. It is remarkable, however, that a system very like that of Mr. Hare had, without his knowledge, been adopted on a small scale in Denmark as early as 1855. It was due to a distinguished statesman named Andreae, who was also a distinguished mathematician; and, with some modifications and restrictions, it still continues.[5]

Two other methods have been proposed for giving representation to minorities which, though much less perfect than the plan of Mr. Hare, diverge much less from the current notions about representation. One is the system of three-cornered constituencies—that is, of constituencies returning three members, in which every elector has only a right to two votes, and in which a minority exceeding a third could, in consequence, secure one representative. This system was proposed by Lord John Russell in 1854, but was not received with favour. In 1867 the House of Lords, on the motion of Lord Cairns, introduced it into the Reform Bill, and it became law, but without any wide redistribution of seats. If the three-cornered system had been made general, it would probably have been readily accepted, and soon been looked upon as natural; but, being applied only to thirteen constituencies, it was an exceptional thing, and not popular. Birmingham and one or two other great towns resented the addition of a third member, whose vote in a party division might counteract that of one of the two representatives they already possessed, and therefore diminish instead of increase their political strength. In cases where the majority equalled or slightly exceeded two-thirds much difficult and expensive organisation was required to enable it to retain the three seats to which, according to its numbers, it was entitled. Bright, who himself sat for Birmingham,

---

[5] See *La Représentation Proportionnelle*, published by the Société pour l'Étude de la Représentation Proportionnelle (Paris, 1888), pp. 338–66.

opposed the system with great bitterness and persistence, and the Radical party were generally hostile to it. It was accordingly abolished in the Reform Bill of 1885, which broke up the great majority of the constituencies into smaller divisions, each retaining one member. It was contended that such subdivision improved the chances of a minority; but the case of Ireland abundantly shows how little reliance can be placed on this security,[6] and the adoption of such seats greatly added to the difficulty of establishing any general system of minority representation.

'Nothing is more remarkable,' writes Mr. Hare in speaking of this episode, 'than that the attempts to retrace the steps that have been made towards rendering the representative bodies comprehensive, and not exclusive in their character, should all emanate from members of the Liberal party, which is understood to insist upon equality in political freedom, without partiality in favour of person or place. The abolition of the restricted vote was put forward as a pretended vindication of electoral rights, while, by delivering the electoral power of every community over to the majority, it would practically disfranchise a third, or even more, of the electors.'[7]

The other system is that of the cumulative vote, by which, in a constituency returning three or more members, each elector has a right to as many votes as there are members, and may either distribute them, or concentrate them, if he pleases, on a single candidate. This method is more likely to be popular than the limited vote, as it gives a privilege instead of imposing a restriction, and it would undoubtedly be effectual in enabling any considerable minority to return a member. It was strongly, but unsuccessfully, advocated by Mr. Lowe in 1867, and it was introduced into the school board elections in 1870. Various inequalities and anomalies have been pointed out in its working, but, on the whole, it is undoubtedly efficacious

---

[6] See on this subject an admirable pamphlet by Mr. Aubrey de Vere, called *Ireland and Proportional Representation* (1885).

[7] Hare *On the Election of Representatives*, 4th ed. p. 14.

in giving minorities a real representation. It is manifest, however, that it can only be really useful in constituencies represented by more than two members.

These various methods are attempts to attain an end which was, on the whole, roughly though unsystematically attained under the older methods of representation. Various other devices have been proposed, which, however, have at present no chance of being accepted. Perhaps the only exception is a low educational qualification, obliging the electors at least to be able to read and write. Such a qualification was much recommended by Mill, and it has passed into several democratic constitutions. It was first introduced in the French Revolutionary Constitution of 1795, but it was not reproduced in any of the subsequent French constitutions. It exists, however, in Portugal, Italy, and Roumania, and in some of the republics of South America.[8] The most recent and most extensive instance of the adoption of plural voting has been in the new Constitution of Belgium. The electors are divided into three classes. One vote is given to all male persons above twenty-five years of age who have resided for a year in one constituency; an additional vote is given to married men and widowers, of not less than thirty-five years, with families, paying a personal tax of five francs to the State on the buildings they inhabit, and also to the owners of property of a certain amount; while a third and smaller class, formed out of men who have received a higher education, filled a public function, or belonged to a learned profession, are entitled to three votes. In this very democratic constitution a form of compulsion is introduced which does not, I believe, exist in any other contemporary constitution. All voters who have not obtained a special exemption from a judge are compelled to vote, and are liable to a fine if they abstain.

It is too soon to form a conclusive opinion on either the value or the permanence of the Belgian system of plural voting, incorporated in an extremely democratic constitution. It

---

[8] *Revue de Droit International*, xxiv. 97.

is especially interesting to English observers, as being an attempt to carry out in some measure one of the favourite ideas of Mill.

Mill was not insensible to the danger and injustice of dissociating the power of voting taxes from the necessity of paying them, and to the fact that unqualified universal suffrage leads plainly and rapidly to this form of robbery. Universal suffrage he valued in the highest degree as a system of education, and he was quite prepared, for educational purposes, to give the most incompetent classes in the community an enormous power of determining the vital interests of the Empire, regulating the industry, and disposing of the property of their neighbours. He imagined that he could mitigate or avert the danger by two expedients. One was to extend direct taxation to the very lowest class, imposing a small annual tax in the form of capitation on every grown person in the community. If this direct tax could be made to rise or fall with the gross expenditure of the country, he believed that every elector would feel himself directly interested in wise and economical administration. Paupers and bankrupts, and those who had not paid their taxes, were to be excluded from the suffrage. Is it a rash thing to say that the very first measure of a Radical Chancellor of the Exchequer who desired to win a doubtful election under the system of universal suffrage would be to abolish this capitation tax?

The other expedient was a very great extension of plural voting. Every man and every woman, according to Mill, should have a vote, but in order to correct the great dangers of class legislation and a too low standard of political intelligence, large classes should be strengthened by a plurality of votes. Employers of labour, foremen, labourers in the more skilled trades, bankers, merchants, and manufacturers, might all be given two or more votes. Similar or greater advantages might be given to the members of the liberal professions, to graduates of universities, to those who had passed through different kinds of open examination. The old system, according to which those who possessed property in different constituencies had a vote in each, should be preserved, although it was an imperfect one; but it should be considerably extended. 'In any future Reform Bill which lowers greatly the pecuniary conditions of the suffrage it might be a wise provision to allow all graduates of universities, all persons who had passed creditably through the higher schools, all members of the liberal professions, and perhaps some others, to be registered specifically in these characters, and to give their votes as such in any constituency in which they choose to register, retaining, in addition, their votes as simple citizens in the localities in which they reside.'[9]

It is sufficiently obvious how utterly opposed all these views are to the predominating tendency of modern English Radicalism, with its watchword of one man, one vote, and its steadily successful efforts to place the property and the liberty of the Empire under the complete dominion of the poorest and the most ignorant. In the first cast of the Reform Bill of 1867 Disraeli introduced a number of qualifications very much in the spirit of those which had been advocated by Mill. While enormously extending and lowering the suffrage connected with the ownership and occupation of property, he proposed to confer a number of votes of another description. There was an educational franchise, to be conferred on all graduates of universities, on all male persons who had passed at any senior middle-class examination of any university of the United Kingdom, on all priests and deacons of the Established Church, all ministers of other denominations, all barristers, pleaders, attorneys, medical men, or certificated schoolmasters. There was a pecuniary franchise, to belong to every man who, during the preceding two years, had a balance of not less than fifty pounds in a savings bank, or in the Bank of England, or in any parliamentary stock, or who paid twenty shillings for assessed taxes or income-tax; and there was a clause enabling voters in a borough to be registered on two different qualifications, and to exercise in consequence a dual vote.

---

[9] Mill *On Representative Government*, pp. 165–71.

It was intended by these franchises to qualify the ascendency of mere numbers by strengthening in the electorate intelligence, education, property, and frugality. All such attempts, however, were opposed by Mr. Gladstone and his followers, and the new franchises were very lightly abandoned by their author. They were usually condemned and ridiculed as 'fancy franchises'—a curious instance of the manner in which, in English politics, a nickname that is neither very witty nor very descriptive can be made to take the place of serious argument.

No such efforts to improve the electorate are now likely to obtain even a respectful hearing. Whether, however, they have passed for ever is another question. When the present evils infecting our parliamentary system have grown still graver; when a democratic house, more and more broken up into small groups, more and more governed by sectional or interested motives, shall have shown itself evidently incompetent to conduct the business of the country with honour, efficiency, and safety; when public opinion has learnt more fully the enormous danger to national prosperity, as well as individual happiness, of dissociating power from property, and giving the many an unlimited right of confiscating by taxation the possessions of the few, some great reconstruction of government is sure to be demanded. Fifty, or even twenty-five years hence, the current of political opinion in England may be as different from that of our own day as contemporary political tendencies are different from those in the generation of our fathers. Expedients and arguments that are now dismissed with contempt may then revive, and play no small part in the politics of the future.

One great possible constitutional change, very new to English public opinion, has risen with remarkable rapidity into prominence in the last few years, and is perhaps destined hereafter to have an extensive influence. I mean the Swiss Referendum. Rousseau, in his 'Contrat Social,' maintained that all laws ought to be voted by universal male suffrage, and that no law which had not received this direct sanction was binding. It is probable that in this, as in some other parts of his political philosophy, he was much influenced by his Swiss experience, for the old form of government known as the Landsgemeinde, according to which all the adult males assemble twice a year to vote their laws and elect their functionaries by universal suffrage, existed widely in his time, both in the town governments and the canton governments of Switzerland. It is a form of government which has played a great part in the early history of mankind, but it is manifestly unsuited to wide areas and large populations. It was abolished in our own century in Zug and in Schwytz, but it may still be seen in Uri, Unterwalden, Appenzell, and Glarus. The French Convention, in 1793, attempted to carry out the doctrine of Rousseau by introducing into its Constitution a provision that, in case a certain proportion of the electors desired it, there should be a popular vote upon every law; and although this Constitution was never put into force, the same doctrine was, as we have seen, in some degree carried out in the shape of plebiscites directly sanctioning several changes of government.

In Switzerland it has taken the form of the Referendum, which appears to have grown out of the Landsgemeinde. It became a regular and permanent element in Swiss government after the French Revolution of 1830, and in recent times it has been largely extended. The Referendum is not intended as a substitute for representative government, but as a final court of appeal, giving the electors, by a direct vote, the right of veto or ratification upon measures which had already passed the legislative chambers. For many years it was confined to the separate cantons, and it took different forms. Sometimes it was restricted to new taxes and changes in the constitutions of the cantons. In several cantons it is chiefly optional, taking place only when a specified number of electors demand it. In other cantons it is compulsory, the constitution providing that all laws passed by the representative body must be submitted to a direct popular vote in order to acquire validity. In all the cantons there is now a compulsory Referendum on every proposition to alter the cantonal constitution, and in many cantons there is a compulsory Referendum on every expenditure of public money, beyond a certain specified sum, varying according to their extent and population. The Catholic canton of Fribourg is now the only one which confines it to questions of constitutional revision.

The Referendum was introduced into the Federal system by the Constitution of 1848, but it was only made applicable to the single case of constitutional revision. Every change in the Constitution made by the Federal Legislature required the ratification of a direct popular vote. In the Constitution of 1874, however, the province of the Referendum was largely extended, for it was provided that all Federal laws, as well as general Federal decrees which were not of an urgent nature, should be submitted to the popular vote on the demand of 30,000 qualified voters or of eight cantons. A remarkable provision was also inserted in this Constitution giving the people some right of initiative, as well as ratification, in matters of constitutional revision. If 50,000 voters demanded it, a popular vote must be taken on the question whether the Constitution should be revised; and, if it was in favour of revision, the two Federal Councils were renewed for the purpose of undertaking the task. A revision of the Constitution which was carried in 1891 went much further. It entitled 50,000 voters to obtain a popular vote which might decree directly the introduction of a new article, or the abolition or modification of an old article of the Helvetic Constitution.[10] In all these ways the nation directly intervenes to dictate or to make its own laws, and the power of the representative bodies is to that extent abridged. A corresponding tendency to give the popular vote an initiative in legislation has appeared in some of the separate cantons.

Laveleye has collected an interesting series of examples of the manner in which this power has been used.[11] On the whole the popular vote, when it extends over the entire Con-

---

[10] Dareste, *Constitutions Modernes*, ii. 658.

[11] Laveleye, *Le Gouvernement dans la Démocratie*, ii. 146–70. See, too, the chapter on the Swiss Referendum in Oberholtzer's *Referendum in America*, pp. 10–14.

federation, more frequently negatives than ratifies the measures submitted to it. The tendencies which it most strongly shows are a dislike to large expenditure, a dislike to centralisation, a dislike to violent innovation. The Referendum is more frequently employed in cantonal than in Federal legislation. Between the enactment of the Constitution of 1874 and July 1891 about 130 laws passed through the Federal Chamber. Of these, sixteen only, exclusive of some constitutional modifications, were submitted to the popular vote, and, of these sixteen, eleven were rejected. The chief charges that have been brought against the popular vote are, that it refuses adequate stipends to public servants, and is very niggardly in providing for works of public utility, especially when they relate to interests that are not easily appreciated by agricultural peasants. On the whole, it has been decidedly conservative, though there have been a few exceptions. It sanctioned the severely graduated taxation which exists in some of the Swiss cantons; but in Neuchatel the system of graduated taxation, having been accepted by the Grand Council, was rejected by the Referendum, and the same thing has happened still more recently in the canton of Berne.[12] One remarkable vote, which was taken in 1879, restored to the different cantons the power of introducing capital punishment into their criminal codes, which had been taken from them by the Constitution of 1874. A somewhat curious recent vote has prohibited the Jews from killing their cattle in the way prescribed by their law. In this case the anti-Semitic feeling and a feeling of what was supposed to be humanity to animals probably blended, though in very unequal proportions.

The popularity of the Referendum in Switzerland is clearly shown by the rapidity with which its scope has been ex-

---

[12] See the *Report on Graduated Taxation in Switzerland* presented to the Foreign Office in 1892, p. 15. Mr. Buchanan, the author of this Report, mentions the remarkable fact that in this canton 'the Radical party was returned to power by a very large majority on the same day that witnessed the rejection of the most important measure which it had passed in the previous session of the Cantonal Grand Council.' This shows how clearly the Referendum vote can be kept separate from party questions.

tended. There is a very remarkable movement of the same kind in America, where in State politics the tendency runs strongly in favour of a substitution of direct popular legislation for legislation through the medium of representative bodies. Every change in a State Government is now made by summoning a convention for that express purpose, and the revision determined on by this convention must be sanctioned by a direct popular vote. In this respect, therefore, the State constitutions of the United States rest on exactly the same basis as the cantonal governments of Switzerland, and the same system has been widely extended to various forms of municipal and county government. In many State constitutions it is prescribed that the State capital can only be changed by a popular vote, and in one or two constitutions the same restriction applies to transfers of great local institutions. In a large number of cases, as I have already noticed, the extreme corruption of the State legislatures has led the people to introduce clauses into their State constitutions limiting strictly the power of the legislatures to impose taxes or incur debts, and obliging them to submit all expenditure beyond the assigned limits to a direct popular vote.

This is, however, only a small part of the legislation which is now carried by direct popular vote. Conventions summoned for the purpose of amending the State constitutions have taken the largest possible view of their powers: they have laid down rules relating not only to organic constitutional change, but to every important subject of legislation, withdrawing those subjects wholly, or partially, from the competency of the State legislatures, and every enactment made by these conventions requires for its validity the ratification of a direct popular vote.

This movement is but little known in England, and although I have already referred to it in another connection, it is sufficiently important to warrant some repetition. In England, a large class of politicians are now preaching a multiplication of small democratic local legislatures as the true efflorescence and perfection of democracy. In America, no

fact is more clearly established than that such legislatures almost invariably fall into the hands of caucuses, wirepullers,
and professional politicians, and become centres of jobbing
and corruption. One of the main tasks of the best American
politicians has, of late years, been to withdraw gradually the
greater part of legislation from the influence of these bodies,
and to entrust it to conventions specially elected for a special
purpose, and empowered to pass particular laws, subject to
direct ratification by a popular vote. I can here hardly do better
than to quote at some length the American writer who has
recently treated this subject with the fullest knowledge and
detail. 'It is very usual,' writes Mr. Oberholtzer, 'for conventions in late years, at the time of submitting constitutions, to
submit special articles or sections of articles for separate consideration by the people. These pertain to subjects upon
which there is likely to be much public feeling. . . . Subjects
so treated by the conventions have been slavery, woman's
suffrage, the prohibition of the liquor traffic, the location of
state capitals, &c. . . . There has been within recent times a
radical change in our ideas in regard to State constitutions,
and our conceptions as to what matters are suitable for a place
in these instruments. At the beginning they were, as constitutions are supposed to be, statements of the fundamentals
of government. . . . Now, however, very different constitutional standards obtain, and in the States of every section of
the country the same tendency is visible, until we have to-
day come to a point when our State constitutions are nothing
short of codes of laws giving instruction to the Legislature
and the other agents of Government on nearly every subject
of general public concern, and often stating the methods
which shall be used in legislating, if not, indeed, actually
legislating, on local questions. . . . The constitutions have
been the repositories for much of the legislation which before
was left to be enacted by the legislatures.'[13]

---

[13] Oberholtzer, *The Referendum in America*, pp. 38–44 (Philadelphia, 1893).

This writer then proceeds to show how the State constitutions as amended by the conventions now make pamphlets of from fifty to seventy-five pages long, including almost all matters of education, taxation, expenditure, and local administration; the organisation and regulation of the railroads, of the militia, of the trade in drink, of the penal and reformatory institutions; clauses prohibiting lotteries, prize fights, or duels, establishing a legal day's work, even defining the relations of husbands and wives, and debtors and creditors.

All these subjects are withdrawn from the province of the State legislature, and are dealt with by conventions ratified by a direct popular vote. 'Indeed,' continues our writer, 'there are now few matters which are subjects for legislation at all that, according to the new conception of a constitution, may not be dealt with by the conventions. It is only after considering the nature of this new conception that the Referendum as exemplified in America is seen to have its closest likeness to the institution as it exists to-day in Switzerland.'

'Side by side with this movement to make codes of laws of our constitutions, and to restrict in many ways the powers of the State legislatures, has grown up a movement tending directly to the almost entire abolition of these bodies. In nearly all the States, by the development of the last few years, the conventions have substituted biennial for annual legislative sessions. These sessions, now being held only half as often, are further limited so that they may not extend over more than a certain number of days. . . . Those States which still retain the system of annual sessions—as, for instance, New York and New Jersey—constantly find cause for dissatisfaction, and the feeling of distrust for these bodies is taking deeper hold of the people every year. The feeling, indeed, has reached a conviction nearly everywhere that the powers of the legislatures should be still further curtailed, and in but one State—Georgia—has there been shown any inclination to return to original principles.'

'With the change in the character of the constitutions, has of necessity come a change in the character of constitutional amendments. Statute legislation, of late years, has been more and more disguised in these amendments, and sent to the Referendum. No better evidence of this is to be found than in the frequency of amendments to prohibit the manufacture and traffic in intoxicating liquors, a subject as far removed as any well could be from the original idea as to a proper matter for treatment in a constitution. Of these elections, in nine years there were nineteen, beginning with Kansas, Nov. 2, 1880, and closing with Connecticut, Oct. 7, 1889.'[14]

These passages are, I think, very significant, as showing certain tendencies of democracy which are as yet little recognised in England, but which are probably destined to contribute largely towards moulding the governments of the future. I must refer my reader to the curious work which I am citing for detailed evidence of the many instances in which, in different States of the American Republic, local measures about taxation and debt, changes in the State territorial boundaries, jurisdiction, or municipal arrangements, or in the suffrage, the system of representation, or the liquor laws, have been settled by a direct popular vote of the same character as the Swiss Referendum. This system appears to have almost wholly arisen in America since 1850,[15] and it has grown rapidly in public favour. It has been the subject of many, and sometimes conflicting, decisions in the law courts, but in the great majority of States it has obtained a firm legal footing, and it is transforming the whole character of State government.

It is not surprising that the Referendum is now beginning seriously to occupy those political thinkers who can look beyond the contests of the hour and the immediate interests of a party. Laveleye has devoted much attention to it,[16] and it

---

[14] Oberholtzer, *The Referendum in America*, pp. 45–46. See, too, the chapter of Mr. Bryce on Direct Legislation by the People, *The American Commonwealth*, ii. 67–82.

[15] Oberholtzer, p. 105.

[16] Laveleye, *Le Gouvernement dans la Démocratie*, ii. 169–70.

was much discussed in Belgium during the recent democratic revision of the Constitution. It was proposed, as a safeguard against the dangers to be feared from that great and sudden change, that the King should possess the power of submitting measures which had passed through the Chambers to a direct popular vote in the form of a Referendum. The proposal was (as I think, unfortunately) defeated, but there have been several minor indications of its growing popularity. The Referendum has, in more than one case, been employed in Belgium in questions of municipal government. The vote which is required in England for the establishment in any borough of a free library supported by the rates, and the system of local option so strenuously advocated by many temperance reformers, and which a growing party desires to apply to the hours of labour in different trades, belong to this category. The Referendum now occupies a prominent place in the programme of the Labour party in Australia, and in most of the Socialist programmes in Europe, while its incorporation in the British Constitution has of late years found several advocates of a very different order of opinion, and has been supported by the brilliant pen and by the great authority of Professor Dicey.[17]

It is a question which is indeed well worthy of serious consideration. If such a system could be made to work, it would almost certainly do something to correct, by an eminently democratic method, democratic evils that are threatening grave calamities to the Empire. It would make it possible to introduce into England that distinction between constitutional questions and ordinary legislation which in America and in nearly all continental countries not only exists, but is maintained and fortified by the most stringent provisions. In the days when the balance of power between the different ele-

---

[17] See an admirable article by Professor Dicey on this subject in the *Contemporary Review*, April 1890. The subject has been also ably discussed in the *National Review* for February, March, and April 1894.

ments in the Constitution was still unimpaired, when the strongly organised conservative influences of class and property opposed an insuperable barrier to revolutionary change, such a distinction might be safely dispensed with. In the conditions of the present day, no serious thinker can fail to perceive the enormous danger of placing the essential elements of the Constitution at the mercy of a simple majority of a single Parliament, a majority, perhaps, composed of heterogeneous and discordant fractions, combined for a party purpose, and not larger than is required to pass a Bill for regulating music-halls or protecting sea-birds' eggs.

The Referendum, in its first and most universal application, is intended to prevent this evil by making it impossible to carry constitutional changes without the direct and deliberate assent of the people. It would also have the immense advantage of disentangling issues, separating one great question from the many minor questions with which it may be mixed. Confused or blended issues are among the gravest political dangers of our time. Revolutionary and predatory measures are much less likely to be carried on their merits than because their proposers have obtained a majority by joining with them a sufficient number of other measures appealing to different sections of the electorate. With the multiplication of groups this evil is constantly increasing, and it is in this direction that many dangerous politicians are mainly working. In the House of Commons, a measure may often be carried which would never have had a chance of success if the members could vote on their own conviction of its merits; if they could vote by ballot; if they could vote as they thought best, without destroying a ministry, or endangering some wholly different measure which stood lower down in the ministerial programme. Motives of the same kind, absolutely distinct from an approval or disapproval of one great measure, govern the votes of the electorate, and largely determine the course of parties and legislation. It would be a great gain to English politics if a capital question could be decided by the electorate on its own merits, on a direct and simple issue. If the nation is moving towards revolution, it should at least do so with its eyes open, and with a clear and deliberate intention.

It would probably be found that such a vote would prove the most powerful bulwark against violent and dishonest change. It would bring into action the opinion of the great silent classes of the community, and reduce to their true proportions many movements to which party combinations or noisy agitations have given a wholly factitious prominence. It might restore in another form something of the old balanced Constitution, which has now so nearly passed away. The transcendently important function of the House of Lords in restraining the despotism of the Commons, and referring great changes to the adjudication of the people, is now rarely exercised and violently assailed. If, when the House of Lords differed on a question of grave national importance from the Commons, it possessed, or, if possessing, it would exercise, the power of submitting that question to the direct vote of the electorate, the most skilful demagogue would find it difficult to persuade the people that it was trampling on their rights. If the power of insisting on a Referendum was placed, as in Switzerland, in the hands of a large body of voters, it would still form a counterpoise and a check of the most important kind.

It is contended for it that it would not only extricate one capital measure from the crowd of minor measures with which it is associated, but would also lift it above the dominion of party, and thus greatly increase the probability of its representing the genuine wishes of the electorate. It would enable the nation to reject a measure which it dislikes, without destroying a ministry of which it approves. The vote would not be on the general policy of the Government. It would be exclusively on the merits of a single measure, and it would leave the ministerial majority in the House of Commons unchanged. Few persons will doubt that a measure brought in this manner before the electorate would be voted on with a much fuller consideration and a much more serious sense of responsibility than if it came before them mixed up with a crowd of other measures, and inseparably connected with a party issue. At a general election, the great majority of votes are given for a party or a statesman, and the real question is, which side should rule the country. By the Referendum the electorate can give its deliberate opinion, not upon men, but upon measures, and can reject a measure without placing the Government of the country into other hands.

It is often said that there are large classes of questions on which such a popular opinion could be of little worth. To this I have no difficulty in subscribing. It is very doubtful whether a really popular vote would have ratified the Toleration Act in the seventeenth century, or the abolition of the capital punishment of witches in the eighteenth century, or Catholic Emancipation in the nineteenth century, or a crowd of other measures that might be enumerated. It is now, however, too late to urge such an argument. Democracy has been crowned king. The voice of the multitude is the ultimate court of appeal, and the right of independent judgment, which was once claimed for the members of Parliament, is now almost wholly discarded. If the electorate is to judge policies, it is surely less likely to err if it judges them on a clear and distinct issue. In such a case it is most likely to act independently, and not at the dictation of party wirepullers. It is to be remembered, too, that the Referendum is not intended as a substitute for representative government. All the advantages of parliamentary debate would still remain. Policies would not be thrown before the electorate in a crude, undigested, undeveloped state. All measures would still pass through Parliament, and the great majority would be finally decided by Parliament. It would only be in a few cases, after a measure had been thoroughly discussed in all its bearings, after the two Houses had given their judgment, that the nation would be called to adjudicate. The Referendum would be an appeal from a party majority, probably made up of discordant groups, to the genuine opinion of the country. It would be an appeal on a question which had been thoroughly examined, and on which the nation had every means of arriving at a conclusion. It would be a clear and decisive verdict on a matter on which the two branches of the Legislature had differed.

It is argued against the Referendum that many of the differences between the two Houses are differences not of principle, but of detail. A Bill is before Parliament on the general policy of which both parties and both Houses are agreed, but one clause or amendment, dealing with a subsidiary part, produces an irreconcilable difference. The popular vote, it has been said, would be an instrument wholly unfit to discriminate between the portion of a Bill that should be preserved and the part that should be rejected. I do not, however, think that there is much weight in this argument. After all discussions of details, a Bill, if it is to become law, must now pass through its third reading, and be accepted or rejected as a whole by a single vote. All that is proposed by the Referendum is, that there should be one more step before its enactment. If the House of Lords objected essentially to some Bill which the House of Commons had more than once adopted, it might pass that Bill with the addition of a clause providing that it should not become law until it had been ratified by a direct popular vote. If the two Houses, agreeing upon the general merits of the Bill, differed irreconcilably upon one clause, instead of the Bill being wholly lost the Houses might agree that it should be passed in one or other form with a similar addition. By this simple method the Referendum might be put in action, and as the appeal would be to the existing electorate, no insuperable difficulties of machinery would be likely to arise.

Another objection is, that the Referendum would have the effect of lowering the authority of the House of Commons, which is now, in effect, the supreme legislative authority in the Empire. This is undoubtedly true, and, in my own judgment, it would be one of its great merits. The old saying of Burghley, that 'England never can be ruined but by her Parliament,' was never more true than at the present time, and the uncontrolled, unbalanced authority of a single representative body constituted like our own seems to me one of the gravest dangers to the Empire. In our age we must mainly look to democracy for a remedy. According to the theories which now prevail, the House of Commons has absolutely no right as against its electors, and it is to the electors that the Referendum would transfer, in a far more efficient manner than at present, the supreme authority in legislation. If the House of Commons moves during the next quarter of a century as rapidly on the path of discredit as it has done during the quarter of a century that has passed, it is not likely that many voices would be found to echo this objection.

The foregoing arguments seem to me, at least, to show that the Referendum is not a question to be lightly dismissed. It might furnish a remedy for great and growing evils which is very difficult to cure, and it would do so in a way which is in full accordance with the democratic spirit of the time. Further than this I should not venture to go. To carry out successfully a scheme so widely diverging from old English modes of thought, to foresee and guard against the possible evils connected with it, would need the experience and discussion of many minds. It is obviously much easier to apply such a system to a small and sparse population like that of Switzerland, than to a dense population like our own; and the ascendency of party has so long been supreme in England that it is not likely that the Referendum could withdraw questions wholly from its empire. It is probable that the vote would often be taken under the glamour of a great name; its result would be looked upon as a party triumph, and for some time it would not be easy to persuade the British public that a ministry should remain in power when its capital measure had been defeated. The experience, however, of Switzerland and America shows that, when the Referendum takes root in a country, it takes political questions, to an immense degree, out of the hands of wirepullers, and makes it possible to decide them mainly, though perhaps not wholly, on their merits, without producing a change of government or of party predominance.

Difficulties arising from both Houses of Parliament would,

no doubt, have to be encountered. The House of Commons would naturally dislike to surrender any part of its power, even into the hands of its masters. The House of Lords, as at present constituted, is viewed with such suspicion by large classes that they would object to a measure which might increase its power, even though that increase was wholly derived from association with the most extreme form of democracy. The great and pressing question of the reform of the Upper House would probably have to precede the adoption of the Referendum.

It seems to me also clear, that in a country like England the Referendum could never become an habitual agent in legislation. Perpetual popular votes would be an intolerable nuisance. To foreign politics the Referendum would be very inapplicable, and in home politics it ought only to be employed on rare and grave occasions. It should be restricted to constitutional questions altering the disposition of power in the State, with, perhaps, the addition of important questions on which, during more than one Parliament, the two Houses of the Legislature had differed.

Within these limits it appears to me full of promise, and it is to be hoped that political thinkers may keep their minds open upon the subject. For some considerable time to come all questions are likely to be submitted to the adjudication of the greatest number, and statesmen must accept the fact, and endeavour to make it as little dangerous as possible. It has been the opinion of some of the ablest and most successful politicians of our time that, by adopting a very low suffrage, it would be possible to penetrate below the region where crotchets and experiments and crude Utopias and habitual restlessness prevail, and to reach the strong, settled habits, the enduring tendencies, the deep conservative instincts of the nation. Such an idea was evidently present in the minds both of Louis Napoleon and of Lord Beaconsfield, and it probably largely influenced the great statesman who based the German Constitution on universal suffrage. How far it may be true I do not here discuss. It is probable that the recent turn in

English politics has added considerably to the number of those who believe in it. It seems to me, at least, certain that popular opinion is likely to be least dangerous if it is an unsophisticated opinion on a direct issue, as far as possible uninfluenced by agitators and professional politicians. It is very possible that its tendencies might be towards extreme Conservatism; but the pendulum has moved so long and so violently in the opposite direction that a period of pause, or even of reaction, might not appear an evil.

The welcome the reader will extend to such considerations will depend largely upon his view of the existing state of the Constitution. If he believes that parliamentary government in its present form is firmly established, working well, and likely to endure, he will naturally object to any change which would alter fundamentally the centre of power. If he believes that some of the most essential springs of the British Constitution have been fatally weakened, and that our system of government is undergoing a perilous process of disintegration, transformation, and deterioration, he will be inclined to look with more favour on possible remedies, even though they be very remote from the national habits and traditions.

Another method by which the evils of a decaying parliamentary system may be in some degree mitigated is by the extension of the powers of committees. The only possible manner in which a large assembly of men can directly and efficiently discharge much business is by the strict organisation of parties, which throws the whole initiation and direction into a few competent hands. But under the best organisation a large assembly is unfit for the investigation of details, and when the discipline of Parliament and of parties gives way its incapacity becomes very manifest. In the United States, as is well known, congressional, or, as we should say, parliamentary, legislation is almost entirely in the hands of committees. Fifty or sixty committees of the House of Representatives, and a somewhat smaller number of committees of the Senate, are appointed at the beginning of every Congress. Each of them usually consists of about eleven members; they sit for two years, and they are entrusted with unlimited powers of curtailing, altering, or extending the Bills that come before them. They do not receive those Bills after discussion in the Chambers. Both the first and second readings are granted as a matter of course, and it is in the committees that Bills receive their full investigation and definite shape. The deliberations there are usually secret, and nearly always unreported. The great majority of the Bills are stifled in committee, either by long postponement or by unfavourable reports. Those which are favourably reported have to receive the sanction of Congress; but they are usually only discussed in the shortest and most cursory manner, and in the vast majority of cases the task of framing legislation lies in reality, not with the Chambers, but with these small delegated bodies. Mr. Bryce has described the process in detail, and he observes that 'the House has become not so much a legislative assembly as a huge panel from which committees are selected.'[18]

The system is extremely unlike our own. The ministers do not sit in Congress, and therefore cannot guide it; and they

---

[18] Since Mr. Bryce's book appeared, an American politician, discussing the decline of oratory in the United States, says: 'A change in the method of conducting business in legislative bodies, which has become general, must also be taken into account. Legislation by committees, instead of the whole body, is the prevailing method of the present day. Almost the entire consideration and shaping of the most important measures which now come before legislative bodies is done in the committee-room before they are reported for action. Little more than ratification of committee work remains after a measure leaves the committee-room. There are exceptions, but this is the rule. Consequently, the opportunity for debate is greatly abridged, and for extended oration almost entirely cut off. . . . Add to this modern method that other invention of recent years, which takes up legislation thus prepared in the committee-room, and puts it in charge of another committee of three, to determine beforehand when it shall be considered by the bodies who are to pass upon it, for how long a time, and in what shape, and by what number of supporters and opponents, to be selected as prize combatants are selected by the opposing sides in a ring, and the hour by the clock when such considerations shall cease—does any one conceive it possible that anything deserving the name of oratory or eloquence can be the outcome of such a contest?' (The Hon. Henry Dawes in *The Forum*, October 1894, p. 153).

do not depend for their tenure of office upon its approval. The Speaker, who in England represents the most absolute impartiality, is, in America, the most powerful of party leaders, for he nominates the members of the committees, by whom legislation is virtually made. As Mr. Bryce observes, Congress loses its unity and much of its importance, and parliamentary oratory dwindles into insignificance. The public, who know that the real business of legislation is transacted in small secret bodies, come to look on Congress and its proceedings with great indifference; and legislation being mainly the product of a number of small and independent bodies, is much wanting in cohesion and harmony.

If these were the only consequences, they might readily be accepted. Some of them, indeed, would appear to many of us positive advantages. Unfortunately, the corruption, log-rolling, and intrigue that so deeply infect American politics appear to be abundantly displayed in the work of the committees.[19]

The system, however, is essentially different from parliamentary government. It places the task of framing laws in the hands of small groups of shrewd business men, who work without any of the disturbing influences of publicity; and it diminishes, though it certainly does not destroy, the injurious influence on public business of anarchy and deterioration in Congress. In France a different system prevails, but most legislation is practically done in 'bureaux,' or subdivisions of the Chamber, which are appointed for the consideration of particular subjects. In England the action of the whole House is much greater; but the committee system appears to be the healthiest part of our present parliamentary system, and it has been considerably extended by the adoption of standing committees in the House of Commons in 1883, and in the House of Lords in 1891.[20] The committees are of several kinds. There are the select committees, which are appointed by either House for the purpose of investigating complex subjects, and

---

[19] Bryce's *American Commonwealth*, i. 204–18
[20] May's *Parliamentary Procedure* (Palgrave's edition).

which have the power of calling witnesses before them. The new Standing Committees of Law and Trade, commonly called grand committees, consist of from sixty to eighty members, representing different sections of the House, and they generally include Cabinet ministers. Various Bills are referred to them from the committee stage by a process of devolution, and their divisions on disputed points are duly recorded. Besides these there is the Committee of Public Accounts, which, with the assistance of the departmental officials, exercises a close and useful supervision over the details of finance.[21]

It is probable that the power, and perhaps the number, of the committees will be increased, and that in this manner the much-impaired business capacity of the House may be considerably recruited. The process of devolution is likely, in some manner and under some conditions and restrictions, to be extended, either by special parliamentary committees, or in other ways, to bodies representing different portions of the Empire. The expense of carrying to London great masses of non-political private business which might be as efficiently and much more cheaply settled at home, is a real and serious grievance; and the obstruction to parliamentary business caused by the introduction of many matters that ought never to be brought before the supreme legislature of an empire, is now keenly felt. Sooner or later some change in this system must be effected, and a much larger proportion of Irish and Scotch business than at present is likely to be entrusted to bodies specially representing those countries. I do not propose to enter at large into this question. The two limitations that should be observed are, I think, sufficiently obvious. The one is, that no body should be set up which would be likely to prove in times of danger a source of weakness or division to the Empire. The other is, that Parliament should never so far abdicate its supreme duty of doing justice to all sections of the people as to set up any body that is likely to oppress or plunder

---

[21] There is an excellent account of the working of these committees in Sir R. Temple's *Life in Parliament*.

any class. If these two conditions are fully and efficiently secured, local government may be wisely and largely extended.
There is, however, no greater folly in politics than to set up a
political body without considering the hands into which it is
likely to fall, or the spirit in which it is likely to be worked.

One change in the internal regulation of Parliament has also
been powerfully urged for the purpose of correcting the instability and intrigue which a multiplication of independent
parliamentary groups is certain to produce. It is, that a government should not consider itself bound either to resign or
dissolve on account of an adverse division due, perhaps, to a
chance or factious combination of irreconcilable minorities,
but should retain office until a formal vote of want of confidence indicates clearly the desire of the House of Commons.
It does not, however, appear to me that this change would be,
on the whole, an improvement. The fact that it has never been
made in France, where the evil of instability in the government
arising from the group system in Parliament has attained its
extreme limits, shows how difficult it would be to implant it
in parliamentary institutions. A defeat in the House of Lords
does not overthrow a ministry; a defeat in the House of Commons on a particular question may be always remedied, if the
House desires it, by a vote of confidence. If the change we are
considering would mitigate the evil of parliamentary disintegration, it would, as it seems to me, aggravate the not less serious evil of the despotism of party caucuses. It continually
happens that a government, long before the natural duration
of a Parliament has expired, loses the confidence of the House
of Commons and of the country, and it is very undesirable
that, under these circumstances, it should continue in office.
It is, however, seldom likely that its majority would be destroyed by a formal vote of want of confidence. Liberals would
hesitate to vote definitely as Tories, or Tories as Liberals, and
the pressure of party organisations would override genuine
opinions. It is on side-issues or incidental questions that the
true feeling of the House is most likely to be displayed and a
bad ministry defeated.

After all due weight has been given to the possible remedies that have been considered, it still seems to me that the parliamentary system, when it rests on manhood suffrage, or something closely approaching to manhood suffrage, is extremely unlikely to be permanent. This was evidently the opinion of Tocqueville, who was strongly persuaded that the natural result of democracy was a highly concentrated, enervating, but mild despotism.[22] It is the opinion of many of the most eminent contemporary thinkers in France and Germany, and it is, I think, steadily growing in England. This does not mean that Parliaments will cease, or that a wide suffrage will be abolished. It means that Parliaments, if constructed on this type, cannot permanently remain the supreme power among the nations of the world. Sooner or later they will sink by their own vices and inefficiencies into a lower plane. They will lose the power of making and unmaking ministries, and it will be found absolutely necessary to establish some strong executive independently of their fluctuations. Very probably this executive may be established, as in America and under the French Empire, upon a broad basis of an independent suffrage. Very possibly upper chambers, constituted upon some sagacious plan, will again play a great restraining and directing part in the government of the world. Few persons who have watched the changes that have passed over our own House of Commons within the last few years will either believe or wish that in fifty years' time it can exercise the power it now does. It is only too probable that some great catastrophe or the stress of a great war may accelerate the change.

I do not speak of the modern extensions of local government in the counties or towns as diminishing the authority of democratic Parliaments. These extensions have been themselves great democratic triumphs, transferring to bodies resting on a very low suffrage powers which were either in the hands of persons nominated by the Crown, or in the hands

---

[22] *La Démocratie en Amérique*, 4me partie.

of persons whose election depended on a high property qualification, and especially on the possession of landed property.
The preceding pages will have abundantly illustrated the dangers that are to be feared from unchecked democracy in this
field. In England there is a great belief in the educational value
of this kind of government. It is true that an honest, well-
meaning local government may begin by making many mistakes, but will soon acquire the habits of good government.
On the other hand, if local government falls into the hands
of corrupt, self-seeking, dishonest men, it will promote quite
other habits, and will have very little tendency to improve.
Prolonged continuity of jobbing is not an education in which
good statesmen are likely to be formed, and few things have
done so much to demoralise American political life as the
practices that prevail in municipal government and in the
management of 'the machine.'

On the whole, it can hardly be questioned that, in spite of
great complexities and incoherences of administration, and
of many strange anomalies, England has been for many years
singularly happy in her local governments. The country
gentlemen who chiefly managed her county government, at
least discharged their task with great integrity, and with a very
extensive and minute knowledge of the districts they ruled.
They had their faults, but they were much more negative than
positive. They did few things which they ought not to have
done, but they left undone many things which they ought to
have done. There was in general no corruption; gross abuses
were very rare, and public money was, on the whole, wisely
and economically expended; but evils that might have been
remedied were often left untouched, and there was much
need of a more active reforming spirit in county administration.

Our town governments, also, since the great Municipal Act
of 1835, have been, on the whole, very successful. They have
not fallen into the hands of corrupt politicians like the greater
number of the municipal governments in America; the statesmen of the period of the first Reform Bill never failed to main-

tain a close connection between the power of taxing and the obligation of paying rates and taxes, and the strong controlling influence they gave to property in municipal government, and in the administration of the poor laws, secured an honest employment of public money. The first and most vital rule of all good government is, that those who vote taxes should contribute, to some appreciable extent, to paying them; that those who are responsible for the administration of affairs should themselves suffer from maladministration. This cardinal rule is, if possible, even more applicable to local than to imperial government. Imperial government is largely concerned with wide political issues. Local government is specially, and beyond all things, a machine for raising and employing money. In every sound company the directors must qualify for their post by being large shareholders, and the shareholders who have the largest interest have the greatest number of votes. This is the first and most obvious rule for obtaining an honest and frugal administration of money, and the success and purity of English local government have been largely due to the steadiness with which the great statesmen who followed the Reform Bill of 1832 acted upon it.

It has been reserved for the present generation of statesmen to do all that is in their power to destroy it. It has come to be regarded as a Liberal principle that it is a wrong thing to impose rating or property qualifications on those who vote rates and govern property. Thus, by the Act of 1894 all property qualifications for vestrymen and poorlaw guardians have been abolished. The rating qualification for voting is no longer necessary. The ex-officio and nominated guardians, who were always men of large experience and indisputable character, have been swept away; the obviously equitable rule that ratepayers should have votes for guardians in proportion to the amount of their contributions has been replaced by the rule of one voter, one vote. The old property qualifications for the electors of district boards have been abolished, and at the same time those boards have acquired additional powers over different kinds of property. With many politicians the evident ideal of city government is, that a great owner of town property, who necessarily pays the largest proportion of the municipal taxation, whose interests are most indissolubly associated with the prosperity of the city, and who, from his very prominence, is specially likely to be made the object of predatory attacks, should have no more voice than the humblest tenant on his estate in imposing, regulating, distributing, and applying municipal taxation.

It would be difficult to conceive a system more certain to lead to corruption and dishonesty; and other circumstances contribute to enhance the danger. If taxation were as limited in its amount, and public expenditure restricted to as few objects as in the past generation, it would signify comparatively little how its burden was distributed. But one of the most marked tendencies of our time is the enlargement of the area of State functions and the amount of State expenditure. The immense increase of local taxation, and especially local debt, that has taken place within a very few years has long excited the alarm of the most serious politicians in England. The complications of local taxation are so great that it is probably not possible to obtain complete accuracy on this subject, but there can be no question of the appalling rapidity with which the movement has advanced. In a very useful paper published under the auspices of the Cobden Club in 1882, it was calculated that the local indebtedness of England and Wales had risen between 1872 and 1880 from 80,000,000l. to 137,096,607l.[23] In 1891, it was stated in the House of Commons to be 195,400,000l.In the following year it was stated that, in the preceding fifteen years, the national debt had fallen from 768,945,757l. to 689,944,-026l., but that during the same period the municipal debt had risen from 92,820,100l. to 198,671,312l.[24] There seems no sign of this tendency having spent its force, and schemes involving

---

[23] *Local Government and Taxation of the United Kingdom* (Cobden Club), p. 480.

[24] See some facts collected by Lord Wemyss in an *Address on Modern Municipalism* (1893), p. 11.

vast increases of municipal expenditure are manifestly in the air. It is at this time that the policy of separating the payment of taxes from the voting of taxes is almost largely adopted. Unfortunately, the very tendencies that make it so dangerous increase its popularity, and therefore its attractiveness to politicians, whose great object is to win votes and tide over an election.

The enormous increase which has also taken place in the State taxation of nearly every civilised country during the last forty-five years is certainly one of the most disquieting features of our time. It is to be attributed to several different causes. The worst is that gigantic increase of national debts and of military expenditure which has taken place in Europe since the Revolution of 1848. National indebtedness has reached a point that makes the bankruptcy of many nations an almost inevitable result of any prolonged European war; and the immense burden of unproductive expenditure that is drawn from every nation for the purpose of paying the national creditors, gives revolutionary literature a great part of its plausibility, and forms one of the strongest temptations to national dishonesty. The incentive is the stronger as most national debts are largely held by foreigners, and as there is no international organisation corresponding to a bankruptcy court for coercing or punishing a defaulting nation. Of this military expenditure it will here be sufficient to say that it is far from measured by the direct taxes which are raised; and the withdrawal of a vast proportion of human effort from productive employment, and the enslavement, during the best part of their lives, of a vast proportion of the population of Europe, have probably contributed, as much as any other single cause, to the revolutionary tendencies of our time.

England need not, I think, take to herself much blame in these respects. If she has not done all that she might have done since the great French war to diminish her debt, she has at least done very much, and far more than any other European country, while her military and naval expenditure has usually been rather below than above what is needed for her

absolute security. The growth, however, of this expenditure
has been very great. Between 1835 and 1888 it is said to have
increased by no less than 173 per cent.[25] This is, however,
mainly due to the gigantic armaments on the continent, and
to the enormous increase in the cost and the constant changes
in the type of ships and guns. The burden is a terrible one;
but every one who will look facts in the face must recognise
that the existence at each given moment of an English fleet of
overwhelming power is the first and most vital condition of
the security of the nation. An island Power which cannot
even support its population with food; which depends for its
very existence on a vast commerce; which from the vastness
of its dominions and interests is constantly liable to be involved in dispute with other Powers, and which presents
peculiar temptation to an invader, could on no other condition maintain her independence, and it is a healthy sign that
English public opinion realises the transcendent importance
of the fact, and has more than once forced it upon politicians
who were neglecting it.

What may be the final result of this growing expenditure
no man can say. It is possible, and by no means improbable,
that the increasing power of guns and torpedoes may make
large ships useless in war, and may again revolutionise, and
perhaps greatly cheapen, naval war. It is possible, and perhaps probable, that the means of defence may obtain an overwhelming preponderance over the means of attack. Small and
poor nations which have taken an honourable part in the
naval history of the past find it impossible to enter into serious
competition with the costly navies of the present, and it is
probable that the richest nations will, sooner or later, find it
impossible without ruin to maintain at once the position of a
first-rate military and a first-rate naval Power. The time may
come when some great revolution of opinion or some great
internal convulsion may check or reverse the tendency of the
last half-century, and bring about a great movement for dis-

[25] Leroy-Beaulieu, *Traité des finances*, ii. 168.

armament. Till that time arrives there can be little hope of any serious diminution of this great branch of national expenditure.

I know few things more melancholy or more instructive than to compare the present state of Europe in this respect with the predictions of the Manchester school, and of the writers who, within the memory of many of us, were looked upon as the most faithful representatives of advanced thought. Some of my readers will doubtless remember the enthusiasm and admiration with which, in 1857, the first volume of Buckle's great History was welcomed. In spite of much crudeness, many shortcomings, and great dogmatism, it was a book well fitted to make an epoch on its subject. The vast horizons it opened; the sweep and boldness of its generalisations; its admirable literary qualities, and the noble enthusiasm for knowledge, for progress, and for liberty that animated it, captivated and deeply influenced a whole generation of young men. One of the most confident of Buckle's predictions was, that the military spirit had had its day; that the 'commercial spirit,' which is now 'invariably pacific,' would speedily reduce it to insignificance; that, although it might linger for a time among the most backward and semi-barbarous nations of Europe, like Russia and Turkey, all the higher talent, all the stronger ambitions, all the force of public opinion in the civilised world, would be steadily against it.

The American Civil War, the war of France and Italy against Austria, the war of Prussia and Austria against Denmark, the war of Prussia and Italy against Austria, the great Franco-German War of 1870, speedily followed, and Europe in time of peace has become a gigantic camp, supporting armies which, in their magnitude and their perfection, are unparalleled in the history of the world. It was estimated in 1888 that Germany, Austria, France, Italy, and Russia, could probably together put in the field more than sixteen millions of soldiers in time of war, and that their united armies in time of peace were not less than 2,315,000 men.[26]

---

[26] *Revue de Droit International*, xi. 99.

Two facts connected with this military development are especially significant. One is, that the trading and commercial spirit has now become one of the chief impulses towards territorial aggrandisement. 'Trade,' as it has been truly said, 'follows the flag.' With the present system of enormous manufacturing production and stringent protective barriers, it has become absolutely necessary for a great manufacturing State to secure for itself a sufficient market by incorporating new territories in its dominions. In hardly any period of her history has England annexed so much territory as in the last half-century, and although many of these annexations are due to the necessity which often compels a civilised power as a mere measure of police and self-defence to extend its frontier into the uncivilised world, much also must be attributed to commercial enterprise.

England has not been alone in this respect. Few more curious spectacles have been exhibited in the present century than that of the chief civilised nations of Europe dividing among themselves the African continent without even a shadow or pretext of right. Experience has already shown how easily these vague and ill-defined boundaries may become a new cause of European quarrels, and how often, in remote African jungles or forests, negroes armed with European guns may inflict defeats on European soldiers which will become the cause of costly and difficult wars.

Another very remarkable fact has been the growing feeling in the most civilised portions of Europe in favour of universal military service. Not many years ago it would scarcely have found a conspicuous defender, except perhaps Carlyle, outside purely military circles; but no competent judge can fail to observe the change which has of late years taken place. The system has now struck a deep root in the habits of continental life, and in the eyes of a considerable and able school it is rather a positive good than a necessary evil.

Its defenders contend, in the first place, that these gigantic armies make rather for peace than for war. The tremendous force of the weapon, the extreme difficulty of managing it; the uncertainty that more than ever hangs over the issue of a struggle; the complete paralysis of all industrial life that must now accompany a great war, and the utter ruin that may follow defeat, impose a severe restraint on the most ambitious statesman and the most excited population; while vast citizen armies, which must be dragged from domestic life and peaceful industry to the battlefield, will never be pervaded with the desire for war that animates purely professional soldiers. I have heard, indeed, one of the most competent judges of the political and military state of Europe predict that the most dangerous period of European peace will be that which follows a disarmament, reducing the armies of the rival Powers to moderate and manageable dimensions.

But, in addition to this consideration, a strong conviction has grown up of the moral and educational value of military discipline. It is urged that, in an age when many things contribute to weaken the national fibre and produce in large classes a languid, epicurean, semi-detached cosmopolitanism, universal service tends strongly to weld nations together, to strengthen the patriotic feeling, to form a high standard of civic duty and of self-sacrificing courage, to inspire the masses of the population with the kind and the intensity of enthusiasm that is most conducive to the greatness of nations. It carries the idea and sentiment of nationhood to multitudes whose thoughts would otherwise have never travelled beyond the narrow circle of daily wants or of village interests. The effect of universal service in Italy in civilising half-barbarous populations, in replacing old provincial jealousies and prejudices by the sentiment of a common nationality, has been abundantly displayed. In some cases a measure of ordinary education is now combined with military service, and the special education which discipline in itself produces is, it is contended, peculiarly needed in our day. 'The true beginning of wisdom,' a wise old Hebrew writer has said, 'is the desire of discipline,'[27] and it is probably on this side that modern education is most defective. Military service at least pro-

---

[27] Wisdom of Solomon, vi. 17.

duces habits of order, cleanliness, punctuality, obedience, and respect for authority, and, unlike most forms of popular education, it acts powerfully on the character and on the will. A few years spent in this school and amid the associations of the barrack will not tend to make men saints, but it is likely to do much to strengthen and discipline their characters, and to fit them to play a useful and honourable part in civil life. It at least gives them the tastes and habits of civilised men, corrects many senseless prejudices, forms brave, steady, energetic, and patriotic citizens. It mitigates the problems of the unemployed and of pauperism, and exercises a reforming influence on the idlest and most disorderly elements in society. Such men are far more likely to be reclaimed by the strong, steady pressure of military discipline than by any teaching of the Churches or the schools.

In all countries, it is truly said, when peace has continued long, and when wealth and prosperity have greatly increased, insidious vices grow up which do much to corrode the strength of nations. Lax principles, low ideals; luxurious, self-indulgent, effeminate habits of thought and life prevail; the robuster qualities decline; the power of self-sacrifice is diminished, and life in all its forms takes a less serious cast. The catastrophe of a great war is often Nature's stern corrective of these evils, but every wise statesman will look for remedies that are less drastic and less perilous. Of these, a few years of universal military discipline is one of the most powerful. It is the best tonic for a debilitated system.

Some admirers have gone even further. There is a theory, which, I believe, took its rise in Germany, but which has found adherents in England, that the gigantic armies of the Continent in reality cost nothing, for the productive powers of men are so much increased by a few years of military discipline that society is amply compensated for the sacrifice it has made. Two or three years of a life are taken from productive employment and supported from national funds, but the remainder is rendered greatly more productive.

I have endeavoured to state the case of the supporters of

universal service in its strongest form. I do not think that it can be doubted that it contains some truth; but, like much truth that has been long neglected, it has been thrust into an exaggerated and misleading prominence. The question is one of extreme importance for the English-speaking race, for, if the education of universal military service does all that is attributed to it, the continental nations which have generally adopted it must necessarily, in the long run, rise to a higher plane than the English race, who, on both sides of the ocean, have steadily rejected it. To me, at least, the theory of the inexpensiveness of the continental military system seems to be a complete paradox, in the face of the overwhelming and ever-increasing burden of debt and taxation distinctly due to the military system, which is crushing and paralysing the industry of Europe and threatening great nations with speedy bankruptcy. It is true that military discipline often forms valuable industrial qualities; but it is also true that the conscription breaks the habits of industrial life at the very age when it is most important that they should be formed, and that, in countless cases, the excitements and associations of military life utterly unfit men for the monotony of humble labour, pursued, perhaps, in some remote hamlet, and amid surroundings of abject poverty.

With the present gigantic armies, wars have, no doubt, become less frequent, though they have become incomparably more terrible; but can any one seriously contend that the unrestrained and reckless military competition of the last few years has given Europe any real security, or that either the animosities or the aspirations that threaten it have gone down? Are its statesmen confident that an ambitious monarch, or a propitious moment, or an alliance or an invention that materially changes the balance of forces, or some transient outburst of national irritation injudiciously treated, might not at any moment set it once more in a blaze? To strew gunpowder on all sides may, no doubt, produce caution, but it is not the best way of preventing an explosion. Never in the history of mankind have explosive elements of such tremendous potency been accumulated in Europe, and, with all our boasted democracy, the issues of peace or war have seldom rested so largely with three or four men. In the present condition of the world, it would be quite possible for the folly of a single ruler to bring down calamities upon Europe that might transfer the sceptre of civilisation to the other side of the Atlantic.

The security of internal peace given by a great army, and the influence of military discipline in forming habits of life and thought that are opposed to anarchical and revolutionary tendencies, have been much dwelt on. But if the military system does much to employ and reclaim the dangerous classes, if it teaches loyalty and obedience and respect, it also brings with it burdens which are steadily fomenting discontent. Certainly, the great military nations of the world are not those in which Anarchy, Socialism, and Nihilism are least rife. Of all the burdens that a modern Government can impose on its subjects, incomparably the heaviest is universal compulsory military service, and, to a large minority of those who undergo it, it is the most irritating and the most crushing servitude. Nor should it be forgotten that, if this system furnishes Governments with tremendous engines of repression, it is also preparing the time when every revolutionary movement will be made by men who have the knowledge and experience of military life. A great military Power continually augmenting its army in hopes of repressing anarchy presents a spectacle much like that which may be seen at a Spanish bullfight when the banderilla has been planted by a skilful hand, and when every bound by which the infuriated animal seeks to shake off the barb that is lacerating its flesh only deepens and exasperates the wound.

No reasonable man will deny that a period of steady discipline is, to many characters, an education of great value—an education producing results that are not likely in any other way to be equally attained. It is especially useful in communities that are still in a low stage of civilisation, and have not yet attained the habits of order and respect for authority, and in communities that are deeply divided by sectional and provincial antipathies. It is, I think, equally true that improvements have been introduced into modern armies which have greatly raised their moral tone. But, when all this is admitted, the shadows of the picture remain very marked. Deferred marriage, the loosening of domestic ties, the growth of ideals in which bloodshed and violence play a great part, a diminished horror of war, the constant employment of the best human ingenuity in devising new and more deadly instruments of destruction—all these things follow in the train of the great armies. It is impossible to turn Europe into a camp without in some degree reviving the ideals and the standards of a military age.

Discipline teaches much, but it also represses much, and the dead-level and passive obedience of the military system are not the best school of independent thought and individual energy. To the finer and more delicate flowers of human culture it is peculiarly prejudicial. Strongly marked individual types, highly strung, sensitive, nervous organisations, are the soils from which much that is most beautiful in our civilisation has sprung. Beyond all other things, enforced military service tends to sterilise them. Among such men it is difficult to overestimate either the waste and ruin of high talent, or the amount of acute and useless suffering that it produces. To democracies these things are of little moment, and they seem lost in the splendour and pageantry of military life. But the statistics that are occasionally published, exhibiting the immensely disproportionate number of suicides in some of the chief armies of the Continent, show clearly the suffering that is festering beneath.

Taine has devoted to the growth of the military system several pages of admirable power and truth, and he justly describes conscription as the natural companion or brother of universal suffrage—one of the two great democratic forces which seem destined for some time to rule the world.[28] The levelling and intermingling of classes it produces renders it congenial to a democratic age, and the old system of obtaining

---

[28] *Origines de la France Contemporaine: Le Régime Moderne*, i. 284–96.

exemptions and substitutions for money has been generally abolished. In the majority of cases, those who desired exemption were men with no military aptitude, so the army probably gained by the substitution. It was a free contract, in which the poor man received what the rich man paid, and by which both parties were benefited. It gave, however, some privilege to wealth, and democracy, true to its genuine instinct of preferring equality to liberty, emphatically condemned it.

There is, however, another aspect of the question which has impressed serious observers on the Continent. In spite of the affinity I have mentioned, it would be hardly possible to conceive a greater contrast in spirit and tendency than exists in some essential respects between the highly democratic representative Governments and the universal military service, which are simultaneously flourishing in a great part of Europe. The one is a system in which all ideas of authority and subordination are discarded, in which the skilful talker or demagogue naturally rules, in which every question is decided by the votes of a majority, in which liberty is perpetually pushed to the borders of license. The other is a system of the strictest despotism and subordination, of passive obedience without discussion or remonstrance; a system with ideals, habits, and standards of judgment utterly unlike those of popular politics; a system which is rapidly including, and moulding, and representing the whole adult male population. And while parliamentary government is everywhere showing signs of growing inefficiency and discredit, the armies of Europe are steadily strengthening, absorbing more and more the force and manhood of Christendom. Some observers are beginning to ask themselves whether these two things are likely always to go on together, and always to maintain their present relation—whether the eagles will always be governed by the parrots.

The great growth of militarism in the latter half of the nineteenth century has, I think, contributed largely, though indirectly, to the prevailing tendency to aggrandise the powers of government and to seek social reforms in strong coercive organisations of society. It is also the chief source of the immense increase of taxation, which has so seriously aggravated the dangers of a period of democratic transformation. It is not, indeed, by any means the only source. Something is due to the higher wages, the better payment of functionaries and workmen of every order, which has followed in the train of a higher standard of life and comfort. This beneficent movement was much accentuated in a period of great prosperity, and it has continued with little abatement, though economical conditions have much changed.

A much more considerable cause, however, of the increase of national expenditure is to be found in the many new duties that are thrown upon the State. The most important of these has been that of national education. Hardly any change in our generation has been more marked than that which made the education of the poor one of the main functions of the Government. In 1833, a parliamentary grant of 20,000*l.* was, for the first time, made in England to assist two societies engaged in popular education. In 1838, the parliamentary grant was raised to 30,000*l.* a year. It soon passed these limits; but the great period of national expenditure on education is much more recent. Before the Act of 1870 the State, in encouraging primary education, confined itself to grants in aid of local and voluntary bodies. It built no schools, and it made no provision for education where local agencies were wanting. The Act of 1870 providing for the establishment of a school in every district where the supply of education was deficient, the Act of 1876 making it penal for parents to neglect the education of their children, and the Act of 1891 granting free education, were the chief causes of the rapid rise in this branch of expenditure. In 1892 the total expenditure of school boards in England and Wales amounted to the enormous sum of 7,134,386*l.* The number of free scholars was about 3,800,-000, and the number of children paying fees or partial fees was about 1,020,000.[29]

---

[29] See the statistics in *Whitaker's Almanack* for 1894, pp. 601, 605.

England has, in this respect, only acted on the same lines as other civilised countries. She has acted on the supposition that, in the competition of nations, no uneducated people can hold its own, either in industrial or political competitions, and that democratic government can only be tolerable when it rests on the broad basis of an educated people. Probably few persons will now altogether doubt these truths, though something of the old belief in the omnipotence of education may have passed away, and though some qualifying considerations may have come into sight. The old Tory doctrine, that national education may easily be carried to a point which unfits men for the manual toil in which the great majority must pass their lives, was certainly not without foundation. Formerly the best workman was usually content to remain in his class, and to bring up his children in it. He took a pride in his work, and by doing so he greatly raised its standard and character. His first desire is now, much more frequently, to leave it, or at least to educate his children in the tastes and habits of a class which he considers a little higher than his own. That a man born in the humbler stages of society, who possesses the power of playing a considerable part in the world, should be helped to do so is very desirable; but it is by no means desirable that the flower of the working class, or their children, should learn to despise manual labour and the simple, inexpensive habits of their parents, in order to become very commonplace doctors, attorneys, clerks, or newspaper writers. This is what is continually happening, and while it deprives the working classes of their best elements, it is one great cause of the exaggerated competition which now falls with crushing weight on the lower levels of the intellectual professions.

Education, even to a very humble degree, does much to enlarge interests and brighten existence; but, by a melancholy compensation, it makes men far more impatient of the tedium, the monotony, and the contrasts of life. It produces desires which it cannot always sate, and it affects very considerably the disposition and relations of classes. One common result is the strong preference for town to country life. A marked and unhappy characteristic of the present age in England is the constant depletion of the country districts by the migration of multitudes of its old healthy population to the debilitating, and often depraving, atmosphere of the great towns. The chief causes of this change are, no doubt, economical. In the extreme depression of agriculture, every farmer finds it absolutely essential to keep his wage bill at the lowest point, and therefore to employ as few labourers as possible. Machinery takes the place of hand labour. Arable land, which supports many, becomes pasture land, which supports few. But every one who has much practical acquaintance with country life will, I believe, agree that the movement has been greatly intensified by the growing desire for more excitement and amusement which, under the influence of popular education, has spread widely through the agricultural labourers. Hopes and ambitions that are too often bitterly falsified draw them in multitudes to the great towns.

This restlessness and discontent produce considerable political effects. Education nearly always promotes peaceful tastes and orderly habits in the community, but in other respects its political value is often greatly overrated. The more dangerous forms of animosity and dissension are usually undiminished, and are often stimulated, by its influence. An immense proportion of those who have learnt to read, never read anything but a party newspaper—very probably a newspaper specially intended to inflame or to mislead them—and the half-educated mind is peculiarly open to political utopias and fanaticisms. Very few such men can realise distant consequences, or even consequences which are but one remove distant from the primary or direct one. How few townsmen, in a political contest, will realise that the neglect or depression of agriculture beats down town wages, by producing an immigration of agricultural labourers; or that a great strike in times of manufacturing depression will usually drive the industry on which they depend for their food, in part at least, out of the country; or that a highly graduated system of taxation, which at first brings in much money at the cost of the few, will soon lead to a migration of the capital which is essential to the subsistence of the many. Every politician knows how difficult it is in times of peace to arouse the public to the importance of the army and navy, on which the very existence of the Empire may depend, or to questions affecting national credit, or to questions affecting those distant portions of the Empire which feed, by their commerce, our home industries. Few men clearly realise that each popular exemption from taxation, each popular subsidy that is voted, means a corresponding burden imposed on some portion of the community; or that economies which leave Civil Servants underpaid almost always lead to wastefulness, inefficiency, and corruption. Men seldom bestow on public questions the same seriousness of attention that they bestow on their private concerns, and they seldom look as far into the future. National interests continually give way to party or to class interests. The ultimate interests even of a class are subordinated to the immediate benefit of a section of it. Proximate ends overshadow distant consequences, and when the combative instinct, with all its passion and its pride, is aroused, even proximate interests are often forgotten. In few fields have there been more fatal miscalculations than in the competition and struggle of industrial life, and they are largely due to this cause.

All classes are liable to mistakes of this kind, but they are especially prevalent among the half-educated, who have passed out of the empire of old habits and restraints. Such men are peculiarly apt to fall under misleading influences. They are usually insensible to the extreme complexity of the social fabric and the close interdependence of its many parts, and to the transcendent importance of consequences that are often obscure, remote, and diffused through many different channels. The complete illiteracy of a man is, no doubt, a strong argument against entrusting him with political power, but the mere knowledge of reading and writing is no real guarantee, or even presumption, that he will wisely exercise it. In order to attain this wisdom we must look to other methods—to a wide diffusion of property, to a system of representation that gives a voice to many different interests and types. The sedulous maintenance of the connection between taxation and voting is perhaps the best means of obtaining it.

These considerations are not intended to show that education is not a good thing, but only that its political advantages have not always proved as unmixed and as great as has been supposed. In the age in which we live, the incapacity and impotence that result from complete illiteracy can hardly be exaggerated, and every Government, as it seems to me, should make it its duty to provide that all its subjects should at least possess the rudiments of knowledge. It is also a matter of much importance to the community that there should be ladders by which poor men of real ability can climb to higher positions in the social scale. This is an object for which private endowments have largely and wisely provided, and, unless the flow of private benevolence is arrested by the increasing action of the State, endowments for this purpose are sure to multiply. Another order of considerations, however, comes into play when great revenues are raised by compulsion for the purpose of establishing a free national education which has more the character of secondary than primary education. The childless are taxed for the education of children, and large classes of parents for the support of schools they will never use. Parental responsibility, as well as parental rights, are diminished, and a grinding weight of taxation, for a purpose with which they have little or no real sympathy, falls upon some of the most struggling classes in the community.

There can be little doubt that this form of taxation is likely to increase. A large party desire to provide at the expense of the State, not only free education, but also free school books, free recreation grounds, and at least one meal during school hours. Sectarian jealousies and animosities, in more than one country, add largely to the cost of education by an unnecessary multiplication of schools, or by establishing a ruinous competition between State schools and schools established by voluntary subscription or supported by religious denominations. At the same time, the standard of popular and free, or, in other words, State-paid education, seems steadily rising. A crowd of subjects which lie far beyond the limits of primary education are already taught, either gratuitously or below cost price. In most countries, education in all its stages seems becoming more and more a State function, bearing more and more the State stamp, and more and more supported from public funds.

This is one main cause of the increase of the revenue drawn by the Government from the people. There are others, on which we may, I think, look with more unhesitating approval. The great work of sanitary reform has been perhaps the noblest legislative achievement of our age, and, if measured by the suffering it has diminished, has probably done far more for the real happiness of mankind than all the many questions that make and unmake ministries. It received its first great impetus in the present century from the Public Health Act of 1848, and in our own generation it has been greatly and variously extended. There can be no nobler or wiser end for a statesman to follow than to endeavour to secure for the poor, as far as is possible, the same measure of life and health as for the rich. Among the many addresses that were presented to the Queen in her Jubilee year, none appeared to me so significant as that which was presented by the sanitary inspectors, summing up what had been done in England during the first fifty years of the reign. They observed that the general health of Her Majesty's subjects had advanced far beyond that of any great State of Europe or of the United States; that the mean duration of life of all the Queen's subjects had been augmented by three and a half years; that in the last year's population of England and Wales there had been a saving of 84,000 cases of death, and of more than 1,700,000 cases of sickness, over the average rates of death and sickness at the beginning of the reign; that the death-rate of the home army had been reduced by more than half, and the death-rate of the Indian army by more than four-fifths.

All this cannot be done without the constant intervention

of Government. On the subject of sanitary reform the case of the extreme individualist will always break down, for disease is most frequently of a contagious and epidemical character, and the conditions from which it springs can never be dealt with except by general, organised, coercive measures. The real justification of the law imposing compulsory vaccination on an unwilling subject is, not that it may save his life, but that it may prevent him from being a centre of contagion to his neighbours. In all legislation about drainage, pollution of rivers, insanitary dwellings, the prevention of infection, and the establishment of healthy conditions of labour, spasmodic and individual efforts, unsupported by law, will always prove insufficient. As population increases, and is more and more massed in large towns; as the competition for working men's houses within a limited area grows more intense; as industry takes forms which bring great numbers of working men and women under the same roof, and as multiplying schools increase the danger of children's epidemics, the need for coercive measures of sanitary regulation becomes more imperious.

A Government can have no higher object than to raise the standard of national health, and it may do so in several different ways. It may do much to encourage those most fruitful and beneficial of all forms of research—research into the causes of disease and the methods of curing it. It may bring within the reach of the poorest class the medical knowledge and appliances which, in a ruder state of society, would be a monopoly of the rich. It may make use of the great technical knowledge at its command to establish qualifications for medical practice which will restrain the quack, who trades on the fears and weaknesses of the ignorant much as the professional money-lender does on their improvidence and inexperience. It may also greatly raise the health of the community by measures preventing insanitary conditions of life, noxious adulterations, or the spread of contagion.

In this, no doubt, as in other departments, there are qualifications to be made, dangers and exaggerations to be avoided. Sanitary reform is not wholly a good thing when it enables the diseased and feeble members of the community, who in another stage of society would have died in infancy, to grow up and become parent stocks, transmitting a weakened type or the taint of hereditary disease. The diminution of mortality which sanitary science effects is mainly in infant mortality, and infant mortality is a far less evil than adult mortality, and in not a few cases it is a blessing in disguise. It is true, too, that mere legislation in this, as in other fields, will prove abortive if it is not supported by an intelligent public opinion. As one of the wisest statesmen of our age has truly said, 'Sanitary instruction is even more essential than sanitary legislation, for if in these matters the public knows what it wants, sooner or later the legislation will follow; but the best laws, in a country like this, are waste paper if they are not appreciated and understood.'[30]

It is possible that a Government, acting at the dictation of a professional which is strongly wedded to professional traditions and etiquette, and which at the same time deals with a subject very far removed from scientific certainty, may throw obstacles in the way of new treatments and remedies that may prove of great benefit to mankind. It is also possible, and indeed probable, that it may carry the system of regulation to an exaggerated extent. Some portions of the Factory Acts are open to this criticism, though it will usually be found that in these cases other than sanitary considerations have entered into this legislation. It is, however, a universal rule that when a system of regulation has begun, it will tend to increase, and when men entrusted with sanitary reforms become a large profession, they will naturally aggrandise their power, exaggerate their importance, and sometimes become meddlesome and inquisitorial. M. Léon Say has lately pointed out the dangers of this scientific protectionism, which is leading sanitarians to attempt to watch our lives in the minutest detail; and another distinguished French authority has bluntly declared

---

[30] *Speeches and Addresses of Lord Derby*, i. 176.

that a new '89 will be needed against the tyranny of hygiene, in order to regain our liberty of eating and drinking, and to limit the incessant meddling of sanitarians in our private lives.[31] Legislators constantly overlook the broad distinction between lines of conduct that are injurious, but injurious only to those who follow them, and lines of conduct that can be clearly shown to produce danger or evil to the community. In the latter case Government interference is always called for. In the former, in the case of adults there is at least a strong presumption against it. As a general rule, an adult man should regulate his own life, and decide for himself whether he will run exceptional risks with a view to exceptional rewards.

But, when all this is admitted, there is hardly any other field in which Governments can do, or have done, so much to alleviate or prevent human suffering. Neither Governments nor their advisers are infallible; but in this case Governments act with the best lights that medical science can give, and they act, for the most part, with perfect good faith, and without any possibility of party advantage. The prolongation of human life is much. The diminution or alleviation of disease and suffering is much more. Sanitary reform cannot be effectually carried out without a heavy expenditure, which is borne in the shape of taxes by the community. But, looking at this expenditure merely from an economical point of view, no expenditure that a Government can make is more highly remunerative. Sir James Paget has estimated the loss of labour by the wage classes from excessive preventible sickness at twenty millions of weeks per annum. Sir Edwin Chadwick writes: 'The burden of lost labour, of excessive mortality, and of excessive funerals from preventible causes were largely underestimated in 1842 at two millions per annum in the Metropolis. In England and Wales, those same local burdens of lost labour and excessive sickness may now be estimated at upwards of twenty-eight million pounds per annum.'[32]

---

[31] See an essay by M. Raffalovich in Mackay's *Plea for Liberty*, p. 217.
[32] Chadwick on *Unity*, p. 63.

A very similar line of reasoning may be employed to justify the great increase of national expenditure in England, and in most other countries, in the field of prisons and reformatories. The enormous improvements that have taken place in the prison system during the present century have added largely to the expenditure of nations, but they have put an end to an amount of needless suffering, demoralisation, and waste of human character and faculty that it is difficult to overestimate. 'The best husbandry,' as Grattan once said, 'is the husbandry of the human creature.' To distinguish between crime that springs from strongly marked criminal tendency and crime that is due to mere unfavourable circumstances, or transient passion, or weakness of will; to distinguish among genuine criminal tendencies between those which are still incipient and curable, and those which have acquired the force of an inveterate disease, is the basis of all sound criminal reform. It cannot be carried out without much careful classification and many lines of separate treatment. The agencies for reclaiming and employing juvenile criminals; the separate treatment of intoxication; the broad distinction drawn between a first offender and an habitual criminal; the prison regulations that check the contagion of vice, have all had a good effect in reducing the amount of crime. Most of these things cost much, but they produce a speedy and ample return. Money is seldom better or more economically spent than in diminishing the sum of human crime and raising the standard of human character. In this case, as in the case of sanitary reform, it may be truly said that legislators act under the best available advice and with perfect singleness of purpose. On such questions very few votes can be either gained or lost.

The same thing cannot be said of all extensions of Government functions. No feature is more characteristic of modern democracy than the tendency to regulate and organise by law countless industries which were once left to private initiative and arrangement; to apply the machinery of the State to countless functions which were once discharged by independent bodies, or private benevolence, or cooperation. A vast increase in many forms of expenditure and in many different kinds of officials is the inevitable consequence, imposing great additional burdens on the taxpayer, and each new departure in the field of expenditure is usually made a precedent and a pretext for many others. I cannot go as far as Mr. Herbert Spencer and some other writers of his school in denouncing this as wholly evil, though I agree with them that the dangerous exaggerations and tendencies are chiefly on this side. Much of this increased elaboration of government seems to me inevitable. As civilisation becomes more highly organised and complex, as machinery increases and population and industries agglomerate, new wants, interests, and dangers arise, which imperiously require increased regulation. It is impossible to leave a great metropolis or a vast, fluctuating, industrial population with as little regulation as a country village or a pastoral people. Compare the old system of locomotion by a few coaches or wagons with our present railway system; or our old domestic industries with our present gigantic factories, stores, and joint-stock companies; or the old system of simple isolated cesspools with the highly complex drainage on which the safety of our great towns depends, and it will be evident how much new restraining and regulating legislation is required. The growth of philanthropy, and the increasing light which the press throws on all the sides of a nation's life, make public opinion keenly sensible of much preventible misery it would have either never known or never cared for, and science discloses dangers, evils, and possibilities of cure of which our ancestors never dreamed.

All these things produce a necessity for much additional regulation, and a strong pressure of public opinion for much more. If Governments, as distinguished from private companies, have some disadvantages, they have also some important advantages. They can command a vast amount of technical skill. They can act with a simultaneity and authority and on a scale which no private organisation can emulate, and in England, at least since the old system of patronage has been replaced by the present system of examination and constant control, the State can usually count upon a very large supply of pure and disinterested administrators. On some subjects Governments are much less likely than private companies to be deflected by corrupt or sinister motives, and an English Government has the great advantage of possessing the best credit in the world, which enables it to give many enterprises an unrivalled stability and security, and to conduct them with unusual economy. The application of British credit to schemes for the benefit of the poor, or the solution of great social questions, has of late years been largely extended, and seems likely steadily to advance. There is also some difference between the action of a representative Government, including, utilising, and commanding the best talent in all classes, and a despotic or highly aristocratic Government, which is in the hands of a few men, and acts under very little restraint and control, like a kind of Providence apart from the nation.

In many departments the conveniences of State action are very great. Few persons, for example, would withdraw the post-office from Government hands. Private enterprise might perform its functions with equal efficiency in the chief centres of population, but Government alone could carry on the enterprise uniformly and steadily, in all countries, in the districts that are unremunerative as well as in those which are profitable. It would be difficult to conceive a more flagrant violation of the English fetish of Free Trade than the regulation of cab fares by authority; but the convenience of the system is so great that no one wishes to abolish it. Banking for the benefit of private persons is certainly not a natural business of Government, but Government machinery and Government credit have built up a system of savings banks and post-office banks which has been a vast blessing to the poor, encouraging among them, to an eminent degree, providence and thrift, and at the same time giving them a direct interest in the stability of the Empire and the security of property. Few things have conferred more benefits on agriculture than the large sums which have been advanced to landlords for drainage, at a rate of interest sufficient to secure the State from loss, but lower than they could have obtained in a private market. Of all the schemes that have been formed for improving the condition of Ireland, the most promising is that for the creation of a peasant proprietary by means of loans issued at a rate of interest which the State, and the State alone, could command, and repaid by instalments in a defined number of years. This is a type of legislation which is almost certain in the future to be widely and variously applied.

All these excursions outside the natural sphere of Government influence should be carefully and jealously watched; but there are some distinctions which should not be forgotten. Government enterprises which are remunerative stand on a different basis from those which must be permanently subsidised by taxation, or, in other words, by forced payments, in most cases largely drawn from those who are least benefited by them. If it be shown that the State management of some great enterprise can be conducted with efficiency, and at the same time made to pay its expenses; if it can be shown that, by the excellent credit of the State, a State loan or a State guarantee can effect some useful change or call into being some useful enterprise without loss to the State or to its credit, a large portion of the objections to this intervention will have been removed. It is also very important to consider whether the proposed intervention of the Government lies apart from the sphere of politics, or whether it may become a source or engine of corruption. It may do so by placing a large addition of patronage in the hands of the executive, and it may do so still more dangerously by creating new and corrupt reasons for giving or soliciting votes. Few persons, for example, can doubt that, if the Socialist policy of placing the great industries of the country in the hands of municipalities were carried out, numbers of votes would be systematically given for the sole purpose of obtaining advantages for the workmen connected with these industries, at the cost of the community at large.

Another element to be considered is, whether the things the State is asked to assist are of a kind that can flourish with-

out its aid. There are forms of science and literature and research which can by no possibility be remunerative, or at least
remunerative in any proportion to the labour they entail or
the ability they require. A nation which does not produce and
does not care for these things can have only an inferior and
imperfect civilisation. A Government grant which would appear almost infinitesimal in the columns of a modern Budget
will do much to support and encourage them. Expenditure
in works of art and art schools, in public buildings, in picture
galleries, in museums, adds largely to the glory and dignity
of a nation and to the education of its people. It is continually
increasing that common property which belongs alike to all
classes; and it is a truly democratic thing, for it makes it possible for the poor man to know and appreciate works of art
which, without State intervention, he would have never seen,
and which would have been wholly in the hands of the rich
and cultivated few. The total indifference of English Governments during a long period to artistic development is one of
the great causes that art has flowered so tardily in England.

In many countries in Europe dramatic art is assisted by subsidies to the opera and the classical theatre. Such subsidies
stand on a different ground from those which I have just noticed, for they minister directly to the pleasures of the rich;
though a brilliant theatre, by drawing many strangers to the
metropolis, probably ultimately benefits the poor. It is not
likely that English democratic opinion would tolerate an expenditure of this kind; and it may be observed that the connection between Governments and amusement is much
closer in most continental countries than in England. In these
countries a large portion of the money raised for the relief of
the poor and the suffering is levied upon public amusements.[33]

The objections to the vast extension of State regulations
and of State subsidies are very many. There is, in the first
place, what may be called the argument of momentum, which

---

[33] See *Le droit des pauvres sur les spectacles en Europe*, par Cros-Mayrevielle
(1889).

Herbert Spencer has elaborated with consummate skill and force.[34] It is absolutely certain that, when this system is largely adopted, it will not remain within the limits which those who adopted it intended. It will advance with an accelerated rapidity; every concession becomes a precedent or basis for another step, till the habit is fully formed of looking on all occasions for State assistance or restriction, and till a weight of taxation and debt has been accumulated from which the first advocates of the movement would have shrunk with horror. There is the weakening of private enterprise and philanthropy; a lowered sense of individual responsibility; diminished love of freedom; the creation of an increasing army of officials, regulating in all its departments the affairs of life; the formation of a state of society in which vast multitudes depend for their subsistence on the bounty of the State. All this cannot take place without impairing the springs of self-reliance, independence, and resolution, without gradually enfeebling both the judgment and the character. It produces also a weight of taxation which, as the past experience of the world abundantly shows, may easily reach a point that means national ruin. An undue proportion of the means of the individual is forcibly taken from him by the State, and much of it is taken from the most industrious and saving, for the benefit of those who have been idle or improvident. Capital and industry leave a country where they are extravagantly burdened and have ceased to be profitable, and even the land itself has often been thrown out of cultivation on account of the weight of an excessive taxation.

The tendency to constantly increasing expenses in local taxation is in some degree curtailed by enactments of the Imperial Parliament limiting in various ways the powers which it concedes to local bodies of raising taxes or incurring debts. That the restrictions are very unduly lax, few good judges will question; yet it is the constant effort of local bodies, which are under democratic influence, to extend their powers. Parliament itself

---

[34] *The Man versus the State.*

is unlimited, and Parliament, on financial questions, means simply the House of Commons. The constituencies are the only check, but a vast proportion of the expenditure of the State is intended for the express purpose of bribing them. Democracy as it appeared in the days of Joseph Hume was pre-eminently a penurious thing, jealously scrutinising every item of public expenditure, denouncing as intolerable scandal the extravagance of aristocratic government, and viewing with extreme disfavour every enlargement of the powers of the State. It has now become, in nearly all countries, a government of lavish expenditure, or rapidly accumulating debt, of constantly extending State action.

It is, I believe, quite true that the functions of Government must inevitably increase with a more complicated civilisation. But, in estimating their enormous and portentously rapid aggrandisement within the last few years, there is one grave question which should always be asked. Is that aggrandisement due to a reasoned conviction that Government can wisely benefit, directly, different classes by its legislation? Or is it due to a very different cause—to the conviction that, by promising legislation in favour of different classes, the votes of those classes may most easily be won?

A large portion of the increased expenditure is also due, not to subsidies, but to the increased elaboration of administrative machinery required by the system of constant inspection and almost universal regulation. Nothing is more characteristic of the new democracy than the alacrity with which it tolerates, welcomes, and demands coercive Government interference in all its concerns. In the words of Mr. Goschen, 'the extension of State action to new and vast fields of business, such as telegraphy, insurance, annuities, postal orders, and parcel post, is not the most striking feature. What is of far deeper import is its growing interference with the relations between classes, its increased control over vast categories of transactions between individuals. . . . The parent in dealing with his child, the employer in dealing with his workmen, the shipbuilder in the construction of his ships, the shipowner in the treatment of his sailors, the houseowner in the management of his house property, the landowner in his contracts with his tenants, have been notified by public opinion or by actual law that the time has gone by when the cry of *laissez-nous faire* would be answered in the affirmative. The State has determined what is right and wrong, what is expedient and inexpedient, and has appointed its agents to enforce its conclusions. Some of the higest obligations of humanity, some of the smallest businesses of everyday life, some of the most complicated transactions of our industrial and agricultural organisations, have been taken in hand by the State. Individual responsibility has been lessened, national responsibility has been heightened.'[35]

Nor can the change of tendency in this respect be measured merely by actual legislation. It is to be seen still more clearly in the countless demands for legislative restriction that are multiplying on all sides; in the Bills which, though not yet carried into law, have received a large amount of parliamentary support; in the resolutions of trade-union congresses, or county councils, or philanthropic meetings or associations; in the questions asked and the pledges exacted at every election; in the great mass of socialistic of semi-socialistic literature that is circulating through the country. Few things would have more astonished the old Radicals of the Manchester school than to be told that a strong leaning towards legislative compulsion was soon to become one of the marked characteristics of an 'Advanced Liberal,' and 'all contracts to the contrary notwithstanding'—a favourite clause in democratic legislation.

Accompanying this movement, and naturally growing out of the great change in the disposition of power, is the marked tendency to throw taxation to a greater extent on one class of the community, in the shape of graduated taxation. In certain forms and to a certain measure this has always existed in England. The shameful exemption from taxation enjoyed by

---

[35] *Laissez faire; or, Government Interference*, by the Right Hon. G. Goschen. Address delivered at Edinburgh, 1883, p. 4.

both nobles and clergy in nearly all continental countries up to the eve of the French Revolution was unknown in England, and it had always been an English custom to impose special taxes on the luxuries of the rich. Tocqueville, in the remarkable passage, which has been often quoted, observed that 'for centuries the only inequalities of taxation in England were those which had been successively introduced in favour of the necessitous classes. . . . In the eighteenth century it was the poor who enjoyed exemption from taxation in England, in France it was the rich. In the one case, the aristocracy had taken upon its own shoulders the heaviest public charges in order to be allowed to govern. In the other case, it retained to the end an immunity from taxation in order to console itself for the loss of government.'[36] Arthur Young, in a little speech which he made to a French audience at the beginning of the Revolution, described vividly the difference subsisting in this respect between the two countries. 'We have many taxes,' he said, 'in England which you know nothing of in France, but the *tiers état*—the poor—do not pay them. They are laid on the rich. Every window in a man's house pays, but if he has no more than six windows he pays nothing. A seigneur with a great estate pays the *vingtièmes* and *tailles*, but the little proprietor of a garden pays nothing. The rich pay for their horses, their carriages, their servants, and even for liberty to kill their own partridges; but the poor farmer pays nothing of this; and, what is more, we have in England a tax paid by the rich for the relief of the poor.'[37]

Both the window tax and the house tax of the eighteenth century were graduated taxes, rising in an increased proportion according to the value of the dwelling. A similarly progressive scale of taxation was introduced by Pitt for carriages, pleasure-horses, and male servants, the duty on each of these rising rapidly according to the numbers in each establishment.

---

[36] *L'Ancien Régime*, pp. 146–47.
[37] Pinkerton's *Voyages*, iv. 200.

The doctrine that revenue should be raised chiefly from luxuries or superfluities has been very largely recognised in English taxation, and since the great fiscal reforms instituted by Sir Robert Peel it has been carried out to an almost complete extent. A working man who is a teetotaller and who does not smoke is now almost absolutely untaxed, except in the form of a very low duty on tea and on coffee. In the opinion of many good judges, this movement of taxation, though essentially beneficent, has been carried in England to an exaggerated point. It is not right, they say, that any class should be entirely exempt from all share in the imperial burden, especially when that class is entrusted with political power, and has a considerable voice in imposing and adjusting the expenditure of the nation. Taxes on articles of universal consumption are by far the most productive. They ought always to be kept low, for when they are heavy they produce not only hardships, but injustice, as the poor would then pay an unduly large proportion of the national revenue; but, on the other hand, their complete repeal is a matter of very doubtful expediency.

In England, however, the policy of absolutely abolishing the taxes on the chief objects of a poor man's necessary consumption has been steadily carried out by both parties in the State. Tory Governments abolished the salt duty in 1825 and (after many reductions) the sugar duty in 1874; while Liberal Governments abolished the coal duty and the tax on candles in 1831, the last vestige of the corn duty in 1869, the taxes on soap and on licenses for making it in 1853 and 1870. Both parties have also concurred in freeing nearly every article of a working man's attire by removing the duties on wool, calico, and leather.[38] It may be questioned whether this policy has been carried to its present extreme because legislators believed it to be wise, or because they believed that it would prove popular with the electors. Such measures furnish exactly the kind of topic that is most useful on the platform.

---

[38] Dowell's *History of Taxation.*

There is another principle of taxation which has been advocated by Bentham and Mill, and which, before their time, was propounded by Montesquieu. It is that a minimum income which is sufficient to secure to a labouring family of moderate size the bare necessaries, though not the luxuries, of life, should remain exempt from all taxation. Strictly speaking, this principle is, no doubt, inconsistent with the imposition of taxation on any article of first necessity; but it has been largely adopted in England in the exemption of the poorest class of houses from taxation, and in the partial or complete exemption of small incomes from the income tax. Successive Acts of Parliament have wholly freed incomes under 100*l.*, under 150*l.*, and under 160*l.* a year from the tax, and have granted abatements in the case of incomes under 200*l.*, under 400*l.*, and, finally, under 500*l.* a year. The large majority of the electors who return the members of the House of Commons now pay nothing to the income tax.

By all these measures a system of graduated taxation has steadily grown up. A few lines from a speech made by Lord Derby in 1885 give a clear picture of what in his day had been done. 'Take the income tax. We exempt altogether incomes up to a certain point, and we exempt them partially up to a higher point. Take the house tax. What have you got there? Total exemption of all that class of houses in which working men usually live. Take the death duties. They absolutely spare property below a certain limited amount. Take the carriage tax. The class of conveyances used by poor persons, or used otherwise than for purposes of pleasure, are made specially free of charge. Take the railway-passenger tax. It falls on first and second class passengers, and leaves the third class untouched. . . . In our poor law, now 300 years old, we have adopted a system so socialistic in principle that no continental Government would venture even to look at it.'[39]

Articles of luxury or ostentation used exclusively by the rich are, in many instances, specially taxed. Such, for example, are

---

[39] *The Times*, November 2, 1885.

the taxes on armorial bearings, on the more expensive qualities of wine, on menservants, and on sporting. In some cases taxes of this kind have been abolished, because the expense of collecting them, or the expense of distinguishing between the better and the cheaper descriptions of a single article, made them nearly wholly unproductive. But, on the whole, the strong leaning of our present system in favour of the poor cannot reasonably be questioned; and it becomes still more apparent when we consider not merely the sources, but the application, of the taxes. The protection of life, industry, and even property, is quite as important to the poor man as to the rich, and the most costly functions which Governments have of late years assumed are mainly for his benefit. Primary education, the improvement of working men's dwellings, factory inspection, savings banks, and other means of encouraging thrift, are essentially poor men's questions.

Adam Smith, in a well-known passage, has laid down the principle on which, in strict equity, taxation should be levied. 'The subjects of every State ought to contribute to the support of the Government as nearly as possible in proportion to their respective abilities; that is, in proportion to the revenue which they respectively enjoy under the protection of the State. The expense of government to the individuals of a great nation is like the expense of management to the joint tenants of a great estate, who are all obliged to contribute in proportion to their respective interests in the estate.'[40]

According to this principle, the man with 1,000*l.* a year should pay ten times the taxes of a man with 100*l.* a year, and the man with 10,000*l.* a year ten times the taxes of a man with 1,000*l.* a year. In the words of Thiers, 'every kind of revenue, without exception, ought to contribute to the needs of the State, for all depend upon it for their existence. Every exemption from taxation is an injustice. . . . The true principle, which was established in 1789, is that every man, without exception, in proportion to what he gains or what he pos-

---

[40] *Wealth of Nations*, Book v. chapter ii.

sesses, should contribute. To exempt labour in order to strike property, or to tax property in exorbitant proportions, would only be to add a new iniquity as great as that which was abolished in 1789. . . . Society is a company of mutual insurance, in which each man should pay the risk in proportion to the amount of property insured. If he has insured a house of the value of 100,000 francs (the rate being 1 per cent.), he owes 1,000 francs to the company. If the insured house is worth a million, he owes 10,000 francs. . . . Society is a company, in which each man has more or less shares, and it is just that each should pay in proportion to their number, whether they be ten, or 100, or 1,000, but always according to the same rate imposed on all. There should be one rule for all, neither more nor less. To abandon this would be as if a merchant were to say to his customers, "You are richer than your neighbour, and must therefore pay more for the same goods." It would only lead to endless confusion, and open out boundless, incalculable, possibilities of arbitrary imposition.'[41]

The great majority of serious economists have, I believe, agreed that, as a matter of strict right, this doctrine is the true one. Adam Smith, however, clearly saw that human affairs cannot, or will not, be governed by the strict lines of economic science, and he fully recognised that it may be expedient that taxes should be so regulated that the rich should pay in proportion something more than the poor. In England, the system of graduated taxation which I have described has passed fully into the national habits, and is accepted by all parties. The taxation of luxuries, as distinguished from necessaries, has been productive of much good, and is much less liable than other forms of graduated taxation to abuse. The exemption of small incomes from all direct taxation undoubtedly brings with it grave dangers, especially when those who are exempted form the bulk of the electorate, and are thus able to increase this taxation to an indefinite extent, without any manifest sacrifice to themselves. At the same time, few per-

---

[41] *La Propriété*, livre iv. chaps. ii., iii.

sons will object to these exemptions, provided they are kept within reasonable limits, are intended solely as measures of relief, and do not lead to lavish expenditure. It does not necessarily follow that, because a class are a minority in the electorate, they are in grave danger of being unduly taxed. As long as they still form a sufficiently considerable portion to turn the balance in elections, they have the means of vindicating their rights. It is the duty of the Government to provide that the taxes are moderate in amount, and are levied for the *bonâ fide* purpose of discharging functions which are necessary or highly useful to the State. There is, however, another conception of taxation, which has of late years been rapidly growing. It has come to be regarded as a socialistic weapon, as an instrument of confiscation, as a levelling agent for breaking down large fortunes, redistributing wealth, and creating a new social type.

The growing popularity of graduated taxation in the two forms of an exemption of the smaller incomes from all direct taxation, and of the taxation of large incomes on a different scale or percentage from moderate ones, is very evident, and it is accompanied by an equally strong tendency towards a graduated taxation of capital and successions. Precedents may, no doubt, be found in earlier times. A graduated income tax existed in ancient Athens, and was warmly praised by Montesquieu. Graduated taxation was imposed with much severity and elaborated with great ingenuity in Florence in the fourteenth, fifteenth, and sixteenth centuries. But it is chiefly of late years, and since democratic influence has predominated, that the question of graduated taxation has been pushed into the forefront. It exists, though only to a very moderate degree, in Prussia and most of the German States, and a Prussian law of 1883 considerably enlarged the number of exemptions.[42] It prevails in slightly different forms in a large number of the Swiss cantons, and especially in the cantons of

---

[42] Leroy-Beaulieu, *Traité des Finances*, i. 139–74; Say, *Solutions Démocratiques de la Question des Impôts*, ii. 184–224.

Vaud, Zürich, Geneva, Uri, and the Grisons. Thus, in the Canton de Vaud real property is divided into three classes—properties of a value not exceeding 1,000*l.*, properties that are valued between 1,000*l.* and 4,000*l.*, and properties of a value above 4,000*l.* The first class are taxed at the rate of 1*l.*, the second at the rate of 1*l.*10*s.*, and the third at the rate of 2*l.* per 1,000*l.* Personal property is divided into seven classes, each of them taxed at a separate rate. Fortunes exceeding in capital value 32,000*l.*, and incomes exceeding 1,600*l.*, are subject to the highest rate. In Zürich a different system is adopted. Though both capital and income are progressively taxed, the rate of that tax is the same for all, but the amount liable to taxation becomes proportionately larger as the fortune or the income increases. Thus five-tenths of the first 800*l.* of a capital fortune, six-tenths of the next 1,200*l.*, seven-tenths of the next 2,000*l.*, eight-tenths of the next 4,000*l.*, and ten-tenths of anything above it, are taxed.[43]

In the Netherlands the capital value of every fortune has, by a recent law, to be annually stated, and it is taxed according to that value on a graduated scale. Ten thousand florins are untaxed; after that the tax on capital gradually rises from one to two in a thousand. There is also a progressive tax on revenue, but with exemptions intended to prevent capital from being twice taxed. In New Zealand and the Australian colonies there is much graduated taxation, chiefly directed against the growth of large landed properties. In New Zealand the ordinary land tax is thrown upon 12,000 out of 90,000 owners of land. There is an additional and graduated land tax on properties which, after deducting the value of improvements, are worth 5,000*l.* and upwards. It rises from 1/8*d.* to 2*d.* in the pound, and there is also a special and graduated tax on absentees. The income tax is 6*d.* in the pound on the first taxable 1,000*l.*, and 1*s.* in the pound on higher rates.[44] In Victoria

---

[43] See a Foreign Office Report on Graduated Taxation in Switzerland (1892).

[44] *New Zealand Official Yearbook*, 1894, pp. 245–47.

there is a graduated succession duty, varying from 1 to 10 per cent.[45] In France the question of graduated, or, as it is called, progressive, taxation has of late been much discussed; but, with the exception of a graduated house tax,[46] attempts in this direction have, until quite recently, been defeated. In the United States, as I have noticed in a former chapter, proposals for graduated taxation have received a serious check in the decision of the Supreme Court in 1894, which appears to establish that, in the imposition of direct Federal taxation, the Congress must only recognise State divisions and the number of citizens. During the war of secession, however, a graduated income tax for a short time existed. The first war income tax, which was established in 1861, taxed all incomes above 800 dollars at the same rate; but the second income tax, which was enacted in July 1862, established a system of graduation, which was, however, nearly all repealed in 1865. The English Budget of 1894 went far in the direction of graduated taxation, both by the additional exemptions granted in the income tax and by the new system of graduation.

Recent discussions have made the arguments which have been adduced by economists against graduated taxation very familiar. It is obvious that a graduated tax is a direct penalty imposed on saving and industry, a direct premium offered to idleness and extravagance. It discourages the very habits and qualities which it is most in the interest of the State to foster, and it is certain to operate forcibly where fortunes approach the limits at which a higher scale of taxation begins. It is a strong inducement at that period, either to cease to work or to cease to save. It is at the same time perfectly arbitrary. When the principle of taxing all fortunes on the same rate of computation is abandoned, no definite rule or principle remains. At what point the higher scale is to begin, or to what degree it is to be raised, depends wholly on the policy of Governments and the balance of parties. The ascending scale

---

[45] Dilke's *Problems of Greater Britain*, ii. 277.

[46] Ibid. pp. 278–79.

may at first be very moderate, but it may at any time, when fresh taxes are required, be made more severe, till it reaches or approaches the point of confiscation. No fixed line or amount of graduation can be maintained upon principle, or with any chance of finality. The whole matter will depend upon the interest and wishes of the electors; upon party politicians seeking for a cry and competing for the votes of very poor and very ignorant men. Under such a system all large properties may easily be made unsafe, and an insecurity may arise which will be fatal to all great financial undertakings. The most serious restraint on parliamentary extravagance will, at the same time, be taken away, and majorities will be invested with the easiest and most powerful instrument of oppression. Highly graduated taxation realises most completely the supreme danger of democracy, creating a state of things in which one class imposes on another burdens which it is not asked to share, and impels the State into vast schemes of extravagance, under the belief that the whole cost will be thrown upon others.

The belief is, no doubt, very fallacious, but it is very natural, and it lends itself most easily to the claptrap of dishonest politicians. Such men will have no difficulty in drawing impressive contrasts between the luxury of the rich and the necessities of the poor, and in persuading ignorant men that there can be no harm in throwing great burdens of exceptional taxation on a few men, who will still remain immeasurably richer than themselves. Yet no truth of political economy is more certain than that a heavy taxation of capital, which starves industry and employment, will fall most severely on the poor. Graduated taxation, if it is excessive or frequently raised, is inevitably largely drawn from capital. It discourages its accumulation. It produces an insecurity which is fatal to its stability, and it is certain to drive great masses of it to other lands.

The amount to be derived from this species of taxation is also much exaggerated. The fortunes of a few millionaires make a great show in the world, but they form in reality a very insignificant sum, compared with the aggregate of moderate fortunes and small savings. Unless the system of graduation be extended, as in Switzerland, to very moderate fortunes, it will produce little, and even then the exemptions that accompany it will go far to balance it. It is certain, too, that it will be largely evaded. There is, it is true, a great distinction to be drawn in this respect between real and personal property. Land is of such a nature that it cannot escape the burden which is imposed on it, but there are many ways in which personal property can escape. Confidential arrangements between members of a family or partners in a business, foreign investments payable to foreign bankers, an increasing portion of wealth sunk in life annuities, insurances made in companies that are not subject to British taxation, securities payable to bearer, which it will be impossible to trace, will all multiply, and the frauds that are so much complained of in income-tax returns will certainly increase. No graver error can be made by a financier than to institute a system which is so burdensome and so unjust that men will be disposed to employ all their ingenuity to evade it. With the vast and various field of international investment that is now open to them they are sure, in innumerable instances, to succeed, and no declaration, no oath, no penalty will effectually prevent it. Taxation is ultimately the payment which is made by the subject for the security and other advantages which he derives from the State. If the taxation of one class is out of all proportion to the cost of the protection they enjoy; if its members are convinced that it is not an equitable payment, but an exceptional and confiscatory burden imposed upon them by an act of power because they are politically weak, very many of them will have no more scruple in defrauding the Government than they would have in deceiving a highwayman or a burglar.

It would be pressing these arguments too far to maintain that a graduated scale of taxation is always and necessarily an evil. In this, as in most political questions, much will depend upon circumstances and degrees. It is, however, sufficiently clear that any financier who enters on this field is entering on a path surrounded with grave and various dangers. Graduated taxation is certain to be contagious, and it is certain not to rest within the limits that its originators desired. No one who clearly reads the signs of the times as they are shown in so many lands can doubt that this system of taxation is likely to increase. It would be hardly possible that it should be otherwise when political power is placed mainly in the hands of the working classes; when vast masses of landed property are accumulated in a few hands; when professional politicians are continually making changes in the incidence of taxation a prominent part of their electioneering programmes; when almost every year enlarges the functions, and therefore the expenditure, of the State; when nearly all the prevalent utopias take a socialistic form, and point to an equalisation of conditions by means of taxation. Under such conditions the temptation to enter upon this path becomes almost invincible.

It is a question of great importance to consider to what result it is likely to lead. To suppose that any system of taxation can possibly produce a real equality of fortunes, or prevent the accumulation of great wealth, seems to me wholly chimerical; though it is quite possible that legislators in aiming at these objects may ruin national credit, and bring about a period of rapid commercial decadence. Highly graduated taxation, however, is likely to have great political and social effects in transforming the character of wealth. It will probably exercise a special influence on landed property, breaking up or greatly diminishing those vast estates which are so distinctive a feature of English life. The tendencies which are in operation acting in this direction are very powerful. Land, as it is at present held by the great proprietors, is usually one of the least profitable forms of property. The political influence attached to it has greatly diminished. The magisterial and other administrative functions, that once gave the great landlord an almost commanding influence in his county, are being steadily taken away, and county government in all its forms is passing into other hands. If government is effectually di-

vorced from property, and if a system of graduated taxation
intended to equalise fortunes becomes popular, great masses
of immovable land must become one of the most undesirable
forms of property. No other excites so much cupidity, or is so
much exposed to predatory legislation. Under all these circumstances, we may expect to see among the great landowners a growing desire to diminish gradually their stake in the
land, thus reversing the tendency to agglomeration which for
many generations has been dominant.

The change, in my opinion, will not be wholly evil. It is not
a natural thing that four or five country places should be held
by one man; that whole counties should be included in one
gigantic property; that square miles of territory should be
enclosed in a single park. The scale of luxury and expenditure
in English country life is too high. The machinery of life is too
cumbersome. Its pleasures are costly out of all proportion to
the enjoyment they give. Nor, on the other hand, is it desirable that great landed properties should be held together
when the fixed and necessary charges are so great that they
become overwhelming whenever agricultural depression, or
any other form of adversity, arrives, while the girls and
younger children of the family are left to a poverty which
seems all the more acute from the luxurious surroundings in
which they have been brought up. If the result of graduated
taxation should be to produce a more equal division of property between the members of a family; if rich men, instead of
making an allowance to their sons, should seek to avoid death
duties by capitalising and at once handing over the amount;
if the preservation of game should be on a less extravagant
scale; if estates should become smaller and less encumbered,
and the habits of great country houses somewhat less luxurious than at present, these things would not injure the
country.

Other consequences, however, of a far less desirable character are certain to ensue, and they are consequences that will
fall more heavily upon the poor than upon the rich. Only a
very small fraction of the expenditure of a great landowner

can be said to contribute in any real degree to his own enjoyment. The vast cost of keeping up a great place, and the scale of luxurious hospitality which the conventionalities of society impose, count for much. Parks maintained at great expense, and habitually thrown open to public enjoyment; the village school, or church, or institute established and endowed; all local charities, all county enterprises largely assisted; costly improvements, which no poor landlord could afford; much work given for the express purpose of securing steady employment to the poor—these things form the largest items in the budget of many of the great landowners. Nor should we omit to mention remissions of rent in times of depression which no poor man could afford to make, and very low rents kept unchanged during long periods of increasing prosperity.

In every considerable class there will be the good and the bad, the generous and the grasping; but, on the whole, no candid man will deny the extremely liberal spirit in which the large landed properties in England have been administered. Whatever ultimate benefits may be obtained by their dissolution, it is certain that the first effect will be to extinguish great centres of beneficence and civilisation, to diminish employment, to increase the severity of contracts, and in many other ways to curtail the pleasures and augment the hardships of the deserving poor. It is often said that wealthy Americans, not having the ambition of founding families, give more than wealthy Englishmen for public purposes; but I believe that an examination of the unselfish expenditure of the larger English landlords on objects connected with their estates would show that they in this respect fall little, if at all, below the Transatlantic example. It is probably only in England that we frequently see the curious spectacle of men with incomes of several thousands a year overwhelmed by lifelong pecuniary troubles, not because of any improvidence, of luxurious habits or tastes, but simply because their incomes are insufficient to bear the necessary expenses of their great position.

It seems likely, under the influences I have described, that a great change, both for good and evil, will take place. Land will probably, in future, be more divided, will change hands more frequently, will be treated in a more purely commercial spirit than in the past. Country places taken for mere pleasure, and unconnected with any surrounding property or any landlord duties, will be more frequent. It is not probable that yeomen farmers will multiply as long as it is economically more advantageous for a farmer to rent than to purchase his farm; but land will be bought and sold more frequently, in moderate quantities, as a speculation, let at its extreme value, and divested of all the feudal ideas that are still connected with it. The old historic houses will, no doubt, remain, but they will remain, like the French castles along the Loire, memories of a state of society that has passed away. Many will be in the hands of rich merchants or brewers, and perhaps American millionaires. They will often be shut up, as a measure of economy, for long periods. They will no longer be the centres of great landed properties, or represent a great county influence or a long train of useful duties. Parks will be divided. Picture-galleries will be broken up. Many noble works of art will cross the Atlantic. The old type of English country life will be changed, and much of its ancient beauty will have passed away.

Assuming, as is most probable, that these changes are effected gradually and without violent convulsion, they by no means imply the impoverishment of those who are now the great landed proprietors. No one can doubt that, at the present day, the members of this class would be better off if they had less land and more money; if their properties were in such forms that they had more power of modifying their expenditure according to their means. They will have to pass through a trying period of transition, but, as they are remarkably free from the prejudices and narrow conventionalities that incapacitate some continental aristocracies in the battle of life, they will probably soon adapt themselves to their new circumstances. With ordinary good fortune, with skilful management, with the rich marriages they can always command, with the excellent legal advice that is always at their disposal, they will probably succeed in many instances in keeping together enormous fortunes, and the time is far distant when a really able man, bearing an historic name, does not find that name an assistance to him in his career. But the class will have lost their territorial influence. Public life, dominated, or at least largely influenced, by professional politicians of the American type, will become more distasteful to them. They will find themselves with few landlord or county duties, and with much less necessary hospitality to perform, and they will probably content themselves with smaller country establishments, and spend much more of their time in brighter lands beyond the sea.

The effects of highly graduated taxation on personal property will also be considerable, but probably not so great as on real property. It will strengthen the disposition of a rich man to divide as much as possible his investments, as all great masses of homogeneous immovable property will become specially insecure. It will, in this respect, increase a movement very dangerous to English commercial supremacy, which labour troubles and organisations have already produced. Most good observers have come to the conclusion that an appreciable influence in the commercial depression of the last few years has been the reluctance of rich men to embark on extensive enterprises at a time when labour troubles are so acute, so menacing, and so likely to exercise an influence on legislation. Far-seeing men hesitate to commit themselves to undertakings which can only slowly arrive at maturity when they see the strong bias of popular legislation against property, and the readiness with which a considerable number of modern statesmen will purchase a majority in the House of Commons by allying themselves with the most dishonest groups, and countenancing the most subversive theories. Every influence which, in any department of industrial life, increase risk and diminishes profits must necessarily divert capital, and, whatever other consequences may flow from the frequent strikes and the formidable labour organisations of our time, it cannot be denied that they have both of these effects. If, in addition to these things, it becomes the policy of Governments to seek to defray national expenditure more and more by exceptional taxation, levied for the sake of popularity exclusively on the rich, the tendency to abstain from large manufacturing and commercial enterprises will be greatly accentuated. Such enterprises will not cease, but they will become less numerous. Many manufacturers will probably follow the example which some have already set, and throw out branch establishments in foreign countries. A manufacturer who has some thousand pounds on hand, instead of employing them, as he would once have done, in extending his business, will be inclined to divide them in distant investments. It need scarcely be pointed out how dangerous all this is to a country which has a population much beyond its natural resources, and mainly dependent upon the enormous, unflagging, ever-extending manufacturing and commercial enterprise which vast accumulations and concentrations of capital can alone produce.

Another consequence, which has perhaps not been sufficiently considered, is the tendency of large fortunes to take forms which bring with them no clear and definite duties. The English landed system, which seems now gradually passing away, had, to a very eminent degree, associated great fortunes and high social position with an active life spent in the performance of a large number of administrative county and landlord duties. It in this way provided, perhaps as far as any social institution can provide, that the men who most powerfully influence others by their example should on the whole lead useful, active, and patriotic lives. A great manufacturer and the head of a great commercial undertaking is still more eminently a man whose wealth is indissolubly connected with a life of constant and useful industry.

Wealth, however, takes many other forms than these, and, if I mistake not, a conspicuous characteristic of our century has been the rapid multiplication of the idle rich. In the conditions of modern life it is quite possible for a man to have a colossal fortune in forms that require absolutely no labour, and bring with them no necessary or obvious duties. If he is content with the low rate of interest of the very best securities, he need scarcely give a thought to the sources of his income. If, as is probable, the whole or a portion of his fortune is invested in more speculative securities, it will require from him some time and thought, but it will not necessarily bring with it any imperative duties towards his fellow-creatures. It is true that a rich man of this kind is in reality a large employer of labour. As a shareholder he is part proprietor of railroads, steampackets, dockyards, mines, and many other widely different, and probably widely scattered, industrial enterprises and organisations. But he has no real voice in the management of these concerns. He knows nothing of the conditions of the countless labourers who, in many countries and many climes, are toiling for his profit. He looks on his investments simply as sources of income. His sole information concerning them is probably confined to a few statistics about dividends, traffic returns, encumbrances, and trade prospects.

We are all familiar with great numbers of more or less wealthy men whose fortunes are of this description. Under the influences that I have described such fortunes seem to me likely to multiply. The tendency of most great forms of industry is evidently towards vast joint-stock companies with many shareholders. With improved means of communication, the securities and enterprises of many countries are easily thrown into a common market, and national and municipal debts, which create one of the easiest and most important forms of investment, are rapidly increasing. One of the first signs that a barbarous nation is adopting the manners of Occidental civilisation is usually the creation of a national debt, and democracies are certainly showing themselves in no degree behind the most extravagant monarchies in the rapidity with which they accumulate national and local indebtedness. Nor should we forget the effect which frequent revolutions and violent social and industrial perturbations always exercise on the disposition of fortunes. These things

seldom fail to depress credit, to increase debt, to destroy industry, to impoverish nations; but they also furnish many
opportunities by which the skilful, the fortunate, and the unscrupulous rise rapidly to easily acquired wealth. If we take
them in conjunction with the influences that are in so many
directions dissociating great wealth from landed property and
administrative functions, and adding to the risks of extensive
industrial undertakings, it will appear probable that the fortunes of the future will be much less connected with active
duties than those of the past.

The prospect is not an encouraging one. A man of very superior powers will, no doubt, always find his work, and to
such a man a fortune of this description will be an incalculable
blessing. It will save him from years of drudgery and anxiety,
and it will give him at the outset of his career the priceless
advantage of independence. To men of lofty moral qualities
it will at least be no injury. Such men will feel strongly the inalienable responsibilities of wealth, and will find in the fields
of social and philanthropic activity ample scope for their exertions. Many, too, who are not men of conspicuous mental
or moral force will have some strong taste for art, or literature,
or country pursuits, or science, or research, which will secure
for them useful and honourable lives. Yet it can scarcely be
doubted that even these will always be exceptions. The majority of men fail to find their work unless it is brought before
them prominently by circumstances, or forced upon them by
the strong pressure of necessity. Wealth which brings with it
no ties and is obtained and enjoyed with no effort is to most
men a temptation and a snare. All the more dissipated capitals
and watering-places of Europe and America are full of examples of men in this position, living lives of absolute frivolity, dissociated from all serious interests, ever seeking with
feverish eagerness for new forms of pleasure, raising the standard of luxury and ostentation, and often, in still graver ways,
depressing the moral tone of the society in which they live.

Considerations of this kind will probably be treated with
much disdain by Radical critics. They will truly say that the

section of society referred to forms only a very small portion of the population, and they will ask whether nations are to frame their institutions with the object of providing occupation for the spoilt children of fortune, and saving them from their own frivolity or vice. No one, I suppose, would maintain that they should do so; but, in estimating the advantages and disadvantages of different institutions, many weights enter into either scale which would not of themselves be sufficient to turn the balance. It is, however, a grave error to suppose that the evils I have described can be confined to the classes who are immediately concerned. It is impossible that the upper class of a nation can become corrupt, frivolous, or emasculated without affecting deeply and widely the whole body of the community. Constituted as human nature is, rich men will always contribute largely to set the tone of society, to form the tastes, habits, ideals, and aspirations of other classes. In this respect, as in many others, the gradual dissociation of the upper classes from many forms of public duty is likely to prove a danger to the community.

It is an evil which appears wherever democracy becomes ascendant, though its progress varies much in different countries. The strong traditions, the firmly knit organisation of English life, have hitherto resisted it much more effectively than most nations. No one can say that the upper classes in England have as yet abandoned politics. Those who fear this change may derive some consolation from observing how largely the most Radical Cabinets of our time have consisted of peers and connections of peers, and from counting up the many thousands of pounds at which the average private incomes of their members may be estimated. Nor indeed, can it be said that English democracy, on either side of the Atlantic, shows any special love for a Spartan, or Stoical, or Puritan simplicity. Mr. Cecil Rhodes once described a prominent politician as 'a cynical sybarite who was playing the demagogue;' and it must be owned that professions of a very austere democracy have not unfrequently been found united with the keenest appetite for wealth, for pleasure, and even for titles.

The political and economical influences, however, which I have endeavoured to trace have established in England, as elsewhere, a tendency which is not the less real because it has not yet triumphed, and the experience of American political and municipal life throws much light upon the path along which we are moving. The change in the House of Commons is becoming visible to every eye, and one of the most important questions for the future is the possibility of maintaining an Upper Chamber as a permanent and powerful element in the Constitution.

CHAPTER 4

Aristocracies and Upper Chambers

O f all the forms of government that are possible among mankind, I do not know any which is likely to be worse than the government of a single omnipotent democratic Chamber. It is at least as susceptible as an individual despot to the temptations that grow out of the possession of an uncontrolled power, and it is likely to act with much less sense of responsibility and much less real deliberation. The necessity of making a great decision seldom fails to weigh heavily on a single despot, but when the responsibility is divided among a large assembly, it is greatly attenuated. Every considerable assembly also, as it has been truly said, has at times something of the character of a mob. Men acting in crowds and in public, and amid the passions of conflict and of debate, are strangely different from what they are when considering a serious question in the calm seclusion of their cabinets. Party interests and passions; personal likings or dislikes; the power of rhetoric; the confusion of thought that springs from momentary impressions, and from the clash of many conflicting arguments; the compromises of principle that arise from attempts to combine for one purpose men of different opinions or interests; mere lassitude, and mere caprice, all act powerfully on the decisions of an assembly. Many members are entangled by pledges they had inconsiderately given, by some principle they had admitted without recognising the full extent to which it might be carried, or by some line of conduct they had at another period pursued. Personal interest plays no small part; for the consequence and pecuniary interests of many members are bound up with the triumph of their party, while many others desire beyond all things a renewal of their mandate. They know that a considerable part of the constituencies to which they must ultimately appeal is composed of fluctuating masses of very ignorant men, easily swayed by clap-trap, by appeals to class interests or class animosities, and for the most part entirely incapable of disentangling a difficult question, judging distant and obscure consequences, realising conditions of thought and life widely different from their own, estimating political measures according to their true proportionate value, and weighing nicely balanced arguments in a judicial spirit.

The confusion becomes still greater when Parliaments divide into a number of small, independent groups, each of them subordinating general political interests to the furtherance of some particular interests and opinions, and when the art of parliamentary government consists mainly of skill in combining these heterogeneous fractions in a single division. The first condition of good legislation on any particular question, as of most other good work, is that it should be single-minded—that it should represent the application of the best available faculty to a special purpose. There is scarcely a contested question determined in Parliament in which motives wholly different from the ostensible ones, and wholly unconnected with the immediate issue, do not influence many votes. It is also rather the rule than the exception that a general election produces a change of government, and the defeated minority of one Parliament becomes the majority in the next.

There is certainly no proposition in politics more indubitable than that the attempt to govern a great heterogeneous empire simply by such an assembly must ultimately prove disastrous, and the necessity of a second Chamber, to exercise a controlling, modifying, retarding, and steadying influence has acquired almost the position of an axiom. Of all the many parliamentary constitutions now existing in the world, Greece, Mexico, and Servia are, I believe, the only ones in which independent and sovereign nations have adopted the system of a single Chamber, and, among these, Servia is only a partial exception. According to the Constitution of this little country, legislation is, in ordinary times, conducted by the king and a single national assembly, in which one out of every four members must be nominated by the king, and which exercises strictly limited and defined powers; but the sovereign has a right of convoking when he pleases a second and much larger assembly, which alone is competent to deal with grave questions affecting the Constitution and the territory of the State.[1] Norway, being united with Sweden, is not an absolutely independent country, but it is one of the countries where legislative power is virtually in the hands of a single Chamber. The Storthing is a single Chamber, elected at a single election, but, when it meets, it elects out of its own body a second Chamber, consisting of a fourth part of its members. The extreme concentration of power resulting from this system is one of the great causes of the dangerous tension that exists in the relations of Sweden and Norway.

The experience of the past abundantly corroborates the views of those who dread government by a single Chamber. In the English Commonwealth such a system for a short time existed; but the abolition of the House of Lords was soon followed by the expulsion of the Commons, and when Cromwell resolved to restore some measure of parliamentary government, he clearly saw that two Chambers were indispensable, and he revived on another basis the House of Lords. In America, Franklin had strongly advocated a single Chamber; and in the American Confederation, which was formally adopted by the thirteen States in 1781, and which

---

[1] Demombrynes's *Les Constitutions Européennes*, i. 715–24. I do not include the Grand Duchy of Finland, the Provincial Diets in the Austrian Empire, and a few small Powers holding a completely subordinate position in the German system, in which single Chambers exist.

represented the United States in the first years of their independent existence, the Congress consisted of only one
branch. It was invested with very small powers, and was
almost as completely overshadowed by the State rights of its
constituents as the Cromwellian House of Commons had
been by the military power of the Commonwealth. But the
very first article of the American Constitution, which was
framed in 1787, divided the Congress into a Senate and a
House of Representatives. In all the separate States the bi-
cameral system exists, and it also exists in all the British colonies which have self-governing powers. In France, Turgot
and Sieyès advocated a single Chamber, and in the French
Constitution of 1791 all power was placed in the hands of
such a body, the result being one of the most appalling tyr-
annies in the history of mankind. In 1848 the same experiment
was once more tried, and it once more conducted France
through anarchy to despotism.

It is not necessary for my present purpose to enter into any
disquisition about the origin and early evolution of the House
of Lords. For a long period of English history it was a small
and a diminishing body, and in the fifteenth century the spiritual, or life peers, considerably outnumbered the temporal,
or hereditary ones. The Reformation had a capital influence
on the constitution of the House. By removing the mitred
abbots, it made the temporal peers a clear majority, while the
vast distribution of monastic property among some of the
great families added enormously to their influence. From this
time the lay, or hereditary peerage steadily increased. Only
twenty-nine temporal peers had been summoned to the first
Parliament of Henry VII., and fifty-one was the largest number summoned under Henry VIII.; but 119 peers were summoned to the Parliament of 1640, and 139 to the Parliament
of 1661.[2] At the close of the seventeenth century the temporal
peerage amounted to about 150; in the first Parliament of
George III., to 174. In 1642, the bishops were excluded by Act

[2] May's *Const Hist.* i. 232–35.

of Parliament from the House of Lords, which thus became, for the first time in its history, a purely hereditary body; and in 1649 the House of Lords was abolished by the vote of the House of Commons. At the Restoration, this vote being of course treated as null, the House revived, and by an Act of Parliament of 1661 the bishops were again introduced into its ranks.

The Revolution, unlike the Commonwealth, had no injurious effect upon it. The change of dynasty was largely due to the action of the heads of a few great aristocratic families; the House of Lords bore a very conspicuous part in regulating its terms; and it is probably no exaggeration to say that the steady Whig preponderance in that House mainly secured the Revolution settlement during the long period of the disputed succession. It is true that, in the redivision of power which resulted from the decline of royal influence at the Revolution, the larger share fell to the House of Commons, and by the time of Walpole that House, in its corporate capacity, was certainly the strongest body in the State; but individual peers exercised an enormous influence over its composition. The system of small nomination boroughs was chiefly due to the fluctuations in wealth and population in the community, and to the practical annihilation of the old prerogative of the sovereign of revising the representation by summoning new and rising places to send members to the Commons. Most of those seats passed under the patronage of peers, either on account of vast territorial possessions which they had inherited, or by the frequent ennobling of great merchant-princes, who, by means of venal boroughs, had acquired political power, and who obtained their peerages as the reward of political services.

The place which is occupied by the small boroughs in English history is a very great one. At the time when the Revolution settlement was seriously disputed they gave the Whig party a steady preponderance of parliamentary power, thus securing it from those violent fluctuations of opinion which, if the Legislature had been really popular, would have almost certainly proved fatal to the unsettled dynasty. They contributed, also, powerfully to the general harmony between the two Houses, and they enabled the House of Commons to grow steadily in influence, without exciting any hostility on the part of the Upper House. Perhaps the most dangerous moment in the history of the peerage was in 1719, when the ministry of Sunderland and Stanhope endeavoured to make it a close body, by strictly limiting the number of the House, and almost wholly depriving the sovereign of the power of creating new peers. Chiefly by the exertions of Walpole, this measure was defeated in the Commons, and no attempt was made to revive it; and the presence in the House of Commons of large numbers of heirs to peerages, or of younger members of noble families, strengthened the harmony between the two Houses.

The union with Scotland not only introduced sixteen peers into the House of Lords: it also introduced a new principle, as those peers were elected for a single Parliament by their fellow-peers. For a long period they were far from improving the constitution of the House, for this small alien section of an ancient but very poor aristocracy proved exceedingly subservient to Government control. The system of election also tended greatly to the misrepresentation of the peerage; for it was by a simple majority, and the party which preponderated in the Scotch peerage returned, in consequence, the whole body of the representative peers. The position of the minority was at this time very anomalous; for while the method of election made it impossible for them to enter the House of Lords as representative peers, they were at the same time incapacitated by law from sitting in the House of Commons, and the House of Lords, in 1711, passed a resolution declaring that, although the sovereign might confer an English peerage on a Scotch peer, he had not the right of introducing him into their House. The disability was, in some degree, evaded by the device of conferring English peerages on the eldest sons of Scotch peers; but it was accepted as law until 1782, when the question was referred to the judges, who unanimously pronounced the resolution of 1711 to have been unauthorised by the Act of Union, and it was accordingly rescinded by a vote of the House of Lords. From this time the right of conferring English peerages on the minority of Scotch peers who are excluded by their politics from the number of representative peers, has been largely exercised.

On the accession of George III. the position of the House of Lords was greatly changed. Hitherto the Whig party had predominated in its ranks, and the first object of the young King was to break down the power of a group of great Whig peers, who had accumulated masses of borough influence, and who had long dominated in the State. This is not the place to relate the long, and on the whole successful, struggle by which the King attained his ends; but it must be noticed that during his whole reign peers drawn from the Tory party were created in large numbers with the object of giving a new complexion to the House of Lords. The inducement to these creations was probably considerably increased by the abolition of sinecure places under Burke's measure of economical reform, which deprived the minister of a large part of his former means of rewarding political services.

The Irish Union introduced into the House of Lords a new body of twenty-eight representative peers. In Ireland, as in Scotland, the vicious system of election by simple majority, which inevitably gives one party in the peerage a monopoly, was adopted; but no question was ever raised about the power of the Crown to introduce Irish peers into the House of Lords by the bestowal of English peerages; and in other respects the Scotch precedent was not exactly followed. The Scotch peers were elected for one Parliament, but the Irish peers for life. The Scotch peers who were not in the House of Lords were absolutely excluded from sitting in the House of Commons; but an Irish peer who was not a representative peer might sit in the Commons for an English, Scotch, or Welsh constituency. The Scotch peerage was closed at the Union, the sovereign being deprived of all power of creating Scotch peerages. The Irish peerage was only limited at the Union, for the sovereign retained the power of creating one Irish peerage whenever three Irish peerages were extinguished—a useless power, which has in our own day been surrendered.

Another important difference was that, the Scotch Church being Presbyterian, the Scotch Union left the spiritual peers unchanged, while the Irish Union introduced a new body of spiritual peers, sitting by a new principle of rotation. This slight addition of an archbishop and four bishops disappeared when the Irish Church was disestablished; but it represents the only modern increase which has taken place in the number of the spiritual peers to counterbalance the great increase of the temporal ones. Several new English bishoprics, it is true, have been in the present century created; but the legislation that authorised them expressly provided that there should be no increase in the number of bishops in the House of Lords.[3] Two archbishops and the bishops of London, Durham, and Winchester invariably sit in the House; but of the remaining bishops, only the twenty-one senior bishops sit in the House of Lords, and an unwritten conventionality greatly restricts their interference in purely secular politics.

Few things, indeed, in English history are more significant than the change which has taken place in the political influence of the Church. Great Churchmen once continually held the highest offices in the Government. But no clergyman has taken part in an English Government since the reign of Queen Anne, though in Ireland a succession of great governing prelates continued far into the eighteenth century. The spiritual element in the House of Lords has become a small fraction in the House, and the presence of that small element has come to be looked upon as an anomaly. Yet the bishops sit in the House of Lords by an older title than any section of the lay peerage, with the possible exception of the earls, and for a considerable period of English history they formed the majority of the House.[4] They represent, in a certain measure, the

---

[3] See, *e.g.*, 10 and 11 Vict. c. 108, s. 2.
[4] See Freeman's essay on this subject in the fourth series of his *Historical Essays*.

principle of life peerages, to which modern Liberal tendencies are steadily flowing, for, although they sit in the House by an order of succession, it is a succession of office, and not a succession of lineage; and the manner in which they are appointed furnishes a strong presumption that they possess a more than average capacity, a more than average knowledge of the condition of great sections of the English people, and especially a more than average share of that administrative ability which is so valuable in the government of nations.

The strong Tory character that the House of Lords assumed in the reign of George III. has been in many ways a misfortune in English history, but it is far from certain that it was unpopular. The House of Lords was never at this period in as violent conflict with the popular sentiment as the House of Commons in the Wilkes case. The most memorable conflict between the two Houses in this reign took place when the House of Lords overthrew the coalition ministry, which commanded a great majority in the House of Commons, and supported Pitt in holding office for three months in opposition to that majority; but the dissolution of 1784 decisively vindicated the policy of the Lords, and proved that on this question they most truly represented the sentiment of the nation. The strong hostility to reform which undoubtedly prevailed in the House of Lords in the closing years of the eighteenth century and in the early decades of the nineteenth century represented with probably unexaggerated fidelity the reaction of opinion which had passed over England in consequence of the horrors and calamities of the French Revolution, and its anti-Catholic sentiment was fully shared by the English people. The total defeat, at the election of 1807, of the party which advocated a policy of most moderate Catholic concession is a decisive proof. It was not indeed until 1821 that any considerable divergence on this question was shown between the two Houses. It will usually, I think, be found that the House of Lords at this time, in the actions which later periods have most condemned, represented a prejudice which was predominant in the country, though it often represented it in a slightly exaggerated form,

and with a somewhat greater persistence than the House of
Commons. The presence of a spiritual element did not prevent
the Upper House being behind the House of Commons in the
great work of diminishing, and at last abolishing the horrors
of the slave trade; and the authority of some great lawyers who
sat in the House of Lords was the direct cause of its opposition
to some of the most necessary legal reforms, and especially to
the mitigation of the atrocities of the criminal code.

There are, however, two facts which must always be borne
in mind in comparing the House of Lords in the corrupt and
unreforming period between the outbreak of the great French
war and the Reform Bill of 1832 with the House of Lords in
our own day. Whatever may be said in the present day of the
class prejudices, the class apathy, or even the class interests,
of its members, no candid man will deny that it is an eminently independent body, absolutely free from all taint or suspicion of corruption, and there is probably no legislative body
in the world in which motives of mere personal interest bear
a smaller share. In the early period of the century, on the
contrary, a great and dominating section of the peerage consisted of men who were directly bound to the Crown by places
or pensions; while the indirect advantages of the peerage, in
the distribution of the vast patronage in Church and State,
were so great that the whole body was bound to the existing
system of government by personal and selfish motives of the
strongest kind. 'The far greater part of the peers,' wrote
Queen Caroline to George IV. in 1820, 'hold by themselves
and their families, offices, pensions, and emoluments solely
at the will and pleasure of your Majesty. There are more than
four-fifths of the peers in this situation.' Wilberforce mentioned in 1811 that more than half the House of Lords 'had
been created or gifted with their titles' since 1780, and the
special object of these creations had been to make the House
completely subservient to the Crown and to the Executive.[5]

The other consideration is the borough patronage, to which
I have already referred. It identified the interests of the peer-

[5] Walpole's *History of England*, i. 150.

age in the closest degree with opposition to reform. It was not only an interest of power and of family, but also an interest of property, for these boroughs were notoriously bought and sold. Before Curwen's Act, which was passed in 1809, imposing penalties on such sales, they were practised with scarcely any concealment, and after that Act they still continued. The analysis of the representation given in Oldfield's 'Representative History,' which was published in 1816, shows that, out of the 513 members who then represented England and Wales, no less than 218 were returned by the influence or nomination of eighty-seven peers. Scotland was represented by forty-five members, of whom thirty-one were returned by twenty-one peers. Ireland was represented by one hundred members, of whom fifty-one were returned by thirty-six peers. Six peers returned no less than forty-five members to the House of Commons.[6]

It is sufficiently obvious from these facts that, while the forms of the Constitution have remained substantially unchanged, its character and working have been essentially and fundamentally altered by the Reform Bill of 1832, and no one can wonder that the House of Lords should have resisted that Reform Bill with a persistence which nothing short of imminent danger of a revolution and the threat of a great immediate creation of peers could overcome. It is, rather, wonderful that a peerage exercising such power should have been, on the whole, so steadily in touch with the popular feeling; that English legislation should have been so free from the privileges of taxation and many kindred abuses in favour of the aristocracy, which existed in most continental countries; that the system of nomination boroughs should have been so largely employed in bringing poor men of genius and promise into the House of Commons; that so large a number of members of the Upper House should have been in the van of every great movement of reform. Even in the conflict of 1832 this characteristic was clearly shown. Some of the oldest and greatest aristocratic families in the kingdom led the popular cause. It was noticed

---

[6] May, i 282–306; Oldfield, vi. 285–300.

that, of the peers created before 1790, 108 voted in favour of the Bill, and only four against it,[7] while, until the very last stage of the struggle, no class of members in the House of Lords were more strenuously opposed to the Bill than the bishops.

Since this great measure the position of the House of Lords in the Constitution has fundamentally altered. It no longer claims to co-ordinate power with the House of Commons in legislation: it exercises a secondary position in the Constitution. But if it has sometimes retarded measures that were both useful and urgent, it also discharges functions of great and of increasing utility. It exercises a suspensory veto, delaying measures which have acquired only an uncertain, transitory, or capricious majority, until they have become clearly the deliberate desire of the constituencies. In the system of party government it constantly happens that the popularity of a statesman, or the ascendency of a party, or the combination at an election of many distinct interests or motives acting simultaneously on many different classes of electors, brings into power a Government many of whose measures have never received the real sanction of the electors. Sometimes lines of policy of great importance are first started in the course of a session. Often measures of great importance are brought forward in Parliament which at the election had been entirely subsidiary with the electors or with great sections of them, or which had come to them with the disadvantage of novelty, and had never been thoroughly understood or thoroughly canvassed. Public opinion in England rarely occupies itself seriously with more than one great question at a time, and those deliberate and widespread convictions, on which alone a national policy can be firmly and safely based, are only arrived at after a long period of discussion. Nothing can be more frequent than for a measure to obtain a majority in the House of Commons which has never been either approved of or considered by the bulk of the electors by whom that majority was returned. In all such cases it is a matter of

---

[7] Molesworth's *History*, i. 203.

vital importance that there should be a delaying power, capable of obstructing measures till they have been distinctly sanctioned by the electorate, till they have come to represent the reasoned and deliberate opinion of the constituencies.

It is extremely important, too, that something of a judicial element should be infused into politics. In policies that are closely connected with party conflicts, the question of party interest will always dominate in the House of Commons over the question of intrinsic merits. A bad measure will often be carried, though it may be known to be bad, when the only alternative is the displacement of a ministry supported by a majority. Under these circumstances, the existence of a revising Chamber which is so constituted that it can reject a measure without overthrowing a ministry, and which is not dependent on the many chances of a popular election, is one of the best guarantees of sound legislation.

It is also one of the greatest and most distinctive excellences of British legislation that it is in general framed, not on the system of giving a decisive victory to one set of interests, and obtaining perfect symmetry or logical coherence, but with a view of satisfying, as far as possible, many different and conflicting interests, classes, and opinions. The permanence and efficacy of legislation, according to English notions, depends essentially on its success in obtaining the widest measure of assent or acquiescence, and provoking the smallest amount of friction and opposition. In carrying out this policy the action of the House of Lords has been of capital importance. Very frequently it represents especially the minority which is overpowered in the other House. The will of the majority in the stronger Chamber ultimately prevails, but scarcely a great contentious measure passes into the Statute Book without compromises, modifications, or amendments designed to disarm the opposition, or to satisfy the wishes of minorities, or to soften the harsher features of inevitable transitions. The mere consciousness that there is another and a revising assembly, whose assent is indispensable to legislation, has a moderating influence on majorities and ministries which it is difficult to overvalue. The tyranny of majorities is, of all forms of tyranny, that which, in the conditions of modern life, is most to be feared, and against which it should be the chief object of a wise statesman to provide.

It is an easy and frequent device of Radical writers to assail the House of Lords by enumerating the measures of incontestable value which it had for a time rejected or delayed. That it has in its long history committed many faults no candid man will deny, though it is by no means equally clear that they have greatly exceeded those which have been committed by the other House. In my own opinion the side of its policy which, in the present century, has been the worst is that relating to religious disqualifications, and the fact is the more remarkable because, in the generation that followed the Revolution, the House of Lords was incontestably more liberal than the House of Commons in all questions relating to Nonconformists. In more modern times this has not been the case, and the doctrine that the existence of an Established Church implied that State funds should be devoted only to one form of religion, and that the great fields of State power, education, influence, and employment should be guarded by religious qualifications against the adherents of other faiths, prevailed in the House of Lords long after it had broken down in the Commons. It is a doctrine which has played a great, and, as I believe, most mischievous, part in English history. In the present century it has probably found its most powerful defence in the early writings and speeches of Mr. Gladstone.

At the same time, many things may be alleged which will at least mitigate the blame that, on such grounds, may be attached to the House of Lords. An assembly which is essentially representative of property and tradition, whose chief duty is much less to initiate legislation than to prevent that which is hasty and unwise, and which fulfils rather the function of a brake or of a drag than of a propelling force, will inevitably be slower than the other House to adopt constitutional or organic changes. The legislative reforms which the House of Lords is so much blamed for having rejected all became law with its consent; and, on the whole, England need not fear comparison with any other country in the enlightened character of her legislation. If a few countries have moved more rapidly, very few have moved so surely, and the permanence of her reforms and the tranquillity with which they were effected are largely due to the existence of a Chamber which delayed them till they had been thoroughly sifted and incontestably sanctioned by the nation, and which disarmed opposition by introducing compromises and amendments to meet the wants of discontented minorities. Of the measures the House of Lords is accused of mutilating or delaying, many had been repeatedly rejected by the House of Commons itself; or had never been brought clearly and directly before the constituencies; or had been supported in the Lower House by small, doubtful, and diminishing majorities; or had excited little more than an academic interest, touching no real feeling throughout the nation. It has seldom, if ever, rejected measures on which the will of the people had been decisively and persistently expressed.

The moment of its greatest unpopularity was probably that of the Reform Bill of 1832, and it was the firm persuasion of the Radical wing of the triumphant party that one early and inevitable consequence of the extended suffrage would be the destruction, or at least the total transformation, of the House of Lords. The Whig ministers, it is true, gave no countenance to these attacks, but the agitation against the Lords was actively maintained by O'Connell and by a considerable body of English Radicals. One attempt was made to deprive it of its veto, and another to expel the bishops from its walls; and the incompatibility of an hereditary legislative body with a democratic Parliament was continually affirmed in language much like that which we so abundantly heard before the election of 1895. The result of this agitation is very instructive. On some of the questions on which the Houses differed the House of Lords yielded, insisting only on minor compromises. On the important question of the appropriation of Irish Church funds to secular purposes it succeeded in carrying its point. The agitation for an organic change in the Constitution was soon found to excite more alarm than approbation in the country. The current of opinion turned strongly against the agitators, and against the Government which those agitators supported. In less than ten years the revolution of opinion was complete, and the election of May 1841 brought a Conservative minister into power at the head of an overwhelming majority.

We may next consider the advantages and disadvantages of the hereditary principle in the Upper House. It was a saying of Franklin that there is no more reason in hereditary legislators than there would be in hereditary professors of mathematics. In England, however, there is no question of placing the making of laws in the hands of an hereditary class. All that the Constitution provides is, that the members of this class should have a fixed place, in concurrence with others, in accomplishing the task. It is absurd to expect that the eldest son of a single family shall always display exceptional or even average capacity, and this is one of the main arguments against hereditary despotic monarchy, which places in the hands of one man, selected on the principle of strict heredity, one of the most arduous and responsible tasks which a human being can undertake. It is not, however, absurd to expect that more than five hundred families, thrown into public life for the most part at a very early age, animated by all its traditions and ambitions, and placed under circumstances exceedingly favourable to the development of political talent, should produce a large amount of governing faculty. The qualities required for successful political life are not, like poetry or the higher forms of philosophy, qualities that are of a very rare and exceptional order. They are, for the most part, qualities of judgment, industry, tact, knowledge of men and of affairs, which can be attained to a high degree of perfection by men of no very extraordinary intellectual powers. Outside the circle of the leisured classes, most men only rise to great positions in political life at a mature age, and after a long struggle in other spheres. Their minds have already taken their definite ply. Their best thoughts and efforts have, during many years, been devoted to wholly different pursuits. When they come into the House of Commons, they have, in many departments, still to learn the rudiments of their art. Even if they are men of real and solid attainments, they have commonly lost their flexibility, and defects of manner or of tact which might be easily corrected in youth, but which become indelible in mature life, often obstruct a political career far more seriously than much graver causes. Every one who has come in close contact with parliamentary life knows how seriously the popularity and influence of members of very real attainments have been impaired by the professorial manner, or the legal manner, or the purely academic habit of mind, or the egotism and false sentiment that often accompany a self-made man; or the incapacity for compromise, for avoiding friction, for distinguishing different degrees of importance and seriousness, which characterises a man who has not had the education of a man of the world. A man, too, who is not marked out in any way by his position for parliamentary distinction is more tempted than those of another class to make sacrifices of principle and character to win the prize. He is likely to be more absolutely dependent on party organisations, more governed by the desire for office or title or social distinction.

The position of a young man, on the other hand, who has the fortune to belong to one of the great governing families is very different. He usually obtains the best education the country can give him, and he possesses the inestimable advantage of coming from an early age into close, constant, unconstrained intercourse with men who are actively engaged in the government of the country. In many great families the whole intellectual atmosphere is political. Political topics are those which are most constantly discussed around him, and the pride and greatness of the family lie mainly in the political distinction which has been achieved by its members in the past, and the political influence and connections they possess in the present. Examples and incentives are thus formed, which seldom fail to act powerfully on a young man of talent and ambition, and the path that is before him is clearly marked out.

He travels, and knows something of foreign languages, and although his knowledge of the Continent is usually exceedingly superficial, it is above the average that is attained in trade or in the professions; while the social element in which he moves requires from him some tincture of general reading. He has usually the immense advantage of entering the House of Commons when he is still a young man, and he very probably soon fills one of the subordinate offices. As an actual or expectant landlord, as a magistrate, as the political leader of his district, as the initiator or president of many local institutions or movements, he obtains an early aptitude for business, an intimate knowledge of the characters and circumstances of great sections of the people, which will be more useful to him than any lesson that he can learn from books. The manners of a gentleman come to him almost as a birthright, and no good judge will fail to recognise their importance in political life. Self-confidence unalloyed by arrogance or egotism; the light touch, the instinctive tact which lessens friction and avoids points of difference; the spirit of compromise and conciliation, which is so useful in the management of men and in the conduct of affairs, are the natural products of the atmosphere in which he was born. Having a great independent position, he is less accessible than poorer men to the sordid motives that play so large a part in public life; while the standard of honour of his class, though it by no means covers the whole field of morals, at least guards him against that large department of bad acts which can be designated as ungentlemanly.

The reader will, of course, understand that this description has only a very general application. There are many cases in which great names and positions are associated only with lives of mischievous self-indulgence or scandalous vice. There are circles where luxury is carried to such a pitch that men almost come to resemble that strange species of ant which is so dependent on the ministrations of its slave ants that it would starve to death if these were not present to feed it. The enormous and elaborate waste of time, the colossal luxury of ostentation, the endless routine of dressing and gossip and frivolous amusements that prevail in some great country houses, form an atmosphere which is well fitted to kill all earnestness of purpose and conviction. The pleasures of life are made its business. The slaughter of countless beasts and birds is treated as if it were a main object of existence. Life is looked down upon as from an opera-box, till all sense of its seriousness seems to vanish, and the conflicts of parties are followed with a merely sporting interest, much like that which is centred on the rival horses at Newmarket or Ascot.

It is no less true that there are numerous cases in which men who were born in spheres far removed from those of the governing families, have exhibited in high perfection all the best qualities which the aristocratic system is calculated to foster. But we are dealing here with class averages, and few persons, I think, will dispute the high average of capacity for government which the circumstances of English aristocratic life tend to produce. An English aristocracy, as has been often observed, is essentially different from those foreign aristocracies which constitute a separate caste. Its members have always largely intermarried with commoners. Their children, except the eldest, descend speedily into the ranks of commoners; they are usually obliged to make their own positions by their own efforts, and, since the great reforms that have taken place in the bestowal of patronage, without unfair advantages; and there is no part of the British Empire in which members of great British families may not be found sharing alike the most arduous labours and the most hard-won prizes.

It is unfortunately a truth only too abundantly attested that, as a general rule, few greater misfortunes can befall a young man than to inherit at an early age such a fortune as places at his feet an ample range of enjoyments without the necessity of any kind of labour. Strong intellectual tastes and powers, and unusual force of character, will make their way through any circumstances, but the common lot of man is to be commonplace—though there are few imputations which most men more bitterly resent—and it is not natural for a young man of small talent and very ordinary character to devote himself to steady labour when no necessity urges him, and when all the means of self-indulgence are at his disposal. On the Continent such young men commonly gravitate to the towns, where a life of pleasure soon passes into a life of vice. In England, the passion for field sports has at least the advantage of supplying a large sphere of unintellectual and absorbing amusement which is healthy, manly, and innocent; but, as I have already observed, the special preservative in England of the character of such men lies in a social condition which assigns to a wealthy class a large circle of necessary duties, and makes the gratuitous discharge of public functions the appanage and sign of dignity.

Another consideration must be mentioned, of a different and more delicate kind. There can be little doubt that the conditions most favourable for a high average of mortality are to be found in the temperate zones of life, removed from the ignorance, the degrading associations, and the keen temptations of want, and also from the luxurious, enervating, self-indulgent habits of superabundant wealth. The one great moral advantage which specially belongs to the latter sphere is the facility of early marriage which an assured competence gives, and which provides in a very critical period of life a strong regulating influence of character. It will, I think, be found that these marriages are more general among rich men connected with a landed aristocracy than among those whose fortunes have been rapidly made by commerce or speculation. Questions of succession hold a larger place in the lives of the former class. An established position and the possession of a great historic house bring duties of hospitality which make marriage almost a necessity, and which are rarely fully learned except by early practice; and the women who give the tone and the attraction to English aristocratic society seldom fail, even in the most frivolous and pleasure-loving circles, to insist on a degree of decorum in the relation of the sexes which is not always found in corresponding societies in other lands.

The importance of this question of marriage is very great,

and modern science has thrown much light on its far-reaching consequences. Marriages confined to a restricted caste, such as are usual in royal families and, in a less degree, in some foreign aristocracies, seldom fail to result in physical, mental, or moral debility. An aristocracy which marries mainly and habitually for wealth is likely to be a dwindling body. The great heiress who concentrates in her own person the fortunes of a family is commonly such because she comes from a family in which children are usually few, or in which deaths are unusually numerous, and the introduction of such women into a family has therefore a natural tendency to lower the average of its productivity.[8] But where marriages are not unduly limited by conventional restraints, and where wealth is not too exclusively sought, the great advantage of choice which an illustrious position gives in what is called, not quite unjustly, the 'matrimonial market,' has an undoubted tendency to improve and invigorate a race, by grafting into its stock an unusual proportion of more than common physical and mental endowments. Country lives and tastes, and the general character of their marriage, have thus combined to give the upper classes in England a high physical average, which has contributed in no small degree to their influence in the world. Whatever else may be said to them, no one at least can accuse them of being an effete and debilitated class. The energy with which they throw themselves into their sports and travels and political contests, the mark they have made in so many fields, the prominent part they have taken in the initiation of so many enterprises, the skill, industry, and success with which they have managed great properties and guided local affairs, are sufficiently evident.

There is no better sign of the vitality of a class than its flexibility of adaptation; and in this respect the upper classes in England have been, in the present century, abundantly proved. When the great democratic movement deprived them of a monopoly or a preference in vast fields of admin-

---

[8] See Mr. Galton's *Hereditary Genius*, pp. 131–40.

istration and patronage, they did not shrink from public life,
but at once accepted the new conditions, flung themselves
boldly and skilfully into all the competitions of English life,
and retrieved by talent and personal popularity a great part
of the ascendency of which they had been deprived by law.
A still graver trial followed when agricultural depression fell
with terrible effect on the main sources of their income. Few
things are more striking in modern English history than the
courage and high spirit with which the landed gentry of England, both of the higher and lower grades, have, on the
whole, met the trial, discarding conventional rules and restraints which limited their means of acquiring fortune, bearing with uncomplaining fortitude great changes of life and
habits, throwing themselves boldly into a multitude of new
industrial enterprises, sending their children to seek a livelihood in the counting-houses of merchants, the ranches of
Mexico, or the diamond-fields of Africa.

That very shrewd and competent observer, Archbishop
Magee, once remarked that nothing struck him more in the
House of Lords than the large amount of curious special
knowledge possessed by its members. When the most out-of-
the-way subject was started there seemed always, he said,
some obscure peer on the back benches who had made this
subject a study, and knew all about it. In the fields of literature, philosophy, and science, the achievements of members
of that House have been very considerable; and in numerous
cases, where no original work is produced, an unusually high
level of scholarship and research has been attained. But it is
naturally in political life that the superior qualities of the class
have been most displayed. No one who is well acquainted
with English history can fail to be struck with the very large
number of its members who have fully held their own in the
conflicts of the House of Commons, and who have discharged
great public duties with an industry and a skill that have been
universally recognised. A few of these statesmen have been
men who would have risen from almost any rank of life to
power and influence. The majority have been men of good,

but not extraordinary, ability who, if they had been born in humbler spheres, would probably have led creditable and successful lives, but have been little heard of, but who, being placed by their position on the threshold of public life, and enabled from an early age, and with many advantages, to devote themselves to it, have attained a proficiency in statesmanship that has been of great service to their country. Among the Prime Ministers since the Reform Bill of 1832 there have been several who represent names and families that have been for centuries illustrious in English history; and, in our own generation, one of the most brilliant of these Prime Ministers has been able, without incurring the smallest imputation of nepotism, to appoint his eldest son, and another of them to appoint his nephew, to a foremost place in his Administration.

The value of this state of things to the nation at large is very great. There are countries where a public man is nothing before he comes to office, and nothing when he quits office, and almost omnipotent while he holds office, and where this is the case public affairs seldom fail to be corruptly, selfishly, and recklessly administered. It is of no small importance that a nation should possess a class of public men, of undoubted competence and experience, who have a large stake in the prosperity of the country, who possess a great position independent of politics, who represent very eminently the traditions and the continuity of political life, and who, whatever may be their faults, can at least be trusted to administer affairs with a complete personal integrity and honour. In the fields of diplomacy, and in those great administrative posts which are so numerous in an extended empire, high rank, and the manners that commonly accompany it, are especially valuable, and their weight is not the least powerfully felt in dealing with democracies. The monarchy and the aristocracy, which some writers regard as merely ornamental portions of the constitution, contribute in a degree which is not often realised to its greatness and its cohesion. It is not the British House of Commons, but the British Throne, that is the centre of the loyalty and affection of the Colonies. The disruption of America from the British Empire was largely due to the encroachments of Parliament on the ancient prerogative of the Crown; and no small part of the success of English colonial government is due to the class of men who have been appointed governors. They have represented in high perfection the type of aristocratic statesman which English institutions produce, and they have displayed a higher average of competence and character than either hereditary sovereigns or elected presidents. An aristocratic government mainly built up this great Empire in the past. The aristocratic element within it undoubtedly contributes to its successful administration in the present. Nor is it a matter of indifference that a large proportion of the men who have held high office in India and the Colonies return after their period of office to the House of Lords, bringing to it a knowledge of Indian and colonial affairs that is seldom equalled in the House of Commons.

So far I have spoken chiefly of the ancient hereditary element in the House of Lords, but it must not be forgotten that this element is constantly recruited from without. In addition to the members of the episcopal bench, great landlords, great merchants and manufacturers, great lawyers (in superabundant measure), great soldiers, sailors, and administrators, are constantly pouring into the House of Lords; and it is also the resource of many experienced statesmen who for some cause are excluded from a Cabinet or a House of Commons, or who from advancing years, or failing health, or quiet tastes, find the strain of the House of Commons excessive or distasteful. The system of promotion is far from perfect, and some of its defects will be hereafter considered; but it at least gives the House of Lords a diversified and representative character. To those who can look beyond names and forms to the substance of things, it is sufficiently evident that a body which is not elective may be eminently representative, reflecting and maintaining with great fidelity the interests, characters, wishes, and opinions of many different classes in the community. It is equally certain that a body which is elected on the widest popular suffrage may be so largely returned by a single class, or by ignorant men duped by artful men, that it may totally fail to represent in their true proportion and degree the genuine opinions and the various interests of its constituents.

Judging by this test, the House of Lords will, I think, rank very high. Man for man, it is quite possible that it represents more ability and knowledge than the House of Commons, and its members are certainly able to discuss public affairs in a more single-minded and disinterested spirit. In all questions of law; in all the vast range of subjects connected with county government, agricultural interests, and the state of the agricultural poor; in questions connected with the Church and the army, and it may, I think, be added, with foreign policy, and often with Indian and colonial policy, its superiority of knowledge is very marked. It contains important representatives of the great manufacturing and commercial interests, some of the greatest owners of town property, some of the most experienced administrators of distant portions of the Empire. Appointments to the episcopacy are now made in a much more rational fashion than in the days of what were called the 'Greek Play Bishops,' when this dignity was chiefly reserved for men who had attained distinction in classical scholarship. Probably the majority of modern bishops have been rectors of large parishes in town or country; have come into close touch with the lives of the poorer classes in the community; have spent many years in disinterested labour for their benefit, and have had rare opportunities of understanding their real wants, characters, tendencies, difficulties, and temptations. As the reader will have gathered, I do not greatly admire the action of the bishops in the House of Lords on purely ecclesiastical questions, and especially on questions affecting religious liberty. But, on large classes of questions relating to the poor, it is difficult to overrate the indirect value a legislative body derives from the presence of men who possess the kind of knowledge and the kind of ability which are to be found in a superior parish clergyman. Philanthropists who have devoted themselves to social questions with eminent skill and generosity have been found within the House of Lords. It always includes a large amount of matured and experienced statesmanship, and a great majority of those who take an active part in its proceedings have been at least members of the House of Commons.

Such an assembly may have serious defects, and it is certainly not fitted in the nineteenth century to take the leading place in the Constitution; but no candid man will deny that it is largely representative, and that it includes in a rare degree the qualities and the elements that are most needed in revising and perfecting legislation. Its members are the natural heads of the gentry, and especially of the landed gentry, and it represents their sentiments and is supported by their strength. Wise statesmanship will always seek to strengthen government by connecting it with the chief elements of independent influence, power, and popularity that exist throughout the nation. No one who has any real knowledge of the English people will doubt the high place the aristocracy holds among these elements. Every electioneering agent knows that the son of a great peer is one of the best parliamentary candidates he can run. More than 190 members of the present House of Lords have been previously elected to the House of Commons, and a great proportion of them have passed directly from the Lower into the Upper House.[9] In choosing directors for companies, presidents for charities, chairmen for public meetings, initiators for almost every kind of social, industrial, political, or philanthropic movement, the English people naturally turn to this quarter. The adulation of rank in great bodies of men is often irrational, even to absurdity, and is connected with a vein of vulgarity that runs deeply through English nature. But, whatever may be thought of it, it at least shows that the position assigned to the House of Lords in the Constitution is not a mere arbitrary, or exotic, or archaic thing, but represents

---

[9] In a speech by Mr. Curzon, in a debate on the House of Lords (March 9, 1888), it is stated that there were then 194 peers who had sat in the House of Commons. In the *Constitutional Yearbook* for 1893 the number at that time is said (p. 60) to be 192.

a real and living force of opinion and affection. Political leaders may talk the language of pure democracy from the platform, but no Cabinet, however Radical, has ever sat in England which did not consist largely of peers and of men who were connected with peers, while the great majority of the other members have been usually possessors of considerable independent fortunes.

Nor is the popular English sentiment about rank in all respects vulgar or irrational. In a vast crowded population established position does something to raise a man into the clear light of day; it forms some guarantee of independence and of integrity; and something at least of the prevailing feeling is due to a well-founded conviction that the British aristocracy have been distinguished as a class for their high standard both of personal honour and of public duty. It is idle to suppose that great masses will ever judge men mainly by their intellectual or moral qualities. Other and lower measures will inevitably prevail; and, as I have elsewhere said, 'When the worship of rank and the worship of wealth are in competition, it may at least be said that the existence of two idols diminishes by dividing the force of each superstition, and that the latter evil is an increasing one, while the former is never again likely to be a danger.' In England the aristocratic classes have no longer the complete preponderance of wealth they once possessed, and the great depression of land has contributed materially to alter their position; but they are still a very wealthy class, and some of their members are among the richest men in the world. But great wealth in their hands is at least not mere plutocracy. It is connected with, and tempered by, another order of ideas. It is associated with an assured social position, with an hereditary standard of honour, with great responsibilities, with a large circle of administrative duties. If aristocracy were to cease to be a power in England, its social influence would chiefly pass to mere wealth, and its political influence would largely pass to the managers of party organisations and to demagogues.

The evils that spring from mere plutocracy are great, and

increasing. One of the most evident is the enormous growth of luxurious living. The evil does not, in my opinion, lie in the multiplication of pleasures. Amusement, no doubt, occupies a very disproportionate place in many lives, and many men grossly mismanage their pleasures, and the amount of amusement expected by all classes and ages has within the last generation greatly increased. But those who have realised the infinite pathos of human life, and the vast variety of human tastes, characters, and temptations, will hesitate much to abridge the sum of human enjoyment, and will look with an indulgent eye on many pleasures which are far from cultivated, elevating, and refined, provided they are not positively vicious, and do not bring with them grave and manifest evils. What is really to be deplored is the inordinate and ever-increasing expenditure on things which add nothing, or almost nothing, to human enjoyment. It is the race of luxury, the mere ostentation of wealth, which values all things by their cost.

This feeling is wholly distinct from the love of art. To minds infected with it beauty itself is nothing if it is common. The rose and the violet make way for the stephanotis and the orchid. Common fruits and vegetables are produced at great expense in an unnatural season. The play is estimated by the splendour of its scenery. Innumerable attendants, gorgeous upholstery, masses of dazzling jewellery, rare dishes from distant countries, ingenious and unexpected refinements of costly luxury, are the chief marks of their entertainments, and the hand of the millionaire is always seen. Nor is the evil restricted to the small circle of the very rich. From rank to rank the standard of social requirement is raised, making society more cumbrous, extravagant, and ostentatious, driving from it by the costliness of its accessories many who are eminently fitted to adorn it, and ruining many others by the competition of idle, joyless, useless display. It is a tendency which vulgarises and materialises vast fields of English life, and is preparing great catastrophes for the future.

The acquisition of gigantic fortunes in trade or speculation, and the desire to attain by these fortunes a high social position,

are the main causes of this increasing luxury, which is so prominent in England and America, and which contrasts so unfavourably with the far simpler and more human social
intercourse of many foreign countries. Economists perhaps
press their case too far when they assert that this kind of expenditure is wholly unproductive. The attraction of luxury,
and of the social consideration it implies, is a great spur to labour, and especially to the continuance of labour after a moderate competence has been acquired. But economists are not
wrong in pointing out the enormous waste of the means of
happiness which it implies, and its moral and political evils are
at least as great as its economical ones.

An aristocracy occupying an undisputed social position
might do much to check this tendency. At a time when the
class whom they specially represent are passing through the
dark shadow of a ruinous agricultural depression, it would
be peculiarly graceful and patriotic if those among them who,
through their urban properties or their mineral wealth, have
escaped the calamity, would set, without compulsion, the
example of a simpler scale of living. Some of them have done
so. Others have themselves retained, amid very luxurious
surroundings, much personal simplicity of life and tastes. The
doctrine of the moral obligation attaching to wealth is one of
the oldest of the moral convictions of mankind. 'If thou art
exalted after having been low,' says an Egyptian writer who
is believed to have lived no less than 3,800 years before the
Christian era,[10] 'if thou art rich after having been needy,
harden not thy heart because of thy elevation. Thou hast but
become a steward of the good things belonging to the gods.'
On the whole, this truth is probably more acted on by rich
men whose properties are connected with land than by any
others. England always furnishes many examples of great
fortunes expended with noble, judicious, and unselfish munificence, sometimes in public works which no moderate for-

---

[10] *The Prisse Papyrus.* See Miss Edwards's *Pharaohs, Fellahs, and Explorers,*
p. 220.

tune could undertake, very often in raising the whole level of comfort and civilisation over an extensive property. One of the greatest landlords in England told me that he calculated that, in his own case, for every 100*l*. that came out of land, 75*l*. went back to it. Many others, as patrons of art, have blended their personal gratification with much benefit to the country.

Much, too, of what appears luxury is not really selfish. The vast parks that surround so many great country houses are in numerous cases thrown open with such a liberality that they are virtually public property, though supported exclusively by private means; and those houses themselves, and the art treasures which they contain, have been for the most part freely exhibited to the world. It must, however, be acknowledged that the great wave of increasing luxury which has swept over England has been fully felt in aristocratic circles, and especially in country life. Among the not very numerous mistakes that have been made by the great English landed gentry as a class, one of the most conspicuous has, I think, been that enormous overpreservation of game which grew up in the last years of the eighteenth century,[11] and has steadily increased to our own day. It has diminished the productiveness of great areas of English land, brought into the country a new form of extravagant luxury, and essentially altered and lowered the character of field sports. The Epicurean sportsman who, without even the trouble of loading his guns, shoots down by hundreds the pheasants which are bred like chickens upon his estates, and which are driven by an army of beaters into his presence, is by no means a beautiful figure in modern country life, however great may be the skill which he displays.

But the worst aspect of plutocracy is the social and political influence of dishonestly acquired wealth. While most of the

---

[11] See the article on 'Battue Shooting' in Blaine's *Encyclopædia of Field Sports*. Battue shooting has existed for some time in some continental countries before it was introduced into England.

fields of patronage and professional life have been greatly purified during the present century, the conditions of modern enterprise in the chief European countries, and still more in the United States, give much scope for kinds of speculation and financing which no honest man would pursue, and by which, in many conspicuous instances, colossal fortunes have been acquired. It is an evil omen for the future of a nation when men who have acquired such fortunes force their way into great social positions, and become the objects of admiration, adulation, and imitation. One of the first duties, and one of the chief uses, of courts and aristocracies is to guard the higher walks of society from this impure contact; and when courts and aristocracies betray their trust, and themselves bow before the golden idol, the period of their own downfall is not far distant.

No one who is acquainted with society in England, France, and America can be blind to the disquieting signs of the increasing prominence of this evil. With the decline of rank and the breaking down of old customs, conventionalities, and beliefs, the power of wealth in the world seems to grow. Where cynicism and scepticism have sapped the character, wealth comes too frequently to be looked on as the one reality of life, and as atoning for every misdeed. When the decent interval has elapsed, when the period of colossal swindling has been duly succeeded by the period of lavish and splendid hospitality, mingled perhaps with ostentatious charity, the love of pleasure and luxury begins to operate, and the old social restrictions give way. In England it may be truly said that the existence and social supremacy of an aristocracy is some barrier against the predominance of ill-gotten riches. Peerages are often granted to men whose chief claim is their wealth, but, with few and doubtful exceptions, this has been only done when wealth has been honestly acquired, and, on the whole, usefully, or at least respectably, employed. In political life, it is to be feared, the standard is less high. If modern British Governments are not greatly maligned, there have been instances in which peerages and other honours have been very literally bought, though by a circuitous process, in the shape of large contributions to party funds; and other instances where they have been notoriously given to fix waverers, to reward apostasies, to induce politicians to vote for measures which they would otherwise have opposed. But it is perhaps not too much to say that this is the only form of dishonesty which has of late years been rewarded by a seat in the House of Lords. For the most part, the influence of Court and aristocracy has been on the side of social purity and financial integrity, though there have been obvious and lamentable exceptions.

The foregoing considerations will, I think, serve to show that the hereditary element exercises a more serious and far-reaching influence over the wellbeing of the nation than is sometimes supposed. At the same time, it is impossible to deny that the House of Lords does not occupy the position, and that its deliberations do not carry with them the weight, that might be expected from the elements of which it is composed. An assembly seems sometimes strangely greater, and sometimes strangely less, than its members, and few things are more curious than the contrast between the too evident debility of the House of Lords in its corporate capacity, and the great weight and influence of a large number of individual peers. As Bagehot has justly observed, the peers who exercise the greatest influence in county life are seldom those who appear most prominently in the debates of the House of Lords. Except on great and critical occasions, the attendance in the House is very small: on an average only about a fifth part of its members are present, and important decisions have sometimes been taken in the presence of not more than a dozen members.[12] Every peer who passes from the House of Commons to the House of Lords is struck by its chilling, well-bred apathy, by the inattention and indifference of the few men

---

[12] See May's *Constitutional History*, i. 271–72. In his speech on the reform of the House of Lords (March 19, 1888), Lord Rosebery stated that in the session of 1885 the average attendance in the House of Lords was 110, which was almost exactly a fifth part.

who, on normal occasions, are scattered over its empty benches while some statesman of first-class eminence is unfolding his policy. A few remarks, chiefly addressed to the reporters, by the leader of the House, by the leader of the Opposition, by a great lawyer on each side, and perhaps—if the dinner-hour is not too near—by one or two independent peers, usually constitute its debates. There are few atmospheres in which young and rising talent has so much difficulty in emerging.

No such apathy is displayed by individual peers in the affairs of their counties; or in the special Committees of the House of Lords, which often do admirable work; or by the members of that House who take part in the joint Committees of the two Houses; and in the few questions which strongly rouse the interest of the House its debates are often models of grave, eloquent, and exhaustive discussion. Many causes conspire to the prevailing tone. The rule that only three members were needed to form a quorum had a very mischievous effect, and a considerable improvement has been produced by a recent standing order which provides that if on a division thirty lords are not present the business on hand shall be adjourned.

Another slight improvement was the suspension, in 1868, of the old privilege of the peers to vote by proxy. It was not, perhaps, a matter of great practical importance, for votes are very rarely determined by debate, and on party questions men's opinions are early formed, and may be easily anticipated. The system of pairing, even for long periods, is fully recognised in the House of Commons, and proxies, as is well known, are largely employed in the very important meetings for the management of companies. At the same time, it was easy to attack, and impossible altogether to defend, a system by which the men who gave the verdict were not those who heard the arguments; and that system had also the disadvantage of strengthening two of the worst characteristics of the House—the scanty attendance of its members, and the excessive power often exercised by a single peer. It also increased the political importance of the class of peers who, by their tastes and habits, are most unfit to be legislators, and who, in fact, are habitual nonattendants. Many members of the House of Lords are conscious that they have no personal competence or turn for legislation. Their tastes are of a wholly different description. They would never have aspired to election, and, finding themselves legislators by accident of birth, and having no ambition or other strong motive to impel them, they are scarcely ever seen within the House, unless they are urgently summoned to some important party division. Under the old system, however, they exercised much habitual influence, as they readily gave their proxies to their party chief.

The absence of such men from a legislative body is certainly not to be regretted. Other members of the House feel that their proper sphere of action is elsewhere. The bishops know that their special work lies in their dioceses, and, although they were very prominent in opposition to the Reform Bill of 1832, an unwritten conventionality now discourages them from taking much part in politics that are unconnected with their profession. Some great nobles are beginning to feel, with Carlyle, that their true work lies in the wise administration of their vast properties, and not in political contests, where they can only play a secondary and somewhat humiliating part. The consciousness that the House of Lords must always, in case of grave difference, yield to the House of Commons; that every expression of independent opinion on its part is followed by insolent threats of revolution, often countenanced or instigated by leaders of one of the parties in the State; that one of its first objects is to avoid coming into collision with the House of Commons, tends to make it distasteful to men of high character and spirit. It deprives it of the moral force and confidence without which it can never have its due weight in the Constitution. There is a widespread feeling among its more intelligent members that a considerable amount of well-bred political languor is very desirable in such a Chamber. If it were animated by a strong and earnest political spirit, it would never acquiesce in the completely subordinate position assigned to it, especially as this position is largely due to usurpation unsanctioned by law. Collisions would inevitably arise, and some organic change would follow.[13]

Two other causes conspire in the same direction. One of them is the jealousy which the House of Commons feels at the initiation of Bills in the House of Lords. A session of the House of Lords usually consists of several months of almost complete inactivity, followed by a few weeks when the pressure of work sent up from the House of Commons is so great, and the time in which it must be accomplished so short, that it is impossible that the work of revision, which is the special task of the Upper House, can be accomplished with proper deliberation. Of all the many wastes of power that take place in English political life, few are more deplorable than this. Social questions have come to be, in our day, of a far more real and pressing importance than purely political ones; and in the House of Lords the country possesses a legislative body which, from its composition, from its comparative leisure, and from its position in the Constitution, is pre-eminently fitted to deal with them. In almost every joint Committee relating to social questions peers have been among the most active and most useful members. Yet during many months of the year the House of Lords is almost idle. Its leaders know that the Commons would look with distrust on any Bill originating with them, and there is little use in introducing Bills which are never likely to become law.

Another cause is the complete exclusion of the House of Lords from all financial legislation. In the opinion of the best historians, taxation was at one period imposed separately and independently by Lords and Commons; but the Lords taxed only their own body, and the Commons the classes they represented. After this, taxes affecting all classes alike were made by the Commons, with the advice and assent of the Lords,

---

[13] See some very just, but wonderfully candid and rather cynical, remarks of Lord Salisbury on this subject in a speech on Lord Rosebery's motion for the reform of the House of Lords (March 19, 1888).

and usually as a result of a conference between the two Houses.[14] The sole right of the Commons to originate money Bills was recognised at least as early as the reign of Richard II., and in the reign of Charles I. the Commons began to omit to make mention of the Lords in the preambles of Bills of Supply, as though the grant were exclusively their own, though the Lords were always mentioned in the enacting words of the Statute. But although the Upper House could not originate money Bills, it had for some centuries the full right of amending them. There are numerous cases of such amendments having been agreed to, and the right was not seriously questioned till after the Restoration. In 1671 the Commons carried a resolution 'that, in all aids given to the King by the Commons, the rate or tax ought not to be altered;' and in 1678 they went still further, and resolved 'that all aids and supplies, and aids to His Majesty in Parliament, are the sole gift of the Commons, and all Bills for the granting of any such aids and supplies ought to begin with the Commons, and that it is the undoubted and sole right of the Commons to direct, limit, and appoint in such Bills the ends, purposes, considerations, conditions, limitations, and qualifications of such grants, which ought not to be changed or altered by the House of Lords.'

The peers were by no means inclined to acquiesce in these claims. In the conferences that ensued they 'utterly denied any such right in the Commons, further than was agreed for the beginning of money Bills only.' 'In all other respects,' they said, 'and to all intents and purposes, our legislative power is as full and free as theirs; we granted as well as they; they could not grant without us, not so much as for themselves, much less for us; we were judges and counsellors to consider and advise concerning the ends and occasions for money as well as they,' with the sole exception that the right of beginning Bills was with the Commons.

Hallam has truly noticed how clearly the preponderance of

---

[14] Stubbs's *Const. Hist.* iii. 282–83, 496–97.

argument and precedent in these conferences was on the side of the peers,[15] and a resolution of the House of Commons alone has no legal validity; but yet the growing power of the Commons enabled them to carry their point. It was never established by law, it was never formally admitted by the other House, but it nevertheless became a received maxim of the Constitution, that the House of Lords was precluded not only from originating, but also from amending, money Bills. After the Revolution this power was tacitly extended by the habit of enlarging greatly the number of Bills which were considered money Bills. Even measures authorising fees, or imposing pecuniary penalties, or making provision for the payment of salaries, or for compensation for abolished offices, have been treated as money Bills, and therefore beyond the amending power of the Lords.[16]

It has been, however, extremely difficult to maintain this position consistently, for large classes of measures which have no financial object have incidental, and sometimes very remote, financial effects, and occasionally, for the sake of public convenience, the House of Commons has slightly relaxed its rule, and allowed amendments to pass which indirectly involved salaries or fees. Thus, for example, the operation of a Bill relating to industrial schools has been prolonged by an amendment in the Lords, although some pecuniary consequences would follow the prolongation. Sometimes the whole financial clause in a non-financial Bill has been rejected by the Lords, this being considered to fall within the class of rejection, and not of amendment. In 1831 a standing order was made

---

[15] Hallam's *Const. Hist.* iii. 28–30 (Cabinet edition).

[16] Hallam's *Const. Hist.* iii. 30–33; May's *Parliamentary Practice* (ed. 1893), pp. 542–46. Mr. Pike, in his *Constitutional History of the House of Lords*, and Mr. Macpherson on *The Baronage and the Senate*, have recently traced in much detail the development of the powers of the House of Lords. See, too, from opposite points of view, Mr. Spalding's *House of Lords*, and Sir W. Charley's *Crusade against the Constitution*, 1895. This last book is especially useful as a collection of facts and speeches relating to its recent history.

directing the Speaker, in cases where an amendment in the Lords involved some pecuniary penalty, to report to the House whether the object of the Lords appeared to be 'to impose, vary, or take away any pecuniary charge or burthen on the subject,' or whether they only intended 'the punishment of offences, and the House shall determine whether it may be expedient in such particular case to insist upon the exercise of their privilege.' In 1849 the Commons agreed that they would not insist on their privilege if the object of a pecuniary penalty was merely to secure the execution of the Act, or the punishment and prevention of offences, or when fees were imposed in respect to a benefit taken or service rendered, or when they form part of a private Bill for a local or personal act. In 1858 they agreed, in the case of private Bills, to accept 'any clauses sent down from the House of Lords which refer to tolls and charges for services performed, and which are not in the nature of a tax.' Sometimes it has been found convenient that non-financial Bills which however involve salaries or fees should originate in the Lords. In these cases financial provisoes have been prepared, discussed, and voted on in the Lords, but withdrawn at the third reading. They were therefore not brought before the Commons as part of the Bill, but they were printed in red ink on the margin, so that the House of Commons had the suggestions of the Lords informally before it, and was, of course, at liberty to treat them as it pleased. By these expedients some difficulties have been overcome and some conveniences attained without altering the received rule that the Lords have no power of originating or amending money Bills.[17]

One power, however, they seemed still to possess. No tax could be legally imposed except by an Act of Parliament, and as there can be no Act of Parliament without the assent of the Lords, the Upper House had at least the power of withholding that assent, and thus rejecting the Bill. Nothing in law, nothing in history, and, it may be added, nothing in reason, denied them this power, and for some time after the right of amend-

---

[17] May's *Parl. Practice*, pp. 544–49; May's *Const. Hist.* i. 482–89.

ment had vanished it was fully acknowledged. But this power also went the way of the royal veto. The doctrine that taxation was essentially a matter for the Commons alone grew and strengthened, especially during the controversies that arose out of the American revolution. 'Taxation,' Chatham once said, 'is no part of the governing or legislative power. The taxes are a voluntary gift and grant of the Commons alone. In legislation the three estates of the realm are alike concerned; but the concurrence of the peers and Crown to a tax is only necessary to clothe it with the form of law. The gift and grant is of the Commons alone.' This doctrine is very far from being beyond controversy, but it had a popular sound, and it was widely accepted. The House of Lords, shrinking from conflicts of privilege, and perhaps content with the indirect influence which its members exercised in the Commons, very rarely even discussed measures which were exclusively or mainly financial, though it frequently rejected or postponed measures incidentally affecting taxation.

The last great conflict on this subject was in 1860, when Mr. Gladstone, as Chancellor of the Exchequer in the Government of Lord Palmerston, proposed the abolition of the paper duties. The repealing measure was introduced in the usual way as a separate Bill, but it formed part of a large and complicated Budget involving extensive remissions of indirect taxation, the imposition of a number of small taxes, the reimposition of the income tax—which was intended to have expired in this year—its increase from 9d. to 10d. in the pound, and a provision for bringing three-fourths of this tax, instead of half only, into the Exchequer within the financial year. The paper duty, which it was determined to repeal, was estimated at 1,200,000l. or 1,300,000l.[18]

Several things contributed to make so great a sacrifice of ordinary revenue at this time seem of doubtful expediency. A commercial treaty with France had just been concluded, and it would involve a great lowering of duties. The political relations with France were also not unclouded, and the prev-

[18] See Sir Stafford Northcote's *Twenty Years of Financial Policy*, pp. 351–56.

Democracy and Liberty

alent feeling of distrust had shown itself in the expenditure
of a very large sum in fortifying our dockyards. A war with
China was raging, and it had assumed more formidable dimensions during the period between the introduction of the
Budget and its completion in the Commons. The renewal and
the high and increasing rate of the income tax fell also heavily
on large classes. The feeling of the House of Commons was
very significantly shown by diminishing majorities. The second reading of the repeal of the paper duties was carried by
a majority of fifty-three. On the third reading the Government
majority had sunk to nine.

When a powerful and popular Government could only
command such a majority on the third reading of a great contested measure, there could be little doubt that the real opinion of the House of Commons was hostile to that measure.
It is probable that most members of the Cabinet would have
gladly postponed to another year the repeal of the paper duties. But it is not easy for a Government to recede from a position which it has formally adopted; and it was impossible
for Lord Palmerston to do so without breaking up his Government when so important a colleague as Mr. Gladstone was
determined at all hazards to carry the measure. The real opinions of Lord Palmerston are clearly disclosed in an extract
which has been published from a letter written by him to the
Queen, announcing to Her Majesty the extremely small majority by which the Bill had passed its third reading in the
Commons. 'This,' he writes, 'may probably encourage the
House of Lords to throw out the Bill when it comes to their
House, and Viscount Palmerston is bound in duty to say that,
if they do so, they will perform a good public service. Circumstances have greatly changed since the measure was
agreed to by the Cabinet, and although it would undoubtedly
have been difficult for the Government to have given up the
Bill, yet, if Parliament were to reject it, the Government might
well submit to so welcome a defeat.'[19]

---

[19] Martin's *Life of the Prince Consort*, v. 100.

The House of Lords acted as Lord Palmerston anticipated and evidently desired. While the other Bills relating to finance were accepted without question, the Bill repealing the paper duties was thrown out by a majority of no less than eighty-nine.

Mr. Gladstone, in a speech of extraordinary eloquence, which was eminently calculated, as it was manifestly intended, to inflame and envenom the difference between the Houses, denounced this proceeding as 'the most gigantic and the most dangerous innovation that has been attempted in our times,' and a large part of the Liberal party, both in the House and in the country, were ready to support him in a violent collision with the Lords. Lord Palmerston, however, in a very difficult position, conducted the controversy with a skill, tact, and moderation that could not be surpassed, and by his eminently patriotic conduct a great danger was averted. A Commission was appointed to examine precedents, and, under the influence of Lord Palmerston, the House of Commons contented itself with carrying three resolutions. The first asserted 'that the right of granting aids and supplies to the Crown is in the Commons alone.' The second, while acknowledging that the Lords had sometimes exercised the power of rejecting Bills relating to taxation, stated that this power was justly regarded by the Commons with peculiar jealousy, as affecting their right to grant supplies; and the third stated 'that, to guard for the future against an undue exercise of that power by the Lords, and to secure to the Commons their rightful control over taxation and Supply, this House has in its own hands the power so to impose and remit taxes, and to frame Bills of Supply, that the right of the Commons as to the matter, manner, measure, and time may be maintained inviolate.'

These resolutions were carried unanimously, though not without much criticism and after a long and instructive debate. It was asserted on the one side, and not denied on the other, that the House of Lords had acted in perfect accordance with the law of the land. In the conferences that had taken place between the two Houses after the Restoration, when the right of amending money Bills was denied to the Lords, the Managers, on the part of the Commons, formally and expressly admitted the right of the Upper House to reject them. This right, it was said, was a settled principle of the Constitution, and it had never been withdrawn, surrendered, or denied. The Constitution, by making the assent of the House of Lords essential to the validity of a tax, clearly implied that the House of Lords had the right of withholding that assent. Blackstone, while enumerating in emphatic terms its disabilities in matters of finance, described its right of rejecting money Bills as absolutely incontestable.[20] Nor was there on this point any real difference of opinion among writers on the Constitution.[21] 'Nothing,' said Lord Lyndhurst in the House of Lords, 'can be found in the Parliamentary Journals, or in any history of parliamentary proceedings, to show that our right to reject money Bills has been questioned.' The Commission which had just been appointed to examine precedents had discovered between 1714 and 1860 about thirty-six cases of Bills repealing duties or imposts of some kind, and a much greater number of Bills imposing charges, which had passed through the Commons, and which had failed in the Lords. In all or nearly all these cases the action of the House of Lords was unchallenged.

In the face of such facts it was surely absurd to argue that the House of Lords was not within its rights in throwing out the paper duties. And if it had a right to do so, it was not difficult to defend the expediency of its act. This great sacrifice of per-

---

[20] It would be extremely dangerous to give the Lords any power of framing new taxes for the subject. It is sufficient that they have a power of rejecting if they think the Commons too lavish or improvident in their grants. But so reasonably jealous are the Commons of this valuable privilege, that herein they will not suffer the other House to exert any power but that of rejecting. They will not permit the least alteration or amendment to be made by the Lords' (*Blackstone*, Book i. chapter ii.).

[21] See Hallam's *History of England*, iii. 31; May's *Parliamentary Practice*, p. 550 (ed. 1893).

manent revenue had been urged on political rather than financial grounds. It had been introduced at a time when both the political and the financial prospects were singularly overclouded, and since its first introduction the circumstances of the country had greatly changed, and the inexpediency of the measure had greatly increased. The small and steadily declining majorities in the House of Commons clearly showed that, without strong party and ministerial pressure, it could not have been carried.

In reply to these arguments it was contended that, though the House of Lords had acted within its technical rights, its conduct in throwing out an important Bill relating to the ways and means of the year was contrary to 'constitutional usage,' and inconsistent with the principle the Commons had frequently asserted, that 'all aids and supplies granted to Her Majesty in Parliament are the sole and entire gifts of the Commons.' By whose authority or action, it was asked would the paper duties be collected in the ensuing year? Would it not be solely by that of the House of Lords? If the Commons had combined in a single measure the increase of the income tax and the repeal of the paper duties, it would have been confessedly beyond the power of the Lords to amend the Bill by accepting one part of it and rejecting the other. Was the course they had actually pursued essentially different from this? To reject an important money Bill, and thereby disturb the balance of the financial arrangements of the year, was in reality a greater infringement of the sole competence of the House of Commons in matters of finance than to introduce into a money Bill some trifling amendment. The precedents that had been adduced were jealously scrutinised, and pronounced to be inapplicable. The Bills that had been rejected had been political Bills, discussed and rejected on political, and not on financial, grounds, and they were Bills by which finance was only slightly, incidentally, and remotely affected. Most of them were measures of protection, encouraging different forms of industry by duties or bounties. Others were measures imposing or remitting penalties, creating or abolishing salaried offices. The rejection of such Bills was a very different thing from an attempt to recast or materially modify the Budget of the year. For two hundred years, it was said, the House of Lords had never taken such a step, never rejected on purely financial grounds a Bill imposing or remitting taxation. Great commercial interests would be affected by its action, and still more by the precedent it established, for men of business had hitherto always assumed that they might take their measures and base their calculations on the Budget as soon as it had passed the Commons.

Whatever may be thought of the weight of argument, the weight of power was on the side of the Commons. As a matter of reason, indeed, resolutions had been adopted and precedents formed which reduced the whole question at issue to hopeless confusion. It was absurd to assert, as the Commons had repeatedly done, that money grants were their 'sole and entire gift,' when they were unable to grant a farthing without the assent of the Lords; and the power of rejection and the power of amendment stood so much on the same ground, and were in some cases so indissolubly connected, that it was very difficult to accept the one and to deny the other. By a tacit understanding, fully acquiesced in, though unestablished by law, the House of Lords had no power of amending money Bills, while its power of rejecting them had been established by a long chain of precedents, formally acknowledged by the House of Commons, and admitted as unquestionable by every serious writer on the Constitution. Yet it was very evident that the one power might be so used as to be practically equivalent to the other. The Commons, however, in the year after this dispute, adopted a method which effectually prevented the Lords from exercising any revising power in finance. They combined the repeal of the paper duties with all the other portions of the Budget in a single Bill, and the Lords had, therefore, no power of rejecting one part unless they took the responsibility of rejecting the whole. This method has since become the usual one. So completely has the sole competence of the House of Commons been recognised, that it has become the custom to levy new duties and increased duties from the time they had been agreed to by the House of Commons, without waiting for the assent of the Lords and of the Crown, which alone could give them the force of law.

Much of the jealousy of the interference of the Lords with financial matters which was displayed at the time of the Restoration was due to the fact that this body was then greatly under the influence of the Crown, and that the chief constitutional conflicts of that period lay between the power of the Commons and the power of the Crown. A still more important consideration was the belief that a tax is the free gift of the people, and that it ought, therefore, to be under the sole control of the representatives of those who give it. Such a control was once considered a guarantee that no one could be taxed unduly, unrighteously, or against his will. The old principle of connecting indissolubly taxation and representation has probably never been more loudly professed than in the present day; but this is only one of the many instances in which men cheat themselves by forms and phrases, while the underlying meaning has almost wholly passed away. The members of the House of Lords are owners of a great proportion of the largest properties in Great Britain, yet they have no part in enacting the imperial taxes they pay. Their House is excluded from all participation in finance, and they have no voice in the House of Commons. At the same time, the whole drift of democratic government is to diminish or to destroy the control which property in England once had over taxation. As I have already observed, the true meaning and justification of the special political powers vested in large taxpayers was, that those who chiefly pay should chiefly control; that the kinds of property which contribute most to support government should have most weight in regulating it; that it is one of the first duties of a legislator to provide that one class should not have the power of voting the taxes, while another class were obliged to pay them. It is plain that this fundamental element in the British Constitution is being rapidly destroyed. One of the most popular and growing ideas in English politics is, that by giving an overwhelming voting power to the poorer classes they may be able to attain a high level of wellbeing, by compelling the propertied classes to pay more and more for their benefit.

A broad distinction must be drawn between the maxim that the Commons alone should have the right to originate taxes, and the maxim that the Upper House should have no power either of amending or rejecting its financial legislation. The former right is recognised, after the English model, in most of the constitutions of free nations, though there are several exceptions. The most remarkable are Austria, Prussia, the German Empire, and the Swiss Federation, in all of which a financial measure may be introduced equally either in the Upper or the Lower House.[22] In the United States the House of Representatives maintains the sole right of originating taxes; but in the State legislatures a different principle prevails, and it is said that there are twenty-one States in which financial measures may be brought forward in either House.[23] In a few continental constitutions the Upper Chamber has the power of rejecting, but not of amending, money Bills,[24] but in most constitutions it is granted both powers; and this is also the system in the United States.

There is a great and manifest danger in placing the most important of all branches of legislation in the uncontrolled power of one House. It leaves the constitution absolutely unbalanced in the department in which beyond all others there is most danger, and where balance and restriction are most required; and it is, I think, much to be desired that, if the Upper House should ever be so remodelled as to carry with it increased weight in the country, it should be entrusted with the same powers of control and revision in matters of finance that are possessed by the American Senate. The evils, however, that might in this department be feared in England from the omnipotence of the House of Commons have been greatly miti-

[22] Morizot-Thibault, *Des Droits des Chambres Hautes en matière de Finances*, pp. 64, 69, 73, 94.
[23] Ibid, p. 82.
[24] Ibid, p. 134.

gated by two facts. The one is, that a very large proportion of the taxes of the country are permanent taxes, and are therefore not the subjects of annual debates. The other is the rule of the House of Commons, which I have mentioned in a former chapter, that no petition, and no motion for a grant or charge upon the public revenue, can be received unless it is recommended by the ministers of the Crown. Though this rule, giving the responsible ministers the sole right of proposing taxation, rests upon no law, but simply on a standing order of 1706, it is no exaggeration to say that it is one of the most valuable parts of the British Constitution. In the great changes that have taken place in the disposition and balance of powers, many of the old constitutional checks have become obsolete, inoperative, or useless; but the whole tendency of modern politics has only increased the importance of the provision which places the initiation in matters of finance exclusively in Government hands. In the present state of Parliaments, and with the motives that at present govern English public life, it is difficult to exaggerate either the corruption or the extravagance that might arise if every member were at liberty to ingratiate himself with particular classes of interests by proposing money grants in their favour.

The exclusion, however, of the House of Lords from every form of financial control naturally deprived it of its chief power in the State; and it is still further weakened by the fact that the creation and overthrow of ministries rest entirely with the other House. In the theory of the Constitution, the sovereign chooses the head of Government, but, except in the very rare cases of nearly balanced claims, the sovereign has no choice. The statesman whom the dominant party in the House of Commons follow as their leader is irresistibly designated, and if he is overthrown it must be by the vote of the House of Commons. Since the resignation of Lord Grey in May, 1832, no ministry has resigned in consequence of a hostile vote of the Lords.

Some other changes may be noticed in the position of the House. In addition to its legislative functions, it is the supreme law court of the country, and this very important privilege has been the subject of extraordinary abuses. It is not here necessary to enter at any length into the curious and intricate history of this power. It seems to have grown out of the right the peers once possessed, as counsellors of the King, to receive petitions for the redress of all abuses; but it was fully organised in successive stages, and in spite of much opposition from the House of Commons, in the sixteenth and seventeenth centuries. The right of hearing judicial appeals extended to all the peers, even to those who were perfectly unversed in matters of law; and for considerable periods after the Revolution, and especially in the reigns of George II. and George III., the Chancellor sat alone in the House of Lords, sometimes to hear appeals from himself, though two lay peers had to be formally present in order to make the requisite quorum. Somers, Hardwicke, Thurlow, Mansfield, and Eldon have all heard appeals in this fashion.[25] After this time lawyers multiplied in the House of Lords, and the appellate jurisdiction was placed by custom exclusively in their hands; though in the case of O'Connell, when party passions were strongly aroused, there was for a short time some danger that the lay lords would insist on their right of intervening. The efficiency of the highest Court was entirely a matter of chance. The Chancellor was usually a good lawyer, but it has sometimes happened that a considerable portion of the remainder of the tribunal consisted of lawyers who, though they had been in their day very eminent, were now suffering from all the debility of extreme old age, and appeals were notoriously from the more competent tribunal to the less competent one.

It seems strange that this state of things should have been so long tolerated; but, in truth, the English people, though they have always been extremely tenacious of their right of making their own laws, have usually been singularly patient of abuses in administering them. They bore during long generations ruinous delays of justice which were elaborately cal-

---

[25] May's *Const. Hist.* i. 247.

culated to prolong litigation through periods often exceeding the natural duration of a lifetime; enormous multiplications of costly and useless archaic forms, intended mainly to swell the gains of one grasping profession. They have suffered judges whose faculties were notoriously dimmed by the infirmities of extreme old age to preside over trials on which lives, fortunes, and reputations depended; and even now this profession, which, beyond almost any other, requires the full clearness, concentration, and energy of a trained intellect, is exempt from the age limit which is so severely imposed on other classes of Civil Servants. It is quite in accordance with this spirit that they should have long endured, with scarcely a murmur, such an appellate jurisdiction as I have described. English writers often dwell, with just pride, on the contrast between the political freedom enjoyed in Great Britain and the political servitude that existed in France in the eighteenth century. If they compared, in their judicial aspects, the House of Lords of that period with the Parliament of Paris, the comparison would be much less flattering to the national pride.

The extremely unsatisfactory condition of the House of Lords, considered as the supreme tribunal of the country, was acutely felt in the present century, and the opinion grew in ministerial circles that the best way of strengthening it was by introducing into the House a certain number of lawyers as life peers. The Cabinet of Lord Liverpool at one time resolved upon this step, but Lord Liverpool himself changed his mind, and it was abandoned. In 1851, Lord John Russell offered a life peerage to an eminent judge, but it was declined;[26] but in 1856 the Government of Lord Palmerston took the startling step of creating by royal prerogative Baron Parke a life peer, under the title of Lord Wensleydale. The fact that he might just as well have been made an hereditary peer, as he was considerably past middle life, and had no living son, gave an unmistakable significance to the creation.

---

[26] See a speech of Lord Granville in the debate on Lord Wensleydale's peerage, February 7, 1856.

As is well known, the attempt was successfully resisted by the House of Lords. The opposition was led with masterly ability by Lord Lyndhurst, and, with the exception of a not very powerful Chancellor, it was supported by all the law lords in the House. It was acknowledged, indeed, that such peerages had been made in remote periods of English history, and that Coke, and Blackstone following Coke, had asserted their legality; but the supporters of the measure were compelled to admit that for the space of 400 years no commoner had been introduced into the House of Lords by such a patent as that of Lord Wensleydale. There had, it is true, been a few peerages for life conferred upon women. It was a dignity which seems to have been specially selected for the mistress of the King, and Charles II., James II., George I., and George II., had in this way raised their mistresses to the peerage. Since the creation of the Countess of Yarmouth by George II., however, there had been no peerage of this kind; and a life peerage conferred on a woman introduced no one into the House of Lords. The only other attempt to establish a modern precedent was derived from the fact that the sovereign possessed, and exercised, the power of conferring peerages on childless men, with remainders to relations to whom they could not, without special permission, have descended. It was obvious, however, that this formed no real precedent, for it was Nature, and not patent, that prevented these peers from transmitting their peerages in the usual way.

The legal maxim, *Nullum tempus occurrit regi*, was quoted in defence of life peerages; but in spite of it the lawyers contended, as it seems to me with good reason, that a prerogative which had been for 400 years unexercised, and which was exercised only at a time when the position of the sovereign and the aristocracy in the Constitution was utterly different from what it now is—at a time when it was not unusual to summon to the House of Lords commoners who were married to peeresses to represent their wives—at a time when the House of Lords was able, of its own authority, to select a Regent for the kingdom, ought not to be revived by a mere act of power.

No reasonable man, indeed, will now regard the direct influence of the sovereign as a danger to English liberty; but revivals of long-dormant royal prerogatives should be carefully watched, for they are certain to pass into the hands of the Cabinet ministers. It was a clear and well-established prerogative of the Crown to remodel the representation by summoning unrepresented places to send members to the House of Commons, or by discontinuing to summon places which had hitherto been represented. This prerogative had been exercised at a much later period than that on which the precedents for Lord Wensleydale's creation were based, and it had even been heard of in our own century. In the course of the debates on the Reform Bill of 1832, an Irish Solicitor-General had suggested that the obstruction of the House of Lords might be overcome by simply using the royal prerogative of creating or disenfranchising constituencies in accordance with the provisions of the Bill; and O'Connell contended that it was in the full legal power of the sovereign to annul the Irish Union, without the intervention of either Lords or Commons, by summoning Irish constituencies to send their representatives to Dublin. No one can for a moment imagine that a modern House of Commons would tolerate such an exercise of the prerogative, however well supported by historical and legal authority; nor would any Government venture to attempt it. The prerogative of creating life peers had not been resorted to by the ministers who took the strongest measures to overcome the resistance or to increase the numbers of the Upper House. Harley had not thought of it when he made twelve peers to carry the Peace of Utrecht; or Pitt when, by lavish creations, he carried the Irish Union; or Grey when he obtained the King's assent to the creation of a sufficient number of peers to carry the Reform Bill of 1832. On the whole, therefore, the House of Lords seems to me to have been thoroughly justified in maintaining that the sovereign could not, by a patent of life peerage, introduce new members into the House of Lords. Another patent was accordingly made out, and Lord Wensleydale entered the House on the same terms as his brother-peers.

The conduct of the House of Lords on this occasion has been much blamed by some considerable authorities. Freeman has denounced it with extreme violence, as a departure from the precedents of early English history,[27] and Bagehot, with much more reason, has lamented that the House neglected a great opportunity of invigorating its constitution by making possible a gradual infusion of life peers.[28] Powerful, however, as are the arguments in favour of life peerages, I do not think that they ought to have been created by a simple revival of a long-dormant prerogative, without statutory authority or limitation. An attempt was made by Lord John Russell, in 1869, to introduce life peers under the authority of an Act of Parliament, limiting the number to twenty-eight, and providing that not more than four should be made in one year. It was defeated on its third reading; and a very similar but rather more extensive measure, which was introduced by Lord Salisbury in 1888, was abandoned on account of the hostility of Mr. Gladstone.

The only object of the Government at the time of the Wensleydale peerage seems to have been to strengthen the appellate jurisdiction by bringing into the House competent lawyers whose fortunes were perhaps deemed inadequate for an hereditary peerage, and who would not add to the very considerable number of noble houses with a legal origin. The state of the appellate jurisdiction continued for several years to be a matter of constant complaint, and it gave rise to much discussion and to some abortive measures. At length, in 1873, Lord Selborne, as the Chancellor of a Liberal Government, succeeded in carrying a Bill transferring all English appeals from the House of Lords to a new tribunal. Irish and Scotch appeals were left to be dealt with in a separate Bill in the ensuing year, and the measure that was actually carried was only to come into force in the November of 1874. Before that date an election and a change of government took place, and

---

[27] Freeman's *Historical Essays*, 4th series, pp. 473–75.
[28] *On the Constitution.*

it devolved upon Lord Cairns, as the Conservative Chancellor, to carry out the new policy.

He had in the preceding year supported, though not without some reluctance, the measure of Lord Selborne, and his first intention on arriving at power was to complete it on the same lines by transferring Scotch and Irish appeals to the new tribunal. It soon, however, appeared that a strong hostile feeling had grown up in the country. In England it was found to be an unpopular thing to deprive the House of Lords of its ancient jurisdiction; while Scotland and Ireland protested against the transfer of their appeals to any less dignified body than a branch of the Imperial Legislature. It was observed that a special clause of the Scotch Act of Union had provided that there should be no right of appeal from a Scotch to an English court. On the other hand, it was generally felt that it would be inexpedient to have different courts of appeal for the different parts of the British Isles. In the face of this strong demonstration of opinion Lord Cairns changed his policy. The operation of Lord Selborne's Bill was for a short time postponed, and the Government resolved to revert in form, though not in substance, to the old system. It was enacted that all appeals from Great Britain and Ireland should be heard in the House of Lords by a court consisting of those members of the House who had held high judicial offices in the State, with the addition of two, and ultimately of four, eminent lawyers, who were to be life peers, created under the statute, and receiving large salaries. The presence of three members was made necessary to form a court. The life peers might speak and vote on all questions like other peers, as long as they continued to exercise their judicial functions; but if they resigned these they lost their seats, though they retained their titles. It was also provided that this judicial body might continue its sittings when Parliament was prorogued.

It is, I think, no paradox to say that, of all the many Reform Bills which have been carried in our time, this reform of the House of Lords has been the most successful. It had a limited and defined object, and it perfectly accomplished it without producing any countervailing evil. From the time of Lord Cairns's law, the appellate jurisdiction of the House of Lords has carried with it all the weight that should attach to the supreme tribunal of a nation, and one, at least, of the old reproaches of the House has been wiped away.

A modification of this law, which has considerable constitutional importance, was proposed and carried in 1887 by a Conservative Government. It provided that the law peers, if they resigned their judicial offices and salaries, should still retain their seats in the House, and be allowed to vote and speak like other peers. In this way, for the first time in modern days, life peers without official positions might sit in the House of Lords. Another slight change in the constitution of the House of Lords had been made in 1871 by an Act which deprived bankrupt peers of the right of sitting and voting.

Other changes far less favourable to it have taken place. In no previous period of English history have creations in the peerage been so numerous as in the later portion of the present reign. A long succession of short ministries has contributed to increase the number, each ministry being desirous of marking its term of office by some creations, and the destruction, through the competititve system, of most of the old methods of rewarding politicians has had the same effect. Much, too, is due to a certain vulgarisation or cheapening of honours that has undoubtedly characterised the second half of the present century; and to the increased pressure of newly made wealth seeking social position.

An examination of these creations furnishes some rather curious results. If we take as our starting-point the accession of Lord Grey to power in November of 1830, when the movement towards parliamentary reform acquired a decisive strength, we shall find that from that period till the death of Lord Palmerston, in October 1865, creations were comparatively few. Sir Robert Peel especially had a strong sense of the danger of lowering the dignity of the peerage, and in his two ministries only twelve peers were created. In the whole of this period of thirty-five years, 148 hereditary peers were created;

123 of them by Liberal, and twenty-five by Conservative, ministries. During this space of time the Liberal party were in power for rather more than twenty-six years.[29]

If we now pass to the twenty-seven years from the beginning of 1866 to the end of 1892, we find no less than 179 hereditary peerages created—eighty-five of them by Liberal, and ninety-four by Conservative, ministers. As the Liberals during this period were in power for rather more than eleven, and the Conservatives for rather more than fifteen, years, the proportion of peerages created by the two parties was not very different. On both sides the increased profusion of creations is very great, and it is remarkable that, even in the earlier period which I have reviewed, the number of creations was considered by good judges both extravagant and dangerous.[30]

It will hardly, I think, be contended that modern creations have added greatly to the weight and lustre of the peerage. There have, no doubt, been many exceptions. In the field of politics a few very eminent men have entered the Upper House while retaining all their mental, though not all their physical, powers. Others, of respectable, or even more than respectable, ability, have gone into it because they have passed under a cloud, because they have lost an election, or been unsuccessful in an office, or come into collision or rivalry with a colleague, or because a prime minister wished to moderate or to muzzle them, or because he desired to make room in his Cabinet for younger, stronger, or more popular men.

---

[29] A table of the additions to the hereditary peerage made during each ministry since 1830 will be found in the *Constitutional Yearbook* for 1893, p. 63.

[30] Thus, McCulloch, writing in 1846, says: 'There can be no doubt that the prerogative of creating peers has been far too liberally exercised, not to say abused, since the Revolution, and more especially since the accession of George III. Mr. Pitt, and the ministers by whom he has been followed, with the single exception of Sir Robert Peel, have lavished peerages with a profusion that has been injurious alike to the dignity and legitimate influence of the peers and to the independence of the Commons (McCulloch's *Account of the British Empire:* 'House of Lords').

A few recruits, who would have done honour to any assembly, have been drawn from diplomacy, from the army and navy, from the permanent offices, or from those great fields of Indian administration in which so much of the strongest character and most masculine intellect of our generation is formed. Kinds of eminence that lie outside the circle of Government employment and the legal profession have been slightly touched. A great historian who had been an active Whig politician, and who supported his party powerfully both by his voice and his pen, and a great novelist who had been for many years a conspicuous Tory member of Parliament, were raised to the lowest grade in the peerage; and the same dignity has been more recently conferred on one writer, who (if we except his almost honorary Government post of Laureate) had no special claim beyond the fact that, for at least forty years, he was universally recognised as one of the very greatest of living Englishmen, the foremost poet of his own country, and, with perhaps one exception, the foremost poet then living in the world. But the bulk of the accessions to the peerage come from other quarters. Great wealth, even though it be accompanied by no kind of real distinction, especially if it be united with a steady vote in the House of Commons, has been the strongest claim; and, next to wealth, great connections. Probably a large majority of those who have of late years risen to the peerage are men whose names conveyed no idea of any kind to the great body of the English people.

It can scarcely be questioned that an infusion into the aristocracy of a certain number of rich merchant-princes is an advantage. They represent a distinct and important element in English life, and carry with them great influence and capacity. It should not be forgotten that the most enduring aristocratic government that the modern world has known was that of Venice, the work of a landless and mercantile aristocracy. It is as little doubtful that the immense place given to undistinguished wealth in the modern peerage has contributed to lower its character. The existence of a peerage has been always defended, among other reasons, on the ground that it furnishes a reward for great achievements; and British Governments undertake, though in a fitful and casual way, to distribute State honours for many kinds of eminence. Perhaps it would be better if they did not do so; but, if they attempt to measure kinds of eminence that are not political, they should, at least, do so in a way that bears some relation to the true value of things. An Upper House depends much more than an elective Assembly on the personal weight and brilliancy of its members, and perhaps the only kind of Upper House that is likely in the long run to form some real counterpoise to a democratic Assembly is one which includes a large proportion of a nation's greatest men, representing supreme and acknowledged achievement in many fields.

The House of Lords represents much, but it certainly does not represent this. If we ask what England in the present century has contributed of most value to the progress of the world, competent judges would probably give a foremost place to physical science. In no other period of the world's history have the discoveries in these fields been so numerous, so majestic, or so fruitful. In no other period has so large a proportion of the highest intellect taken this direction. In no other department have English achievements, by the acknowledgment of the whole scientific world, been so splendid. There is, I believe, only a single very recent example of purely scientific eminence being recognised by a peerage.

Closely akin to science, and perhaps even more important among the elements of national wellbeing, are the great healing professions. Here, too, our century ranks among the most illustrious in the history of the world. It has seen the discovery of anæsthetics, which is one of the greatest boons that have ever been bestowed upon suffering humanity. It has produced the germ theory of disease; the antiseptic treatment in surgery; a method of removing ovarian tumours which has successfully combated one of the most terrible and most deadly of diseases; a method of brain surgery which has already achieved much, and which promises inestimable progress in the future. It has vastly extended our knowledge of disease by the invention of the stethoscope, the clinical thermometer, the laryngoscope, the ophthalmoscope, and in many other ways which it is not here necessary to enumerate. England may justly claim a foremost place in this noble work,[31] and many of her finest intellects have been enlisted in its service. In no single instance has this kind of eminence been recognised by a peerage. It is clearly understood that another and lower dignity is the stamp of honour which the State accords to the very highest eminence in medicine and surgery—as if to show in the clearest light how inferior in its eyes are the professions which do most to mitigate the great sum of human agony, to the professions which talk and quarrel and kill.

Art forms another important element in the full development of national life. In this field, it is true, England cannot claim any place at all comparable to that which she has won in science or in the healing professions; but if measured, not by a doubtful comparison of three or four of the greatest names, but by the number of men of undoubted genius who have appeared in a single generation, English art has never, I believe, ranked so high as at present, and never compared so favourably with the art of other nations. In 1896, for the first time, a peerage was conferred on an English artist. The doors of the Upper House were never opened to the men who, in this century, have rendered the greatest services to the State and to humanity—to Simpson, whose discovery of chloroform has prevented an amount of human suffering which it would need the imagination of a Dante to realise; to Stephenson, whose engineering genius has done more than that of any other man to revolutionise the whole economical and industrial condition of England; to Chadwick, the father of that great movement of sanitary reform which has already saved more human lives than any, except perhaps the very greatest, conquerors have destroyed; to Darwin, who has

[31] An excellent sketch of English achievements in this field will be found in the essay by Dr. Brudenell Carter on Medicine and Surgery in Ward's *Reign of Queen Victoria*.

transformed our conceptions of the universe and whose influence is felt to the farthest frontiers of speculative thought. For their own sakes it is not to be regretted that the claims of such men were not thrown into humiliating competition with those of the acute lawyers and politicians, the great country gentlemen and the opulent brewers, who throng the approaches to the Upper House; but if such a House is to continue, and, in a democratic age, is to retain its weight and influence in the State, it is not likely that elements of this kind can for ever be neglected.

The position of an hereditary Chamber in a democratic age is a problem of much difficulty and obscurity. I have traced in a former chapter the force and the danger of the current which is making all parts of the political machinery of a piece, breaking down all the inequalities, diversities of tendency, counterbalancing and restraining influences, on which the true liberty and the lasting security of nations so largely depend. Such a movement is naturally inimical to the hereditary principle in legislation, and the danger has been intensified by the enormous increase during the last few years in the political difference between the House of Lords and one of the great parties in the State. This fact is especially significant, as about two-thirds of the numerous creations that have been made in the present reign have been made by Liberal Governments, while an appreciable number of the earlier peerages consist of members of those great Whig houses which have been the oldest and steadiest supporters of civil and religious liberty. It is true, as I have said, that an Upper House is naturally a moderating, restraining, and retarding body, rather than an impelling one; that the bias of an hereditary class is naturally on the side of habit and tradition; and that a very opulent class is inevitably conservative in questions relating to property. But these considerations are far from accounting for the full measure of the change that has taken place. Till the death of Lord Palmerston there was no great or steady party preponderance in the House of Lords. It grew up mainly under the policy of Mr. Gladstone; but it only acquired its overwhelming magnitude when that statesman announced his determination to place the government of Ireland in the hands of the party which he had shortly before described as aiming at public plunder and the dismemberment of the Empire. The great body of the Liberal peers refused to follow him, and although he had himself, in his different ministries, created about eighty peerages, his followers in the House of Lords soon dwindled into little more than a small number of habitual office-holders.[32]

The disproportion was very great; but it must be acknowledged that it would have been impossible to form, by any fair means, an Upper Chamber consisting of men of large property and considerable and independent positions, in which opinions hostile to Irish Home Rule did not greatly preponderate. It must also be added, that the elections of 1886 and 1895 have shown beyond all possibility of doubt that, on the Home Rule question, the House of Lords represented the true sentiments of the democracy of the country.

And certainly the very remarkable parliamentary history of England from 1892 to 1895 does not weaken the conclusion. It appears that, under our present conditions, some desire for a change of representation and government at every election acts with an almost tidal regularity on the constituencies, though the strength or weakness of the revulsion depends upon the policy of the rival parties. In the election of 1892, and after a Conservative Government which had lasted for more than six years, the Home Rule party obtained a small and precarious majority of forty votes. In England, and especially in the great towns of England, it was utterly defeated; in Great Britain as a whole it was in a minority; but the skilful organisation and large over-representation of the Irish peasantry, and the strength of the Church disestablishment party in Wales, turned the balance, and a Government was formed

---

[32] In his speech on the reform of the House of Lords, March 19, 1888, Lord Rosebery estimated the number of the Home Rule peers at about thirty, or about 5 per cent. of the House of Lords.

depending for its support on a small majority, consisting of a number of discordant factions. The remarkable House of Commons that sat in those years passed a Bill placing the government of Ireland in the hands of a separate Parliament, at the same time leaving a powerful contingent of eighty Irish members in the Parliament at Westminster; it passed a vote in favour of the establishment of a separate Parliament in Scotland; it passed another vote in favour of breaking up the British Isles into a federation, with a number of distinct leg-islatures. It carried by a small majority, though it afterwards rescinded, an amendment to the Address, in March 1894, praying her Majesty 'that the power now enjoyed by persons not elected to Parliament by the possessors of the parliamen-tary franchise to prevent Bills being submitted to your Maj-esty for your Royal approval shall cease,' and expressing a hope that 'if it be necessary your Majesty will, with and by the advice of your responsible ministers, use the powers vested in your Majesty to secure the passing of this much-needed reform.'

The members of the Government clearly saw that it was impossible to carry Home Rule by a direct appeal to the na-tion. When the Home Rule Bill, which was a capital portion of their policy, was rejected by an overwhelming majority in the Lords, they did not venture to dissolve upon the question, and submit it to the adjudication of the constituencies. They hoped to secure a Home Rule majority on other grounds, by creating and stimulating an agitation against the House of Lords. The last speech delivered in Parliament by Mr. Glad-stone was truly described by Mr. Balfour as 'a declaration of war against the House of Lords.' This and the Home Rule policy were the two legacies which the retiring statesman be-queathed to his party.

As early as 1888 no less than seven members who after-wards sat in the Radical Cabinet of 1892, voted in favour of a resolution of Mr. Labouchere stating 'that, in the opinion of this House, it is contrary to the true principles of represen-tative government, and injurious to their efficacy, that any person should be a member of one House of the Legislature by right of birth, and it is therefore desirable to put an end to any such existing rights.'[33] It is not surprising that such men should have eagerly taken up the war against the House of Lords, and Cabinet ministers took the foremost part in leading the assault. The policy of 'filling the cup' was openly avowed, and it meant that measure after measure was to be introduced which was believed to be popular, in order that the House of Lords might reject them, and might in this way be discredited with the electors. It was hoped that by such a policy the tide of democratic feeling would rise with irresistible force against the hereditary House. Mr. Morley rarely made a speech on the platform without denouncing the hereditary legislators. Mr. Shaw Lefevre informed his constituents that 'the wisest course at the moment is to reduce still further the power of the Lords by depriving them of the power of veto,' thus reducing them to an absolutely impotent body, with no power of even retarding legislation. Sir William Harcourt declared 'that a majority of a single vote in the House of Commons is a more accurate representation of the popular will than a majority of four hundred in the House of Lords.'[34]

Other ministers, and their supporters in Parliament, followed suit, and outside the House Radical organisations and Radical speakers and writers vied with one another in the violence of their denunciations, in their contemptuous or arrogant predictions that the hereditary principle had had its day. Catalogues of the pretended misdeeds of the House of Lords during the last fifty years were drawn up, without the slightest intimation that it had ever fulfilled any one useful purpose. One of the most malevolent and grossly partial of these works was widely circulated with the warm recommendation of Mr. Gladstone. Another popular Radical writer observed, in a highly jubilant strain, that at the election of 1892

---

[33] See Charley, *The Crusade against the Constitution*, pp. 514–16.
[34] Ibid., pp. 437, 462.

the country had given a clear mandate to the House of Commons to enact a Home Rule measure; that this was pre-eminently 'one of the acts upon which a great and serious people never go back;' and that the House of Lords was nothing more than a farce and a nuisance, which must be speedily crushed. He graciously added that its opposition might be overcome by raising 500 sweeps to the peerage.[35]

There were signs, however, that all was not moving as the leaders of this party desired. It was a curious and significant fact that, on the retirement of Mr. Gladstone, the party found it necessary or expedient, after much heartburning, to go to the House of Lords for their leader, putting aside the claims of their leader in the Commons. Under the new system of local government a vast multitude of elections were taking place on an exceedingly democratic basis, and, to attentive observers, no feature of these elections was more remarkable than the extraordinary popularity of peers as candidates, even in places where they had no special local interests. It is only necessary to look through the elections of the London County Council to recognise this fact. It was evident, too, that the attempt to create a popular agitation against the Lords was proving very impotent. Neither Great Britain nor indeed Ireland showed the smallest indignation because the House of Lords had rejected the Irish Home Rule Bill, and because it had refused to consent to the scheme for restoring, at the cost of a large sum of public money, the tenants who had been evicted because they had joined the conspiracy called 'the Plan of Campaign.' Nor were the ministers more successful in their attempts to persuade the working men that the House of Lords had injured them because it had introduced into the Employer's Liability Bill an amendment providing that, if any body of workmen expressed by a clear two-thirds vote their desire to make their own insurance arrangements with their employers, and to contract themselves out of the Bill, they

---

[35] Mr. Frederic Harrison, 'How to drive Home Rule Home' (*Fortnightly Review*, September, 1892).

should be allowed to do as they wished. Divisions multiplied;
bye-elections were unfavourable, and at last, after a feeble life
of three years, the Government fell, and the inevitable dissolution speedily followed. On the eve of the election Lord
Rosebery clearly and emphatically told the country that the
real and supreme question at issue was the House of Lords,
and that Home Rule and all the other government measures
were involved in the destruction of what he somewhat absurdly called its 'legislative preponderance.'

The country had now the opportunity of expressing its
opinion about these men, their objects, and their methods,
and it gave an answer which no sophistry could disguise and
no stupidity could misunderstand. The complete, crushing,
and unequivocal defeat of the Radical party in 1895 is certainly
one of the most memorable events in the present generation.
No circumstance of humiliation was wanting. The majority
against the late Government was greater than any which had
been seen in England since the election of 1832. In addition
to several less important members of that Government, four
Cabinet ministers, including those whose attacks on the
House of Lords I have quoted, were defeated at the poll. In
nearly every portion of the kingdom, and in town and country alike, the verdict was the same. In constituencies where
the members of the party escaped disaster they usually did
so by a greatly decreased vote. But most conspicuous of all
was the emphatic condemnation of the New Liberalism, not
only in London, but also in the overwhelming majority of the
great provincial towns, where industrial life is most intense,
where vast masses of working men are agglomerated, and
where the older Liberalism had found its strongest and most
enthusiastic support.

The lesson was a salutary one, and it is not likely to be
forgotten. It proved beyond dispute what many had begun
to doubt—the profound conservatism of the great masses of
the English people, and their genuine attachment to the institutions of their country. It showed clearly which section of
the Liberal party in the great Home Rule schism most truly

reflected the sentiments and the conviction of the nation. It showed how enormously men had overrated the importance of the noisy groups of Socialists, faddists, and revolutionists that float upon the surface of English political thought like froth-flakes on a deep and silent sea. It showed also not less clearly how entirely alien to English feeling was the log-rolling strategy which had of late been growing so rapidly in English politics.

It would be uncandid and untrue to represent this election as having turned solely on the question of the House of Lords. As is always the case, many different elements conspired to the result, and among them must be included that periodical tidal movement to which I have already referred. At the same time, the question of the Upper House was in the very foreground of the battle, and was as directly at issue as it is ever likely to be in England, unless she should adopt the system of a Referendum. The result of the election clearly showed that the House of Lords had represented the opinion of the nation much more truly than the House of Commons between 1892 and 1895; that the country had no wish to overthrow it, or to destroy its power, or to extirpate its hereditary element, and that, as long as its members discharge their duty faithfully, fearlessly, and moderately, they are not likely to want popular support.

At the same time, there could be no greater error than to infer from the triumph of 1895 that there is no need of any change or reform in the Upper House, widening its basis, increasing its strength and its representative character. With the overwhelming power that is now placed in the hands of the House of Commons; with the liability of that House to great and sudden fluctuations; with the dangerous influence which, in certain conditions of politics, small groups or side-issues, or personal dissensions or incapacities, may exercise on the course of its decisions; with the manifest decay of the moderate and moderating elements in one of the great parties of the State, and with a Constitution that provides none of the special safeguards against sudden and inconsiderate organic change that are found in America and in nearly all continental countries, the existence of a strong Upper Chamber is a matter of the first necessity. It is probable that the continuance, without a great catastrophe, of democratic government depends mainly upon the possibility of organising such a Chamber, representing the great social and industrial interests in the country, and sufficiently powerful to avert the evils that must, sooner or later, follow from the unbridled power of a purely democratic House of Commons. There is no question in politics of a more serious interest than the elements from which such a body should be composed.

A brief glance at the constitutions of some other countries may here be instructive. The most illustrious of all examples of a great controlling aristocratic assembly is the Senate of ancient Rome, a body which existed for no less than 1,300 years, and which, at least during the period of the Republic, contributed more than any other to mould the fortunes and the character of the only State which both achieved and long maintained supreme power in the world. Like the House of Lords, it was at once a legislative and a judicial body, though its legislative functions were confined to sanctioning laws which had been voted by the people, and were, as time went on, greatly impaired. It had, however, the right of imposing and applying taxes. It had complete authority over foreign policy, over the administration of the provinces, and over the conduct of war. It watched, as a supreme body, over the security of the State, and had even a right in time of great danger to suspend the laws and confer absolute powers on the consuls. Though it was essentially a patrician body, it was not, until a late period of the Empire, an hereditary body. One order of magistrates possessed as such the right of entering into it; the bulk of the senators were chosen for life, first by the consuls, and afterwards by the censors, but chosen only out of particular classes. In the earlier period they were exclusively patricians; but they were afterwards chosen from those who held magisterial functions, and, as the magistrates were elected by the whole people, though by a very unequal suffrage, the democratic influence thus obtained a real, though indirect, influence in the Senate.

During the last days of the Republic, and under the Empire, the Senate went through other phases, which it is not necessary for us to follow. Though greatly changed and greatly lowered, it survived every other element of Roman freedom, and even after the establishment of the Byzantine Empire and amid the anarchy of the barbaric invasion it played no small part in Roman history. It is here sufficient to notice that in the days of its vigour and greatness it was neither an elective nor an hereditary body, though both election and heredity had some influence over its composition; and that, next to its own wisdom, it owed its power chiefly to the number and importance of the great functions that were confided to it.[36]

If we pass over the great chasm which separates the Roman Republic from our modern day, we shall find little difference of opinion, among competent judges, that the American Senate is the Upper Chamber, out of England, which has hitherto ranked the highest. Until very recent days all critics of the American Constitution would have agreed with Story, that the Senate is not only 'a most important and valuable part of the system,' but is even 'the real balance-wheel, which adjusts and regulates its movements.'[37] A few discordant voices have of late been heard, but as a work of constructive and prescient statesmanship it unquestionably ranks very high, though one of its most important characteristics is less due to deliberate foresight than to an inevitable compromise. The smaller States refused to join in the federation unless they obtained, in at least one House, the security of an equal vote, and were thus guaranteed against the danger of absorption by their larger colleagues. In the Continental Congress, which first met in

---

[36] See Merivale's *Hist. of Rome*, iv. 9–14; Bluntschli, *De l'Etat*, pp. 384–85; Laveleye, *Gouvernement dans la Démocratie*, ii. 19–22. See, too, the notices of the Senate in Mommsen and Gibbon, and, on its later history, Gregorovius, *Hist. of Rome in the Middle Ages*.

[37] *Commentaries on the Constitution of the United States*, ii. 182.

1774, it had been agreed that each State should, in voting, count for only one; and this system was afterwards adopted in the Senate, with one slight modification. In the Continental Congress the vote had been by States. In the Senate each State was represented by two members, but they voted as individuals, and might therefore take different sides.

By this process a powerful counterpoise was established to the empire of mere numbers which prevailed in the Lower House. Two members represented the smallest as well as the largest State, and they were chosen, not by a directly popular vote, but by the State legislatures, which, like the Federal Legislature, consisted of two Houses.[38]

The next question that arose was the length of time during which the senators should hold their office. Montesquieu had maintained that a senator ought to be chosen for life, as was the custom in Rome and in the Greek republics. Alexander Hamilton, the foremost political thinker of America, and probably Jay, desired to adopt this system;[39] but it was ultimately agreed to adopt a limited period, considerably longer than that which was assigned to the members of the House of Representatives. In this latter House the term of office is only two years. In the Senate it is six years, one-third of the Senate being renewed every two years by the State legislatures. The Senate is thus a permanent body subject to frequent modifications. It was the object of its framers to combine a considerable measure of that continuity of policy which should be one of the first ends of a legislator with close and constant contact with State opinion; to place the Senate above the violent impulses, the transient passions, the dangerous fluctuations of uninstructed masses, but not above the genuine and steady currents of national feeling. The qualifications of a senator were also different from those of the members of the other House. He must have been a citizen for nine years, whereas in the other House seven years only were

---

[38] For the method of election see pp. 57, 58 of this volume.

[39] Story, ii. 189. See, too, Hamilton's *Works*, i. 334.

required. He must be at least thirty years old, while the members of the Lower House need only be twenty-five. The age of thirty was probably adopted in imitation of the Roman Senate.

The body, representing only the States, is a very small one. It at first consisted of twenty-six members, and with the multiplication of States has gradually risen to eighty-six.[40] As might be expected from the manner of election, nearly all its members are experienced politicians, who have sat in the State legislatures or the House of Representatives, or have held high official posts, and in intellect, character, and influence they rise considerably above the average of American public men. The Senate is presided over by the Vice-President of the United States, who, however, is not chosen by it, and who has no vote in it, except in the event of equal division. As a legislative body it has the same powers as the other House, except that it cannot originate money Bills, though it may both alter and reject them. It is not, like the House of Lords, the supreme court of appeal, but public men accused of violations of public trusts and duties may be impeached before it by the House of Representatives. Its position in this respect resembles, but not exactly, that of the British House of Lords. In America two-thirds of the members present must concur for a conviction; the senators in cases of impeachment vote on oath, or on affirmation, and not, like English peers, on their honour; their sentence does not extend further than a removal from office and a disqualification from holding office, and it leaves the convicted persons still liable to indictment and punishment according to law. If the person impeached is the President of the United States, the Chief Justice of the Supreme Court presides over the Senate, as the Vice-President would have a personal interest in the issue. It must be added that impeachment has long been obsolete in England, but is still sometimes employed in the United States. Subject to the limits and condi-

---

[40] Including the senators for the new State of Utah.

tions which the American Constitution lays down, it is a valuable and much-needed restraint upon corruption.

But the most distinctive feature of the American Senate is its large share in what in most countries would be considered the functions of the Executive. In foreign policy it exercises a commanding and most salutary influence. The American Constitution has carefully provided against the passion for organic change which is natural to democracy; but it was more difficult to provide against the extreme dangers that may ensue when foreign policy falls into the hands of demagogues, is treated as a mere shuttlecock of party, and conducted with a view of winning votes. The United States has certainly not escaped this evil. In few other countries has the language of public men, even in responsible positions, been more frequently insulting to other nations, and especially to Great Britain, on occasions when by such means some class of electors might be won. If America had been a European continental power, surrounded by great military empires, the attitude of her public men, and even of her legislative bodies, towards other nations and their affairs would have drawn her into many wars. Fortunately for her, she escapes by her situation the chief dangers and complications of foreign policy. In England, at least, the motives that inspire the language of her public men whenever an election is impending are now well understood, and foreign affairs, before they reach the stage whenever words are translated into acts, pass into a calmer and wiser atmosphere. No treaty with a foreign Power can be contracted, and no ambassador or other negotiator can be appointed, without the assent of the Senate, and the whole subject of foreign policy is therefore brought under the supervision of the standing committee of that body.

Like the English Cabinet, it on these occasions deliberates and decides in secret. It is, indeed, one of the most remarkable characteristics of the American democracy, how much of its working is withdrawn from the public eye. As I have already mentioned, in the earlier period of its history the sittings of the Senate were altogether secret,[41] and the rule of secrecy still prevails in its 'executive sessions,' though, on a demand of a fifth of the members present, the votes of the members may be published. On the whole, this arrangement does much to secure a true, thorough, and impartial examination of foreign policy, free from the claptrap and popularity-hunting that too often accompany public discussion, and the corruption and intrigue that usually follow complete secrecy.

In the last place, the Senate has a great part, in concurrence with the President, in distributing the patronage of the State. It is the President, indeed, and the President alone, who selects, but the consent of the Senate is required to the appointment. This applies not only to the diplomatic and great executive appointments, but also to the appointment of the judges of the Supreme Court. Until 1867 the assent of the Senate was only required to appointments, but not to removals; but a law of that year restricted the sole power of the President to that of suspending an official when Congress is not in session.[42]

Such, in its general outlines, is this illustrious body, which plays so important a part in American history, and has excited the envy and admiration of many European statesmen and writers on politics. Its merits are great and manifest, though there has been of late some tendency to believe that they have been exaggerated, and although it is unfortunately but too clear that they have not been wholly retained. The sketch which I have drawn in a former chapter of the later course of American politics sufficiently proves it, and sufficiently indicates the cause. The excellent system of indirect and double election, which the framers of the Constitution considered the best way of freeing democracy from its baser and more foolish elements, has not been able to withstand the pressure and the ingenuity of caucuses and managers. The men who are en-

---

[41] Bryce, i. 149.
[42] Ford's *American Citizen's Manual*, p. 13.

trusted with the task of voting for the President have long since been deprived by their electors of all liberty of choice, and are strictly pledged to vote for particular candidates. In the election of senators a similar process has gradually, though more imperfectly, prevailed. The State legislatures are essentially the creatures of the caucus, and the members are pledged when elected to vote for particular candidates for the Senate. The system of the equality of the States has been very valuable in counteracting one great danger of democracy, but it introduced a danger of another kind. The desire of the free and slave sections of the country to multiply States of their own complexion, in order to acquire or maintain a preponderance in the Senate, was one main cause of the great Civil War. The Senators are usually the most prominent statesmen of legislatures that are often exceedingly corrupt, and the stream which springs from a tainted fountain cannot be wholly pure. In spite of their small number and their careful selection, the members of the American Senate have not been free from the taint or suspicion of personal corruption.[43]

Though in some respects greatly superior to the British House of Lords as an Upper Chamber, the Senate ranks in this respect clearly below it, and below most of the Upper Houses in Europe. One of the worst results of democracy, and especially one of the worst results of the influence of American example upon politics, is the tendency which it produces to overrate the importance of machinery, and to underrate the importance of character in public life. It is not surprising that it should be so, for the American Constitution is probably the best example which history affords of wise political machinery. Nor are the great men who formed it to be blamed if their successors, by too lax laws of naturalisation and by breaking down all the old restrictions and qualifications of race, colour, and property, have degraded the electorate, and in some serious respects impaired the working of

---

[43] See the admirable pages on the Senate in Mr. Bryce's *American Commonwealth*.

the Constitution. To me, at least, it seems more than doubtful whether there is any political advantage which is not too dearly bought if it leads to a permanent lowering of the character of public men and of the moral tone of public life. In the long run, the increasing or diminishing importance of character in public life is perhaps the best test of the progress or decline of nations. It is an ominous sign for a nation when its governors and legislators are corrupt, but it is a still worse sign when public opinion has come to acquiesce placidly in their corruption.

On the whole, however, the influence of the American Senate has been eminently for good; but careful observers believe that it has become more subservient than it once was to the corrupt party influences that sway American politics. Its veto upon public appointments has been, I believe, of great advantage, but it has not always been exercised as it ought. There is no diplomatic service in the world which has included men of higher abilities or purer characters than that of America; but there is also, I suppose, no other civilised nation where it would be possible for a Government, for the purpose of ingratiating itself with a particular class of voters, to select as their national representative in a foreign country a man of another nation who had recently fled from justice under the gravest of imputations. The lines with which, not long since, one of the best English observers, and one of the most sincere English admirers of American institutions, sums up his impressions of the Senate are not encouraging. 'So far as a stranger can judge,' writes Mr. Bryce, 'there is certainly less respect for the Senate collectively, and for most of the senators individually, now than there was eighteen years ago, though, of course, there are among its members men of an ability and character which would do honour to any assembly.'[44]

I have dwelt at some length upon the constitution of the American Senate, as it is, on the whole, the most remarkable

---

[44] Bryce's *American Commonwealth*, i. 161.

of all modern instances of a successful Upper Chamber not
based on the hereditary principle. It is, however, evident that
much which is distinctive in it, and which has contributed
most to its peculiar importance, is so alien to English ideas
that it could not be reproduced. It is hardly within the range
of possibility that the foreign policy of England and the administration of the chief patronage of the Crown should be placed
under the direct control and supervision of an Upper Chamber
sitting and deciding in secret, nor are there any abuses in these
departments sufficiently grave to require so great a change.

It will not be necessary to bestow more than a cursory glance
on a few typical examples of the Senates, or Upper Houses, of
European countries.[45] In the French Republic, by the constitutional law of 1875, the Senate consisted of 300 members, of
whom seventy-five were elected for life by the two Houses
combined, and afterwards, as vacancies occurred, by the Senate itself, while 225 were elected for nine years by the departments and the colonies. In the case of this latter class the
American system of indirect election is adopted, deputies,
delegates from the municipal councils and some other local
authorities being the electors. A third part of this portion of
the Senate is renewed every third year, and this system of
partial renewal is largely adopted in European Senates. It will
be found in those of Spain, Belgium, the Netherlands, Denmark, and Roumania, though the periods and proportions of
renewal are somewhat varied. In France, as in Denmark, the
Netherlands, and Switzerland, the senators receive a small
payment like the members of the Chamber of Deputies. The
French Senate can be converted into a court of justice for the
trial of political offences. It possesses the same legislative

---

[45] Full particulars of these constitutions will be found in the works of
Dareste and Demombrynes, which I have already quoted. The revised
Belgian Constitution is later than these works, and is, of course, pub-
lished separately. The reader may also consult Desplaces, *Sénats et
Chambres Hautes*, 1893; Morizot-Thibault, *Droits des Chambres Hautes en
matière de Finances, 1891*.

powers as the Lower Chamber, except that it cannot originate money Bills; and it has one special prerogative—that the President can only dissolve the Chamber of Deputies with its consent. By a law of 1884 an important change was introduced into its composition. The life peers were not removed, but it was enacted that no more should be created, and that all vacancies in this class should be filled up, in the usual manner, by departmental election. The whole body will thus spring from the same elective source.

In the German Empire, the Bundesrath, or Federal Council, is so unlike the usual type of Upper Chambers that some writers hesitate to include it in that category. It bears indeed, in some respects, a strong resemblance to a privy council or a council of ministers. It consists of fifty-eight members, appointed by the governments of the different States in the German Empire. In this representation, however, the American system of giving equal weight to all States has not been adopted. The States are represented according to their importance, Prussia having seventeen voices. The Chancellor of the Empire who is himself chosen by the Emperor, presides, and it is provided that the presidency can only be in the hands of a representative of Prussia or of Bavaria.

The powers of this body are very extensive and very various. No measure can become a law of the Empire, no treaty relating to the common affairs of the Empire can become valid, without its consent. No change in the Constitution of the Empire can be effected if fourteen members of the Federal Council oppose it. Its members have a right to appeal and speak in the Reichstag, though they cannot be members of it. It proposes measures which are to be brought before the Reichstag, and new taxes are among the number, and it sends delegates into that body to support them. It has great administrative powers. It establishes from among its members permanent commissions to preside over the great departments of affairs which are common to the Empire. On each of these commissions at least four States must be represented, besides the Emperor; and there are provisions, which it is not here necessary to describe, for giving special privileges on special subjects or occasions to particular States. It has the right, with the consent of the Emperor, to dissolve the Reichstag, and, except in the case of an attack on German territory, its assent is required for a declaration of war. It has the power of pronouncing that States in the Imperial Confederation have failed in fulfilling their federal obligation, and it can authorise the Emperor to coerce them. Differences between the members of the Confederation that are not provided for by the letter of the Constitution, or cannot be settled by legal tribunals, pass before the Federal Council, but it does not possess in these cases a coercive authority. It has also some right of supervision over the administration of justice, especially in cases of socialistic or anarchical agitation. The power of the Emperor and the power of the Federal Council form together such a formidable weight in the German Empire that the real influence of the Reichstag has hitherto been much less than that of the popular House in most constitutional countries.

The constitutions of the States that compose the German Empire are very various, and I will here only refer briefly to that of Prussia, which is the most important. Its Upper House is composed of several distinct classes. There are members by hereditary right. There are a small number who hold their seats by virtue of great posts which they occupy. There are members who are nominated for life absolutely by the King, or on the presentation of certain classes of great proprietors, of the universities, and of the principal towns. The whole body consists of rather more than 300 members, and sixty must be present to form a House. The Prussian House of Lords can only accept or reject financial measures which are sent to it from the Lower House. It can neither originate nor alter them.

The Austrian Upper Chamber is framed on much the same composite principle as that of Prussia. In 1895 it consisted of the princes of the Imperial Family who had attained their majority, sixty-eight hereditary members, seventeen Catholic

prelates, and 131 members named for life.[46] Delegations from
Austria and Hungary, equal in numbers and elected in stated
proportions from the two Houses of the two countries, sit
alternately at Vienna and Buda-Pesth, and manage those imperial affairs which are common to both nations.

In Italy the composition of the Senate is more simple. With
the exception of the princes of the royal family, it consists
exclusively of members nominated for life by the King. No
limit of numbers is imposed, but the limit of age is forty years,
and the members have to be selected from eight categories.
They are chosen from the clergy, from the great scientific
academies, from the Chamber of Deputies and provincial
councils, from the high functionaries of the State, from the
magistracy, the army, and the heads of families who pay the
highest taxes, and, finally, from those who by their services
or eminent merits have deserved well of their country. The
Italian Senate has all the legislative powers of the Lower
Chamber, with the exception of the origination of taxes, and,
like most other senates, it has the right of judging as a judicial
body grave political offences.

In Spain the Senate is composed of 360 members. Half of
these are elected in different proportions by the clergy, the
learned societies, the universities, the provincial councils,
and by delegates from the most-taxed commoners. These
elected members are renewed by halves every five years, and
the sovereign has also the right of dissolving this portion of
the Senate. The other half are permanent, and sit for life.
Some of them sit by their own right. To this category belong
the chief grandees of Spain and a number of important functionaries in Church and State. The remainder are nominated
for life by the Sovereign, and are chosen out of particular
classes, much in the same way as in Italy. The powers of the
Senate are substantially the same as in Italy. In Spain no mea-

---

[46] *Almanach de Gotha*, 1896, p. 716.

sure can become law unless it has been voted for by a majority of all the members who constitute each Chamber.

In Switzerland the American system is adopted of having one Chamber, elected by the population in proportion to its numbers, while the other Chamber is elected by the different cantons, each canton being equally represented by two deputies.[47] The respective provinces of the Federal Government and of the governments of the cantons are minutely traced by the Constitution, but the two Federal Assemblies have almost equal, though in some respects slightly differing, powers, and, as I have already noticed, neither has any special privilege in matters of taxation. A curious feature of the Council of States is, that there is no uniformity in the election of its members and in the duration of their mandate. Each canton has a right to send two deputies, but it may determine for itself the mode of their election and the time for which they are to sit. Sometimes these deputies are chosen by the legislative bodies of the cantons, and sometimes by direct popular election, and they are generally chosen for either one year or three years. The two Chambers usually sit separately, but for some purposes they deliberate together, and in this case, in the event of a difference, the greatly superior numbers in the more popular House give it an overwhelming preponderance. The two Houses sitting together choose the seven members of the Federal Council, which is the executive Government of the Confederation, and they select, out of the seven members, the two who are to hold during the ensuing year the position of President and Vice-President of the Swiss Republic. The whole position of the legislative bodies in Switzerland is materially lowered by the Referendum, or power of appealing directly to a popular vote upon proposed measures, which, as we have already seen, is the most remarkable feature in the Swiss Republic.

In the Netherlands the Upper Chamber is elected by the provincial States, and its members sit for nine years, with a

---

[47] In some cases a canton has been split into two, and in these cases each half canton sends one member.

partial renewal every three years. With the exception of a few important functionaries, they must have a considerable property qualification, which is measured by the taxation they pay. By a singular, and, as it seems to me, most unwise provision, the Upper Chamber has no right either of initiating or of amending laws, and it therefore cannot exercise that influence of modification or compromise which is the most valuable function of most Upper Houses. Its sole power in legislation is to accept or reject in their totality the measures that have been voted by the other Chamber. It does not possess the power, which most Senates possess, of trying ministers who are impeached by the Lower Chamber. This right of trial belongs to the High Court of Justice; and the members of this court are nominated by the King out of a list of candidates which is submitted to him at each vacancy by the Second Chamber. In the reform of the Constitution which took place in 1887, the number of members in the Upper Chamber was increased from thirty-nine to fifty, and that in the Lower House from eighty-six to 100.

In Belgium, by the Constitution of 1831 the Senate was elected in a manner which is quite different from those I have hitherto described, and which is pronounced by the best Belgian writer on constitutions to be 'detestable.'[48] It was elected directly, and on the basis of mere numbers, by the same electors as the House of Representatives. The principal differences between the two Houses were, that the Senate was only half as large a body as the Chamber of Deputies; that it was elected for eight instead of four years; that its members were unpaid, and that they could only be selected from the larger taxpayers of the country. The Senate is renewed by halves every four years; but the King has also the power of dissolving it, either separately, or conjointly with the other Chamber. It has the same legislative powers as the other House, except that financial measures and measures relating to the contingent of the army must be first voted by the Lower House. It has no judicial

---

[48] Laveleye, *Le Gouvernement dans la Démocratie*, ii. 455.

functions, these being reserved exclusively for the regular tribunals. By the Constitution of 1893 great changes have been
made in the composition of the Senate, as well as of the Lower
House. A number of senators equalling half the number of the
members of the Chamber of Deputies are now directly elected
by the voters in the provinces, in proportion to their population, and with the provision that the electors must be thirty
years old. But, in addition to these, there is another class,
chosen by the provincial councils, each council returning from
two to four senators, according to the population of the province it represents. The first of these two classes of senators
must be chosen from among citizens who pay a certain amount
of direct taxation. For the second class no pecuniary qualification is required. The sons of the sovereign, or, if he has no
sons, the Belgian princes who come next in the order of succession, are senators in their own right.

The foregoing examples will be sufficient to illustrate the
different manners in which the problem of providing an efficient Upper Chamber can be met. On the whole, these
Chambers in the continental constitutions have worked well,
though they have in general not yet had a very long experience, and most of them—especially those of a composite character—have included a large proportion of the chief elements
of weight and ability in their respective countries. In the colonial constitutions under the British Crown, where responsible Governments have been established, the usual type has
been one elective and popular Chamber and a smaller Chamber, consisting of members who are either nominated for life
directly by the Crown, or who sit by virtue of high offices to
which they have been appointed by the Crown, or, more frequently, of a combination of both classes. In some cases, however, election and nomination are mixed, and in others the
Upper House is completely elective, but subject to a property
qualification for the electors or members, or for both. There
are no less than seventeen colonies under the British Crown
with responsible governments. Many of them are so small
that inferences drawn from them are scarcely applicable to a

great country, but a few of the Senates of the larger colonies may be briefly sketched.[49]

Thus, in the Dominion Parliament of the great Canadian confederation the Senate consists of eighty-one members, nominated for life by the Governor-General under the great seal of Canada, and selected in stated proportions from the different provinces in the confederation. Each senator must be at least thirty years old. He must have property to the value of four thousand dollars and a residence in the province which he represents, and he receives a payment of one thousand dollars a year. Each province also has its own separate Parliament, but they are not all constructed on the same type.

In Newfoundland there is an extremely democratic constitution, for both the Legislative Council and the House of Assembly are elected by manhood suffrage, though a property qualification is retained for the members.

In Africa the Senate of the Cape of Good Hope consists of twenty-two members, elected for ten years, and presided over by the Chief Justice of the colony. There is a property qualification both for electors and members, and the members of both Houses are paid. Full responsible government in this colony only exists since 1872. The neighbouring colony of Natal was made a distinct colony in 1856. Its Legislative Council is formed of five official and two nominated members, together with twenty-three members who are elected for four years by electors possessing a certain property qualification. Vast territories lie outside these colonies, which are administered by commissioners; while the West African dependencies, with their large native and almost infinitesimal European populations, and the more important islands adjacent to Africa, are managed by governors, with the assistance of councils.

In the numerous islands or island groups which are subject to the British Crown there is much variety of constitution.

---

[49] An excellent summary will be found in a little work of Mr. Arthur Mills, called *Colonial Constitutions*, 1891. See, too, Martin's *Statesman's Yearbook*.

Thus, in the Bahamas, in Barbadoes, and in the Bermudas, we find the threefold constitution consisting of a governor, a popular elected Assembly, and a Legislative Council nominated by the Crown. In the Leeward Islands, which were combined into a single Government in 1882, the Federal Government consists of a governor and a Legislative Council of ten nominated and ten elected members, representing the different islands. In Jamaica there is now no representative Assembly, but the governor is aided by a Privy Council and a Legislative Council of eighteen members, of whom four are official, five nominated by the governor, and nine elected by colonists who pay a certain level of taxation. It is specially provided in the Constitution that six of the elected members can, if unanimous, carry any financial measure. Most of the small islands are administered by a governor and a Legislative Council consisting partly of official members and partly of members nominated by the Crown. It has been remarked that there is a strong tendency of opinion in the island colonies hostile to representative institutions, and in favour of more concentrated government honestly administered. Thus, in Grenada and St. Vincent representative institutions were abolished at the request of the people in 1876 and 1877, and a form of government by a governor and Legislative Council, partly official and partly unofficial, has been adopted. A very similar change had been effected, a few years earlier, in several of the islands which formed part of the Leeward Islands. Jamaica, in 1866, surrendered a representative Constitution that had existed for 200 years, and accepted a far less democratic Constitution; and on the coast of Central America representative institutions, after an experience of seventeen years, were abolished in British Honduras in 1870.

In Australia the colonial governments have passed through several phases, and questions relating to the formation of an Upper Chamber, its power over money Bills, and its relations to the governor and the Lower House, have been fiercely debated, and usually argued chiefly upon British precedents. It is here only necessary to state the nature of the Upper Council in each colony. In New South Wales the Legislative Council is nominated for life by the governor. The minimum number is fixed at twenty-one; but this number has been largely exceeded, and there was one unsuccessful attempt, in the premiership of Sir Charles Cowper in 1861, to overbear the Council by nominating a large number of members in order to win a majority. It was strongly condemned, both by public opinion in the colony and by the authorities in England.[50] Four-fifths of the members must be persons not holding any paid office under the Crown, but this is not held to include officers in the sea and land forces or retired officers on pension.[51] In Queensland the Legislative Council is formed on the same principle of nomination; in Victoria, in South Australia, in Western Australia, and in Tasmania, it is an elective body, directly elected for limited periods, but usually under a special property qualification. In New Zealand the less democratic method is adopted, and the Legislative Council consists of members nominated by the governor. Before 1891 they were appointed for life; but an Act of that year made all new appointments tenable for seven years only, though the councillors may be reappointed.[52]

If we turn now from these various consitutions to our own, we shall find, I think, a very general agreement among serious political thinkers that it would be an extreme misfortune if the upper, or revising, Chamber in the Legislature were abolished, and an agreement, which, if less general, is still very wide, that it must, in some not far distant day, be materially altered. For my own part, I should consider it a misfortune if the hereditary element, of which it is now mainly composed, were not still largely represented in it. The peerage occupies a vast place in English history and tradition. It has a widespread influence and an indisputable popularity; and,

---

[50] See Coghlan's *Wealth and Progress of New South Wales*, p. 500. Rusden's *History of Australia*, iii. 258–62.

[51] Coghlan, p. 501.

[52] *New Zealand Yearbook*, 1894, p. 14.

as I have endeavoured to show, its members possess in a high degree some of the qualities and capacities that are most useful in the government of men. Their political prominence not only represents, but also sustains and strengthens, a connection between the upper classes of the country and political life, to which England owes very much, and in an age as democratic as our own it may qualify some evils, and can produce no danger.

It must also be remembered that, without resorting to revolutionary measures, no reform of the House of Lords can be carried without its own assent, and it is scarcely within the limits of possibility that it would sanction a law which extinguished its hereditary element. To carry such a measure in spite of it would probably prove a long and most serious task. It has become a fashion of late years, at times when the House does, or threatens to do, something which is thought unpopular to organise great London demonstrations against it. Some thousands of men and women, largely swollen by mere holiday-seekers, and representing at most a very doubtful voting preponderance in two or three London constituencies, are accustomed to assemble in Hyde Park, and by the mouth of men who, for the most part, would be unable to find a single constituency that would send them into Parliament, to proclaim themselves the voice of the nation, and hurl defiance at the Upper House. In England these things have little weight. In France they have been more serious, for more than one revolution, for which the immense majority of the French people had never wished, has been accomplished by the violence of a Paris mob. There can, however, be little doubt that, if a proposal for the violent destruction of the House of Lords were brought authoritatively before the country, that House would find in the great silent classes of the nation a reserve of power that would prove very formidable. Nor is it possible to predict what results and what reactions would ensue if once the barriers of law were broken down, and the torrent of revolutionary change let loose. It is not likely that true liberty would gain by the struggle.

The British aristocracy, as we have seen, contains a large number of members who possess every moral and intellectual quality that is needed for a good legislator. It includes also many members who have neither the tastes, nor the knowledge, nor the capacity of legislators, and whose presence in the House of Lords probably tends more than any other single circumstance to discredit it in the country. The obvious remedy is, that the whole peerage should elect a certain number of their members to represent them. Eighty or 100 peers returned in this way to the Upper House would form a body of men of commanding influence and of the highest legislative capacity. The Irish and Scotch peerages already furnish examples of peers of the realm who are not members of the Upper House, though they are eligible for that position. It is much to be desired that this class should be increased. Among other advantages, it would meet the case of men who, having attained great eminence, or performed great services in fields very widely removed from politics, are deserving of the highest dignity the State can bestow, but who have no natural aptitude for the task of a legislator. On the whole, few better constituencies can be conceived than the whole body of the peerage; but the elected peers should be chosen by a cumulative vote, or by some other method which would secure the proportionate representation of all shades of opinion, and not, as is now the case in Ireland and Scotland, by a method that practically extinguishes minorities. Those peers who were not elected, or who did not wish to be elected, to the Upper House should have the right of standing like other men for the Lower one.

To these ought, I think, to be added a number of life peers limited by statute. Some of them might be what are called 'official peerages.' Great positions of dignity or responsibility, which are rarely attained without exceptional ability and experience, which make men the natural and official representatives of large classes, and bring them into close touch with their interests, sentiments, and needs, might well carry with them the privilege of a seat in the Upper House. But, in addition to these, the Crown should have the power of conferring life peerages on men who, in many different walks, are eminently distinguished by their genius, knowledge, or services. In this way it would be possible vastly to increase both the influence and the efficiency of the Upper House, and to bring into it men who do not possess the fortunes that are generally supposed to be needed for an hereditary peerage. The life peerages that are already possessed by the bishops and by some law lords furnish a precedent.

Whether beyond the limits I have stated, the representative principle should be introduced into the British Upper House is a more difficult question. In comparing England with the Colonies, it must always be remembered that a genuine aristocracy is a thing which the Colonies do not possess, and which it is not possible to extemporise. It should be remembered, too, that a new country, where few traditions have been formed, where all the conditions of life and property and class relations are very simple, and where the task of legislation is restricted to a narrow sphere, may be well governed under constitutions that would be very unsuited to a highly complex and artificial society, which is itself the centre of a vast and most heterogeneous empire. American experience shows that the system of double, or indirect election, cannot retain its distinctive merits in times or countries where party spirit runs very high. The men who are elected by this method simply represent the opinions of a party majority in the electing body, and are designated by the organisation by which that electing body is created.

Some statesmen of considerable authority would vest county councils and municipalities with large powers of electing members to the Upper House. Whether these for the most part very recently constructed bodies are as yet so conspicuous for their influence or their judicial wisdom that they could be safely entrusted with this task seems to me very doubtful. If the projects which are now vaguely agitated for breaking up the United Kingdom into a federation should ever in any form or measure be accomplished, something might be done to mitigate the weakness and the danger that such a disintegration would inevitably produce, by receiving in the Upper House the representatives of local legislatures; and a similar system might with great advantage be extended to the distant parts of the Empire. Distant colonies, which lie wholly outside the range of English party politics, and have no English party objects to attain, would almost certainly send to an Upper House men of superior character and abilities, and their presence might have some real effect in strengthening the ties that bind the Empire together.

It is impossible to predict what form public opinion on these matters may assume. Some pressing party interest, or passion, or personal ambition, will probably in the last issue determine its course, unless timely wisdom in dealing with this momentous question is displayed by the true lovers of the Constitution.

Some other and minor reforms of the House of Lords seem also to be loudly called for. One of these is the conversion of an unlimited into a limited veto. A power of preventing for all time measures which both the House of Commons and the constituencies desire should not be lodged with any non-elected legislative body, and an unlimited creation of peers is the only means which the Constitution provides for overcoming the resistance of the House of Lords. That House, in fact, never attempts to exert its full theoretical power on any large question, though there have been occasional and deplorable instances of its rejecting, through long successions of Parliaments, in spite of constant majorities in the Lower House, reforms affecting small classes of people and exciting no widespread interest. But on great questions, and on questions involving party issues, this is never done; and the very magnitude of the power theoretically vested in the House of Lords is an obstacle to its moderate exercise. A veto limited and defined by law would be more fearlessly exercised and more generally accepted. The English system of veto resembles in some respects the English system of parliamentary impeachment, which, extending to life, liberty, and the confiscation of goods, is a weapon of such tremendous force that it has become completely obsolete; while in America, impeachment, carrying only very moderate penalties, is sometimes, though rarely, employed.

It is well understood that, on all great questions, the veto of the House of Lords is now merely suspensory, securing that no important measure can be carried which does not represent the distinct, the deliberate, the decided opinion of the nation. When a policy which the House of Commons has adopted and the House of Lords rejected has been clearly ratified by the nation, voting on a distinct issue, and by considerable and sustained majorities, the House of Lords invariably accepts it. But the importance of the function it exercises in delaying great changes until this sanction has been obtained can hardly be overestimated. As I have already said, many measures pass through the House of Commons which the constituencies never desired, or even considered, because they were proposed by ministers who, on totally different questions, had obtained a parliamentary majority. Other measures are the result of transient excitement arising from some transient cause. Others are carried, in the face of great opposition, by a bare, or perhaps languid, divided, and dwindling majority. Other measures are accepted, not because they are desired, but because they cannot be rejected without overthrowing a ministry.

With the increasing influence of ignorance in the electorate, and the rapid disintegration of Parliaments into independent groups, the necessity of a strong revising tribunal, exercising a suspensory veto, becomes continually greater. It is extremely desirable that the negative of the House of Lords should at least extend over one Parliament, so that the particular questions at issue should be brought directly before the electors. It would also be very desirable that it should be finally overcome, not by a bare majority of the House of Commons, but by a majority of at least two-thirds.

The adoption of provisions making such majorities necessary in many branches of legislation and administration would furnish a powerful safeguard against revolutionary or tyrannical measures. In America a two-thirds majority must exist in both Houses in order to overcome the veto of the President; and we have already seen the still stronger precautions that are taken in the American Constitution against parliamentary attacks on the Constitution, on contract, property, or individual freedom. In theory the unlimited power of veto vested in the House of Lords forms a sufficient barrier against such attacks. In practice this protection has become far from sufficient. Without the existence of a real Constitution, limiting parliamentary powers, and protected, as in America, by a Supreme Court, England will never possess, in these vital points, the security which exists beyond the Atlantic. Perhaps the best protection that could be obtained without such a fundamental reorganisation would be a law providing that no measure should be carried against the resistance of the Upper House unless it had been adopted by two successive Houses of Commons, and by majorities of at least two-thirds.

Such a change would, in theory, diminish the powers of the House of Lords. In practice it would, I believe, considerably increase them; and, if it were accompanied by reforms such as I have indicated, it would render the House very powerful for good. In the days when government was mainly in the hands of classes who were largely influenced by traditions, precedents, and the spirit of compromise, tacit understandings, unrecognised by law, were sufficient to define the provinces, to support, and at the same time to limit, the powers of the different parts of the Constitution. Power in England has now passed into other hands; another spirit prevails, and it is very necessary that every function and capacity should be clearly recognised and accurately limited by law.

Another reform which would, I think, be very advisable would be that in England, as in most continental countries, Cabinet ministers should have the right of opposing or defending their measures in both Houses, though their right of voting should be restricted to the House to which they belong. The great evil of the present system is especially felt when the most powerful minister is in the House of Lords, while the decisive verdict on his policy lies with the Commons. A policy explained by subordinates or delegates has never the same weight of authority as when it is expounded by the principal. It is a manifest defect in the Constitution that when the existence of a ministry depends on a House of Commons decision on some question of foreign policy, such a minister as Lord Salisbury or Lord Rosebery should be excluded. It is also a great evil that a Prime Minister, when forming his ministry, should be restricted in his choice of the men who are to fill posts of immense responsibility, by a consideration of the House to which they belong. A change which made such a restriction unnecessary would certainly add to the efficiency of ministries, and its benefits would far outweigh its disadvantages. These disadvantages appear to be a slight increase of the labour thrown on Cabinet ministers, and an unbalanced increase of the debating (though not voting) powers of the ministry, arising from the fact that the chief ministers would have the power of speaking in two Houses, while the leaders of the Opposition would be confined to one.[53] The appearance, however, of a Cabinet minister in the House to which he did not belong ought, I think, to be optional, and not obligatory.

The last reform I would suggest would be some relaxation of the present rule by which all the stages through which a measure has passed are lost if the measure is not completed in a single session. A complete abolition of this rule, which would enable the House of Commons to take up at the beginning of a session the measures which were left unfinished in the last, at the stages which they had then reached, provided there had been no dissolution in the interval, has been often advocated. It has been argued that the present system involves an enormous waste of time and power, that this waste becomes continually more serious with the increase of public

---

[53] It would be, of course, possible to extend the privilege to members of either House who had held Cabinet rank.

business, that it gives a great encouragement to deliberate obstruction. Few things, indeed, seem more absurd than that a measure which has been thoroughly discussed and repeatedly sanctioned by the House of Commons should be lost at its last stage, not because of any parliamentary defeat, but simply because the House, by mere pressure of business, has been unable to complete its work before it is prorogued for its holiday, and that in the ensuing session the whole ground has to be trodden again by the same men. Such is the method of doing business which is adopted by one of the busiest, and also one of the most loquacious, assemblies in the world. In most foreign legislatures a different method is pursued. In Belgium, Denmark, France, Greece, the Netherlands, Portugal, Spain, Sweden, Norway, and the United States, unfinished legislation may be taken up in the following session in the stage in which it was left when the prorogation took place.[54] Yet in none of these countries, with the possible exception of America, is the pressure of business as great as in the British Parliament.[55]

There are, however, real arguments in favour of the British system. It enables the House of Commons easily to get rid of many proposals which it does not consider ripe or fit for immediate legislation, but which for various reasons it does not wish to meet with a direct negative. There is also another consideration, which I have already indicated, and which, though it is not often openly expressed, is, I believe, widely felt. It is, that the House of Commons, as it is at present constituted, with its practically unlimited powers, may become, under the direction of a rash or unscrupulous minister, so great an evil and danger in the State that whatever seri-

---

[54] See Dickinson's *Constitution and Procedure of Foreign Parliaments*, 2nd ed., p. 9.

[55] One result of this system is the great obstacle it throws in the way of legislation initiated by private members. Mr. Dickinson has given some curious statistics about the fate of public Bills introduced by private members in five years, from 1884 to 1889; 960 were introduced, 110 only became law (p. 8).

ously clogs the wheels of the machine is rather an advantage than a disadvantage. Great as is the scandal arising from deliberate obstruction or the unbridled license of loquacious vanity; great as are the evils of the postponement of much necessary legislation, or the hasty and perfunctory discharge of duties which do not lend themselves to party exigencies, these things, in the eyes of many, are not too high a price to pay for an exemption from the calamities that would follow, if a party majority and an ambitious minister could swiftly do their will in tearing to pieces the old institutions and settled social conditions of the country, in order to build up their own power on their ruin. As long as England is governed under its present system 'the declining efficiency of Parliament' will be watched by many patriotic men with no unmingled regret. The downward progress is at least a slow one. In spite of the destruction of all the balances and restrictions of the Constitution, the men who desire to revolutionise find many obstacles in their way, and the men who, in order to win votes in their constituencies, have pledged themselves to revolutionise, without wishing to do so, find easy pretexts for evading their promises.

No serious evil, however, I think, would follow if it were provided that, when a measure had passed through all its stages in the Commons, its consideration in the Lords, and the consideration of the Lords' amendments in the Commons, might be adjourned to, or extended over, the ensuing session. The detailed revision and amendment of elaborate measures, which is one of the most useful and uncontested duties of an Upper House, cannot be properly performed when those measures are only sent up to it at the very end of a session, and have to be hurried through all their stages in a few days. Careful and well-considered legislation is, after all, the great end of a legislative body; and it would be much more fully attained in England if the consideration of laws, which is unduly protracted in one House, were not unduly hurried in the other.

CHAPTER 5

Nationalities

The effects of democracy on the liberty of the world are not only to be traced in the changes that are passing over the governments and constitutions of the different nations, and in the wide fields of religious, intellectual, social, and industrial life; they are also powerfully felt in international arrangements, and especially in the growth of a doctrine of nationalities as the basis of a new right of nations, which has been one of the most conspicuous features of nineteenth-century history. It is essentially different from the old doctrine of the divine right of kings, which regarded great tracts of the world as the rightful dominion of particular dynasties; and also from the doctrine of the balance of power, which prevailed at the Peace of Westphalia, and governed most of the capital changes in Europe during the two succeeding centuries. According to the great politicians and political philosophers of the seventeenth or eighteenth century, the maintenance of European stability is the supreme end of international politics. The first object in every rearrangement of territory should be to make it impossible for one great Power to absorb or dominate over the others; and, by multiplying what are called buffer States, and by many artificial divisions and apportionments of territory, they endeavoured to diminish the danger of collisions, or at least to limit as much as possible their number and their scope. Territorial changes, in their view, should be regarded mainly with a view to these objects, and justified or condemned in proportion as they attained them. The more modern doctrine is, that every people, or large section of a nation, has an absolute and indefeasible right to the form of government it pleases, and that every imposition upon it of another rule is essentially illegitimate.

It is not here necessary to trace in much detail the genesis of this view. It was prominent among the original doctrines of the French Revolution, but it was not long consistently maintained. Popular votes taken under the pressure of an occupying army, and largely accompanied by banishments, proscriptions, and *coups d'état*, had, it is true, some place in the first conquests of the Revolution. The Convention proclaimed in the loftiest language its determination to respect the inalienable right of every people to choose its own form of government,[1] and the Republic made much use of the doctrine of the rights of nationalities to kindle revolts; but it also made those revolts powerful instruments for effecting its own territorial aggrandisement, and it was speedily transformed into a military despotism the most formidable, the most aggressive, the most insatiably ambitious the modern world has ever seen. The strength and tenacity of the sentiment of nationality were, indeed, seldom more forcibly displayed than in the struggle of Spain and of the Tyrol against the Emperor who professed to be the armed representative of the French Revolution.

After Waterloo the rights of nationalities suffered a long eclipse. The Congress of Vienna and the arrangements of the peace divided countries and populations among the victorious Powers, with the most absolute disregard for national antecedents and national wishes. The old republic of Genoa was handed over to Piedmont, which it detested. The still

[1] Sorel, *L'Europe et la Révolution Française*, iii. 154–55, 169–70.

older republic of Venice became a province of Austria. Saxony was divided, and a great part annexed to Prussia. Poland was again partitioned. Catholic Belgium was united with Protestant Holland, and the Catholic electorates on the Rhine with Protestant Prussia. The doctrine of the divine right of kings, and a formal repudiation of the right of nations to choose their forms of government, were the basis of the new 'Holy Alliance,' of the resolutions of the Congress of Laybach, and of the whole Policy of Metternich, and in accordance with these principles an Austrian army put down insurrection in Naples, and a French army in Spain.

There were, however, signs that the doctrine of nationalities was not extinct, and there were movements in this direction which excited hopes that were not fully justified by the event. The enthusiasm evoked by the emancipation of Greece, by the revolt of the Spanish colonies in America, and by the foreign policy of Canning, marks the turn of the stream, and the French Revolution of 1830 kindled a democratic and a nationalist movement in many countries much like that which accompanied the Revolution of 1848. There were insurrections or agitations in many of the States of Italy, in Germany, Denmark, Poland, Hungary, Belgium, and Brazil. Most of them were speedily suppressed. Russia crushed with merciless severity insurrection in Poland. An Austrian army put down revolt in the Pontifical States. In Germany and Austria and Italy politics soon moved along the old grooves, and the spirit of reaction was triumphant; but the separation of Belgium from Holland marked a great step in the direction of the rights of nationalities; the government of France now rested on a parliamentary basis; popular institutions were introduced into Denmark; the aristocratic cantons of Switzerland were transformed, and the Reform Bill of 1832 placed English politics on a more democratic basis. Neither Louis Philippe nor Lord Palmerston desired to propagate revolution, and their alliance was chequered and broken by many dissensions; but, on the whole, it served the cause of liberty in Europe, and still more the cause of non-intervention.

The French Revolution of 1848 again changed the aspect of affairs, and in a few months nearly all Europe was convulsed. The revolutions which then took place were essentially revolutions of nationality, and though most of them were for a time suppressed, they nearly all eventually accomplished their designs. I do not propose to relate their well-known history. It is sufficient to say that the French Government, in the manifesto which was issued by Lamartine in the March of 1848, while disclaiming any right or intention of intervening in the internal affairs of other countries, asserted, perhaps more strongly than had ever been before done in an official document, the legitimacy of all popular efforts for national independence, and clearly intimated that when such risings took place the Republic would suffer no foreign intervention to suppress them.

The doctrine of nationalities has been especially formulated and defended by Italian writers, who in this field occupy the foremost place. The aspiration towards a common nationality that slowly grew up among the Italian people, in spite of the many and ancient political divisions that separated them, may be probably traced to the traditions of the old Roman power. Dante and Macchiavelli at once displayed and strengthened it, and it has greatly coloured the Italian political philosophy of our century.

The first question to be asked is, What constitutes a nationality? Vico had defined it as 'a natural society of men who, by unity of territory, of origin, of customs, and of language, are drawn into a community of life and of social conscience.' More modern Italian writers, among whom Mancini, Mamiani, and Pierantoni are conspicuous, have employed themselves in amplifying this definition. They enumerate as the constituent elements of nationality, race, religion, language, geographical position, manners, history, and laws, and when these or several of them combine they create a nationality. It becomes perfect when a special type has been formed; when a great homogeneous body of men acquires, for the first time, a consciousness of its separate nationality, and thus becomes 'a moral unity with a common thought.' This is the *cogito ergo sum* of nations, the selfconsciousness which establishes in nations as in individuals a true personality. And as the individual man, according to these writers, has an inalienable right to personal freedom, so also has the nationality. Every government of one nationality by another is of the nature of slavery, and is essentially illegitimate, and the true right of nations is the recognition of the full right of each nationality to acquire and maintain a separate existence, to create or to change its government according to its desires. Civil communities should form, extend, and dissolve themselves by a spontaneous process, and in accordance with this right and principle of nationality. Every sovereign who appeals to a foreign Power to suppress movements among his own people; every foreign Power which intervenes as Russia did in Hungary, and as Austria did in Italy, for the purpose of suppressing a national movement, is essentially criminal. On the other hand, any war for the emancipation of struggling nationalities, such as that of France with Austria, and Russia with Turkey, derives its justification from this fact, quite irrespective of the immediate cause or pretexts that produced it.[2]

Such, pushed to its full extent and definition, is the philosophy which, in vaguer and looser terms, pervades very widely the political thought of Europe, and has played a great part in the historic development of the nineteenth century. It may be observed that, though the idea of nationality is greatly affected by democracy, it is in itself distinct from it, and is, in fact, very frequently separated from it. The idea and passion of nationality blend quite as easily with loyalty to a dynasty as with attachment to a republican form of government, and nations

---

[2] An excellent review of the Italian school of writers on nationality, by Professor von Holtzendorff, will be found in the *Revue de Droit International*, ii. 92–106. See, too, a valuable essay by Professor Padeletti, ibid. iii. 464. M. Emile Ollivier, in his *Empire Libéral*, has discussed the French views on the subject.

that value very little internal or constitutional freedom are often passionately devoted to their national individuality and independence. It may be observed also, that the many different elements of nationality which have been mentioned rarely concur, and that no one of them is always sufficient to mark out a distinct nationality. As a matter of history, all great nations have been formed, in the first instance, by many successive conquests and aggrandisements, and have gradually become more or less perfectly fused into a single organism. Race, except when it is marked by colour, is usually a most obscure and deceptive guide, and in most European countries different race elements are inextricably mixed. Language and religion have had a much greater and deeper power in forming national unities; but there are examples of different creeds and languages very successfully blended into one nationality, and there are examples of separations of feeling and character, due to historical, political, and industrial causes, existing where race, creed, and language are all the same.

In the opinion of some writers, even the will of the people must be disregarded when questions of race, or language, or geography, demand an annexation, and in each country the prevailing theory of nationality is very manifestly coloured by national circumstances. Thus German writers, in defending the annexation of Alsace, have not contented themselves with arguing that this province was acquired in repelling an unjust invasion, and that its retention is essential to the security of Germany. While recognising fully that an overwhelming majority of Alsatian votes would be given in favour of France, they have justified the annexation on the ground of the doctrine of nationalities, as restoring to Germany an essentially German province, which had been torn from her in part by gross fraud, and which is inhabited by a population who, though not German in sentiment, were at least German in origin, in character, and in language. French writers have defended their designs upon the Rhine on the ground that the Rhine boundary is clearly the natural frontier of France, and that she is, therefore, only completing her nationality by annexing a territory exclusively inhabited by a loyal German population. Italian writers have demanded the absorption or annexation of Italian-speaking communities in Switzerland and Austria because they are Italian, entirely irrespective of all other considerations.

A more considerable section, however, of the upholders of the doctrine of nationalities maintain that annexations can only be justified, and can always be justified, by a plebiscite of the whole male population, and it was one of the great objects of Napoleon III. and of Count Cavour to introduce this principle into the public right of Europe. It was adopted when Savoy and Nice were annexed to France, and in the case of the different Italian States which, through their own spontaneous action, were incorporated in the Italian unity. When, after the War of 1866, the Austrian Emperor, in order to avoid the humiliation of treating directly with Italy, placed Venetia in the hands of Napoleon III., it was transferred by that sovereign to Italy subject to the consent of the population by a plebiscite. So, too, the invasion of Neapolitan territory in 1860, and the capture of Rome in 1870 by Piedmontese troops, without any declaration of war or any real provocation, and in violation of plain treaty obligations, were held to have been justified by the popular votes which shortly after incorporated Naples and Rome in the Italian Kingdom. In the Treaty of Prague, which was concluded in 1866, and which, among other things, made Prussia the ruler of Schleswig-Holstein, there was a clause promising that if the inhabitants of the northern parts of Schleswig expressed by a free vote their desire to be reunited to Denmark, their wish should be conceded; but, in spite of a largely signed petition for such a vote, this promise, to the great dishonour of Germany, has never been fulfilled.[3] The last case, as far as I am aware, of the employment of a plebiscite to sanction an annexation was in 1878, when the little island of St. Barthélemy, in the Antillas, was ceded by the King of Sweden and Norway to the French Republic.[4]

---

[3] *Revue de Droit International*, ii. 325–26.
[4] See *Les Annexions et les Plébiscites dans l'Histoire Contemporaine*, par E. R. De Card (1880).

Sometimes, as in Italy, the movement of nationality is a movement of sympathy and agglomeration, drawing together men who had long been politically separated. More frequently it is a disintegrating force, and many of its advocates desire to call into intense life and self-consciousness the different race elements in a great and composite empire, with the hope that they may ultimately assert for themselves the right of distinct national individuality.

Within certain limits, the doctrine of nationalities undoubtedly represents a real and considerable progress in human affairs. The best, the truest, the most solid basis on which the peace of the civilised world can rest is the free consent of the great masses of its population to the form of government under which they live. The increased recognition of this fact, the increased sensitiveness of the European conscience to the iniquity of destroying wantonly the independence of a civilised nation, or maintaining one civilised nation under the yoke of another, is a genuine sign of moral progress. At the same time there can, I think, be little question that the doctrine of nationalities has assumed forms and been pushed to extremes which make it a great danger to the peace of the world. It becomes the readiest weapon in the hands both of a conqueror and of a revolutionist, and, by discrediting the force of all international treaties, deepening lines of division, and introducing elements of anarchy and rebellion into most great nations, it threatens the most valuable elements of our civilisation.

Scarcely any one would apply it to the dealings of civilised nations with savages, or with the semi-civilised portions of the globe. It is, indeed, most curious to observe the passion with which nations that are accustomed to affirm the inalienable right of self-government in the most unqualified terms have thrown themselves into a career of forcible annexation in the barbarous world. Nor is it easy to obtain a true judgment of the opinion even of civilised communities. A plebiscite is very rarely the unforced, spontaneous expression of a genuine national desire. It is usually taken to ratify or indemnify an accomplished fact. It is taken only when there can be no doubt about the result, and a strong centralised government has, on such occasions, an enormous power of organising and directing. In all countries a great portion, in most countries a large majority, of the people take no real interest in political affairs, and if a great constitutional or dynastic question is submitted to their vote by a strongly organised government, this government will have no difficulty in dictating the response. Tolstoi, in one of his later works, has made some remarks on this subject which, though very little in harmony with prevailing ideas, contain, I believe, a large measure of truth. 'I have always,' he writes, 'noticed that the most serious and the most respectable members of the labouring class show a complete indifference to, and even contempt for, patriotic manifestations of every kind. I have observed the same thing among the labouring class in other nations, and my observation has often been confirmed by cultivated Frenchmen, Germans, and Englishmen, when speaking of their own fellow-citizens. The labouring population is too intensely and too exclusively occupied with the care of providing for its own subsistence to take an interest in those political questions which lie at the root of patriotism. Such questions as Russian influence in the East, the unity of Germany, the restoration of France of her severed provinces, do not really touch the people, not only because they scarcely ever know the first elements of the problem, but also because the interests of their lives lie wholly outside the circle of politics. A man of the people will never really care to know what is the exact line of the national frontier. . . . To him his country is his village or his district. He either knows nothing of what lies beyond, or it is a matter of perfect indifference to him to what government these territories belong. If a Russian emigrates, he will not care whether his new home is under the dominion of Russia, or Turkey, or China.[5]

---

[5] Tolstoi, *L'Esprit Chrétien et le Patriotisme*, pp. 88–9, 93. It is curious to contrast this judgment with the remarks of Goethe to Eckermann. 'In

But even putting this consideration aside, can it seriously be maintained that a great and ancient nation is obliged to acquiesce in its own disintegration whenever a portion of its people can be persuaded to desire a separate political existence? If a popular movement can at any time destroy the unity of the State, the authority of the sovereign power, and the binding force of international treaties, the whole public order of Europe must give way. Some of the countries which play the most useful and respectable parts in the concert of nations, such as Switzerland, Belgium, and the Austrian Empire, would be threatened with immediate dissolution; and there is scarcely a great country in Europe which does not contain districts with distinct race and religious elements, which might easily be quickened into separate agitation. As in marriage the conviction that the tie is a life tie, being supported by all the weight of law and opinion, is sufficient in the vast majority of cases to counteract the force of caprice or temporary disagreement, and produce acquiescence and content, so, in the political world, the belief in the sovereign authority of the State, and in the indissoluble character of national bonds, gives stability and unity to a nation. Divorce in families, and revolution in States, may sometimes be necessary, and even desirable, but only under very grave and exceptional circumstances.

If the bonds of national unity are lightly severed; if the policy of disintegration is preached as in itself a desirable thing; if the constituent elements of a kingdom are encouraged or invited to assert their separate individuality, nothing but anarchy can ensue. The door will be at once opened to endless agitation and intrigue, and every ambitious, restless,

---

general, national hatred has this special characteristic, that you will always find it most intense, most violent, in proportion as you descend the scale of intellectual culture. But there is a degree where it altogether disappears—where men rise, so to speak, above the lines of nationhood, and sympathise with the happiness or unhappiness of a neighbouring nation as if it consisted of compatriots.'

unscrupulous conqueror will find his path abundantly prepared. It is the object of all such men to see surrounding
nations divided, weakened, and perhaps deprived of important strategical positions, through internal dissensions. One
of the great dangers of our age is that wars are likely to be
carried on, in the French phrase, 'à coup de révolutions,' that
is, by deliberately kindling democratic, socialist, or nationalist
risings. It has been stated on good authority, that the decision
of German statesmen to adopt universal suffrage as the basis
of their constitution was largely due to the desire to guard
against such dangers. From the French revolutionists, who
begin their career of invasion by promising French assistance
to every struggling nationality, to the modern Panslavist, who
is often preaching the right of nationalities in the mere interest
of a corrupt and persecuting despotism, this doctrine has
been abundantly made use of to cloak the most selfish and
the most mischievous designs. Those men are not serving the
true interests of humanity who enlarge the pretexts of foreign
aggression, and weaken the force of treaties and international
obligations, on which the peace and stability of civilisation so
largely depend.

Such considerations sufficiently show the danger of the
exaggerated language on the subject of the rights of nationalities which has of late years become common. It will, indeed, be observed that most men use such language mainly
in judging other nations and other policies than their own.
One of the most remarkable test cases of this kind which have
occurred in our generation has been that of the United States.
This great nation is one of the least military as well as one of
the freest and most democratic in the world, and its representative writers, and sometimes even its legislative bodies,
are fond of very absolute assertions of the right of revolution
and the inalienable supremacy of the popular will. Yet in its
own acquisitions the American Republic has never adopted
the principle of plebiscite. Texas was admitted into the Union
by a treaty with a State which was considered independent;
Upper California was conquered from Mexico; New Mexico

was acquired by purchase; Louisiana was purchased from Napoleon in 1803; Florida was acquired by treaty with Spain in 1821; but in no one of these cases were the people consulted by a popular vote.[6]

But most significant of all was the attitude assumed by the Federal Government in dealing with the secession of the South. Long before that secession some of the best observers had clearly pointed out how the influence of climate, and much more the special type of industry and character which slavery produced, had already created a profound and lasting difference between the North and the South. Both Madison and Story had foreseen that the great danger to the United States was the opposition between the Northern and Southern interests.[7] Calhoun was so sensible of the difference that he proposed the establishment of two presidents, one for the free, and the other for the slave States, each with a veto on all national legislation.[8] Guizot[9] and Tocqueville[10] had both distinctly recognised the same truth. Though language and religion were the same, and though race was not widely different, two distinct nations had grown up, clearly separated in their merits and their defects, in character, manners, aspirations, and interests.

After the election of President Lincoln the long-impending disruption came. The Southern States proclaimed the right of nationalities, demanded their independence, and proved their earnestness and their unanimity by arguments that were far more unequivocal than any doubtful plebiscite. For four long years they defended their cause on the battle-field with

---

[6] See an article by Professor Lieber on Plebiscites, *Revue de Droit International*, iii. 139–45.

[7] Story's *Commentaries on the Constitution of the United States*, ii. 177.

[8] Goldwin Smith's *The United States*, p. 184.

[9] See a very remarkable passage (exceedingly creditable to the sagacity of Guizot, when it is remembered that these lectures were delivered between 1828 and 1830) in the *Hist. de la Civilisation*, XVIIIᵐᵉ leçon.

[10] *Démocratie en Amérique*, tom ii. ch. x.

heroic courage, against overwhelming odds, and at the sacrifice of everything that men most desire. American and indeed European writers are accustomed to speak of the heroism of the American colonies in repudiating imperial taxation, and asserting and achieving their independence against all the force of Great Britain. But no one who looks carefully into the history of the American revolution, who observes the languor, the profound divisions, the frequent pusillanimity, the absence of all strong and unselfish enthusiasm that were displayed in great portions of the revolted colonies, and their entire dependence for success on foreign assistance, will doubt that the Southern States in the War of Secession exhibited an incomparably higher level of courage, tenacity, and self-sacrifice. No nation in the nineteenth century has maintained its nationhood with more courage and unanimity. But it was encountered with an equal tenacity, and with far greater resources, and, after a sacrifice of life unequalled in any war since the fall of Napoleon, the North succeeded in crushing the revolt and establishing its authority over the vanquished South.

The struggle took place at a time when the recent emancipation of Italy had brought the doctrine of the rights of nationalities into the strongest relief. That doctrine had been accepted with enthusiasm by nearly all that was progressive in Europe, and nowhere more widely and more passionately than in England. It is curious and instructive to observe the attitude of English opinion towards the contest that ensued. At the opening of the war the secession of the South was very generally blamed, and throughout the war a majority of the population remained, I believe, steadily on the side of the North. With the great body of the working classes the question was looked on simply as a question of slavery. The North was represented as fighting for the abolition of slavery, which it certainly was not, and as fighting to prevent the extension of slavery to the new territories, which it certainly was; and the cause of democracy was deemed inseparably connected with the maintenance and the success of the great Republic of the

West. But, on the other hand, a majority of the upper, and perhaps of the middle, classes soon came to sympathise decidedly with the South, and they were the classes who were most powerfully represented in the press, in society, and in Parliament.

Their motives were very various. Some were, no doubt, unworthy, or purely frivolous. There was the contrast, which was then often drawn, between 'the gentlemen of the South' and 'the shopkeepers of the North.' There was jealousy of the increasing power of the United States, and of the increasing attraction of its form of government. There was resentment excited by many unscrupulous acts and many insulting words of American statesmen and writers; and the ignorance of American politics was so great that few Englishmen realised that the aggressive side of American policy had been mainly due to Southern statesmen acting in Southern interests. The enmity which led the United States to declare war against England in 1812, at the time when England was engaged in a desperate struggle for her existence and for the liberty of Europe against the overwhelming power of Napoleon, was not wholly forgotten,[11] and the more recent sympathy of America with Russia during the Crimean war, had, perhaps, still some slight influence. There were also powerful considerations of present English interests involved in the war. The North was strongly Protectionist, and had begun the war by enacting an ultra-Protectionist tariff, while the South was the fervent champion of Free Trade, and it was from the South that the English cotton manufacture obtained its supplies, while the Northern blockade was reducing to extreme distress the population of Lancashire. Nor should we omit that 'sporting spirit' which, it has been truly said, largely governs English interest in every foreign struggle. A comparatively small Power, encountering with consummate skill, with desperate courage, and for a long time with brilliant success, a gigantic but unwieldy and less

---

[11] See some excellent remarks on this war in Goldwin Smith's *United States*, pp. 166–74.

skilful adversary, was certain to awake strong popular interest, quite irrespective of the merits of the case.

But it would be a grave injustice to attribute to such motives the great body of serious and deliberate opinion in England which desired the recognition of Southern independence and the cessation of the war. One large class emphatically condemned the original secession; but they either believed, with most experienced European statesmen, that the final subjugation of the South was impossible, and that the prolongation of the war was, in consequence, a mere useless waste of life, or that, if the South were finally subjugated, it would reproduce in America that most lamentable of all European spectacles, the spectacle of a subjugated Poland. Another large class believed that, on the principle of the American Constitution, the South was acting within its constitutional rights. They contended that when the separate States agreed on carefully defined conditions to enter into a bond of union, they never meant to surrender the right, which they had so lately vindicated against Great Britain, of seceding from it if the main body of their citizens desired it. This was the doctrine of Calhoun, and it was supported by a great weight both of argument and authority. There were some who, like Sir Cornewall Lewis, detested slavery, but who contended that the differences between North and South were so grave that separation was the only solution, and that it would ultimately prove a great blessing to America, as well as to the world, if the Northern States developed as a separate republic, untainted by the deteriorating influences of negro slavery and a tropical climate.[12] But the strongest argument on this side was the doctrine of the rights of nationalities. I can well remember how the illustrious historian, Mr. Grote, whose political leanings were strongly democratic, and who, at the same time, always formed his opinions with an austere independence and integrity, was accustomed to speak on the

---

[12] See a letter by Sir Cornwall Lewis prefixed to his *Administrations of Great Britain*, p. 19.

subject, and how emphatically he dissented from the views
of Mill and of a large proportion of those with whom he usually acted. He could not, he said, understand how those who
had been so lately preaching in the most unqualified terms
that all large bodies of men had an absolute, unimpeachable,
indefeasible right to choose for themselves their form of government, and that the growing recognition of this right was
one of the first conditions of progress and liberty, could support or applaud the Federal Government in imposing on the
Southern States a government which they detested, and in
overriding by force their evident and unquestionable desire.

The inconsistency was real and flagrant, and the attitude
of the North, and of its supporters in Europe, could only be
justified on the ground that the right of nationalities was not
the absolute, unlimited thing which it had been customary to
assert. In the Northern States public opinion never faltered.
Before the war began, it is true, there were some men, among
whom Horace Greeley was conspicuous, who maintained
that if the Southern States generally desired to secede they
ought not to be prevented; and there were many men who
throughout the war tried to persuade themselves that a strong
unionist sentiment was latent in the South. But the question
of submitting the integrity of the Republic to a popular vote
in the several States was never entertained, though there was
a proposal, which was defeated by the Republican party, of
submitting to a direct popular vote a compromise about slavery which might have averted the war.[13] It was at once felt
that the question at issue was a question of national preservation, to which all other considerations must be subordinated, and the best men maintained that, by preserving the
integrity of the republic, even against the wishes of an immense section of the people, they were most truly serving the
interests of humanity. Three fatal consequences would have
followed the triumph of the South. Slavery would have been
extended through vast territories where it did not hitherto

---

[13] This was the Crittenden compromise. See Rhodes's *History of the United States*, iii. 150, 254–67. See, too, on Greeley's opinion, pp. 140–42.

prevail. A precedent of secession would have been admitted which, sooner or later, would have broken up the United States into several different Powers. And as these Powers would have many conflicting interests, the European military system, which the New World had happily escaped, would have grown up in America, with all the evils and all the dangers that follow in its train.

The judgment of the North was justified by the event, and this great struggle added one more to the many conspicuous instances of the fallibility of political predictions. The overwhelming majority of the most sagacious politicians in Europe believed, either that the North would never attempt to restrain by force the Southern States if they desired to secede; or that an armed revolt of many entire States, guided by their legislatures, could not possibly be suppressed; or that, if it were suppressed, it could only be through a general rising of the enslaved negroes, which they anticipated as one of the most certain consequences of the prolongation of the war. Each one of these predictions was signally and absolutely falsified. The speedy and complete acquiescence of the defeated South in the result of the war was no less surprising to European statesmen; while the fact that the cotton produced in the South by free labour greatly exceeds that which was produced by slavery,[14] shows that the Southern belief that utter and imminent ruin must follow abolition was an absolute delusion. How different might have been the course of American history, how much bloodshed and misery might have been spared, if, even at the last moment, the policy proposed by President Lincoln in 1862 had been accepted, and the slave States had agreed to gradual enfranchisement, receiving Government bonds to the full value of their slaves![15]

---

[14] See some remarkable figures on this subject in Mr. Rhodes's *History of the United States from the Compromise of 1850*, i. 314. The annual average produce of cotton in the South between 1865 and 1886 exceeded that of the last twenty years of slavery by no less than 65·3 per cent.

[15] Rhodes's *History of the United States from the Compromise of 1850*, iii. 634–35; *Annual Register*, 1862, p. 231.

The regeneration of Italy had preceded the contest in America, and, more than any other event, it gave popularity to the doctrine of the rights of nationalities. It was one of the most genuine of national movements, and very few who were young men when it took place, still fewer of those who, like the writer of these lines, then lived much in Italy, can have failed to catch the enthusiasm which it inspired. Though some provinces sacrificed much, there was no province in which the Italian cause did not command the support of overwhelming majorities, and though two great wars and an overwhelming debt were the cost, the unity of Italy was at last achieved. The mingled associations of a glorious past and of a noble present, the genuine and disinterested enthusiasm that so visibly pervaded the great mass of the Italian people, the genius of Cavour, the romantic character and career of Garibaldi, and the inexpressible charm and loveliness of the land which was now rising into the dignity of nationhood, all contributed to make the Italian movement unlike any other of our time. It was the one moment of nineteenth-century history when politics assumed something of the character of poetry.

The glamour has now faded, and, looking back upon the past, we can more calmly judge the dubious elements that mingled with it. One of them was the manner in which the annexation of Naples was accomplished. The expedition of Garibaldi to Sicily consisted of so few men, and could have been so easily crushed if it had encountered any real popular resistance, that it scarcely forms an exception to the spontaneous character of the movement towards unity. But the absolutely unprovoked invasion of Naples by Piedmontese troops, which took place without any declaration of war when the Neapolitan forces had rallied at Gaeta, and when the Garibaldian forces were in danger of defeat, was a grave violation of international obligations and of the public law and order of Europe, and it can only be imperfectly palliated by the fact that similar interventions at the invitation of a sovereign and in the interests of despotism had not been uncommon.

Much the same thing may be said of the subsequent invasion of Rome, and in this case another and still graver consideration was involved. A great Catholic interest here confronted the purely national movement. In the opinion of the head of the Catholic Church, and in the opinion of the great body of devout Catholics throughout the world, the independence of the head of the Church could only be maintained if he remained the temporal sovereign of his diocese; and there was therefore a cosmopolitan interest of the highest order at issue. The possession of Rome and the adjoining territory to the sea would have met the Catholic requirement for the independence of the Pope, and it was urged by men who had a warm general sympathy with the right of nations to choose their rulers, that in this case the less must yield to the greater, and that, in the interest of the whole Catholic population throughout the world, the small population of Rome and the adjoining territory must be content with a position which was in most respects privileged and honourable, and forego their claim to unite with Italy.

Gioberti had taught that the true solution of the Roman question was an Italian federation under the presidency of the Pope, and at the Peace of Villafranca Napoleon III. and the Emperor of Austria agreed to do their utmost to carry out this scheme. It was, however, from the first doomed to failure. One part of it was the restoration of the dispossessed princes, which could only be effected by force. Another was the introduction of Austria, as the ruler of Venetia, into the confederation, which excited the strongest Italian antipathy. 'The large measure of reform' which the two Emperors agreed to use their influence to obtain from the Pope proved wholly unacceptable to that potentate, while the honorary presidency of the confederation, to which he did not object, was equally unacceptable to Italy. Italian feeling flowed irresistibly towards unity, and the great prestige of Rome, which alone could command an indisputable ascendency among the Italian cities, marked her out as the natural capital. It is, however, not altogether impossible that some compromise with the Catholic interest might have been effected if there had been any real intelligence at the Vatican. Unfortunately, in this quarter incapacity and obstinacy reigned supreme. The Pope had, it is true, a cardinal-minister who possessed to an eminent degree the superficial talents that enable a statesman to write clever despatches and to conduct skilfully a diplomatic interview; but neither he nor his master showed the smallest real power of governing men, of measuring wisely the forces of their time, and of averting revolution by skilful, timely, and searching reform.

The part which was played by England in these transactions was very remarkable. Though she had not sacrificed a man or a guinea in the cause, she intervened actively and powerfully at every stage of its development; she had always an alternative policy to propose, and in nearly every case this policy ultimately prevailed. Lord John Russell conducted her foreign policy, and he was warmly supported in the Cabinet by Lord Palmerston. He dissented strongly from the leading articles of the Peace of Villafranca, and clearly pointed out the impossibility of carrying them into effect. He urged persistently that the Italian people should be left to form their own governments freely, without the intervention of either France or Austria. He was the only statesman who officially approved of the Piedmontese invasion of Naples, which he defended by a quotation from Vattel, and by the part played by William III. in the English revolution of 1688. He steadily advocated the withdrawal of French troops from Rome, and the treatment of the Roman question as a purely Italian one. He exasperated foreign statesmen not a little by his constant lectures on 'the right which belongs to the people of every independent State to regulate their own internal government,' and on the iniquity of every foreign interference with their clearly expressed will. 'With regard to the general question of interference,' he wrote, 'in the internal affairs of other countries, Her Majesty's Government holds that non-intervention is the principle on which the Governments of Europe should act, only to be parted from when the safety of a foreign State or its permanent interests require it.'[16]

At the same time, in the true spirit of an English Whig, he refused to lay any stress on the verdict of universal suffrage as expressed by a plebiscite, and regarded the regular vote of duly authorised representative bodies as the only decisive and legitimate expression of the voice of the people. Speaking of the annexation to the Italian State of Naples, Sicily, Umbria and the Marches, he wrote to Sir J. Hudson: 'The votes by universal suffrage which have taken place in those kingdoms and provinces appear to Her Majesty's Government to have little validity. These votes are nothing more than a formality following upon acts of popular insurrection, or successful invasion, or upon treaties, and do not in themselves imply any independent exercise of the will of the nation in whose name they are given. Should, however, the deliberate act of the representatives of the several Italian States . . . constitute those States into one State in the form of a constitutional monarchy, a new question will arise.'[17]

It is probable that the emphasis with which Lord John Russell dwelt upon this distinction was largely due to the fact that the annexation of Savoy to France had been sanctioned and justified by a popular vote. The British Government treated this vote and the pretended popular wish with complete disdain, as a mere device of the two Governments concerned, for the purpose of veiling the character of a secret and dangerous intrigue; and Lord John Russell denounced the whole transaction in language which might easily have led to war.[18]

This policy undoubtedly represented the predominant public opinion of Great Britain, and it was eminently successful. In the very critical state of Italian affairs, and amid

---

[16]See the despatches on Italy in the second volume of *Lord Russell's Speeches and Despatches.*

[17] Lord J. Russell to Sir J. Hudson, Jan. 21, 1861.

[18] Walpole's *Life of Russell*, ii. 319–21.

the strongly expressed disapprobation of the great Continental Powers, the steady countenance and moral support of England gave both force and respectability to the Italian cause, and broke the isolation to which it would have otherwise been condemned. The obligation was fully felt and gratefully acknowledged; and there is a striking contrast between the extreme unpopularity of France in Italy within a few months, it may be almost said within a few weeks, after Solferino. The promise that Italy should be freed 'from the Alps to the Adriatic,' and uncontrolled by any foreign Power, was falsified by the Peace of Villafranca, which left Austria the mistress of Venetia, and if its provisions had been carried out would have made her the dominant power in the peninsula. Imperious considerations of French interests might be truly alleged to justify this unexpected peace, but it is not surprising that it should have sent a thrill of exasperation through the Italian people. The claim of the Emperor on the gratitude of the Italians was still further weakened when he demanded Nice and Savoy as a payment for his services, and his attempt to support two great but essentially incompatible interests by maintaining with French bayonets the dominion of the Pope at Rome, while he acquiesced, though slowly and reluctantly, in the annexation of the other portions of Italy to the new kingdom, and in the abandonment of his favourite scheme of an Italian federation, had the very natural effect of exciting anger and distrust on both sides. England, on the other hand, had but one voice, and her simple policy of leaving Italy, without any foreign intervention, to construct her own government fully met the Italian desires.

History has certainly not said her last word about Napoleon III., a sovereign who has of late years been as extravagantly depreciated as he was once extravagantly extolled. More justice will one day be done to his manifest and earnest attempts, under circumstances of extreme difficulty, to reconcile a great and real Catholic interest, which was very dear to a large section of his subjects, with his earnest desire to free Italy from foreign control. The obstacles he had to encounter were enormous: the stubborn resistance of the Papal Court to the reforms and compromises he recommended; the furious indignation of French Catholic opinion at his acquiescence in the annexation of Romagna, Umbria, and the Marches; the irresistible torrent of Italian opinion impelling Italian policy in the direction of unity. The great continental countries disapproved of his policy as unduly liberal, while, on opposite grounds, English disapprobation greatly increased his difficulties. He desired manifestly and sincerely to withdraw his troops from Rome, if he could do so without destroying the temporal power. At one moment he had almost attained his end, and the evacuation was actually ordered, when Garibaldi's invasion of Sicily threw the South of Italy into a flame, and changed the whole aspect of affairs. Projects for establishing a neutral zone under European guarantee; for garrisoning Rome with Neapolitan troops; for reorganising the Papal army on such a scale that it might be sufficient to secure the independence of Rome, were constantly passing through his mind. At one time he proposed a congress to deal with the question. At another he authorised and inspired a pamphlet maintaining that the city of Rome alone, without any other territory, would be sufficient to secure the independence of the Pope. At another he ordered inquiries to be made into the government of the city of London by the Lord Mayor and Corporation, under the strange notion that this might furnish some clue for a double government at Rome. The secret despatches of his minister, which have now been published, furnish a curious and vivid picture of the extreme difficulties of his task, but also, I think, of the sincerity with which, amid many hesitations and perplexities, he endeavoured to accomplish it.[19]

History will also pronounce upon the policy of England during this crisis, and, if I am not mistaken, it will be less eulogistic than contemporary English opinion. It will scarcely, I think, approve of that strange and famous despatch in which

---

[19] Thouvenel, *Le Secret de l'Empereur.*

Lord John Russell justified the Piedmontese invasion of Naples, and it may well pronounce the Roman policy of England to have been an unworthy one, though it was both popular and successful. This question was pre-eminently one on which a great and cosmopolitan Catholic interest had to be weighed against a question of nationality, and in such a dispute the intervention of a Protestant Power seems to me to have been wholly unjustifiable. The bitter resentment it excited among the Irish Catholics was, in my opinion, not without foundation.

Whether the unity of Italy has been to the Italian people the blessing that we once believed may also be greatly doubted. The political movements and combinations that make most noise in the world, and excite the largest measure of enthusiasm, are often not those which affect most deeply or most beneficially the real happiness of men. The elements of true happiness are to be found in humbler spheres, and are to be estimated by other tests. Italy has had many good fortunes, but the peace which left her with the acquisition of Lombardy, and the certainty before her of another great war for the acquisition of Venetia, was one of the chief disasters in her history. Proposals, it is true, were then circulated, with some authority, for the sale of Venetia by Austria to Italy, and if such a sale had been effected the whole course of recent European history might have been changed. Italy might have been saved from financial ruin, and the financial position of Austria would have been enormously improved. It would have been possible for Austria to have carried out both more promptly and more efficiently her transformation into a really constitutional empire; and as Italy would have had no motive for joining with her enemies, the war of 1866 might either have been averted, or have ended differently.

But a false point of honour, in which the Austrian Emperor undoubtedly represented the prevalent feeling of his subjects, prevented such a cession, and opened a new chapter of events almost equally disastrous to Austria and to Italy. In the terrible years of preparation for a great war the debt of Italy rose rapidly to unmanageable dimensions, and the dangers, the responsibilities, the gigantic army and navy of a great Power, soon created for her a burden she was wholly unable to bear. Most of the Italian States, before the war of independence began, were among the most lightly taxed in Europe, but no other European country, in proportion to its means, is now so heavily taxed as Italy. Those who have observed the crushing weight with which this excessive taxation falls, not only on the upper and middle classes of the Italian people, but also on the food and industry of the very poor, the grinding poverty it has produced, and the imminent danger of national bankruptcy that hangs over Italy, may well doubt whether her unity has not been too dearly purchased, and whether Napoleon's scheme of an Italian federation might not, after all, have proved the wiser. A very competent writer has computed that, in the years of perfect peace between 1871 and 1893, the taxation of Italy has increased more than 30 per cent.; that the national debt has been increased in twenty-three years of peace by about four milliards of francs, or 160 millions of pounds; and that the interest of this debt, without counting the communal debts or the floating debt, absorbs one-third of the whole revenue.[20]

It has been truly claimed, however, for Italy that she represents the triumph of the doctrine of nationalities in its best form. Nowhere else do so many elements of nationality concur—language, religion, a clearly defined geographical unity, a common literature, and common sentiments. In German unity genuine sympathy bore a great part, but in some portions of the Empire force alone carried out the policy. In some quarters race is represented as the most essential element of nationality, and the doctrine of nationality has blended closely with a doctrine of races which seems destined to be a great disturbing influence in the affairs of the world.[21]

---

[20] See Geffcken's article on the 'War Chests of Europe,' *Nineteenth Century*, August 1894.
[21] See *Revue de Droit International*, iii. 458–63.

The unity of the Latin race, to be established partly by absorptions, and partly by alliances in which France should hold the ruling place, was a favourite French doctrine in the time of Napoleon III., though it has now greatly faded, owing to the profound antipathies that divide France and Italy. Michel Chevalier, among others, powerfully advocated it; it was given as one of the chief reasons for the unfortunate expedition to Mexico; it gave colour to French aspirations to dominion both in Belgium and French Switzerland; and a school of writers arose who represented the establishment of an equilibrium between the great races as the true balance of power, the future basis of international politics. The unity of the Teutonic race has had corresponding adherents in Germany, and their eyes have been greedily cast, not only towards Austria and towards Alsace, but also towards Holland, towards the German provinces of Belgium, and towards the Baltic provinces. The Panslavist movement is the latest, and perhaps the most dangerous, on the stage, and it seeks the disintegration not only of Turkey, but of Austria. It must be observed, too, that in proportion to the new stress given to the claims of nationality comes an increased desire among rulers to extirpate in their dominions all alien national types, whether of race, or language, or creed, which may some day be called into active existence.

Few things are more curious to observe than the conflicting tendencies which are, in the same period of history, drawing nations in diametrically opposite directions. The tendency to great agglomerations and larger political unities has in our day been very evident. Railroads, and the many other influences producing a more rapid interchange of ideas and commerce, and more cosmopolitan habits and manners, act strongly in this direction; and the military and naval systems of our time throw an overwhelming power into the hands of the great nations. On the other hand, there has been in many forms a marked tendency to accentuate distinct national and local types.

It has been very clearly shown in national languages. As late as the days of Frederick the Great, French had a complete ascendency, even at the Prussian Court; and long after that date it seemed in many countries likely to displace all local languages in the common usage of the upper classes. Nearly everywhere this tendency has been checked, and national languages now fully maintain their ascendency. The late Queen Sophie of the Netherlands was accustomed to relate that, at the time of her marriage in 1839, some of her counsellors told her that it was scarcely necessary for her to learn Dutch, as the use of it was so rapidly passing away among the upper classes in Holland; but she lived to see that usage constant and universal. It was, I believe, only under Nicholas that Russian superseded French as the Court language at St. Petersburg, and, according to competent judges, the same change has in the present generation extended widely through all Russian society. In Belgium there has been a marked and most significant movement for maintaining the Flemish language and Flemish nationality; a similar tendency prevails in Bohemia and Hungary, and even at home it may be seen in the greatly increased stress laid upon the Welsh language. The war of 1870 strengthened it, and French has lost much of its cosmopolitan character as the language of diplomacy, while no other single language has taken its place. At no previous period, I suppose, has so large an amount of interest and research been devoted to the study of local customs, literatures, traditions, and antiquities. Education, if it widens interests, also contributes to kindle political life in small areas, and the extension of the suffrage and of a local government, and perhaps still more the growth of a local press, have all their effect in accentuating local divisions and awakening local aspirations. The vast military systems of the Continent may, perhaps, in some degree divert the minds of the great disciplined masses from internal and constitutional politics, and they weaken the lines of provincial differences, but they also bring into stronger and sharper relief national distinctions and national antagonisms.

Among the problems that weigh heavily on the statesmen of our age, few are more serious than those of reconciling local and particularist aspirations with the maintenance of imperial strength and unity, and with the stability of European peace. In all such questions many various, and often conflicting, circumstances must be considered, and no general and inflexible rule can be laid down. England, in 1864, made a remarkable concession to the rights of nationalities when, in response to a strongly expressed local wish, she abandoned her protectorate over the Ionian Isles and permitted their annexation to Greece. She certainly would not have acted in the same way if Malta, or Ireland, or some other vital portion of her Empire had demanded to be annexed to a foreign Power. Every great empire is obliged, in the interest of its imperial unity and in the interest of the public order of the world, to impose an inflexible veto on popular movements in the direction of disintegration, however much it may endeavour to meet local wishes by varying laws and institutions and compromises. Nations, too, differ very widely in the strength of their national types, in their power of self-government, in their power of governing others, in their power of assimilating or reconciling alien types. There are cases where the destruction of an old nationality, or even of a nationality which had never fully existed, but had been prematurely arrested in its growth, leaves behind it in large classes hatreds which rankle for centuries. There are other cases where, in a few years, a complete fusion is effected, where every scar of the old wound is effaced, where all distinctions are obliterated, or where they subsist only in healthy differences of type, tendency, and capacity, which add to the resources without in any degree impairing the strength and harmony of the nation. There are cases where an extension of local representative institutions will amply satisfy local aspirations and appease local discontents, and where such institutions are certain to be justly and moderately used. There are other cases where they would be infallibly turned into instruments for revolution, plunder, and oppression, where they would only increase dissension, and perhaps lead to civil war.

All these elements of the problem must, in each separate case, be duly estimated. On the whole, the doctrine of the absolute and indefeasible right of nationalities to determine their own form of government seems to me now less prominent among the political ideas of the world than it was in 1848, and at the period of the emancipation of Italy. Both England and America have learnt, from their own experience, the dangers that may spring from its too unqualified assertion; Eastern Europe has shown how easily it may be converted into an instrument of aggression and intrigue; and the institution of the plebiscite has been much discredited since the fall of the second French Empire. France was once the most ardent champion of this doctrine in its extreme form, partly, perhaps, because her own territory is singularly compact, homogeneous, and well assimilated; but since 1870 her aspirations and alliances have carried her in very different directions. At the same time, the movement towards international Socialism, which has spread widely through the working classes of the Continent, is wholly alien to the idea of nationality, appeals to a different kind of enthusiasm, and seeks to divide the world by other lines. The chief apparent exception has been the greatly increased importance which the Irish Home Rule movement has assumed since the Irish suffrage was so extended as to give an overwhelming power to the lowest orders, since Parnell organised his agitation, and since Mr. Gladstone accepted his demands. But the nation, in 1886 and 1895, condemned this policy with an emphasis that it is impossible to mistake; nor would the movement in Ireland ever have attained its formidable magnitude if it had not allied itself with motives and interests very different from the pure nationalism of Grattan and of Davis.

CHAPTER 6

Democracy and Religious Liberty

There are few subjects upon which mankind in different ages and countries have differed more widely than in their conceptions of liberty, and in the kinds of liberty which they principally value and desire. Even in our own day, and among civilised nations, these differences are enormously great. There are vast countries where the forms of liberty to which the English race are most passionately attached, and which they have attained by the most heroic and persistent efforts, would appear either worthless or positively evil. There are nations who would recoil with horror from the unlimited liberty of religious discussion and propagandism which has become the very life-breath of modern Englishmen; who care little or nothing for the unrestricted right of public meeting and political writing; who deem complete commercial liberty, with its corollary of unrestricted competition, an evil rather than a good; who regard the modern relaxations of the restrictions of creed or sex in employments and appointments as subversive of the best moral elements in the community, and in whose eyes an Englishmen's absolute right to bequeath his property as he wills is the source of enormous injustice. In some Western, and in nearly all Eastern nations, good administration is far more valued than representation, and provided men can obtain a reasonable amount of order, peace, security, and prosperity at a moderate charge, provided their habits and religions are undisturbed, they care very little by whom or in what way their rulers are appointed, and gladly dismiss the whole subject of politics from their thoughts.

On the other hand, numerous restraints, prohibitions, and punishments exist in England, and are strongly supported by English opinion, which would in other zones of thought be bitterly resented. It would seem, in many countries, a monstrous tyranny that poor parents should be compelled to send their children to school, and should be fined by a magistrate if they kept them at home in times when they most needed their services. The English Sunday wears to many continental minds at least as repulsive an aspect as the Star Chamber would wear to a modern Englishman. That a man who wished to work on that day should not be allowed to do so; that a struggling shopkeeper should be forbidden, if he desired it, to open his shop; that a farmer should be prevented from reaping his own harvest when every fine day is of vital consequence to his interests; that poor men should be excluded by law on their one holiday from their place of meeting and refreshment; that nearly all forms of amusement, and even most of the public picture galleries, museums, and libraries should be closed on the day on which they could give the widest pleasure, would seem to many quite as serious an infringement of liberty as those acts against which Magna Charta and the Bill of Rights were directed.

A severity of censorship is maintained in England, with the full sanction of public opinion, over theatres and music-halls, and over most forms of gambling, which in some parts of the Continent would excite at least as much discontent as a censorship of the Press. To a man of Spanish blood, a legal prohibition of bull-fights would probably appear quite as oppressive as a restriction of his electoral rights, and a very similar sentiment has of late years grown up in a great part of the South of France. If this example may be thought an extreme one, it is at least certain that on the whole subject of the treatment of animals English opinion and practice differ enormously from the general continental standard in the number and the severity of their restrictions. In no other country are scientific experiments on living animals restrained by law, and in most countries public opinion would be wholly against such legislation. A special Act of Parliament makes it in England a criminal offence to yoke a dog to a cart,[1] which in Holland, Belgium, and many other very civilized countries is done every day, without exciting the smallest disapprobation. The manufacture of 'pâté de foie gras,' which is accomplished by artificially producing a disease, is an important industry in France and Germany; it would probably be suppressed in England by law, and what in other countries is considered the very ordinary process of dishorning cattle has been pronounced, though with some conflict of judicial opinion, to be illegal.

Laws against wanton cruelty to animals exist in most countries, but in their scope, their stringency, and above all in their administration, there is an immense difference between England and the Continent. An amount of overdriving, overworking, and other ill-treatment of animals[2] which in most countries—certainly in most Southern countries—does not excite any reprobation or attention is in England punishable by law. In France there is the well-known Grammont law, which was enacted in 1850, for the protection of animals. But it is confined to domestic animals which are 'publicly and abusively' treated: it is clearly laid down by French lawyers that it gives no inquisitorial power of interfering with what is done in a private house, or court, or garden; it can only be put in force by public functionaries, and its penalties range from a fine of 5 to 15 francs, or a maximum sentence of five

---

[1] 17 & 18 Vict. c. 60, s. 2.

[2] *e.g.*, England is, I suppose, the only country in Europe where a peasant woman may be arrested and brought before a magistrate because she has carried her fowls to market with their heads downwards.

days of prison.[3] In England the corresponding penalty is two months' imprisonment; there is no exception of acts done in private houses, and private persons may put the law in force. Few societies are more warmly supported in England than one which annually prosecutes about 6,000 persons, chiefly very poor men, for offences against animals, the immense majority of which would be on the Continent unpunished, and probably even unblamed. At the same time, there are few countries in the civilized world in which the killing of animals enters so largely as in England into the amusements of the upper and middle classes of society, and lines of distinction are drawn which, though fully recognised by English opinion, would in many countries be resented. The magistrate who sends a poor man to prison for taking part in a cock-fight or a dog-fight, for baiting a badger or worrying a cat, very probably protects his own game by setting steel traps for vermin and strychnine for stray dogs, and takes part without reproach in a coursing match, a stag hunt, or a battue.

A similar contrast may be found in other fields. In the English marriage law there is at least one restriction on the contraction of marriages, and there are many restrictions on the dissolution of unhappy marriages which nearly all other Protestant countries have abolished. The licensing laws, the factory laws, the laws on sanitation, bristle with restrictions and penal clauses that in many other countries are unknown, and there are great communities in which the law which treats attempted suicide as a crime would be deemed a violation of natural freedom. Political freedom and social freedom do not necessarily go together, and it will often be found that restraints and prohibitions are being multiplied in one department while they are being relaxed or abolished in another. It is probable that the lives of men were more variously and

---

[3] The questions raised in connection with the Grammont law have been treated in full by N. A. Guilbon, *Des mauvais traitements envers les animaux domestiques*.

severely restricted under the censorship of the Roman republic than under the tyranny of the Cæsars; under the rule of
the Puritans during the Commonwealth, or in Scotland and
New England, than in many of the despotisms of the Continent.

These few examples may illustrate the variety and the difficulty of the subject, and it may not be a useless thing to take
stock of our present conceptions of liberty, to observe the
changes that are passing over them, and to ascertain in what
directions modern legislation and opinion are realising, enlarging, or abridging them.

One most important form of liberty, which in our generation has been almost completely achieved, both in England
and in most foreign countries, has been religious liberty. In
England, at least, complete liberty of worship and of opinion
had been practically attained in 1813, when Unitarians at last
received the legal recognition which had long been granted
to other Dissenters. It is true that, if we looked only on the
letter of the law, this statement would not be absolutely true.
A number of wholly obsolete laws directed against Roman
Catholics, or against those who abstained from the Anglican
service, were only repealed in 1844 and 1846.[4] Unrepealed
clauses in the Catholic Emancipation Act of 1829 even now
make it an offense punishable by banishment for life for Jesuits, or members of other male religious communities, to
come into the kingdom, and for any person in England to join
such bodies, or to introduce others into them;[5] and an Act of
William III. is still on the Statute Book, according to which,
in the opinion of very competent lawyers, the gravest and
most solid works impugning the Christian religion and the

---

[4] 7 and 8 Vict. c. 102; 9 and 10 Vict. c. 59.

[5] 10 George IV. c. 7, ss. 28–34. There was an exception in favour of nat-
ural-born subjects who had been Jesuits or members of other religious
orders before the Act passed, and who were only required to register
themselves. A Secretary of State might also give other Jesuits a special
license to remain in England for not longer than six months.

Divine authority of the Old and New Testaments might be made subjects to prosecution.[6] These laws, however, have become entirely absolute, and it is not too much to say that every form of religious worship which does not directly offend morality, and every form of religious opinion which is expressed in serious and decent language, are, in England, perfectly unrestricted.

The practice of the law is in this respect fully supported by public opinion. No change in English life during the latter half of the nineteenth century is more conspicuous than the great enlargement of the range of permissible opinions on religious subjects. Opinions and arguments which not many years ago were confined to small circles and would have drawn down grave social penalties, have become the commonplaces of the drawing-room and of the boudoir. The first very marked change in this respect followed, I think, the publication in 1860 of the 'Essays and Reviews,' and the effect of this book in making the religious questions which it discussed familiar to the great body of educated men was probably by far the most important of its consequences. The power and popularity of the works of Buckle and Renan; the long controversies that followed Bishop Colenso's criticism on the Pentateuch; the writings of Darwin, and their manifest bearing on the received theologies; the gradual infiltration into England of the results that had been arrived at by the Biblical critics of Germany and Holland, have all had a powerful influence, and the tendency has been greatly accelerated by the fashion, which sprang up in England in 1865, of publishing magazines consisting of signed articles by men of most various and opposing opinions. The old type of magazine represented a single definite school of thought, and it was read chiefly by those who belonged to that school. The new type appeals to a much larger and more varied circle, and its editors soon discovered that few things were more acceptable to their

---

[6] Stephen's *History of the Criminal Law*, ii. 468–76.

readers than a full discussion by eminent men of the great problems of natural and revealed religion. Opinions the most conservative and the most negative appeared side by side, were read together, and are now habitually found in the drawing-rooms of men of the most different opinions.

Custom so soon establishes its empire over men that we seldom realise the greatness and the significance of this change. Every Church—even the most intolerant one—seems to have accepted it in England. On hardly any subject has the Church of Rome been more imperative than in her efforts to prevent her members from coming in contact with any form of heterodox opinion. Many of my readers will probably remember how, to the very end of the temporal power of the Pope, English newspapers and magazines at Rome were subject to a stringent censorship, and continually arrived with whole passages carefully excised, lest anything inconsistent with the doctrines of the Church should penetrate into Rome, even in a foreign tongue and to a stranger community. In French Canada, where the old spirit of Catholicism probably retains a stronger hold over the people than in any other country, a stringent censorship of the Press is still maintained. In 1869 there was a case, which excited much attention in England, of a Canadian who was excommunicated and denied Christian burial because he had been a member of a Canadian institute which had refused to exclude from its library books and journals disapproved of by the Church. A pamphlet published by a leading member of that institute in defence of its policy was condemned in such terms that every Catholic who, after being properly warned, retained it in his house could only be absolved by the bishop or his vicars-general. As recently as 1892 a sentence was read in all the Canadian Catholic churches forbidding, under penalty of refusal of the Sacraments, any Catholic to print, sell, distribute, read, or possess two Catholic journals which had offended the bishop. Their offence appears to have been that they had published and commented on a gross instance of clerical immorality which had been clearly proved, and that one of them had proposed to publish 'Les Trois Mousquetaires' of Alexandre Dumas.[7] In England, there are probably few houses of the Catholic gentry where periodicals may not be found in which men like Herbert Spencer and Huxley expound their views with perfect frankness. Among the contributors to these magazines there have been at least two cardinals and many other Catholic divines.

Men will differ much about the good and evil resulting from this fact; but it at least indicates a great change of public feeling in the direction of religious liberty, and it is in the highest degree improbable that in England, and in most of the leading countries of the world, theological opinions could be again repressed on the ground of their theological error. It is possible, however, for religious expression and worship to be unfettered, but at the same time for its professors to be gravely injured by disqualifications and disabilities. In the full concession of political rights to Nonconforming bodies, England has been much behind some other nations. The United States led the way, and one of the articles of its Constitution declared in clear, noble, and comprehensive language, that 'no religious test shall ever be required as a qualification to any office or public trust under the United States.' In the words of Judge Story, 'The Catholic and the Protestant, the Calvinist and the Arminian, the Jew and the infidel, may sit down at the common table of the national councils without any inquisition into their faith or mode of worship.'[8] In France, though gross religious intolerance accompanied and followed the Revolution, the general principle of severing political privileges from theological beliefs was at least clearly laid down. In 1789 the National Assembly threw open all civil and military posts and privileges to Protestants, and in 1791 to Jews; and, in spite of the many vicissitudes which French government afterwards

---

[7] Goldwin Smith's *Canada*, p. 15. See, too, a Canadian book, Doutre, *Ruines Cléricales*. There has been a more recent case of a Catholic bishop in Ireland excommunicating the readers of a newspaper of which he disapproved.

[8] Story *On the Constitution*, iii. 731.

experienced, these privileges were never seriously infringed. It was a significant fact that the jew Crémieux was a member of the Provisional Government of 1848. The Belgian Constitution of 1831 followed the example of the United States, and gave Belgians of all creeds absolute religious freedom and full constitutional privileges. Prussia was and is a very conservative country, but in the Constitution of 1850 it was expressly provided that civil and political rights were independent of religious beliefs.

In England, it is somewhat humiliating to observe how slowly this constitutional equality was attained. By an Irish Act of 1793, and by English Acts of 1813 and 1817, all ranks of the army and navy were gradually opened to Catholics and Dissenters; while the abolition of Test and Corporation Acts in 1828 placed Protestant Dissenters on an equality with the members of the Established Church in corporate and civil offices. Then followed the Catholic Emancipation Act of 1829, and in 1833 and 1838 Acts were carried permitting Quakers, Moravians, and some other persons who had conscientious objections to swearing, to substitute in all cases an affirmation for an oath. The conflict about the emancipation of the Jews raged long and fiercely; but in 1839 they were permitted to take oaths in the form that was binding on their consciences, in 1845 they were admitted into corporate offices, in 1858 they made their way into the House of Commons, and at a much later period a distinguished living Jew has been raised to the peerage and made Lord Lieutenant of his county. The admission, after a long struggle, to the House of Commons of an avowed atheist, in the person of Mr. Bradlaugh, completed the work of abolishing religious disqualifications in England.

I do not include in the struggle for religious liberty such measures as the abolition of compulsory Church rates, the disestablishment and disendowment of the Irish Church, the alterations that have been effected in the law of tithes. These seem to me to belong to a different category, and must be regarded as episodes in the conflict between the supporters and opponents of an established Church. Among the great achievements of religious liberty, however, may undoubtedly be counted the important measure carried by Lord John Russell in 1836, enabling Dissenters to celebrate their marriages in their own chapels and by their own rites, and establishing a system of civil marriage for those who desired it, and also a comprehensive and secular system for the registration of births, deaths, and marriages. To the same class belongs the Act of 1870 permitting scrupulous unbelievers, who rejected all forms of oath, to give evidence in the law courts on affirmation, the penalty of perjury being still retained as a protection against false witness. The measure of 1880, also, which, following a precedent that had long been established in Ireland, permitted Nonconformist burial services and burials without religious services in parish churchyards, was partly, but not wholly, inspired by hostility to the Established Church. In many instances a deeper and holier feeling made Nonconformists wish to be laid at rest with parents or ancestors of the established faith, and in country districts, where no other burial-places existed, it was a real grievance that Nonconformist burials could only be effected with an Anglican service.

The most important, however, of all modern conquests of religious liberty have been those which placed at the disposal of men of all creeds the best education the nation could afford. The great work of the establishment of undenominational primary education in England will be hereafter considered. Its accomplishment had been preceded by that long and arduous struggle for the admission of Nonconformists to the studies, degrees, and emoluments of the English universities which forms one of the noblest pages in the history of the Liberal party, when English Liberalism was at its best. The rise of the High Church party in 1833 greatly retarded it, and to the last that party strained every effort to close the doors of higher education against all who refused to accept the Anglican creed. The same spirit that led ecclesiastics in the eighteenth century, in the interests of their monopoly, to defend the law which degraded the sacrament into an office test, still prevailed, and the scandalously profane system of compelling boys fresh from school to purchase their admission into Oxford by signing the Thirty-nine Articles, which not one in a hundred had seriously studied, was strenuously supported. Dublin University has the honourable distinction of having long preceded the English universities in the path of true Liberalism, for even before 1793 Catholics and Nonconformists were admitted among its students, and after 1793 they were admitted to its degrees, though not to its scholarships and fellowships. In the Scotch Universities, also, there was no religious test against Dissenters. In Cambridge, Nonconformists might become students, but no one could obtain a degree without subscribing the Thirty-nine Articles. At Oxford, Nonconformists were repelled on the very threshold, for the subscription was exacted at matriculation. English Dissenters were not only excluded from the inestimable advantage of higher education, and from the many great prizes connected with the universities—they were also seriously impeded, by the want of a university degree, in their subsequent professional careers.

This last grievance was removed by the foundation of the London University in 1836. Being a mere examining body, it could not offer the teaching advantages, nor did it possess the splendid prizes, of the older universities; but it at least conferred degrees which were highly valued, and which were encumbered by no theological test. Measures for opening Oxford and Cambridge to the Dissenters were again and again introduced by Liberal ministers, again and again carried in the Commons, again and again rejected in the Lords. In 1854, Nonconformists were allowed to obtain the B.A. degree in the old English universities, but they could not obtain higher degrees, and although they might compete at examinations for the great university prizes, they could not enjoy them. At last, in 1871, a great measure of enfranchisement, which was originally placed in the hands of Mr. Coleridge, and had failed five times in the Lords, became law, opening nearly all offices and degrees in the universities without theological restriction.

Seven years later the few remaining distinctions, with the very proper exception of degrees and professorships of divinity, were abolished by a Conservative Government. In Dublin University, the grievance of the restriction of fellowships and scholarships to members of the Established Church was mitigated in 1854 by the institution of non-foundation scholarships open to all creeds, and the whole body of the remaining restrictions was swept away by the Act of 1873. There is still, it is true, a Divinity School in Trinity College for the benefit of candidates for orders in the Protestant Episcopal Church. It corresponds to Maynooth, which is exclusively devoted to the education of priests, and which was set up and established by a large expenditure of public money. But, with the exception of the divinity professorships connected with this school, every post in the great Irish university, from the highest to the lowest, is now open to the members of all religious creeds.

The long delay in opening the English universities to Dissenters has been a great misfortune. It shut out whole generations from one of the best boons that a nation could offer to her children. It added something to the acerbity and much to the narrowness of the Nonconformist spirit, and the unworthy and reactionary attitude of the House of Lords on this and on kindred religious questions contributed perhaps more than any other cause to alienate from that House the Liberal sentiment of England. The evils resulting from that alienation are very great, though there are clear recent signs that it has been diminishing. The battle of religious disqualification is now substantially won. The balance of power has shifted. Other questions have arisen, and the dangers to be feared and to be guarded against lie in other directions. But the bias that was formed, the passions that were generated by bygone contests, are not wholly extinct, and they make it more difficult to save the State from the dangers of an unbridled democracy.

In the universities, the evils that were predicted from the abolition tests have never taken place. Many and various opinions are openly avowed, and truth has gained much by the avowal; but the religious sentiment has not decayed, and it is certainly not less genuine because it is no longer fortified by privilege, or connected with interested and hypocritical assents. While the foundation by private munificence of denominational colleges within an unsectarian university has preserved the best features of the old system, the juxtaposition of opposing creeds has produced no disorder, and university sentiment speedily accepted the changed situation. It was once my privilege to receive an honorary degree from the University of Oxford in company with a great and venerable writer, who had long been the most illustrious figure in English Unitarianism, as well as one of the chief defenders of a spiritualist philosophy. I can well remember the touching language in which Dr. Martineau then described the dark shadow which his exclusion on account of his faith from English university life had thrown over this youth, and the strange feeling with which he found himself entering, at the age of eighty, an honoured and invited member, where fifty or sixty years before he and all other Dissenters had been so rigidly proscribed.

The force and steadiness of the current which has, during the last half-century, been moving in the direction of the establishment of religious liberty and of the abolition of religious disqualifications cannot be mistaken. It has been accompanied by a corresponding movement in favour of an enlargement of the lines of the Established Church. I do not think that the hold of this Church upon the affections of the English people has, in the present generation, been really weakened, although some of the forces opposed to it have acquired additional strength, and although the growth within its borders of a ritualistic party may very possibly one day lead both to disruption and disestablishment. But the lines of defence and of attack have been somewhat changed. Both the doctrine that a State establishment of religion is an essentially anti-Christian thing, and the doctrine that every nation is bound in its corporate capacity to profess a religion, and that the maintenance of an established Church is therefore the first of national duties have, I think, lost much of their old power. The belief that the Church, as a continuous organisation, has the same indefeasible right to its tithes and glebes as a private individual to the property which he has earned or inherited, and the belief that the diversion of property from religious to secular purposes is an act of sacrilege, have certainly not passed away, but they are no longer governing forces in English politics.

The main defence of the Church of England as an establishment now rests upon its utility. It is, it is said, a great corporation, which is indissolubly bound up with the best elements in the national life and history, which has shown itself in these latter days as far as possible from dormant and effete, and which is exercising over a vast area and in multifarious ways a beneficent, moralising, and spiritualising influence. If its revenues in the aggregate seem large, no other revenues are so little abused, are so constantly associated with moral and useful lives, are so largely and so steadily employed for the benefit of the community. Its parochial system places in the poorest and most unattractive parish an educated and cultivated resident gentleman, who is not dependent on his parishioners, and whose whole life is spent in constant intercourse with the poor, in constant efforts to improve their condition, to raise their morals, to console them in their troubles. Like the dew of heaven, the silent continuous action of this system falls over great tracts of human life and suffering which the remedies of the politician can never reach. There are no more beautiful or more useful lives than those which may be often found in some backward and deserted district, where the parish clergyman and his family are spreading around them a little oasis of cultivation and refinement, and, by modest, simple, unobtrusive and disinterested work, continually alleviating suffering and raising the moral level of those among whom they labour. What a contrast do they often present to the noisy demagogue, to the epicurean party gambler, who is seeking for votes or power by denouncing them! It is impossible to doubt that the whole of the system would be greatly impaired if the Church were broken into fragments, and if its ministers degenerated into mere narrow sectarians, representing a lower plane of education and refinement, and depending for their subsistence on the good pleasure of their parishioners.

And the parochial system is but one of the many benefits that may be traced to the Establishment. The maintenance of a learned clergy, who play a great part in the fields of literature and scholarship; the cathedral system, which adds so largely to the splendour and beauty of English life; the existence, both at home and abroad, of an order of men to whom British subjects of all creeds and classes have a right in time of trouble to appeal; the wider latitude of opinion which an established Church seldom fails to give; the importance of a State connection, both in restraining the excesses of sacerdotal tyranny and in diminishing the temptations to clerical demagogism, are all advantages which may be truly alleged and largely amplified. Many of them extend far beyond the limits of convinced Anglicans, and affect most beneficially the whole national life. Is it the part of a true statesman to destroy or weaken a machine which is doing so much good in so many ways? Is it probable that its revenues would be more wisely or more usefully employed if they were flung into the political arena, to be struggled for by contending parties?

But in order to strengthen these lines of defence two things are necessary. The one is, that the disadvantages attending the existence of an established Church should be reduced to the smallest possible limits; the other is, that the benefits of the establishment should be as largely as possible extended. The first object has been attained by the complete abolition of religious disqualifications and disabilities. These were once defended as inseparable from an establishment, and the best fortifications for its defence. They are now more justly looked upon as the most serious arguments against it, for they were restrictions and injuries imposed on different classes of the community in order that it might subsist. As we have seen, it has been one of the great works of the nineteenth century to sweep these disqualifications away.

The other object is to comprehend the largest possible portion of the English people in the Established Church. In this respect reformers are following faithfully the root idea of the Church, which was intended to be a national, or, in other words, a representative, Church, representing and including the two great sections of the community that were separated from the See of Rome. One of these sections, though repudiating the pretensions of the Papacy, leant strongly towards the theology of Rome; the other frankly adopted the principles of the Reformation on the Continent. The composite and representative character of the Church is clearly exhibited in the Prayer Book, which, if it does not contain positive contradictions of definite doctrine, at least includes very evident contradictions of tendency.

The attempt of the Tudor statesmen to include the whole body of the English people in the National Church failed, and the attempt of the statesmen of the Revolution to bring back the great Puritan body by an Act of Comprehension was equally unsuccessful. The amalgamation of the different Protestant organisations is now plainly impossible, and if it were possible it would be of very doubtful benefit. It is true, indeed, that the original grounds of dissension have in a great measure disappeared. The rigidities and the distinctions of Calvinistic theology, which were once deemed so transcendently important, have lost their old hold on the minds of men, and an amount of ornament and ritual and music has crept into Puritan worship which would have aroused the horror of the early Puritans. The Ritualistic party in the Anglican Church is very widely separated from Protestant Nonconformity, but there is no real difference of principle between the Evangelical section of the Church of England and the great body of the Protestant Dissenters. With many the separation is a mere matter of taste, some persons preferring the written liturgy, and some the extemporaneous prayers. Others object to the Church of England, not because their own type of theology has not a fully recognised place within its borders, but because it also admits doctrines or practices which they condemn. With others, again, the separation depends wholly on the accident of birth and education. Through habit, or interest, or affection, men prefer to remain in the ecclesiastical organisation in which they have been brought up, and with which they are not dissatisfied, rather than go over to another to which they have no objection. The case of Scotland shows how it is possible for three Churches to exist in separation which are identical in their form of worship, identical in their ecclesiastical organisation, and all but identical in their doctrine.

The decay of the doctrinal basis of English Nonconformity, though it is not likely to lead to any amalgamation of Churches, is having one very mischievous consequence. It is giving Nonconformity a far more political character than in the past, and a political character which is sometimes singularly unworthy and unscrupulous. Envy becomes the guiding motive, a desire to break down and diminish the Established Church the chief ground of political action. A characteristic though an extreme example of this spirit was exhibited by certain representatives of Welsh Nonconformity, who actually opposed a Bill to enable the bishops more easily to suppress immorality among their clergy, lest it should tend to increase the efficiency of the Establishment.[9] In some periods of past history England owed much to the political action of Nonconformists, and they raised very appreciably the moral level of English politics. Those who have studied their conduct and their alliances in the present generation will scarcely attribute to them such an influence.

But although it is not possible, and probably not desirable, that the Established Church should absorb rival organisations, the steady tendency of the present generation has been to expand the circle of permissible opinions. An Act of 1865 modified materially the form of subscription to the Articles. Instead of being obliged to subscribe to 'all and everything' in the Thirty-nine Articles and the Prayer Book, the clergyman is now bound only to a belief in the doctrines of the Church

---

[9] See the debates on the Clergy Discipline (Immorality) Bill of 1892. See, too, the remarks of Sir R. Temple on this discussion. *Life in Parliament*, pp. 341–43.

as a whole. The gross tyranny which, under the name of the indelibility of orders, made it illegal for a clergyman who had found it impossible conscientiously to continue in the Church to adopt any other profession, was abolished in 1870, in spite of the strenuous opposition of Bishop Wilberforce, and successive judicial decisions by the Privy Council have established the legal right of each of the three parties in the Church to hold their distinctive doctrines. No feature of the modern Anglican Church is more conspicuous than the great variety of opinions that have now a fully recognised place within its limits.

This movement has been much more a lay movement than a clerical one, and it is mainly due to the influence which establishment gives to the lay element in the government of the Church. It forms a remarkable contrast to the growing ascendency of ultramontanism in the Church of Rome, but it is in full accordance with the spirit that is prevailing in the legislation and the public opinion of nearly all countries. The tendency to multiply restrictions, which is so clearly seen in many departments of modern legislation, does not appear in the sphere of religion. The belief both in the certainty and in the importance of dogma has declined; nearly everywhere great fields of human action are being withdrawn from the empire of the Churches, and the right of men to believe and profess various religious doctrines without suffering molestation or losing civil privileges is now very generally recognised. In some countries and districts the law is certainly in advance of public opinion. In some cases, where the overwhelming majority of the nation belong to one creed, there are restraints upon proselytism; and dissenters from the established creed, or from a limited number of recognised creeds, are forbidden to set up churches, though they may meet in private houses; but with the single exception of Russia, all the countries which in the first decades of the century were most intolerant in their legislation have been touched by the new spirit.

In Sweden, not many years ago, every administrative and

judicial function was strictly limited to the professors of the Lutheran creed. Even the practice of medicine and the right of teaching were confined to them. All attempts to induce a Lutheran to change his creed were penal offences, severely punished, and every Swede who abondoned the religion of his country was liable to banishment for life. It was not until 1860 that the existence of dissenting bodies was, under severely specified conditions, recognised; but in 1862, 1870, and 1873 laws were passed permitting Swedish Lutherans to join other religions, and opening nearly all public posts and employments, as well as the seats in the Legislature, to men of all religions.[10]

Austria, again, not long since was a great centre of religious and political reaction, but it is now one of the best-governed countries in Europe, and there are very few modern legislations which will better repay study than that of Austria since 1860. The Concordat of 1855, which secured the Catholic Church a monopoly, has been annulled, and the Austrian Constitution makes all civil and political rights independent of creed, and guarantees to all subjects perfect liberty of conscience and worship. A distinction, it is true, is drawn between recognised and unrecognised religions. The former, by the organic law of 1867, comprised, in addition to Catholicism, the Protestant religions of the Confession of Augsburg and of the Helvetic Confession, the Greek Church, and the Jewish Synagogue; but a law of 1874 greatly enlarged the circle, by providing that all other creeds might obtain a full legal recognition if they satisfied the Minister of Public Worship that there was nothing in their teaching, worship, or organisation contrary to law or morals, and that they were sufficiently numerous to support a Church. These recognised religions may constitute themselves as corporations, regulating their own affairs, founding establishments, and exercising publicly their religious worship. The adherents of religions

---

[10] Block, *Dict. de la Politique*, article 'Suède.' See, too, Dareste, *Les Constitutions Modernes*, ii. 41, 42, 48, 51.

that are not legally recognised have, however, a full right to celebrate their worship in private houses, provided there is nothing in that worship contrary to law or morals. In the State schools, religious instruction must be given separately to the scholars of different denominations by their own priests or pastors, or by lay teachers appointed by the different religious bodies. A valuable and most significant portion of the law of 1874 provides that the ecclesiastical power must never be used, except against the members of the Church to which it belongs, and that it must never be used with the object of interfering with the observance of the law, or the acts of the civil power, or the free exercise of any civil right.[11]

Spain and Portugal are the last examples that need be given of countries in which, though scepticism and indifference are very rife, the whole population, with infinitesimal exceptions, is of one nominal belief, and in which the steady teaching of the Church and many generations of intolerant legislation have made the establishment of religious liberty peculiarly difficult. According to the judgment of those who are best acquainted with these countries, there exists in both countries, but especially in Spain, a strong determination to secularise the government, to limit Church property, and to restrain ecclesiastical power, accompanied by much indisposition to encourage any multiplication or competition of religions.[12] Few countries have witnessed, in the present century, more confiscations of Church property than Spain, and the political influence of its priesthood is very small, though it is not impossible that the establishment of universal suffrage in 1890[13] may tend to its revival. The Catholic religion is recognised as the religion of the State, but it is provided that no one on

---

[11] See Dareste, Demombrynes. There is an admirable series of papers examining in detail the Austrian legislation since 1860 in the *Revue de Droit International et de Législation comparée.* They are scattered through several volumes. See especially tom. viii. pp. 502–5.

[12] An interesting account of religion in Spain will be found in Garrido, *L'Espagne Contemporaine*, pp. 123–62 (1862).

[13] See Dareste, i. 626.

Spanish soil may be molested for his religious opinions and
for his worship as long as he respects Christian morality,
though 'the public manifestations and ceremonies of the State
religion' alone are authorised. Small congregations of Span-
iards who dissent from the Established Church worship freely
and publicly in the chief towns.

In Portugal the law is very similar. The Catholic religion is
recognised as the religion of the kingdom; all others are permitted to strangers, and they may have edifices destined for
their worship, but they must not have externally the appearance of churches. 'No one may be molested for his religion,
provided he respects that of the State and does not offend
public morality.' At the same time, a Portuguese who publicly
apostatises from the Catholic Church is punished by twenty
years' suspension of political rights.[14] The priests have also
in Portugal a recognised place as registering agents at elections for the Chamber of Deputies and these elections conclude with a religious ceremony.[15]

It will be evident, I think, to those who have taken an extended survey of the subject, that the line of religious liberty
which ought to be drawn in any country, like most other
political lines, is not an inflexible or invariable one, but one
which largely depends on many fluctuating considerations.
The religious legislation of a country where there are grave
differences of opinion will naturally be somewhat different
from the legislation of a country where there is a practical
unanimity, and where opposing creeds can only be introduced by immigration or by proselytism from without, and
considerations of public order may most legitimately modify
and limit religious legislation. Religious processions, demonstrations, or controversies in the streets, which would
probably produce obstruction or riot, or which are intended
to injure some class or person, or which would irritate public

[14] *Revue de Droit International*, xx. 334.
[15] Demombrynes, i. 495, 503–5, 510.

opinion, may be most properly forbidden, while those which are practically harmless are allowed.

There is a broad and intelligible distinction between the right of freely expressing religious or political opinions in churches or meetings to which no one is obliged to come, in books or papers which no one is obliged to read, and the right of expressing them in the public streets, which all men are forced to use, and which are the common property of all. The first and most essential form of liberty is the liberty of performing lawful business without molestation and annoyance, and this liberty is most imperfectly attained when it is impossible for men, women, or children to pass through the streets without having attacks upon their religious belief thrust forcibly upon their attention. In most countries such street controversies are rigidly suppressed. Where they are permitted, they ought surely to be deemed a matter of tolerance, and not of right; to be regulated in each case according to special circumstances. Some years ago it was the habit of a Protestant missionary society to placard the walls throughout the Catholic provinces of Ireland with questions and arguments subversive of the Catholic faith, and missionaries might be seen driving along the roads throwing controversial leaflets to every peasant and into every turf-basket as they passed. In my own judgment, such a method of propagandism ought not to have been permitted, and it is probable that most of those who disagree with me would admit the principle for which I am contending, if the arguments that were disseminated had been directed not against Catholicism, but against Christianity. In France, where a stringent law forbids meetings in the streets, it has been, under the Republic, a common thing to see profane and often obscene caricatures of the most sacred persons and incidents in the Evangelical narratives publicly exposed. The prohibition of such placards in the streets would surely not be a violation, but a vindication, of liberty.

In India, questions of religious liberty of great delicacy and difficulty have arisen. For a long period it was the steady policy of the British Government not only itself to maintain an attitude of strict religious neutrality, but also to discourage proselytism as a grave danger to public order. 'The English,' Lord Macartney declared, 'never attempt to disturb or dispute the worship or tenets of others; . . . they have no priests or chaplains with them, as have other European nations.' In 1793, when the charter of the East India Company was renewed, Wilberforce endeavoured to procure the insertion of clauses to the effect that it was the duty of the English to take measures for the religious and moral improvement of the natives in India, and that the Court of Directors should for that purpose send out and maintain missionaries and schoolmasters, as well as chaplains and ministers for those of their own creed. Owing to the strenuous resistance of the East India directors and proprietors, these clauses were struck out of the Bill at the third reading; the Company for many years refused to grant licenses to missionaries, and they more than once exercised against missionaries the power they possessed of expelling unlicensed Europeans from India. It was not until 1813 that Parliament broke down the barrier, and threw open the doors of India to missionary efforts. It did so in spite of a great preponderance of Anglo-Indian opinion, and of the evidence of Warren Hastings, and this measure marks most conspicuously the increasing power which the Evangelical party was exercising in British politics.[16]

But although India was from this time thrown open to numerous missionary enterprises, the law forbade and forbids, in terms much stricter than would be employed in British legislation, any word or act which could wound religious feelings,[17] and the State endeavours to maintain its own religious neutrality, and to abstain as far as possible from any act that

---

[16] Strachey's *India; Wilberforce's Life*, ii. 24–28, 392–93; iv. 101–26. See, too, on the history of the relations of British law to native religions, Kaye's *Christianity in India*, and Marshman's *Lives of Carey, Marshman, and Ward.*
[17] Stephen's *History of Criminal Law*, iii. 312–13.

could conflict with the religious feelings, observances, and customs of the subject races. It has not, however, always been able to do so. It seems an easy thing to guarantee the free exercise of different forms of worship, but grave difficulties arise when these religions bring with them a code of ethics essentially different from that of the ruling power. Probably the first instance in which the British Government undertook to prohibit a religious observance in India was in 1802, when Lord Wellesley suppressed under severe penalties the sacrifice of children by drowning, which took place annually at the great religious festival at Saugor. The slaughter of female infants, though it does not appear to have grown out of religious ideas, was fully recognised by Hindu morals, and it was practised on such a scale that within the memory of living men there were great districts in which not a single girl could be found in many villages.[18] English law has made this act a crime, and some legislation which is as recent as 1870 has done much to suppress it. The human sacrifices that were once constantly performed before the images of Kali, and were not unfrequent at other shrines, have been abolished, and in 1829 Lord William Bentinck took the bold and most beneficent step of abolishing the suttee, or the practice of immolating Hindu widows on the funeral piles of their husbands.

The horrible fact that several hundreds of women were annually burnt alive within the British dominions, and in the immediate neighborhood of Calcutta, had long occupied the thoughts of British governors, but the practice was so essentially a religious rite that for a long time they did not venture to forbid it. Lord Cornwallis directed public servants to withhold their consent from the ceremony, if it was asked for, but he prohibited them from taking any official step to prevent it. Lord Wellesley consulted the judges about the possibility of suppressing it, but in their opinion such a step would be extremely dangerous. In 1813, Lord Minto, while disclaiming

---

[18] Strachey's *India*, pp. 290–91.

all intention of forbidding it, or of interfering with the tenets of the native religions, undertook at least to introduce some limitations and regulations with the object of diminishing its barbarity. According to the new regulations, it could only be practised after communication with the magistrates and principal officers of police, and in the presence of the police, and they were directed to ascertain that the widow's act was purely voluntary, that no stupefying or intoxicating drugs were employed, that there was up to the very last no violence or intimidation, that the victim was not under the age of sixteen and not pregnant. There does not, however, appear to have been much diminution of the practice, and in 1828, the year preceding its suppression, it was officially reported that 463 widows had been burnt, 287 of them being in the Calcutta division alone.[19] In the ten previous years the annual number of immolations is said to have averaged not less than 600.

The measure of Lord William Bentinck excited many fears and much opposition. It was argued that the practice of suttee had existed for countless centuries in India; that it was in the eyes of the Hindus 'a religious act of the highest possible merit,' a 'sacred duty' and a 'high privilege;' that to prohibit it was a direct and grave interference with the religion of the Hindus, a manifest violation of the principle of complete religious liberty which the British Government had hitherto maintained and guaranteed. Great fears were entertained that the sepoy army in Bengal might resent the suppression; and it was remembered that the religious element was believed to have contributed largely to the formidable sepoy mutiny which had taken place in 1806 at Vellore, in Madras. Lord William Bentinck, however, wisely took the officers of the Bengal Army into his confidence, and he was convinced by their answers that there was no real danger of revolt. He was encouraged by the fact that the custom chiefly prevailed among the effeminate and timid inhabitants of Bengal; that it was almost

---

[19] Mill's *History of India*, ix. 189.

or altogether unknown in great districts of India; that the Mohammedans in bygone days had successfully interfered with Hindu rites to a far greater extent than he proposed. The judges were now of opinion that the suttee might be safely abolished, and the determined policy of Lord W. Bentinck completely triumphed. Suttee was forbidden in Bengal in 1829, in the Madras and Bombay provinces in the following year. There were a few successful and unsuccessful attempts to evade the new law. There was one somewhat serious riot. There was a strong remonstrance, drawn up by leading Hindus. There was an appeal to the Privy Council in England; but when the impotence of all resistance was established, the natives speedily, though reluctantly, acquiesced. In a few years suttee became a mere tradition of the past, and under English influence even native princes made laws for its suppression.[20]

At the same time the Government took the utmost pains to impress upon the natives that they entertained no desire of disturbing their faith. Formal declarations had been repeatedly made that the laws of the Shastra and of the Koran would be maintained, and that Hindu and Mohammedan would be as fully protected in the free exercise of their religions under a Hindu or a Mohammedan Government. The law specially recognised and protected the system of caste,[21] and the rites of idolatrous worship were to a large extent endowed. A tax was levied on pilgrimages, and chiefly expended in defraying the expenses of the temple worship. The worship of Juggernaut and many less important shrines was susbsidised, and the Government exercised a superintending care over the management of the temples and over the vast endowments

---

[20] See Boulger's *Lord William Bentinck*, pp. 77–111, and Mill's *History of British India*, ix. 184–92. Sir John Strachey, in the excellent book which he published in 1888, says; 'The prohibition of the burning of widows was and is utterly disapproved by all but a small minority of Hindus. I do not believe that the majority, even of the most highly educated classes, approve it (*India*, pp. 353–54).

[21] 37 George III. c. 142, sect. 13.

which had been from time immemorial connected with them; prevented the misappropriation of their revenues; sent soldiers and police to protect or dignify idolatrous processions, and contributed very largely by wise and honest administration to the prosperity of the great religious establishments.

The Evangelical party in England agitated fiercely against these measures, and their influence gradually prevailed. In 1833 the Home Government was induced to order the abolition of the pilgrim tax and the discontinuance of all connection between the Government and idolatrous ceremonies. For five years this order seems to have been little more than a dead-letter, but in 1838 more efficacious measures were taken. The management of the whole system of idolatrous worship, and of the revenues connected with it, passed exclusively into the hands of the believers, and all superintending and supporting connection on the part of the Government was withdrawn.

Another difficult and dangerous question, in which considerations of humanity and justice were on one side, and old-established religious custom was on the other, was the question of inheritance. By the Mohammedan and the Hindu laws of inheritance apostasy was equivalent to civil death, and the convert lost all rights of heritage. This law had, in the eyes of the believers, a religious character; and the Hindu law of inheritance had an especially close connection with the Hindu religion, as property descended conditionally on the performance of religious rites, which were believed to be of transcendent importance for the benefit of the dead. Lord William Bentinck, who had already immortalised himself by the suppression of the suttee, resolved, if possible, to abolish the penalty which the native laws imposed on conversion, and in 1832 he introduced a regulation to that effect into Bengal. After long discussion and much opposition this policy at last triumphed, and an Act of Parliament of 1850 abolished through the whole of India every law and usage inflicting forfeiture of property on account of apostasy or exclusion from any faith. Another measure conceived in the same spirit, and directed against some peculiar Hindu superstitions, punished with imprisonment any one who tried to intimidate another by threatening to make him the object of divine displeasure. The marriage of Hindu widows also was legalised. Native converts to Christianity were enabled to obtain a divorce from husbands or wives who had deserted them on account of their conversion. The rights of succession and the power of bequest of natives who did not belong to any native religious community were fully recognised.[22]

These facts show sufficiently that, while the general principle of protecting the worship, revenues, and usages of native religions is fully recognised, there has been an increasing tendency in Indian legislation to allow considerations of humanity, justice, and individual liberty to override religious considerations. The great sepoy mutiny of 1857, which was mainly due to religious fanaticism, sufficiently disclosed the extreme dangers of the subject. After the suppression of the mutiny, also, there was a moment of great peril. A powerful party, supported by the high authority of Colonel Herbert Edwardes, one of the most distinguished of Indian soldiers, attributed the mutiny to the British Government having neglected their duty of bringing home Christian truths to the native population, and Colonel Edwardes issued a memorandum urging that the true policy to be pursued was 'the elimination of all unchristian principles from the government of India.' To carry out this policy he desired that the Bible should be compulsorily taught in all Government schools; that all endowments of native religions from public money, and all legal recognition of caste, should cease; that the English should cease to administer Hindu and Mohammedan law,

---

[22] Stephen's *History of Criminal Law*, iii. 321; Kaye's *Christianity in India*; Leslie Stephen's *Life of Sir James Stephen*, pp. 259–60. See, too, an admirable chapter on 'Our Religious Policy in India' in Sir Alfred Lyall's *Asiatic Studies*.

and to countenance Hindu and Mohammedan processions. This memorandum received a considerable amount of partial or unqualified support, but wiser counsels ultimately prevailed. In the Queen's proclamation of October 1858 there is a remarkable paragraph, which is said to have been due to the direct action of the Queen herself, and which did very much to establish permanent quiet in India. 'We do strictly charge and enjoin,' it said, 'on all those who may be in authority under us, that they abstain from all interference with the religious beliefs and worship of any of our subjects, on pain of our highest displeasure.'[23]

The policy indicated in these words has been, on the whole, carried out with signal sagacity and success, and the large introduction of natives into high offices under the Crown has had a reassuring influence on the native mind. Before the mutiny there were no natives on the bench of any supreme court of India, or in the Legislative Council, or in the higher branches of the Civil Service. Since the mutiny all these great departments have been thrown open to them. British law protects carefully the moral and social types that grow out of the native religions, and especially the Hindu conception of the family, which is widely different from that of Christian nations; and it is mainly through respect for native ideas that the Indian penal code treats adultery as a criminal offence, and punishes it with imprisonment that may extend to five years.[24] At the same time, the prohibition of the suttee and of infanticide has introduced grave changes even into this sphere. The law already violates Hindu notions by permitting the remarriage of widows and modifying the rules of succession, and it is not likely that many years will pass before the pressure of philanthropic European opinion leads to a prohibition of the horrible custom of child marriage, under which girls of ten or twelve years are assigned as wives to old, worn-out, and perhaps dying men. In the protected native States the British Govern-

---

[23] Bosworth Smith's *Life of Lawrence*, ii. 325–26.
[24] Stephen's *Criminal Law*, iii. 318.

ment has repeatedly intervened for the purpose of putting down infanticide, suttee, slavery, the punishment of alleged witches, and punishment by torture or mutilation.[25]

The educational policy of the Government also, which was chiefly adopted at the instigation of Sir Charles Wood in 1854, and which has since then been energetically and successfully pursued, cannot fail to have a real, though indirect and unintended, influence on religious belief. The first principle, it is true, of that policy is that 'the ruling power is bound to hold itself aloof from all questions of religion.' The universities, in which the educational system culminates, are purely secular examining bodies, modelled after the London University; and while grants in aid are accorded to all private educational establishments which impart a good secular education, are under competent management, and are open to inspection by Government officers, the State proclaims and steadily acts upon the principle of rigidly abstaining from all interference with the religious teaching of these establishments. But many of the schools and colleges that have earned grants in aid are missionary establishments. Pure secular education, which the Government especially encourages, is as repugnant to Mohammedan as to Catholic ideas; the mixture of classes and creeds, which the new system fosters, breaks down social divisions that are closely connected with religious beliefs; and the mere spread of scientific conceptions of the universe, of European habits of thought and standards of proof, must do much to shatter the fantastic cosmogonies of the Hindu creeds, and produce a moral and intellectual type profoundly different from that of the old believers. Education as yet touches only a small fraction of the great Indian people; but in this, as in other ways, contrary to its own wishes, the influence of the Government is opposed to the religion of the natives. It is not probable that it is preparing the way for Christian theology, but it is tending to undermine or attenuate old beliefs and to introduce Western types of thought and

---

[25] Lee Warner's *Protected Princes of India*, pp. 292–95.

morals. 'Few attentive observers of Indian history,' writes Sir Henry Maine, 'can fail to see that the morality of modern indigenous literature tends to become Christian morality, which has penetrated further than Christian belief.'[26]

Another case in which the principles of religious liberty have come into collision with principles of morality and public expediency may be found in Mormonism in America. Polygamy was not an original doctrine of the Mormon faith: it was not until 1843, thirteen years after the publication of the Book of Mormon, that Joseph Smith professed to have a revelation authorising it, and it was not until 1852 that it was openly acknowledged to the Gentile world. Long before this period, however, the Mormons had experienced a large amount of severe and illegal mob persecution. The rise and rapid progress of a new religion combining to an extraordinary degree the element of fraud with the elements of fanaticism soon aroused a fierce resistance, which was entirely unrestrained by the provisions of the Constitution giving unrestricted right of religious belief and profession.

In its first form Mormonism was simply a society of men believing in the divine mission and revelations of Joseph Smith, baptised for the dead in a Church which he founded and ruled, placing their property at his disposal, holding some very materialistic views about the nature of the Divinity, and also a strange notion that Christ had preached in America, after His crucifixion, to Children of Israel who already peopled that continent.[27] However eccentric might be these opinions, Mormonism in its general aspect was a sect not wholly differing from many others, and it could move freely within the wide limits which the American Constitution accorded to religious developments. The Mormons were first

---

[26] Ward's *Reign of Queen Victoria*, i. 462. There is an excellent chapter on Indian Education in Sir John Strachey's *India*. See, too, an interesting Blue Book on 'The Results of Indian Administration during the past Thirty Years' (1889), pp. 16–18.

[27] This is stated in the Book of Mormon.

concentrated in considerable numbers in the town of Kirtland, in Ohio, but they soon migrated to the thinly populated district called Jackson County, in Missouri, where about 1,200 were established. In obedience to a revelation of Joseph Smith, they purchased a large tract of land, and streams of fanatics poured in, boasting loudly that the land was to be given to them as an inheritance.

The old settlers, however, resented bitterly the intrusion of this sinister element, and after a long series of acts of violence and several vicissitudes, the Saints, now numbering about 12,000, were compelled to cross the Mississippi into Illinois, where they built the town of Nauvoo. They soon organised a powerful militia, established a regular government, and displayed to an extraordinary degree those industrial qualities for which they have always been remarkable. For a few years their progress was uninterrupted. A vast temple consecrated to their worship was erected, and they grew every month in numbers, power, and wealth; but the same causes that aroused hostility in Missouri made them unpopular in Illinois, and it was strengthened by a well-founded belief that the sect was moving in the direction of sexual license. Internal dissension also appeared; riots broke out, and the State authorities intervened. Joseph Smith and his brother surrendered to stand their trial on the charge of having instigated an attack on the office of a hostile newspaper, and were placed in prison. Then followed one of those tragedies which have always been peculiarly common in America: the prison was stormed and captured by a hostile mob, and Joseph Smith was shot dead. This last event took place in June 1844.

But the new Church survived its founder, and the election of Brigham Young placed at is head a man of very superior powers, who exercised an almost undisputed authority till his death in 1877. It was surrounded by numerous and bitter enemies, who were utterly unrestrained by any considerations of law, and after many months of trouble and violence, after the loss of many lives and the endurance of terrible sufferings, the Mormons who had not already fled from Nauvoo were driven forcibly across the Mississippi. They had, however, before this time taken measures for a migration which is one of the most remarkable incidents in modern history. Inspired by a passionate fanaticism that seems strangely out of place in the nineteenth century and in an intensely industrial society, they resolved to cross the Rocky Mountains, to traverse a space of no less than 1,000 miles, and to establish their Church far beyond the limits of the United States, in a wild and desert country, inhabited only by roving bands of savage Indians. This daring scheme was executed with extraordinary skill, resolution, and perseverance, and in 1847 and 1848 several thousands of fugitives planted the nucleus of a great State on the borders of the Salt Lake.

There is no other instance in history in which a religious fanaticism was so closely blended with an intense industrial spirit, and the speed with which the new colonists transformed a barren waste, built and organised a great city, and planted in this far-off land all the elements of civilisation is one of the wonders of American history. Immigrants poured in by thousands, and it seemed as if the new Church would at last be suffered to develop its own type of life and belief undisturbed. But the ill-fortune that had hitherto pursued it continued. The discovery of Californian gold drew the stream of white emigration across the territory of the Salt Lake, the Treaty of 1848 with Mexico placed the Mormon home within the jurisdiction of the United States, and Arizona and New Mexico grew up on its southern borders.

The Mormons desired to form themselves into a separate State under the name of Deseret, or 'The Land of the Honey-Bee,' and if they had been able to do so they would have obtained almost absolute power of self-legislation; but Congress refused to recognise them, and in 1850 the Mormon district was organised into the Territory of Utah. The position of a Territory is very different from that of a State, for the chief executive officers in it are appointed by the President to the United States, and, although a local legislative body exists, Congress retains great powers of legislation and control.

Brigham Young was appointed the first governor, though he was, a few years after, removed on account of his resistance to the Federal authorities. For a long time the Mormon priesthood were omnipotent in Utah. As might have been expected, their main object was to baffle all interference on the part of the Federal Government and to protect themselves from Gentile intrusion; while their missionaries preached their doctrines far and wide, and many thousands of immigrants from England and Wales, from the Scandinavian countries in Europe, and from other portions of the United States, traversed the vast expanse of desert, and brought to the new colony their strong arms, their burning enthusiasm, and their complete surrender of all individual will and judgment to the orders of the Mormon chief. The Federal officers who were sent to Utah found themselves practically powerless in the face of a unanimous public feeling. All the subordinate functionaries and all the jurymen were Mormons.

The tide, however, of Gentile emigration had set in for the West, and emigrants who were not Mormons began to come to a territory where all the first difficulties of settlement had been overcome. They were naturally far from welcome; in 1857 a large party were massacred at a place called Mountain Meadows, and although Indians were the chief agents in the crime, it was at last clearly traced to a Mormon source. It was not, however, till nearly twenty years after it took place that the chief Mormon culprit was brought to justice.[28] Many minor acts of violence appear to have been committed, and as long as the juries consisted of Mormons it was found impossible to punish them. But the completion of the Union Pacific Railway, and the discovery of some rich silver and lead mines, strengthened the Gentile immigration, and it was vaguely computed, about 1890, that there were some 50,000 Gentiles in Utah and about 110,000 Mormons.[29]

---

[28] Many particulars about his remarkable case will be found in an article in the *Revue des Deux Mondes*, October 15, 1895.

[29] *Encyclopædia Americana*, art. 'Mormonism.' The same well-informed writer computes the whole number of Mormons at at least 250,000.

But before this time the existence and the rapid increase of a polygamous community in America greatly occupied American opinion, and different religious bodies were urging the duty of suppressing it. There was, however, grave difference of opinion on the subject. Deplorable as was the appearance of a polygamist sect in the midst of a Christian land, there were those who contended that polygamy among the Mormons ought to be tolerated, as Christian Governments had always tolerated it among Hindus and Mohammedans. It was clearly the offshoot of a religious system resting on a religious doctrine, and it was a fundamental principle of the United States to give all religions the most ample scope for their development. Polygamy, these reasoners observed, prevails over a vast proportion of the human race. It is supported by clear and incontestable Old Testament authority, and it is not very clearly condemned in the New Testament. When it is the acknowledged doctrine of a well-defined Church it is undoubtedly an evil, but it is much less dangerous than when it is irregularly practised in a generally monogamous society. It does not produce the same confusion of properties and families, the same deception, or the same social stigma and oppression. Much was said of the duty of the Federal Government to intervene on behalf of the oppressed women, who were degraded by polygamy to an inferior and servile condition. It is impossible, however, to overlook the curious and significant fact that the Mormons were the first, or almost the first, people to give the political suffrage to women; that female suffrage existed among them for many years; and that it proved so favourable to polygamy that its abolition by the Congress was one of the measures for suppressing that custom. In the words of one of the latest American writers on this subject, 'woman suffrage existed in Utah for seventeen years, and proved to be one of the strongest bulwarks of polygamy.' 'For more than a quarter of a century the Mormon Church fought, with every weapon that it could command, the laws directed against its favourite insitution. One by one new and more vigorous penalties were enacted by Congress against polygamy. Finding women the most ardent champions of the vicious practice (owing to their stronger religious convictions), Congress in 1887 took away their right of suffrage.'[30]

In the face of such facts it was very difficult to contend that polygamy was generally unpopular among the Mormon women. It was certain that women bore their full proportion among the Mormon converts and the Mormon devotees, and there was strong evidence to support the conclusion that they were in general contented with their lot. Marriage usually took place very early. The wives were persuaded that their state in a future world depended on the happiness they procured their husbands in this; and it was part of a Mormon's religious duty to live equally with his wives, and abstain from favouritism. If they did not observe this duty, they were publicly reprimanded.[31] The Mormons, it was said, only asked to be left alone. They had gone forth, at the cost of terrible hardships, into a distant and lonely wilderness to practise their religion in peace, and whatever civilisation existed in Utah was wholly their work. Nor was that civilisation, even from a moral point of view, a contemptible one. Whatever else might be said of polygamy, it could not be denied that it had extinguished in Utah forms of vice that were the canker of all other American cities. Prostitution, adultery, illegitimate births, abandoned children, were unknown among the Mormons, and the statistics of crime showed that, judged by this test, they were far superior to the Gentiles around them. In intelligent, well-organised, and successful industry they had never been surpassed. Work was taught as the first of duties. Large families,

---

[30] Mr. Glen Miller in the *Forum*, Dec. 1894.

[31] See an interesting description of Mormon life and ideas, by Comte d'Haussonville, *Revue des Deux Mondes*, November 15, 1882; and also an article called 'A New View of Mormonism,' by R. W. Barclay, in the *Nineteenth Century*, January 1884. Mr. Barclay quotes official statistics showing how immensely greater is the proportion of crimes among the Gentiles than among the Mormons at Utah. See, too, Captain Burton's *City of the Saints*.

which in old countries indicate a low industrial civilisation, had a different character in a new country, where the cost of labour was enormously great. Each member worked in his own department for the whole family, and each family became almost wholly self-subsisting.[32]

Had a community of this kind, it was asked, no claim on the forbearance of the Government? Ought it to be treated as a mere seed-plot of vice? Was it in accordance with the religious liberty which was so solemnly guaranteed by the Constitution of the United States; was it becoming in a great and free democracy to enter into a persecuting crusade against a Church, however erroneous, against a practice, however deplorable, which was inseparably connected with a religious doctrine? And was such a crusade likely to have any other consequence than to make martyrs, and to kindle this strange fanaticism into a fiercer flame?

As early as 1862 there had been a law against polygamy, and attempts had sometimes been made to enforce it, but they proved almost absolutely abortive. All the juries were Mormons, and in the space of eighteen years there had not been more than two convictions for polygamy. After the termination of the great Civil War public opinion was more strongly directed to the subject, and more than one stringent law against polygamy was made. The Mormons asserted that polygamy was a tenet of their faith, and therefore entitled to the protection which the Constitution accorded to all forms of religious belief; but the Supreme Court decided that no such article of faith could claim protection under the Constitution.[33] In 1879 the Government of the United States attempted to enlist the services of other countries in the crusade, and a circular letter was sent to the American ministers in Europe, calling the attention of the European Governments to the American enactments against polygamy, and asking them to prevent the preaching of Mormonism and the emigration of

---

[32] Comte d'Haussonville.
[33] Dickinson, *New Light on Mormonism*, p. 174.

professed Mormons to the United States; but the Government of the countries where Mormon missionaries had been most successful replied that they could not undertake to inquire into the religious belief of emigrants. The laws of 1871 and of 1874 proved almost as inoperative as that of 1862. Federal judges were sent down to try cases, but they could try them only with juries that were mainly or exclusively Mormon, and it was almost impossible to induce such a jury to convict in a case of polygamy.

Religious opinion, however, in the United States urged on the Government, and in 1882 they began a life-and-death struggle for the purpose of stamping out polygamy. The Edmunds law, which was carried after long discussion in that year, is a striking illustration of the extreme energy which democratic communities can throw into repressive legislation. Utah had been steadily denied the privileges of a State constitution, and its internal affairs were therefore under the full control of Congress. The Edmunds law provided that in all the 'Territories' of the United States bigamy and polygamy should be punished with a fine of not more than 500 dollars and imprisonment up to five years. In order to overcome the difficulty of obtaining proof of marriage, it provided that any one cohabiting with more than one woman shall be punishable by imprisonment up to six months, or by a fine not exceeding 300 dollars, or by both punishments, at the discretion of the court; and that on trials for bigamy, polygamy, or unlawful cohabitation, any juryman might be challenged who had been living in the practice of any of these acts, or who, without being himself a polygamist, 'believes it right for a man to have more than one living and undivorced wife at the same time, or to live in the practice of cohabiting with more than one woman. Every man as he entered the jury-box might be questioned on oath as to his belief and practice in these matters. Polygamists and their wives were at the same time deprived of all power of voting at elections, and were incapacitated from holding any public place of trust or emolument. All registration and election offices in the Territory of

Utah were declared vacant, and a commission of five persons, appointed by the President of the Republic, was sent down to supersede all Mormon functionaries in matters of election and to appoint new ones.[34]

Under the influence of this most Draconic law polygamy was for the first time severely punished. All who practised and all who sympathised with it being removed from the juries, many convictions were obtained. In the year ending in September 1891 there were no less than 109 convictions.[35] In general the Mormons appear to have welcomed their long sentences of imprisonment in the spirit of martyrs, declaring that they must obey God rather than men, and women constantly refused to give evidence that could convict their husbands. Under the disenfranchising clauses of the Edmunds law about 12,000 men and women were deprived of their votes.[36]

As, however, the actual practice of polygamy was by this law required for disfranchisement, power still remained with the Mormons, and Mormons who believed in polygamy, though they were not known to be themselves polygamists, were almost always elected. But a long series of other measures were taken to break down their political power. By the Federal law which I have already mentioned female suffrage in Utah was abolished, on the ground that it contributed to strengthen Mormonism. It was decided that, the Mormon Church being 'utterly subversive of good morals and the well-being of society,' no alien who is a Mormon could be naturalised, and the funds of the Mormon society for encouraging immigration were confiscated. A local test oath was imposed as a qualification for the suffrage, obliging every voter to swear that he is not a bigamist or polygamist, or a member of any order which encourages and practices plural marriage;

---

[34] See the text of the Edmunds law in Dickinson, *New Light on Mormonism,* pp. 150–53.

[35] *Political Science Quarterly,* 1891, p. 768.

[36] Mr. Barclay says 16,000 (*Nineteenth Century,* January 1884).

and the Supreme Court, in 1890, determined that this test was not contrary to the Constitution. The criminal law against polygamy was steadily enforced, and it was strengthened by new and stringent provisions directed against unwilling witnesses, compelling a full registration of all marriages, depriving illegitimate children of rights of inheritance, and treating, in the spirit of the old Puritan legislation, both adultery and simple fornication as criminal offences.[37] These last measures, of course, both were and were intended to be purely partial in their operation. No one would have dreamed of applying them to Chicago or New York. But by such means the Mormon ascendency in Utah was broken, and in the election of 1890 the Gentile element, for the first time, obtained control of its municipal government.[38] The Mormon Church was itself pronounced to be an illegal corporation, its property was forfeited or escheated; and the forfeiture appears to have been severely enforced. As one of the latest American writers on the subject says, 'Officials sent from the Eastern States to official positions in the Territory as a reward for party services, found indiscriminate denunciation of the Mormons an excellent method of perpetuating political power. It is notorious that not a few who came to Utah poor men enriched themselves at the expense of the Mormon Church. The shrinkage of the Church property escheated by the Government would itself unfold a tale of official rapacity,' and there were 'ugly hints of corruption' extending even to the judicial bench.[39]

It would require an amount of local knowledge to which I can make no pretence, and which only an American writer is

---

[37] The text of the very severe and comprehensive Act of 1884 is given in Dickinson, pp. 153–60. It enacts, among other things (ss. 19, 20), 'that whoever commits adultery shall be punished by imprisonment in the penitentiary not exceeding three years,' and 'that if an unmarried man or woman commits fornication, each of them shall be punished by imprisonment not exceeding six months, or by fine not exceeding 100 dollars.'

[38] *Political Science Quarterly*, 1890, pp. 371–72.

[39] *Forum*, December 1894, p. 464.

likely to possess, to estimate with any confidence the present
and future effects of this crushing legislation. The accounts are
somewhat conflicting, and for some time after the enactment
of the Edmunds law very competent American writers were
exceedingly desponding about the results. They complained
that polygamy had never been more defiantly preached and
more fearlessly practised; that it seemed rather to increase
than diminish; that the whole body of the Mormons acted with
a perfect discipline in obedience to the commands of their
chief, voting together, controlling their schools, and electing
their chief officers. Having been refused the right of state independence for more than twenty years after their population
and wealth were sufficient to entitle them to it, they made it
an object to secure a predominance in the State of Nevada, and
soon acquired there an important influence. They were said
to hold the balance of power in Idaho and Arizona, and to be
rapidly increasing in the Territories of Washington, Montana,
and Wyoming, as well as in Colorado and New Mexico. Rumours of another distant migration were sometimes heard
among them. They were accused of an implacable hatred to
the Federal Government, and the opinion was openly expressed by many of their enemies that even if Mormonism
cleared itself from all suspicion of polygamy, it should be ex-
terminated at any cost; that it was leading rapidly to civil war
in Utah; that if it were not effectually suppressed the Mormon
leaders would, in a few years, rule every State to the west of
the Mississippi.[40]

Whether these statements were exaggerated when they
were originally made I am not able to say. There is, however,
evidently another side to the question, and during the last
few years, and especially since 1891, the aspect of the Mor-

---

[40] *Encyclopædia Americana*, art. 'Mormonism;' Dickinson's *New Light on
Mormonism*, pp. 170–86, 197; Codman's *Solution of the Mormon Problem*.
There are some striking and, I think, just remarks on the persecuting
spirit which has been displayed in the English press on the subject of
Mormonism in Mill *On Liberty*, pp. 163–67 (ed. 1859).

mon question in America has considerably changed. Many powerful influences have been favouring the policy of the Government. It was noticed that among the more wealthy Mormons there was a growing disposition to secede. Such men naturally desired to escape the strict exaction of tithes for the benefit of the Mormon Church, and they felt more keenly than poor men both the legal penalties and the social stigma attaching to their creed. Polygamy had proved, from an economical point of view, possible, and even successful, as long as the family remained fully selfsupporting and all its members were engaged in different industries, but it became far too expensive a luxury to subsist long, under the conditions of American life, in an idle, leisured class. More frequent and more intimate contact with the Gentile world, and the rise of a new generation who had but little of the fierce fanaticism of the early converts, had their influence, and many of the younger Mormons were manifestly indisposed to an institution which brought with it severe social and legal penalties, and obstructed and hampered them at every step of their career. While such a feeling was growing, a formidable schism broke out in the Church. A party called Josephites, or 'Latter-day Saints of the Reorganised Church of Jesus Christ,' appeared, and is said soon to have enlisted 20,000 followers. It was led by Joseph Smith, a son of the founder of Mormonism, and it denounced polygamy as a departure from the original faith.[41]

All these things were preparing a great change in the Mormon Church; and the laws against polygamy appear to have found considerable, though for the most part silent, support among the Mormons themselves. After some hesitation their leaders recognised the fact. The abstract lawfulness of this institution is still a part of the Mormon creed, but its practice under present circumstances has not only been suspended, but been forbidden in the Mormon Church. In September 1890 the head of that Church publicly announced a revelation

---

[41] Dickinson, pp. 215–16.

warning Latter-day Saints against contracting any marriage
forbidden by the law of the land. Whether this abandonment
is final and quite sincere it is difficult to say, but Mr. Glen
Miller, whom I have already quoted as a late authority on the
subject, firmly believes in its reality. 'The institution of polygamy' he says, 'would have gone down eventually of its own
weight under the rush of Gentile immigration. The action of
the Church only hastened the inevitable. In the days of its
strongest hold less than 10 per cent. of the adult males of the
Territory lived in polygamy. No "plural" marriages in any
form are now taking place in Utah. It is a sin within the Mormon Church, as within any other, to live with more than one
woman. The young man who should attempt it would find
himself and his mistress (for such any "plural" wife would be
regarded) subject to the same social ostracism from the Mormons as from society at large.' At the same time, this writer
observes, 'there has been a complete cessation of persecution
for polygamy, and numbers of old-time offenders have re-
sumed relations with their "plural" wives with practical immunity from punishment. But the prop of polygamy—its
social respectability and exaltation as a religious virtue—has
been taken away. These old polygamists visit their younger
wives precisely as a married man in an Eastern community
might consort with a mistress—quietly and stealthily, not
openly or boastfully, as formerly.'

The sharp division between the Mormons and the Gentiles,
which a few years ago was general, is fast disappearing. In-
termarriages are not unfrequent. They mingle largely in the
public schools. They are united in all forms and institutions
of business; and what is perhaps even more important, the
Mormons have ceased to act politically as a purely isolated
body, and have thrown themselves cordially into the great
party contests of the United States.[42] They are said to be exhibiting to a full measure that flexibility of adaptation which
is so remarkable in the American people, and which enables

---

[42] *Forum*, December 1894.

them with a rapidity scarcely known in Europe to accommodate themselves to new conditions.

The authorities in the Federal Government have shown themselves very ready to accept the submission. In the September of 1894, President Cleveland issued a proclamation declaring that he was satisfied that the members of the Mormon Church were now living in obedience to the law, and granting a full amnesty and pardon to those who had been convicted of polygamy and deprived of their civil rights;[43] and in the same year Congress passed a measure under which Utah, in the beginning of 1896, attained its long-sought object, and was admitted as a separate State in the American Union. One of the conditions of the enabling Act is that the new Constitution prohibits polygamy.

The party which was created for the special purpose of opposing Mormonism was formally disbanded at the close of 1893, and both of the great parties in the State are now competing for the Mormon vote. The charge which has recently brought, with most effect, against the Mormons has not been their polygamy, but their susceptibility to Church interference in political life. At the same time the non-Mormon politicians have shown themselves very ready to nominate as candidates officials of the Mormon Church, believing that such candidates are likely to secure the largest number of Mormon votes. A gentleman holding the high position of 'Apostle' in the Church was put forward by the Democratic party as their nominee for the Senate of the United States.[44] So complete to all appearance is the reconciliation between the American Government and the Mormon Church, that it is said to be a Mormon tenet that the American Constitution is an inspired document.[45]

---

[43] *The Times,* July 14, Sept. 29, 1894.

[44] See an article of Mr. Glen Miller's in *Forum,* December 1895. The senators elected, however, were of the Republican party.

[45] *Report of the Commissioners on the Causes of Immigration to the U.S.A.* (House of Representatives, 1892), pp. 185–86.

A future historian must tell the final results of the conflict which I have described between religious fanaticism and repressive legislation, but it is surely a curious sign of the times that the theatre of the struggle should have been the great democracy of the West. When democratic opinion thoroughly favours repression, that repression is likely, in the conditions of modern society, to be stronger and more uncompromising than under a monarchy or an aristocracy. It is difficult to observe without some disquiet the manifestly increasing tendency of democracies to consider the regulation of life, character, habits, and tastes within the province of Governments. On the whole, however, democracies, at least in the Anglo-Saxon race, seem to me favourable to religious liberty. No doctrines have more manifestly declined during the last half-century than the doctrines of salvation by belief, of exclusive salvation, and of the criminality of error, which lay at the root of the great persecutions under Christian rule. No forms of liberty are more prized by English democracies than the liberty of expression, discussion, and association. The prevailing passion for equality favours the rise of various sects, and a great indifference to religious dogma in general prevails among the working class, who have now risen to power.

There is, however, another influence connected with, and scarcely less strong than, democracy which has an opposite tendency, and it is probable that if religious persecution ever again plays a great part in human affairs, it will be closely connected with that growing sentiment of nationality which I have examined in the last chapter. No attentive observer can have failed to notice how frequently it displays itself in a desire to unify the national type, and to expel all alien and uncongenial elements. Religion more than any other single influence perpetuates within a nation distinct types and consolidates distinct interests. Few facts in the nineteenth century have been so well calculated to disenchant the believers in perpetual progress with their creed as the anti-Semite movement, which in a few years has swept like an angry wave over the greater part of Europe. It was scarcely heard of before the latter years of the seventies, but it has already become a great power, not only in semi-civilised countries like Roumania and Russia, but also in Austria and in Germany. In France, which had been prominent for its early liberality to the Jews, the immense popularity of the works of Drumont shows that the anti-Semite spirit is widely spread. I have already noticed how clearly the extravagant French enthusiasm for Russia, at the very time when the Russian Government was engaged in savage persecution of the Jewish race, shows that a question of national interests and national revenge could supersede, in one of the most enlightened nations in Europe, all the old enthusiasm for religious liberty. The recent movement for proscribing, under pretence of preventing cruelty to animals, the mode of killing animals for food, which is enjoined in the Jewish ritual, is certainly at least as much due to dislike to the Jews as to consideration for cattle. It appears to have arisen among the German anti-Semites, especially in Saxony, and in 1893 a law prohibiting the Jewish mode of slaughtering cattle was carried in Switzerland by a popular vote.

In these countries the anti-Semite movement has been essentially a popular movement, a fierce race-hatred, pervading great masses of the people, and for the most part neither instigated nor encouraged by their Governments. Religious fanaticism has mixed with it, but usually, and especially in Germany, it has played only a very minor part. Many causes have conspired to it. The enormous power which Jews have obtained in the press and the money markets of Europe is very evident, and great power is never more resented than when it is in the hands of men who suffer from some social inferiority. Jews, in some countries, are specially prominent in unpopular professions, such as tax-gatherers and small money-lenders, agents, manipulators, and organisers of industry. They have little turn for labouring with their hands, but they have a special skill in directing and appropriating the labour of others. They have come to be looked upon as typical capitalists, and therefore excite the hostility both of Socialists, who would make war on all capitalists, and of the very different class which views with jealousy the increasing power of money, as distinguished from land, in the government of the world; while, on the other hand, they have themselves contributed largely to the socialistic and revolutionary elements in Europe. Among their many great gifts, they have never, as a race, possessed the charm of manner which softens, conciliates, and attracts, and the disintegration of politics, which is such a marked feature of our time, brings every separate group into a clearer and stronger relief. It is as a distinct and alien element in the national life that they have been especially assailed.

The Russian persecution stands in some degree apart from the other forms of the anti-Semite movement, both on account of its unparalleled magnitude and ferocity, and also because it is the direct act of a Government deliberately, systematically, remorselessly seeking to reduce to utter misery about four and a half millions of its own subjects. The laws of General Ignatieff in May 1882, and the later and still more atrocious measures that were taken at the instigation of M. Pobedonostseff, form a code of persecution which well deserves to rank with those that followed the religious wars of the sixteenth century.[46] The Russian legislator does not, it is true, altogether proscribe the Jewish worship, though no synagogue is permitted in any place where there are less than eighty, and no public prayer in any place where there are less than thirty, Jewish houses. Nor does he absolutely and by a formal measure expel the Jews from Russian soil. Such a step has, indeed, been adopted on a large scale in 1891 and 1892, in the case of the poorer Jews of foreign nationality. It is estimated that these number about 150,000, and many of them,

---

[46] An excellent summary of these laws will be found in the report of Messrs. Weber and Kempster to the House of Representatives of the U.S.A.: *Report of Commissioners of Immigration upon the Causes which incite Immigration to the United States* (1892), pp. 149–65.

though of foreign parentage, had been born in Russia, had lived there all their lives, spoke no language except Russian, depended absolutely on Russian industries for their livelihood, and desired nothing more than the naturalisation which was refused them. The small number who consented to abjure their faith were suffered to remain. Multitudes of the others were expelled from their houses, and driven like cattle by bands of Cossacks across the frontier, where thousands have perished by misery and cold.[47]

For the native Jews a different treatment was provided. The legislator contented himself with driving the great body of these Jews, including several hundreds of thousands of persons, out of an immense proportion of the territory and out of the great cities, in which they had long lived unmolested; confining them, in the territory in which they were allowed to dwell, to the overcrowded towns; banishing them by countless restrictions, disabilities, and disqualifications from all honourable and lucrative posts, and from a multitude of the trades and occupations in which they were accustomed to earn their livelihood, and thus deliberately reducing them to such a depth of misery that in some provinces large numbers perished by literal starvation.[48]

The Jews are at the same time subject to a number of taxes which do not fall upon the Christians. Their offences are punished by special laws and harsher penalties. Their military service is more severe than that of Christians, and they are excluded from all the higher ranks of promotion. They are pronounced aliens by law, their condition is regulated by special ordinances, and they are left unprotected to the mercies of the police.

Bribes as well as penalties are employed for their conversion. Every adult convert is rewarded with a gift of from fifteen to twenty roubles from the State, and every child convert

---

[47] See Errera, *Les Juifs Russes* (1893), pp. 40–43. Compare the remarks of Weber and Kempster, p. 165.

[48] Errera, *Les Juifs Russes*, pp. 103–9.

with half that sum. If one partner in a Jewish marriage adopts
the orthodox faith, that partner is at once freed from the marriage tie, and permitted to marry a Christian. All the children
under seven of the sex of the convert are compulsorily bap-
tized. If the couple elect to live together, the convert must
sign a declaration that he or she will endeavour to convert the
other; and if such conversion is not effected, both are prohibited from residing outside the Jewish pale. Though no one,
according to Russian law, can perform a legal act under the
age of twenty-one, Jewish children at the age of fourteen may
be received into the Orthodox Church without the permission
of their parents or guardians.

There are, it is true, a variety of exemptions, some of them
resting upon regular decrees, but a large part purely arbitrary
and precarious. Wealthy Jews are able, after a certain number
of years, to become members of what is called the First Guild,
and are permitted by the payment of a large sum to purchase
the right of living in any part of Russia; and some classes are
exempted from portions of the code on account of their university degrees, or of the practice of certain learned professions. Their number, however, has been carefully limited by
a crowd of recent enactments restricting to very small proportions the Jews who are admitted to the universities and
the professional training schools, and in many other ways
impeding their education.

A more important exception is that of skilled artisans, who,
under the system of passports, annually renewed, are permitted to reside temporarily outside the pale. Their position,
however, is utterly precarious. The passports may be at any
time withdrawn. The permitted trades have never been authoritatively defined, and the limits of exemption have been
frequently and arbitrarily contracted.[49] By a recent enactment
the artisans are only allowed in a small proportion of towns,
where their industry can be under constant supervision.[50] If

[49] Frederic, *The New Exodus*, pp. 166–68.
[50] Errera, p. 69.

through age or infirmity they are unable to work, they are at once banished to the pale, and any intermission of work makes them liable to the same expulsion. It has been a common practice, write the American Commissioners, 'to visit the workshops in which these artisans were employed when they were out delivering work, or perhaps on a holiday, and because they were not found actually engaged in such artisan's work at the time of the visit, they were reported as being fraudulently enrolled in the Artisans' Guild, and thereupon expelled to the pale.[51] In many cases they have been expelled simply because they were not found working on their own Sabbath.[52]

The Jewish artisan outside the pale may bring with him his wife and children, but he must receive no other relatives, not even his father or mother, in his hut. He must sell nothing outside the pale, except what he has himself made, and under this rule tailors have been expelled because the buttons on the coats, and watchmakers because the keys of the watches they sold were not of their own manufacture.[53] Their wives also are under the severest restrictions. In 1891, ten wives of Jewish artisans were expelled from Kieff because they had been found guilty of selling bread and milk.[54] Among the exempted trades is that of midwife, and Jewish midwives are permitted in all parts of the Empire, but they are specially forbidden to keep their children with them when outside the pale.[55] A characteristic provision permits the Jewish prostitute to ply her trade in any part of the Empire. Leroy-Beaulieu mentions a well-authenticated case of a poor Jewish girl who, in order to purchase permission to learn shorthand at Moscow, actually took out the yellow passport of a prostitute, but

---

[51] Weber and Kempster, p. 39.
[52] Frederic, *The New Exodus*, p. 248.
[53] Weber and Kempster, p. 39.
[54] Errera, p. 73.
[55] Ibid. pp. 72–73.

was shortly afterwards expelled by the police, as it was found that she was not practising the permitted trade.[56]

In spite of the shackles that are imposed on the Russian press, and the misrepresentations of official writers, the facts of this persecution have been largely, though no doubt very imperfectly, disclosed. The Government of the United States rendered a great service to history by sending two singularly competent and judicial commissioners to study on the spot the nature and the cause of a persecution which drives tens of thousands of Jewish emigrants to America. Their admirably full and temperate report; the excellent work in which Professor Errera has collected and sifted the best evidence relating to the persecution; the writings of M. Leroy-Beaulieu, who is a capital authority both on Russian and on Jewish questions, and a few well-informed articles which appeared in the foreign press, have brought together a vast mass of well-authenticated evidence, and Mr. Harold Frederic has related the story in a book which is founded on close personal investigation, and which is one of the most powerful and most terrible of our time.

To these writers I must refer the reader for the details of a persecution which far exceeds in atrocity any other that has taken place in Europe in the nineteenth century. It cannot be measured by the mere letter of the law, though few persons who have examined the new code will doubt that it was deliberately and methodically constructed with the object of driving the great bulk of the Jewish population to the alternative of conversion, starvation, or exile. Still more horrible have been the sanguinary outbursts of popular fury, often connived at, if not instigated, by authority, the brutal acts of

---

[56] Errera, p. 31. Mr. Frederic mentions 'two perfectly authenticated cases of young Jewish girls of respectable families and unblemished characters who adopted the desperate device of registering themselves as prostitutes in order to be allowed to remain with their aged parents in the city where they were born' (*The New Exodus*, p. 216). See, too, p. 247, and Weber and Kempster, p. 42.

arbitrary violence by which the persecution at every stage has been continually accompanied.

If the reader suspects this language of exaggeration, he should study the accounts in the writers I have cited of the police raid on the Jewish quarter of Moscow, which began the expulsion of the Jews from that city in 1891 and 1892, when more than 700 men, women, and children, who had committed no shadow of offence, were dragged from their homes in the dead hour of the night, and, in the extreme cold of a Russian winter, first taken to the prison, and then marched in chains out of the city and summarily exiled to the pale.[52] He should read the account of the Jewish settlement of Marina Rostscha, which was surrounded during the night by a band of Cossacks with torches and drawn swords, who dragged at least 300 unsuspecting Jewish families from their beds, and, scarcely giving them time to dress, drove them from their homes, through the woods and over the snow-covered ground, beyond the limits of the province. Utter ruin naturally accompanied the persecution. The Jews were cut off from their only means of livelihood. There was a wholesale repudiation of debts; and this was, no doubt, a leading motive in the tragedy. Those who possessed realised property were prevented from removing it, and forced to sell it at the shortest notice to a hostile population, usually for a minute fraction of its real value.[58] Multitudes of the fugitives perished on the road by cold, or starvation, or fatigue. Some, in the agony of their distress, found a refuge in suicide. Sick Jews in the extreme of suffering were repelled from the Christian hospitals,[59] and tens of thousands, in the utmost destitution to which human beings can sink, have been driven from their

---

[57] The official paper at St. Petersburg denied the employment of chains, but it is established by overwhelming evidence. See Frederic, pp. 289–92; Weber and Kempster, pp. 47–51.

[58] Some striking instances of this at Moscow are given in *The New Exodus*, pp. 222–28.

[59] Weber and Kempster, p. 41.

country to seek a refuge among strangers. According to the careful estimate of Mr. Frederic, in the single year which ended in October, 1892, at least a quarter of a million of Russian Jews have in this way been forced into exile.[60]

Nowhere, indeed, in modern Europe have such pictures of human suffering and human cruelty been witnessed as in that gloomy Northern Empire, where the silence of an iron despotism is seldom broken except by the wailings of the famine-stricken, the plague-stricken, and the persecuted.

> La, sotto giorni brevi e nebulosi,
> Nasce una gente a cui il morir non duole.

Nearly half of the Jewish race is said to have dwelt there, and their persecution is no modern thing, though in the multitude of its victims the persecution under Alexander III. has transcended all that preceded it. The causes which produced the anti-Semite movement in other lands existed in Russia in peculiar intensity, as there was no other country where the Jews were so numerous, and scarcely anywhere the Christians were at once so ignorant and so poor. The charge of Nihilism was made much use of, though in truth but very few Jews have been proved guilty of conspiracy.[61] An evil chance had placed upon the throne an absolute ruler who combined with much private virtue and very limited faculties all the genuine fanaticism of the great persecutors of the past, and who found a new Torquemada at his side. He reigned over an administration which is among the most despotic, and probably, without exception, the most corrupt and the most cruel in Europe; over a people with many amiable and noble qualities, but ignorant and credulous, sunk in poverty far exceeding that of Western Europe, detached by a great economical revolution

---

[60] *The New Exodus*, pp. 283–84.
[61] Frederic (pp. 118–19) and Errera (pp. 144–45), have shown the very small number of Jews among the convicted Nihilists. Errera examines very fully the various charges brought against the Russian Jews.

from their old grooves and guiding influences, and peculiarly subject to fierce gusts of fanatical passion. Among the causes of the great Russian persecutions of Polish Catholics, of Lutherans, of Russian dissenters, and, above all, of Jews, much has been ascribed by the best observers to the mere greed of corrupt officials seeking for blackmail and for confiscations. Much has been due to social collisions; to the hatred aroused by the competition of a more industrious, more intelligent, and more sober race; to the hatred which debtors bear to their creditors; to the natural tendency of oppressed, ignorant, and poverty-stricken men to throw the blame of their very real sufferings upon some isolated and alien race. Religious fanaticism also, which has a deep hold over the Russian nature, and which has shown itself in many strange explosions, has borne a considerable part. But probably not less powerful than any of these motives has been the desire to make Russia purely Russian, expelling every foreign element from the Slavonic soil. It is a feeling which has long smouldered in great strata of Russian society, and to which the Panslavist movement of our own day has given a vastly augmented power and scope. Some of the most disgraceful apologies for the savage persecutions in Russia have come from writers who profess to be champions of nationalities, ardent supporters of liberty and progress.

COLOPHON

The Palatino typeface used in this volume is the work of Hermann Zapf, the noted European type designer and master calligrapher. Palatino is basically an "old style" letterform, yet strongly endowed with the Zapf distinction of exquisiteness. With concern not solely for the individual letter but also the working visual relationship in a page of text, Zapf's edged pen has given this type a brisk, natural motion.

Book Design by JMH Corporation, Indianapolis, Indiana
Typography by Weimer Typesetting Company, Inc., Indianapolis, Indiana
Printed and bound by Halliday Lithograph, Inc., West Hanover, Massachusetts